Readings and Cases
in Information Security
Law and Ethics

Michael E. Whitman

Herbert J. Mattord

D0207207

COURSE TECHNOLOGY
CENGAGE Learning™

Australia • Brazil • Japan • Korea • Mexico • Singapore • Spain • United Kingdom • United States

COURSE TECHNOLOGY
CENGAGE Learning

Readings and Cases in Information Security: Law and Ethics

**Michael E. Whitman,
Herbert J. Mattord**

Vice President, Career and Professional Editorial: Dave Garza

Executive Editor: Stephen Helba

Managing Editor: Marah Bellegarde

Senior Product Manager: Michelle Ruelos Cannistraci

Editorial Assistant: Sarah Pickering

Vice President, Career and Professional Marketing: Jennifer Ann Baker

Marketing Director: Deborah S. Yarnell

Senior Marketing Manager: Erin Coffin

Associate Marketing Manager: Shanna Gibbs

Production Director: Carolyn Miller

Production Manager: Andrew Crouth

Senior Content Project Manager: Andrea Majot

Art Director: Jack Pendleton

For product information and technology assistance, contact us at **Cengage Learning Customer & Sales Support, 1-800-354-9706**

For permission to use material from this text or product, submit all requests online at **cengage.com/permissions**
Further permissions questions can be e-mailed to **permissionrequest@cengage.com**

Microsoft ® is a registered trademark of the Microsoft Corporation.
Library of Congress Control Number: 2010927206
ISBN-13: 978-1-4354-4157-6
ISBN-10: 1-4354-4157-5

Course Technology
20 Channel Center Street
Boston, MA 02210
USA

Cengage Learning is a leading provider of customized learning solutions with office locations around the globe, including Singapore, the United Kingdom, Australia, Mexico, Brazil, and Japan. Locate your local office at:
international.cengage.com/region.

Cengage Learning products are represented in Canada by Nelson Education, Ltd.

For your lifelong learning solutions, visit **course.cengage.com**

Visit our corporate website at **cengage.com**.

Printed in the United States of America
1 2 3 4 5 6 7 14 13 12 11 10

Preface

The need for information security education is self-evident. Education is one of the recognized needs to combat the threats facing information security.

These readings provide students with a depth of content and analytical perspective not found in other textbooks. The fundamental tenet of *Readings & Cases in Information Security* is that Information Security in the modern organization is a problem for management and not a problem of technology—a problem that has important economic consequences and for which management will be held accountable. It is a further observation that the subject of information security is not presently widely included in the body of knowledge presented to most students enrolled in schools of business. This is true even within areas of concentration such as technology management and IT management. This textbook is suitable for course offerings to complement programs that adopt any one of the existing Course Technology textbooks. *Readings and Cases in Information Security* can be used to support *Principles of Information Security*, or *Management of Information Security* to further provide educational support for these texts.

Purpose and Intended Audience

This readings text provides instructors and lecturers with materials that give additional detail and depth on the management overview of information security, with emphasis on the legal and ethical issues surrounding these areas. These readings and cases can support a senior undergraduate or graduate information security class, or information technology class that requires additional depth in the area of information security. The cases can be used to enable individual or team projects, or used to support classroom discussion or writing assignments. This readings text can be used to support course delivery for both information security–driven programs targeted at information technology students and also IT management and technology management curricula aimed at business or technical management students.

Scope

Note that the title denotes support for the management of an information security program or organization. Current information security literature now acknowledges the dominant need to protect information, including the protection of the systems that transport, store, and process it, whether those systems are technology or human based. The scope of the *Readings and Cases* text covers fundamental areas of management of information security and the legal and ethical issues associated with these areas. The authors and many of the contributors are Certified Information Systems Security Professionals and/or Certified Information Security Managers.

Features

- Designed for use with other information security textbook offerings, this text adds current research, informed opinion, and fictional scenarios to your classroom.

- Prepare students for situations in the information security industry with articles, best practices, and cases relating to today's security issues.

- Create an interactive classroom by using the readings as discussion starters and using the scripted questions when provided in several of the cases.

- Some readings and cases have teaching guides to facilitate in-class discussion and learning from the material.

Overview of the Text

In addition to being an introduction to the text, we expect this section will also serve as a guidepost, directing teachers and students to relevant chapters and cases.

Acknowledgments and Thanks

The authors would like to thank the following individuals for their assistance in making *Readings and Cases in Information Security: Law and Ethics* a reality.

- To the hardworking, dedicated development team at Course Technology: thanks for your patience and tolerance in the development of this endeavor.

- All the students in the Information Security and Assurance Certificate courses at Kennesaw State University for their assistance in testing, debugging, and suffering through the various writing projects undertaken by the authors.

- Thanks to the authors who contributed these works, and to the reviewers who made them better.

- Special thanks to Paul Witman, a reviewer of substantial ability and great insight, who greatly contributed to the quality of the book you hold in your hands.

About the Authors

Wasim Al-Hamdani

Dr. Al-Hamdani finished his Ph.D. in Computer Science in 1985 at the University of East Anglia, Norwich, United Kingdom. He is currently an Associate Professor of Cryptography and Information Security at Kentucky State University. Dr. Al-Hamdani plays a leading role at Kentucky State University in developing the Information Assurance master's program and Information Security bachelor's degree. He was at the University of Technology in Baghdad from 1985 to 1999. He has supervised master's and Ph.D. students. He has published six textbooks and more than 53 papers dealing with computer science and cryptography and has contributed six chapters in research books concerning cryptography, information security, and XML security. For the past 19 years he has concentrated his research in cryptography, information security, and standardization.

Tridib Bandyopadhyay

Dr. Tridib Bandyopadhyay is an Assistant Professor of Kennesaw State University (KSU). At KSU, Dr. Bandyopadhyay teaches Systems Analysis, E-Business Systems, and Principles and Management of Information Security. His major research interests are in (i) information security investment issues in the private and public domains including interdependent IT security risks in supply chain management firms and cyber insurance, and (ii) Information and Communications Technology issues in the Low Income Countries (LIC). He is a member of AIS and INFORMS. Prior to his engagements in the academics, Dr. Bandyopadhyay has worked as an electrical engineer, and as a planning manager in the largest energy-generating company in India.

Vinay K. Bansal

Vinay K. Bansal (CISSP, CISA) works as a Senior Security Architect in Cisco System's Corporate Security Program Office. In his current role, Vinay is the global lead for "Web and Application Security Architecture Team," which focuses on improving the Security of Cisco's IT Web Applications, databases, and mobile services. Vinay holds a Master's Degree in Computer Science from Duke University and an undergraduate degree in electronics engineering.

Vinay has more than 17 years of extensive industry experience in successfully leading, architecting, and implementing IT-based solutions with focus on security/Internet/e-commerce applications. During his career, he worked in various positions including Tech-Lead, Enterprise, Security and Systems Architect, Lead Developer, and Project Manager. He holds various industry-recognized certifications, including CISSP, CISA, PMP, and Java Architect.

He also worked in Cisco's Global Government Solutions Group, helping in building Business and IT collaboration in defining organization's enterprise architecture. Vinay was also part of the Cisco's CA organization, where he was security lead for one of the biggest eBusiness initiatives within Cisco (an $86 million project) with a team of more than 200 business, functional, and technical team members. Vinay was instrumental in successful implementation of Oracle's Single-Sign-On, externalization, password management, and defining security best practices. He was also a key member of the earlier CA-Architecture team, where he participated in building base standards around application, integration, security architecture, and defining the architecture governance processes.

Prior to joining Cisco in May 2000, Vinay worked at IBM Global Services as an architect and has worked in a consulting capacity for multiple global Fortune 500 companies like Nokia, Dynamicsoft (now part of Cisco), Experien, and Plessey Telecom (UK). At Duke, as part of his Master's work, Vinay was actively involved with research in the field of virtualization of computing resources using grids and clusters.

Vinay has been an active speaker on the topic of Application Security. Most recently he presented in Triangle InfoSecCon in October 2008 and ISSA Raleigh Chapter (January 2009).

Jennifer L. Bayuk

Jennifer L. Bayuk is an independent information security management and information technology due diligence consultant, experienced in virtually every aspect of the field of information security. She is engaged in a wide variety of industries with projects ranging from oversight policy and metrics to technical architecture and requirements. She has been a Wall Street chief information security officer, a manager of Information Systems Internal Audit, a Price Waterhouse security principal consultant and auditor, and security software engineer at AT&T Bell Laboratories. While in financial services, Ms. Bayuk chaired the Securities Industry and Financial Markets Association Information Security Subcommittee and the Financial Services Sector Coordinating Council Technology R&D Committee. Working with the Department of Treasury's Office of Critical Infrastructure Protection, she coordinated committee activities to support the Department of Homeland Security's National Infrastructure Protection Plan. Ms. Bayuk frequently publishes on IT governance, information security, and technology audit topics. She authored two textbooks for the Information Systems Audit and Control Association and coedited a collection of works on enterprise information security and privacy for Artech House. She has lectured for organizations that include the Computer Security Institute, the Institute for Information Infrastructure Protection, the Information Systems Audit and Control Association, the National Institute of Standards and Technology, and the SysAdmin, Audit, Network, Security Institute. She is a certified information security manager, a certified information systems security professional, a certified information security auditor, and certified in the Governance of Enterprise IT (CISM, CISSP, CISA, and CGEIT). Ms. Bayuk is an Industry professor at Stevens Institute of Technology and has master's degrees in Computer Science and Philosophy. She can be reached at www.bayuk.com.

Shankar Babu Chebrolu

Shankar Babu Chebrolu, PhD(Cand), is an IT architect responsible for securing Web-based applications in Customer Value Chain Management at Cisco Systems, working closely with Cisco Supply Chain partners, Customers, Application Service Providers, Solution Vendors, Functional IT teams, and Corporate Security Programs Organization. Shankar is currently pursuing a PhD in Information Technology at Capella University and holds a Master's Degree in Computer Science & Engineering from Indian Institute of Technology (IIT), Mumbai, India. His research interests include information security management, cloud computing, IT effectiveness, and strategic alignment with business.

Shankar has been an active speaker at various conferences including Siebel Customer World, Oracle Open World, CA World, Oracle Applications User Group, and ISSA's Triangle InfoSeCon presenting in his areas of expertise: Web application security architectures, management of security processes, and integrating third-party security models within Cisco Enterprise.

Shankar holds several certifications, including Certified Information Systems Security Professional (CISSP), Global Information Assurance Certification (GIAC) and Sun Certified Enterprise Architect (SCEA). Shankar is a recipient of "Cisco Security Champion" award for being a security advocate and for his extra efforts in keeping Cisco secure.

Andrew P. Ciganek

Dr. Andrew P. Ciganek earned his Ph.D in Management Information Systems from the Sheldon B. Lubar School of Business at the University of Wisconsin at Milwaukee in 2006. His research interests include examining the managerial and strategic issues associated with the decision-making process of innovative technologies. A particular emphasis is made on decision speed and agility. Dr. Ciganek has published in the *International Journal of Knowledge Management* as well as several referenced conference publications and book chapters examining topics related to knowledge management, mobile computing devices, service-oriented architectures, and enterprise application integration.

Wendy D. Dixie

Wendy D. Dixie received a bachelor's degree in Computer Science from Kentucky State University. She later received an MBA with a concentration in Information Technology from Eastern Kentucky University. She is currently pursuing a master's degree in Computer Science Technology at Kentucky State University where she is working as a manager in the Information Technology Department.

Ms. Dixie has over 13 years of experience in information technology. Prior to working at Kentucky State University, she worked 6 years in information technology at St. Joseph's Hospital in Lexington, Kentucky.

Guillermo A. Francia

Dr. Guillermo A. Francia, III, received his B.S. in Mechanical Engineering degree from Mapua Tech in 1978. His Ph.D. in Computer Science is from New Mexico Tech. Before joining Jacksonville State University in 1994, he was the chairman of the Computer Science department at Kansas Wesleyan

University. Dr. Francia is a recipient of numerous grants and awards. His projects have been funded by prestigious institutions such as the National Science Foundation, the Eisenhower Foundation, the U.S. Department of Education, and Microsoft Corporation. In 1996, Dr. Francia received one of the five national awards for Innovators in Higher Education from Microsoft Corporation. As part of an Eisenhower grant, he codirected a successful summer workshop for secondary teachers on teaching probability through computer visualization in 1993. Dr. Francia served as a Fulbright scholar to Malta in 2007. He has published articles on numerous subjects such as computer security, digital forensics, security regulatory compliance, educational technology, expert systems, client-server computing, computer networking, software testing, and parallel processing. Currently, Dr. Francia is serving as director of the Center for Information Security and Assurance at Jacksonville State University.

Lara Z. Khansa

Lara Khansa is Assistant Professor of Business Information Technology in the Department of Business Information Technology, Pamplin College of Business, at Virginia Polytechnic Institute and State University. She received a Ph.D. in Information Systems, an M.S. in Computer Engineering, and an MBA in Finance and Investment Banking from the University of Wisconsin, Madison, and a B.E. in Computer and Communications Engineering from the American University of Beirut. Her primary research interests include the economics of information security, and regulatory economics with their implications for IT innovation and the future of the IT industry landscape. Dr. Khansa worked at GE Medical Systems as a software design engineer and earned the Green Belt Six Sigma certification. She has published papers in the *European Journal of Operational Research*, *Communications of the ACM*, and *Computers & Security*, among others. She is a member of the Association for Information Systems (AIS), the Institute of Electrical and Electronics Engineers (IEEE), and the Beta Gamma Sigma National Honor Society. She can be contacted at larak@vt.edu.

Jeffrey P. Landry

Jeffrey P. Landry, Ph.D, MBA, is a Professor in the School of Computer and Information Sciences at the University of South Alabama. Dr. Landry is currently working on a federally funded project to develop tools for assessing risks in voting systems. Designed for election officials, the tools seek to rank-order risks in federal elections using Monte Carlo simulation. Dr. Landry has participated in information systems risk analysis and management as exemplified by the CCER Project. As a codirector of the Center for Computing Education Research (CCER-www.iseducation.org), Landry helped identify, assess, and respond to risks using a process similar to that called for by the NIST SP 800-30. The CCER project, begun in 2003 and currently ongoing, involved the development and deployment of a secure, online certification exam. Dr. Landry's information systems ethics research focuses on interpersonal trust in the IS context. Dr. Landry has taught graduate and undergraduate courses, including information systems strategy and policy, project and change management, human computer interaction, research methods, and application development. He received his doctoral degree in Information and Management Sciences from Florida State University in May 1999. He previously worked in the commercial software development sector for eight years as a software engineer, project manager, and software department manager, employed by a Department of Defense contractor developing commercial software sold worldwide to government, commercial, and defense organizations, that conducted reliability and maintainability predictions of electronic equipment, in compliance with government-issued standards, MIL-HDBK-217 and MIL-HDBK-472. Dr. Landry has published in *Communications of the ACM, Journal of Information Systems Education, Information Systems Education Journal*, other journals, and in numerous conference proceedings.

Divakaran Liginlal

Divakaran Liginlal (Lal) is currently an Associate Teaching Professor of Information Systems at Carnegie Mellon University in Qatar. He previously worked as an Assistant Professor of Information Systems at the School of Business, University of Wisconsin at Madison. Lal received a BS in Communication Engineering from the University of Kerala, an MS in Computer Science and Engineering from the Indian Institute of Science, and a Ph.D in Management Information Systems from the University of Arizona. Before joining academics, he worked as a scientist for the Indian Space Research Organization (as a member of the Inertial Guidance System team for India's Satellite Launch Vehicle program). His research interests include information security and privacy, decision support systems, and computational and cognitive models of decision-making and problem solving. He has developed and taught courses such as writing secure code, information security management, information security technologies, building e-commerce systems, XML and web services, communication technologies, enterprise networking, data structures and algorithms, and introduction to computing at the graduate and undergraduate levels. Lal has received funding support for his research and teaching from Microsoft Corporation, Hewlett Packard, CISCO, DOIT at the University of Wisconsin at Madison, and the ICAIR at the University of Florida. His research has been published in such journals as *Communications of the ACM, IEEE TKDE, IEEE SMC-A, European Journal of Operational Research, Decision Support Systems, Fuzzy Sets and Systems*, and *Computers & Security*. Lal received the Mabel Chipman Award for excellence in teaching from the School of Business, University of Wisconsin at Madison in 2007, the University of Arizona Foundation Award for meritorious teaching in 1998, and the Larson grant award for innovation in curriculum design from the School of Business, University of Wisconsin at Madison in 2001 and 2004.

Herbert J. Mattord

Herbert J. Mattord, M.B.A. CISM, CISSP, completed 24 years of IT industry experience as an application developer, database administrator, project manager, and information security practitioner in 2002. He is currently an Assistant Professor of Information Security, on the faculty at Kennesaw State University. He and Michael Whitman are the authors of *Principles of Information Security, Principles of Incident Response and Disaster Recovery, Readings and Cases in the Management of Information Security, The Guide to Firewalls and Network Security: With Intrusion Detection and VPNs*, and *The Hands-On Information Security Lab Manual*, all from Course Technology, Cengage Learning. During his career as an IT practitioner, he has been an adjunct at Kennesaw State University; Southern Polytechnic State University in Marietta, Georgia; Austin Community College in Austin, Texas; and Texas State University, San Marcos. He currently teaches undergraduate courses in information security, data communications, local area networks, database technology, project management, and systems analysis & design. He is the coordinator for the department's Certificate in Information Security and Assurance, and is also an active member of the Information Systems Security Association and the Association for Computing Machinery. He was formerly the manager of Corporate Information Technology Security at Georgia-Pacific Corporation, where much of the practical knowledge found in this and his earlier textbook was acquired. Herb is currently an ABD doctoral candidate, pursuing a Ph.D. in Information Systems at Nova Southeastern University.

Patricia Morrison

Patricia Morrison is an instructor with the Information Technology Department at Cape Breton University. She received a diploma in Information Technology and a Bachelor of Business Administration from Cape Breton University and a Master of Business Administration from City University. She is an I.S.P. designate of C.I.P.S. In 2007 she completed the Cape Breton University Teaching Program. She is the recipient of the President's Award for the pursuit of common purpose and has been involved with a number of committees at Cape Breton University including the Learning Initiative Committee, BTI Degree Committee, Orientation Committee, Chair of Ad Hoc Committee in Instructional Technology, and the Recycling Council. Her involvement on campus has expanded to include membership on the Information Technology and the Aboriginal Task Forces, Academic Performance Committee, Senate, Executive Senate, Chair of the Teaching, Learning, and Evaluation Committee. She was a team member for the United Way Campaign and the Internal Scholarship and Bursary Campaign on campus. Off campus she is the Shannon School of Business representative, serves on the Cape Breton Business Hall of Fame committee, and is currently participating in the Women in Business Breakfast Series. Patricia worked as a microcomputer administrator in the Credit Granting Department, Central Visa Centre of the TD Bank in Toronto. She also worked as computer operator/computer support, payroll officer and learning assistant within Cape Breton University. Community experience includes the development and delivery of the Simulation Project for a period of years 1996 through 2003.

John H. Nugent

John H. Nugent is a board of director member of Digital Defense Group, Omaha, Nebraska, and is the founding director of Center of Information Assurance (IA) and MBA and MM programs in IA, and serves as an Associate Professor at the Graduate School of Management, University of Dallas, where he teaches courses on IA, accounting, auditing, business strategy, wireless, telecommunications, and capstone courses.

Previously, John served as a Fortune 10 subsidiary CEO serving as president and a board of director member of a number of AT&T subsidiaries. There he oversaw the development of over 100 state-of-the-art products ranging from chips, to communication products, to secure switches and satellite systems.

John was awarded the Defense Electronics "10 Rising Stars" award in July 1989 as well as the Diplome de Citoyen D'Honneur, Republic of France in June 1988 for his work there. John is a member of the U.S. Secret Service's North Texas Electronic Crimes Task Force and is a subcommittee chair of several American Bar Association (ABA) committees that research and publish on cyber security, cyber law, privacy, and information assurance matters.

John also serves as a national lecturer for the American Institute of Certified Public Accountants (AICPA) where he leads sessions for state CPA societies on IT security, auditing, internal controls, fraud prevention and detection, IT controls, and the International Financial Reporting Standards (IFRS). He is widely published and has appeared many times on national television and radio, as well as a business and technology expert in leading newspapers.

John has consulted for many organizations including the following:

American Institute of CPAs (AICPA), Bank of America, Canadian Foreign Ministry, Dallas Police Department Intelligence Fusion Center, DLJ (now CSFB), Ericsson, Federal Deposit Insurance Corporation (FDIC), Fujitsu, Haynes & Boone, IBM/LCI—Australia, Language Computer Corporation,

Lymba Corporation, Marconi Communications, MCI/Pace University, METI (formerly MITI, Japan), Nortel Networks, Pension Benefit Guaranty Corporation (PBGC), and the U.S. State Department among others.

J. Harold Pardue

J. Harold Pardue, Ph.D., is a Professor of Information Systems in the School of Computer and Information Sciences at the University of South Alabama. Dr. Pardue has taught graduate and undergraduate courses, including management information systems, systems analysis and design, expert systems, e-commerce, human computer interaction, research methods, n-tier/SOA application using .Net, database and database programming, human computer interaction, production operations management, and business statistics. He received his doctoral degree in Information and Management Sciences from Florida State University in June 1996. Dr. Pardue is currently working on a federally funded project to develop tools for assessing risks in voting systems. Designed for election officials, the tools seek to rank-order risks in federal elections using threat trees and Monte Carlo simulation. As a codirector of the Center for Computing Education Research, Pardue acted as chief technology and security officer. The CCER project, begun in 2003 and currently ongoing, involved the development and deployment of a secure, online certification exam. Dr. Pardue's research interests include trust in computing, IS architectures, HCI, and IS education. His work has been published in the *Communications of the ACM, Information Systems Education Journal, Journal of Informatics Education Research, College & Research Libraries, Review of Business Information Systems, Journal of Engineering Education, Journal of Information Science Education, Engineering Economist, System Dynamics Review, Journal of Psychological Type, Journal of Computer Information Systems*, and numerous national and international conferences.

Russell Shaver

Russell Shaver attended North Georgia College where he graduated in 1970. He then went into the Air Force during the Vietnam conflict where he served as a pilot. After his tour in South East Asia he was stationed in Texas and attended graduate school at St. Mary's University and the University of Texas in San Antonio. He earned a master's degree from each school.

When he left the Air Force, he went to work as an environmentalist for a newly formed regional government, quickly rising to the position of Director of Administration. While in that position, he directed a number of projects and worked closely with the EPA and State Water Agency. Upon leaving the regional government agency, he went to work at Datapoint Corporation, eventually transferring into their R&D group. This group was very instrumental in developing early Local Area Network (LAN) technology, distributed processing, laser printers, systems software, and small server systems. This assignment gained him a thorough knowledge of these topics and also gave him experience working within the realm of technology development. His role grew into that of an operational manager coordinating development projects, controls, personnel, and remote development groups located in California, Canada, and Europe. After Datapoint, he worked in several positions in start-up technology companies such as Technical Concepts Corp. and Performance Technology Inc. Each of these were spin-offs of the original R&D group from Datapoint.

Upon returning home to Georgia in 1990 Russell worked for CBIS and T/R Systems filling operational roles. In 2003 he decided to do something he had always wanted to do and began to teach at the college level, where he remains on the faculty as a Lecturer at Kennesaw State University.

Jeffrey M. Stanton

Jeffrey M. Stanton, Ph.D. (University of Connecticut, 1997), is an Associate Dean for research and doctoral programs at the School of Information Studies at Syracuse University. Dr. Stanton's research focuses on organizational behavior and technology, with his most recent projects examining how behavior affects information security and privacy in organizations. He is the author with Dr. Kathryn Stam of the book *The Visible Employee: Using Workplace Monitoring and Surveillance to Protect Information Assets Without Compromising Employee Privacy or Trust* (2006, Information Today, ISBN: 0910965749). Dr. Stanton has published more than 60 scholarly articles in top peer-reviewed behavioral science journals, such as the *Journal of Applied Psychology, Personnel Psychology, and Human Performance*. His work also appears in *Computers and Security, Communications of the ACM*, the *International Journal of Human—Computer Interaction, Information Technology and People*, the *Journal of Information Systems Education*, as well as *Behaviour & Information Technology*. Dr. Stanton is an expert psychometrician with published works on the measurement of job satisfaction and job stress, as well as research on creating abridged versions of scales and conducting survey research on the Internet; he is on the editorial board of *Organizational Research Methods*, the premier methodological journal in the field of management. Dr. Stanton is an associate editor at the journal *Human Resource Management*. Dr. Stanton's research has been supported through more than ten different grants and awards including the National Science Foundation's prestigious CAREER award. Dr. Stanton's background also includes more than a decade of experience in business both in established firms and start-up companies. In 1995, Dr. Stanton worked as a human resources analyst for Applied Psychological Techniques, a human resource consulting firm based in Darien, Connecticut. His projects at this firm included the development, implementation, and assessment of a performance appraisal system, development of a selection battery for customer service representatives, and the creation of a job classification and work standards system for over 350 positions in the public utilities industry. Dr. Stanton also worked for HRStrategies, Inc. as a human resources consultant, the Connecticut Department of Mental Health as a statistical consultant, and for Inpho Inc. (now Domania.com), AKG Acoustics Inc., and the Texet Corporation in management and engineering positions.

Michael E. Whitman

Michael Whitman, Ph.D., CISM, CISSP, is a Professor of Information Security in the Computer Science and Information Systems Department at Kennesaw State University, Kennesaw, Georgia, where he is also the coordinator of the Bachelor of Science in Information Security and Assurance and the director of the KSU Center for Information Security Education and Awareness (infosec.kennesaw .edu). He and Herbert Mattord are the authors of *Principles of Information Security, Management of Information Security, Principles of Incident Response and Disaster Recovery, Readings and Cases in the Management of Information Security, The Guide to Firewall and Network Security: With Intrusion Detection and VPNs*, and *The Hands-On Information Security Lab Manual*, all from Course Technology, Cengage Learning. Dr. Whitman is an active researcher in information security, fair and responsible use policies, ethical computing, and information systems research methods. He currently teaches graduate and undergraduate courses in information security. He has published articles in the top journals in his field, including *Information Systems Research*, the *Communications of the ACM, Information and Management*, the *Journal of International Business Studies*, and the *Journal of Computer Information Systems*. He is an active member of the Information Systems Security Association, the Association for Computing Machinery, and the Association for Information Systems. Through his efforts and those of Herbert Mattord, his institution has been recognized by the Department of Homeland Security and the National Security Agency as a National Center of Academic Excellence in Information Assurance Education—twice. This text is also part of his institution's Information Assurance Courseware Evaluation certification, also promoted by the NSA, mapped to CNSS standards 4011, 4013, and 4014.

Katherine H. Winters

Ms. Katherine H. Winters is a Lecturer in the College of Engineering and Computer Science at the University of Tennessee at Chattanooga (UTC). She holds B.S. and M.S. degrees in Computer Science and an M.S. in Engineering Management. Her teaching responsibilities include Java 1 and 2, principles of information security, management of information security, computer ethics, and the Capstone Project. In addition, she is the coordinator for the Computer Literacy program. Ms. Winters's research interests include security in software engineering and integration of security throughout the computer science curriculum. She has authored papers on these areas in refereed journals, conferences, and symposiums.

Ms. Winters was instrumental in the mapping activities associated with UTC receiving CNSS 4011 and 4012 certification. She was also instrumental in UTC receiving the Center of Excellence in Information Security. She has been involved in the development of the curriculum for the Computer Science B.S. and M.S. Information Security Concentrations as well as the non-degree certificates corresponding to the 4011 and 4012 certification. Ms. Winters is also involved in various committees and activities across campus including the Technology Strategic Planning Work Group. She is a member of the ACM, IEEE, and Upsilon Pi Epsilon. Prior to joining the faculty at UTC, she taught courses at Chattanooga State Community College. Ms. Winters was employed by the Tennessee Valley Authority where she was involved in analysis and archival of environment data as well as process improvement.

Li Yang

Dr. Li Yang is an Assistant Professor in the Department of Computer Science and Electrical Engineering at the University of Tennessee at Chattanooga. Her research interests include network and information security, databases, and engineering techniques for complex software system design. She authored both pedagogical and research papers on these areas in referenced journals, conferences, and symposiums. She is one of many major forces in the mapping activities associated with the University of Tennessee at Chattanooga (UTC) receiving CNSS 4011 and 4012 certification. She was also instrumental in UTC receiving the Center of Excellence in Information Security. She has been actively involved in the development of the curriculum for the Computer Science B.S. and M.S. Information Security Concentrations as well as the non-degree certificates corresponding to the 4011 and 4012 certification. She is a member of the ACM and Upsilon Pi Epsilon.

Jeffrey S. Zanzig

Dr. Jeffrey S. Zanzig is an Associate Professor of Accounting in the College of Commerce and Business Administration at Jacksonville State University in Jacksonville, Alabama. He received both his Bachelor's and Master's of Business Administration degrees from Jacksonville State University. He also holds a Master's of Accounting from the University of Alabama at Birmingham, a Master's of Science in Computer Systems and Software Design from Jacksonville State University, and a

Ph.D. in Accounting from the University of Mississippi. His professional designations include: Certified Public Accountant, Certified Internal Auditor, Certified Management Accountant, and Certified in Financial Management. He has authored a variety of articles in accounting and auditing and received the 2006 Max Block Distinguished Article Award for Informed Comment from the New York State Society of Certified Public Accountants.

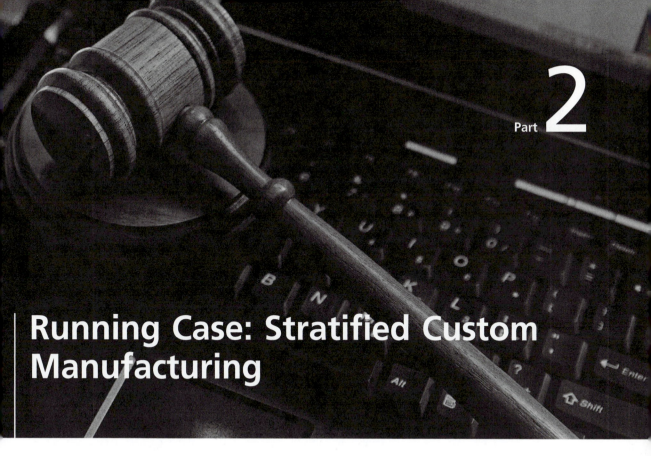

Part 2

Running Case: Stratified Custom Manufacturing

Russell Shaver
Kennesaw State University

Russell Shaver is a Lecturer at Kennesaw State University with a wide range of experience including holding two Masters degrees (MS-Systems Mgmt, MS-Environmental Mgmt), commercial pilot's license, over 25 years' experience working with six start-up ventures, over 20 years in operational roles, 8 years in Human Resource roles, and experience with a Fortune 500 corporation in Sales, Marketing and R&D. He enjoys his current role teaching at the college level and consulting with growing companies as an entrepreneur and risk taker.

Overview

In this chapter you will be introduced to a fictional company to be used in a running case. Each part of the book that follows will conclude with another installment of the running case and will include discussion questions your instructor may ask you to answer. As in life, there are few times when there is only one correct answer with occasions where there are no correct answers, only opinions. The purpose of this case study is to prompt your engagement, open discussion, and expand your worldview on issues of legal and ethical matters. The company described here is not based on any actual organization or even a group of organizations and does not reflect the actual or even the recommended practices of a real company. Many aspects are described that are knowingly dysfunctional and less than optimum in order to illustrate concepts and allow you to explore ideas on the subject of information security management and how legal and ethical considerations are brought to these issues.

Stratified Custom Manufacturing (SCM) was founded by four individuals who shared experiences at Western Central Tennessee Polytechnic University. In the early 1990s a faculty member and two of his students were engaged in a class project with a local electronics fabrication contractor to implement an information systems project at the firm. After successfully implementing the inventory improvement project, the firm's owner, Andrew "Drew" Cubbins, the teacher, Dr. Lisa Murphy, and the two students discovered a shared interest in exploring another project. The students approached Dr. Murphy and Mr. Cubbins about developing a novel business plan for a new type of company, one that performed custom manufacturing for others on either a made-to-order basis for one-of-a-kind, high-value items or a prototype + production basis for manufactured electronics. Jelani "James" Mburi and Susan Adkins spent their final semester as students developing the business plan with the active engagement of Dr. Murphy and Mr. Cubbins. After earning their "A" grades and graduating, the four decided to explore a new type of relationship as entrepreneurial business partners.

Incorporated in the state of Tennessee and named by picking the first word of the new name at random from the dictionary, Stratified Custom Manufacturing was organized in 1996 as a privately held corporation. The initial stockholders were the four principals already noted and Elmer Johnson, Drew's accountant who became the new firm's CFO. Drew was tapped to be the Chief Executive Officer (CEO), President, and Chairman of the Board of Directors. Lisa became the Chief Technology Officer (CTO) and Vice President of Design and Development. James was named Vice President of Sales and Marketing. And Susan became the Vice President of Human Resources and Business Services. Each was able to raise at least $10,000, and a few had access to more capital than that. The initial equity position was $50,000 from the five founders and another $200,000 lent by the founders to the corporation at market rates without voting rights.

The company opened for business on September 15, 1996, in leased space adjacent to Drew's existing business with a contract from that firm for its first product, a custom design project for a one-of-a-kind portable music player that could play music files created on a computer, but without the computer. In 1996 this was a novel concept. Drew thought it was an impractical business idea but planned to give it to his son as a unique gift and wanted to prime the pump by getting some work for the new business.

By mid-year 1997, the firm had grown to 30 employees and sales of about $20,000 per month. At the end of 1997, annual sales had accumulated to just at $350,000 and there were 46 employees at the company's Memphis location. The board of directors, recognizing the value of the concept, reinvested all earnings and the company continued to expand.

By the end of 2000, SCM was manufacturing to order in Memphis and San Jose and had sales offices in Memphis, San Jose, San Antonio, and New York City that brought in roughly $8 million in sales with a margin of about 26%. It was near the end of 2000 when the management team decided to take the firm public with an initial public stock offering (IPO) of $40 million to fund expansion. The IPO was a huge success and the firm expanded quickly into international markets.

Location	Manufacturing	Sales	Customer Technology Center	HR and Business Service Center	Data Center
North American Operations					
Memphis, TN	X	X	X	X	X
San Jose, CA	X	X	X		
Tampa, FL	X	X	X		
New York, NY		X	X		
Los Angeles, CA		X	X		
Seattle, WA		X			X
San Antonio, TX		X	X		X
European Operations					
Milan, Italy		X	X		
London, United Kingdom		X	X		
Ellwangen, Germany	X	X		X	X
Pacific Operations					
Tokyo, Japan		X	X		
Sydney, Australia		X		X	X

Table 2-1 SCM Locations and Functions

Current Structure

This year, the firm is expected to have sales of $790 million operating with a net margin of 22%. Corporate headcount is expected to end the current year at 4,510 employees (3,456 in design and manufacturing, 765 in sales, and the balance in all other functions) and approximately 2,600 subcontract designers used on specific projects as contract needs dictate. In the past two years, sales grew at an average rate of only 4% per year, indicating that they had fairly well dominated the markets in which they were operating. Table 2-1 shows the current locations and the functions served by each.

The current state of SCM's ownership and executive leadership is shown in Figure 2-1. A select view of the current SCM management team is shown in Figure 2-2.

Information Technology

The tasks usually associated with information technology are assigned to two directors. One of them, the Director of Software Engineering, is responsible for all of the software that goes into products designed and built by SCM. This encompasses traditional general-purpose programming for those applications that run on general-purpose computing architectures as well as the embedded programming support for custom processor designs and those using

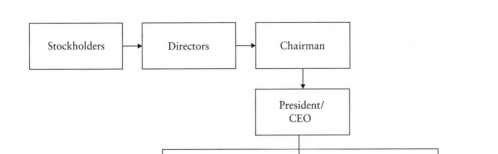

Figure 2-1 SCM Organization: Owners and Executives

Courtesy Course Technology/Cengage Learning

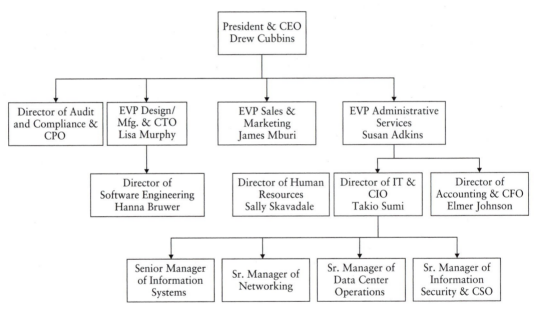

Figure 2-2 SCM Select Management Team Organization

Courtesy Course Technology/Cengage Learning

off-the-shelf logic controllers. The other is the Director of Information Technology, also the Chief Information Officer (CIO). This role fulfills the usual internal computing support role found in most current organizations.

Information Security

The information security role at SCM was reorganized in 2009 to align the functions involved in risk management with the Information Technology (IT) department, which was viewed as the single largest information security concern of the organization. The senior-most security person is the Senior Manager of Information Security who has been named as

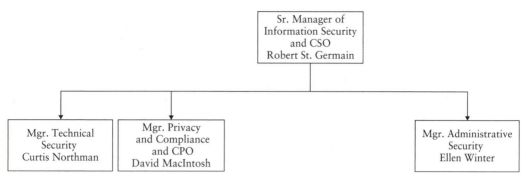

Figure 2-3 SCM Information Security Unit Organization

Courtesy Course Technology/Cengage Learning

Section	Key Policy Text
Statement of Purpose	This document establishes an overarching security policy and direction for our company. Individual departments are expected to establish standards, guidelines, and operating procedures that adhere to and reference this policy while addressing their specific and individual needs.
Protection of Information	Information must be protected in a manner commensurate with its sensitivity, value, and criticality.
Use of Information	SCM company information must be used only for the business purposes expressly authorized by management.
Information Handling, Access, and Usage	Information is a vital asset and all accesses to, uses of, and processing of Company X information must be consistent with policies and standards.
Legal Conflicts	SCM company information security policies were drafted to meet or exceed the protections found in existing laws and regulations, and any SCM company information security policy believed to be in conflict with existing laws or regulations must be promptly reported to information security management.
Exceptions to Policies	Exceptions to information security policies exist in rare instances where a risk assessment examining the implications of being out of compliance has been performed, where a standard risk acceptance form has been prepared by the data owner or management, and where this form has been approved by both information security management and internal audit management.
Policy Non-enforcement	Management's non-enforcement of any policy requirement does not constitute its consent.
Violation of Law	SCM company management must seriously consider prosecution for all known violations of the law.
Revocation of Access Privileges	SCM company reserves the right to revoke a user's information technology privileges at any time.
Use of Information Security Policies and Procedures	All SCM company information security documentation, including, but not limited to, policies, standards, and procedures, must be classified as "Internal Use Only," unless expressly created for external business processes or partners.

Table 2-2 EISP

ISSP Title	Key Policy Coverage
Messaging	Details how all SCM messaging systems are to be used by employees and administered by members of the organization. This includes but is not limited to wire line and wireless telephone, telex, facsimile, email, SMS text messages, Internet Relay Chat, and Instant Messaging.
Internet Usage	Informs all members of the SCM organization how they are expected to make use of the Internet, both for the benefit of SCM and on those occasions when they make use of company resources for personal reasons that are not prohibited by company policy.
Information Systems	Covers how the IT function addresses systems-level security. Major sections include client system configuration, server system configuration, and organizational change management and change control.
IT Networks	Describes how SCM will acquire, configure, and operate its data networks.
Use of Company Assets Away from Company Premises	Details how members of the SCM organization are expected to use company-owned assets when those assets are in locations other than that owned or controlled by SCM.
Connecting Other Assets to SCM Systems and Networks	Covers how members of the SCM organization can connect devices that are not owned by SCM to the SCM data network and allow those devices to interact with SCM systems. This document is the justifications for and the configuration guidance for the SCM Network Access Control (NAC) system.
Intellectual Property at SCM	Informs all members of the SCM organization on intellectual property (IP) ownership issues. This includes how SCM IP is to be protected and how SCM will defend the IP of others including the use of licensed software and the use of digital copies and photocopying equipment owned by SCM.

Table 2-3   ISSP Documents

the Chief Security Officer, responsible for both logical and physical security across the enterprise. The information security organization as operated by the current CSO is shown in Figure 2-3.

Information Security Policy at SCM

The policy environment at SCM grew organically along with the company. Each business function retains ownership of its own policy creation and maintenance. The information security policy was completely revised in a rather large project directed by the CIO when the need to move the information security function from the CTO business area was completed in 2009 and when the responsibilities for information security were reorganized. This "new" approach is documented in the Enterprise Information Security Policy (EISP) of the company. Some highlights of this policy are shown in Table 2-2.

In addition to the effort of developing all new EISP content, existing policies were reorganized into a set of issue-specific security policies (ISSPs). The number and nature of the ISSP documents is shown in Table 2-3.

Part **3**

Personnel and Privacy

Objective

The objective for this section of the text is an examination of the legal and ethical issues associated with the management of security personnel, non-security personnel, and overall privacy issues in the organization. With the increased regulatory emphasis on privacy protection, it is imperative that the student understand the implications that personnel and privacy decisions have for organizational liability and public trust. Breaches of customer and employee privacy will have severe repercussions, which could directly impact an organization's reputation and stakeholder confidence.

Contents

A Reading: Data Privacy: Is It Possible?

John H. Nugent

This reading examines the fundamentals and history of data privacy, the threats faced, and the changing nature of our data, and based on competing national and economic interests, concludes by demonstrating that the threats posed will likely lead to a continued state of technological insecurity. The reading addresses additional key attributes of this dilemma, such as state-based compromises, information warfare, technology (pre-acquisition) exploits, the mitigation of the foundational elements of data privacy (borders and trust), the low economic barriers to carrying out sophisticated data compromises, and the low probability of perpetrators being detected or caught.

B Case: Coordination between an Information Technology Department and a Human Resources Department: A Case Study and Analysis

Jeffrey M. Stanton

A medium-sized U.S. engineering company (< 500 full-time employees), referred to in this case study as Cenartech, has a sophisticated information infrastructure that supports engineering, sales, financial, and human resources functions. The information systems infrastructure comprises application and storage servers, wired and wireless networks, email and text messaging services, and a Web presence. A relatively new director of Information Technology figures prominently in this case, as does a more seasoned Human Resources director. Conflict between these two roles provides the primary pedagogical value of this case.

C Case: IT Ethics and Security in an IT Certification Project

Jeffrey P. Landry and J. Harold Pardue

This fictionalized case revolves around the development and deployment of a secure, online certification exam and is constructed from actual events. The project presented numerous security concerns, technical and managerial, as well as ethical and legal issues that put the project, and the professional reputations of its sponsors, at risk. Some of the issues include cheating, inadvertent and intentional release of exam items, defenses against unauthorized access, risk management, confidentiality, and privacy issues related to the information collected on individuals and institutions. Solutions are provided along with critical case questions for students.

D Reading: An Etymological View of Ethical Hacking

Michael E. Whitman

How we describe something defines it. A specific choice of words can cause irreparable damage to an idea or immortalize it. This paper examines the etymology of "Ethical Hacking." By examining the meaning of the term *ethical hacking* and the way in which it is used, the field of information security can seek to mitigate some of the notoriety hackers enjoy and avoid slighting the ethical work performed by the discipline.

E Running Case

Data Privacy

Is It Possible?

Dr. John H. Nugent, CPA, CFE, CFF, CISM, FCPA
Graduate School of Management, University of Dallas

John Nugent is a Board of Director Member of Digital Defense Group, Omaha, Nebraska, and is the founding director of Center of Information Assurance (IA) and MBA and MM programs in Iowa, and serves as an Associate Professor at the University of Dallas Graduate School of Management. Previously, John served as a Fortune 100 subsidiary CEO and board of director member of a number of AT&T subsidiaries.

Overview

This reading examines the fundamentals and history of data privacy, the threats faced, and the changing nature of our data, and based on competing national and economic interests, concludes by demonstrating that the threats posed will likely lead to a continued state of technological insecurity. The reading addresses additional key attributes of this dilemma, such as state-based compromises, information warfare, technology (pre-acquisition) exploits, the mitigation of the foundational elements of data privacy (borders and trust), the low economic barriers to carrying out sophisticated data compromises, and the low probability of perpetrators being detected or caught.

Introduction

Privacy is generally regarded as "… the expectation that confidential personal information disclosed in a private place will not be disclosed to third parties, when that disclosure would cause either embarrassment or emotional distress to a person of reasonable sensitivities. *Information* is interpreted broadly to include facts, images (e.g., photographs, videotapes) and disparaging opinions."[1]

Data assurance and privacy are governed by a variety of laws across the globe with certain governing bodies being more protective of data and privacy rights than others.[2] Prior to the technology advances we see presently, privacy and data security were easier to maintain as compromise in times past required proximity and physical access. Today, with modern communication systems, which link us all together in a basic virtual "One to All" electronic network (the Internet), the traditional protections afforded by "Borders and Trust" permit parties at long distances to now have virtual proximity and access to our most private data, often with little chance of notice, discovery, or punishment. And this condition is exacerbated via wireless communications where one may literally just take a copy of someone's data from the ether, and remain totally undetected. Today we are basically becoming "digital beings" with vast amounts of personal information collected, aggregated, and presented for sale by firms such as Accurint and ChoicePoint in the United States, among numerous others.[3]

On an individual basis, legislative bodies, legal scholars, courts, practitioners, and ordinary citizens have dealt with the issue of privacy for well over the last two hundred years. A leading article on privacy appeared in the *Harvard Law Review* in 1890 titled the "Right to Privacy."[4] This treatise was followed some seventy-seven years later with a codification of the "principles of privacy," which appeared in the "Second Restatement of Torts," in which its author laid down four principles of privacy rights.[5] These four principles dealt with unreasonable intrusion, appropriation of another's name, publication of private facts, and publication of false facts about another. However, each of these fundamental treatises dealing with privacy did not adequately address the changes technology would bring.

Other Important Data Privacy Regulations

The Organization for Economic Cooperation and Development (OECD)

The OECD, realizing the impact technology was having on privacy and data security, served as the pioneer organization in promulgating multinational guidance on what member nations should do to protect their citizens' private information. In 1980 it issued a set of guidelines that has served as the basis for much of the legislation and policy that exists today regarding privacy and the protection of personal data.[6] Basically this guidance provided for:

- Collection Limitation Principle—This principle set out the need to limit data collected, that any collected data should only be done so by legal means, and where appropriate, the party on whom the data was collected should be notified.

- Data Quality Principle—Data collected should be appropriate to use and should be free from errors, current, and up to date.

- Purpose Specification Principle—The purpose of use should be specified.

- Use Limitation Principle—Personal data should not be disclosed or used for any purpose other than the authorized purpose.

- Security Safeguards Principle—Data collected should be protected against unauthorized access, use, modification, or destruction.

- Openness Principle—Transparency should be established such that parties know the policies of data collection and use, and the physical location of the data controller.

- Individual Participation Principle—The party on whom data is being collected should be able to discern from the data controller or collector that such a party has data concerning the first party. The party should also be able to obtain (for a reasonable fee) the data so collected.

- Accountability Principle—The data controller should be held accountable for data collected.

Following the lead of the OECD, many countries today have developed laws and regulations that govern the collection, control, storage, use, dissemination, and destruction of personal information. The common elements found in these laws and regulations address the following matters:

- Ownership, collection, use, production, reproduction, control, transmission, and destruction of content or databases or elements thereof,

- Outsourcing the production or management of applications or any of the elements described above, and

- Marketing of applications or uses of private data.

Council of Europe's Directive 95/46/EC and the UK's Data Protection Act of 1998[7]

In 1998 there was a harmonization of privacy policy activity regarding personal information and data security in Europe. In this year the Council of Europe issued Directive 95/46/EC, and the United Kingdom issued its Data Protection Act of 1998. These promulgations synchronized major European efforts regarding the protection of privacy data.

One country, Romania, basically cut and pasted the promulgations established in the Council of Europe's Directive 95/46/EC when enacting its Personal Data Processing in the Electronic Communication Domain. In November 2001, the Romanian Parliament enacted Law No. 677/2001 for the Protection of Persons concerning the Processing of Personal Data and the Free Circulation of Such Data. This law follows very closely the Data Protection (1995/46/EC) Directives of the Council of Europe.[8]

The UK's Data Protection Act was specific to the control, use, and export of privacy data from the UK to non-European (non Council of Europe) parties. In particular, the Eighth Data Protection Principle has as its basic requirements the following steps:

- Step 1—Consider whether there will be a transfer of personal data to a third country.

- Step 2—Consider whether the third country and the circumstances surrounding the transfer ensure that an adequate level of protection will be given to that data.

Council of Europe Cyber Crime Convention	The convention is divided into four sections.
	The first section deals with substantive legal issues: illegal access, illegal interception, data interference, system interference, misuse of devices, computer-related forgery, computer-related fraud, offenses related to child pornography, and offenses related to copyright.
	The second section deals with law enforcement issues, including preservation of stored data, preservation and partial disclosure of traffic data, production order, search and seizure of computer data, real-time collection of traffic data, and interception of content data.
	The third section contains provisions concerning traditional and computer crime.
	The fourth section contains the final clauses, which deal with standard provisions in Council of Europe treaties.
U.S. Code Title 18, Part I, Chapter 47, Section 1029	Fraud and related activity in connection with access devices
U.S. Code Title 18, Part 1, Chapter 47, Section 1030	Fraud and related activity in connection with computers
U.S. Code Title 18, Part I, Chapter 65, Section 1362	Communication lines, stations, or systems
U.S. Code Title 18, Part I, Chapter 119	Wire and Electronic Communications Interception and Interception of Oral Communications
U.S. Code Title 18, Part I, Chapter 121, Section 2701	Unlawful access to stored communications
U.S. Code Title 18, Part II, Chapter 206, Section 3121	General prohibition on pen register and trap and trace device use; exception

Table 3A-1 Selected European and U.S. Guidance and Laws on Computer Crime and Privacy Protections

Sources: http://www.tech-faq.com/computer-crime-laws.shtml and http://www.crime-research.org/library/CoE_Cybercrime.html

- Step 3—Consider whether the parties have or can put into place adequate safeguards to protect that data (for instance, by entering into model clauses or establishing binding corporate rules).
- Step 4—Consider if any of the other derogations to the Eighth Principle specified in the Act apply (such as the consent of the Data Subject to the transfer).

In furtherance of the means to make effective the transfer and protection of privacy information, the Eighth Principle also called for the anonymization of data where possible; and for Safe Harbor treatment where responsible parties agreed to specific control and oversight functions.

The Safe Harbor provision provides for a set of principles, which are similar to the principles found in the Data Protection Act, and relates to transfers of privacy data to U.S. entities. It has been operational since November 2000 when the U.S. Department of Commerce opened the online self-certification process for U.S. organizations.[9] The Safe Harbor mechanism provides for a voluntary process whereby U.S. entities providing adequate protection over personal data transferred to them from the EU is recognized by the Commission as providing adequate protection for the transfer of personal data under the terms of the Directive.

In the United States, the Federal Trade Commission is primarily responsible for enforcing the Safe Harbor provision, but the mechanism is not available to many entities such as telecommunications companies and financial institutions. A full list of companies that have signed up to the Safe Harbor regime can be found on the U.S. Department of Commerce's Safe Harbor Web site.[10]

U.S. Sector Approach to Data Protection and Privacy

Unlike Europe where a harmonization approach has been taken relative to data protection and privacy via the Council of Europe, the United States has followed a sector approach to such, with many different and often disparate pieces of legislation dealing with different aspects of privacy and data protection and parties. Such a sector approach makes compliance often difficult with transparency of intent often lost in the muddle.

As an example of the contrast in approaches, Table 3A-1 highlights just a few of the many U.S. laws that deal with privacy and the protection of data.

The International Landscape: Two Segments—Many Issues

The international landscape is comprised of two principal segments: namely, nation-states (sovereign bodies) and everyone else. Non-nation-state parties must obey the law of the land wherever they are; otherwise they may be in violation of civil or criminal statutes or other rules and regulations. Sovereign nations (countries), however, operate in a more or less free form, establishing the rules by which they will administer themselves and their behavior from time to time. Wide ranges exist in the form of government a country establishes and how each conducts itself within and extraterritorially over time.

Sovereign States Activities and Issues

The definition of a sovereign state (country) was established by Article 1 of the Montevideo Convention of 1933.[11] The Convention states a sovereign state or country should possess the following attributes:

1. A permanent population,
2. A defined territory,
3. A government, and
4. A capacity to enter into relations with the other states.

Such a definition provides that each nation-state is sovereign and autonomous. Presently there are 194 countries in the world.[12] And therein lays one of many dilemmas. That is, there is no central authority that has the authority and power to govern or regulate the behavior of all states, despite valiant attempts to administer the behavior of and between states via bodies such as the League of Nations, OECD, the Council of Europe, and the United Nations amongst others.[13] And with significant differences amongst nations regarding ages and stages of being, culture, language, religion, norms, behavior, wealth, natural resources, and self-interest, differences and conflicts arise, sometimes resulting in the major conflagrations and world wars. That is, as interests and leverage shift amongst countries, there is no sole arbiter to regulate and enforce behavior or punishment among sovereign nations.

Moreover, because of this constant state of flux and change in leverage between and among nations, state insecurity drives sovereign nations to fund, develop, staff, operate, and maintain both military and intelligence services that have as their charter to defend against internal as well as external threats. In order to carry out those charter requirements, such defense and intelligence services need to know what other parties who may pose a real or potential threat are doing or are capable of. This aspect of their charter requires them to gain access to the secrets and private data of other states and parties by legal as well as extralegal means.

Such national insecurity driven with a "need to know" mentality may be best summarized by a quote attributed to Ben Franklin, one of the framers of the U.S. Constitution, when he stated: "In order to be safe, you can never be secure!"[14] That is, security is an ongoing process and not an end result.

The growth in electronic attacks is predicated on several changing fundamentals. First, assets today are moving from the physical to the virtual, where a nation's and a person's economic wealth and personal data today are represented by bits and bytes. Second, and just as important, the traditional data protections afforded by distance, time, and borders have been largely mitigated via modern communications systems, which are seamlessly netted together and transgress national and other boundaries. That is, via these modern systems and networks, "Borders and Trust," the foundational elements of data privacy and security have been expanded far beyond the ability of a party to effectively keep one's data private and secure, especially from the security elements of the leading nations.

Large-scale examples of states controlling and gathering the private data of other parties in those other states are replete. For example:

- PTTs—Post Telephone and Telegraph—the government-owned communications body that controlled all public communications including mail, telegraph, and telephone communications. Governments know it takes coordinated communications to carry out significant illegal or improper behavior. So by monitoring all communications, governments could carry out their charter obligations of defending the state. Such control extends to landing points regarding the inflow and outbound communications from the sovereign state. And today, despite many PTTs having a share offering, governments maintain an operating control function within the enterprise.

- Project Rahab—Despite the diligent work of the OECD and Council of Europe in crafting agreements in order to protect the private data of the enterprises and citizens of the signatories to such treaties, we see the German Bundesnachrichtendienst (BND) actively taking their signatories' private data. Pierre Marion, former director of French Intelligence, was quoted as stating, "I know from the organization of the BND, that they are extensively gathering intelligence in the field of economy, technology, and industry. It is a very important preoccupation of the management of the BND."[15] Moreover, the BND had an active program called Project Rahab by which it took vast amounts of private data from U.S. parties and other allies.[16]

- Project Elvis (Elvis+)—Sun Microsystems, in 1997, became proactive regarding the limitation on the length of encryption keys that could be exported from the United States. The issue involved a competitive one because European companies were permitted to export encryption systems with 128 bit keys, while U.S. enterprises were limited to exporting encryption products with only 46 bit keys. This limitation in

3A

perceived encryption strength was deemed to provide unfair competitive advantage to European companies. Sun, being a fierce competitor, decided to establish a joint venture (JV) company in the USSR wherein Sun would only hold a 49% equity position with the USSR parties holding 51%. Such control by the USSR parties made the JV subject to only USSR laws, which permitted exportation of products with 128 bit keys. The business model called for Sun to ship the computer systems to clients around the world with the encryption being sent separately to those clients directly from the USSR.[17]

The only wrinkle to this end around of U.S. export regulations was the reported situation that it was likely possible the JV was actually controlled by USSR Intelligence, and that a trapdoor had possibly been installed in the encryption software during product development. This happening, if true, would have made Sun the unwitting agent of USSR Intelligence. Such a condition, if true, had it come to be, could have compromised the private data of many users.[18]

- Echelon—Perhaps the largest electronic intercept program ever to surface, Project Echelon is a joint program administered by five countries for their mutual benefit. The countries are the United States, Canada, the United Kingdom, Australia, and New Zealand. It was reported in *BusinessWeek*, March 2003, that this Echelon system is capable of intercepting every electronic communication in the world daily.[19] Such massive collection capabilities have led to the development and deployment of Natural Language Processing (NLP) tools, in order to effectively and efficiently process this gargantuan volume of data. These software tools understand the grammar, syntax, and nuance of each respective language, and are being deployed as the end processors of such massive collection efforts. Such a vast collection of data surely challenges the privacy of all.[20]

- Lourdes, Cuba—The Russian intercept facility located at Lourdes, Cuba, was one of the largest such facilities in the world. This facility was claimed to be able to intercept all U.S. communications east of the Mississippi River. At one time it was manned by over 1,500 Russian engineers, scientists, and technicians.[21] This collection site also provides an example of the private data of many that was likely compromised.

- China/Germany 2007—China is claimed to have hacked into the computers of Angela Merkel's Chancellery as well as three other German ministries in a large-scale economic espionage data collection operation.[22] This yet again provides a strong indicator of the degree to which governments are compromising the privacy of others through technology exploits.

- Amdocs—Fox News covered a series of stories focused on the role of the Israeli-based private telecommunications firm, Amdocs. Amdocs has the contracts with the 25 largest telephone companies in the United States. This company provides all of the carriers' directory assistance, calling-record, and billing work, which gives Amdocs real-time access to nearly every telephone in the country, including records of phone calls.[23]

According to Fox, Amdocs has been investigated on numerous occasions by the FBI and other law enforcement agencies, for suspected ties to the Israeli mafia, as well as to espionage. The news report went on to say that in 1999, the National Security Agency (NSA) issued a TOP SECRET/Sensitive Compartmentalized Information

(TS/SCI) report, warning that all American phone records were getting into the hands of foreign governments—particularly the Israeli government.[24]

- Y2K—The Millennium Year Issue: When disk space was a premium, software devel opers hardcoded years in a two-digit format only in order to preserve disk space. Hence, when the turn of the century arrived, systems would not know if the year was 1900 or 2000, as "00" was the only representation of the year coded. Moreover, much of this code was written in COBOL, a programming language largely unused by this time in leading nations. Hence, a significant amount of code that needed to be remediated relative to this issue had to be sent offshore to countries where there were more COBOL programmers. In this regard, both the U.S. FBI and CIA in 1999 made grave warnings about foreign firms performing Y2K software remediation services working hand in hand with the intelligence services in those countries. Here it was reported that these firms were placing trapdoors in the remediated code such that those foreign intelligence services could later enter the customer's systems and compromise private data.[25]

What can be seen from an examination of these few, but meaningful examples is that many, and likely most, governments use modern electronic systems to gain access to other parties' private information for a multitude of reasons. This behavior, often in contravention of the international agreements such parties signed stipulating they would not carry out such activities, leaves little doubt about the ineffective nature of such privacy agreements concerning the behavior of sovereign state enterprises regarding data privacy.

Other Examples of Data Privacy Compromises

From Carnegie Mellon's CERT organization, a growing attempt by others trying to gain access to or take other parties' data may be viewed.

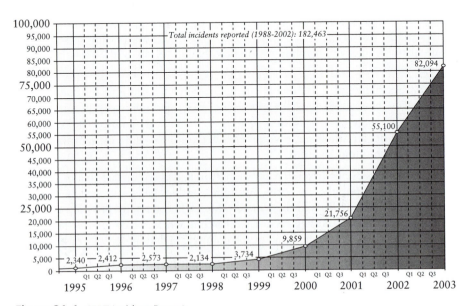

Figure 3A-1 CERT Incident Report

Courtesy Course Technology/Cengage Learning

3A

And just as the number of incidents increase, a like-kind increase in the number of malicious programs being launched on the Internet is also growing.

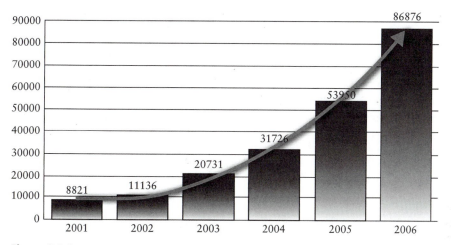

Figure 3A-2 Increase in the Number of New Malicious Programs

Courtesy Course Technology/Cengage Learning

Correlating with the increase in incidents and growth of malicious code is the criminalization or mal-activity carried out over the Internet wherein private data was compromised:

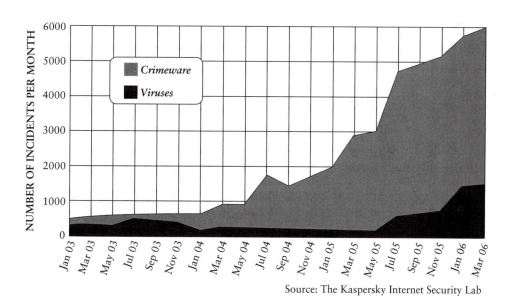

Source: The Kaspersky Internet Security Lab

Figure 3A-3 Computer Attacks: Crimes Versus Viruses

Courtesy Course Technology/Cengage Learning

Such criminal activity regarding others' personal data is also increasing in the dollar damage incurred as seen below.

Worldwide Impact in Billions of U.S. Dollars	
YEAR	**IMPACT**
2005	14.2
2004	17.5
2003	13.0
2002	11.1
2001	13.2
2000	17.1
1999	13.0
1998	6.1
1997	3.3
1996	1.8
1995	.5

Table 3A-2 Financial Impact of Systems and Data Breaches

Source: Computer Economics, 2006

Other selected correlating data regarding noncompliance with data privacy and protection promulgations are as follows:

- *USA Today* reported on December 9, 2007, that for the 300 cases tracked by Attrition.org, 162 million records containing sensitive personal data were lost or stolen in 2007, triple the number from 2006. Such losses were reported by 98 companies, 85 schools, 80 government agencies, and 30 hospitals and clinics in just a half dozen countries.[26] **Arrests or prosecutions have been reported in just 19 of these cases!**
- There is $18 billion a year lost in the United States to Intellectual Property (IP) theft.[27]
- U.S. Secret Service breaks up Shadow Crew, an online criminal consortium comprised of over 3,000 members who compromised other parties' personal data.[28]
- U.S. Federal Trade Commission reports 10 million annual cases of identity theft.[29]
- Kaspersky Labs reports criminal activity on the Internet has doubled in the past year and it sees no diminishment in this trend in the loss and misuse of other parties' personal data.[30]
- TJX lost 45.7 million of its customers' private data records via an electronic criminal breach of its systems.[31]

- The UK Treasury lost 25 million private data records from a benefits database containing sensitive personal information despite warnings of weaknesses in controls going back 3 years.[32]
- Lexis-Nexus, Citibank, ChoicePoint, AICPA, the U.S. Veterans Affairs and Air Force, and many universities among others all report losses of backup tapes or breaches of their systems containing sensitive personal data.
- "Botmaster" admits to infecting 250,000 computers and stealing the personal identities of thousands of people by wiretapping their communications and accessing their bank accounts.[33]

Conclusion

Europe has taken the lead in addressing the risks and issues regarding privacy and data protection in the digital age. Here, the OECD, the Council of Europe, as well as the UK with its comprehensive Data Protection Act of 1998 took a harmonized approach to addressing privacy and data protection issues. The United States chose a sector approach in dealing with these same matters.

The results of both paths (Europe and the United States) in attempting to protect privacy and data in the digital age has been to see such promulgations ignored or thwarted by sovereign states, and complied with in the non-sovereign sector only by parties who choose to follow the law.

Several factors are driving the breaches of the respective promulgations regarding privacy and data security, namely:

- Sovereign state legitimate defense and intelligence needs
- Economic competiveness
- Amalgamation of vast amounts of digitally stored data (an attractive target)
- Digitization of our economic wealth and assets
- Digitization of our "persona" where we have in effect become digital beings
- Economical digital attack tools available to virtually all
- A virtual "One to All" network—the Internet—that compromises the basic tenets of data privacy
- The mitigation of national boundaries via electronic connections
- The inability to determine who breached one's privacy
- The inability to successfully prosecute those breaching a party's privacy or security

Clearly, a number of responsible nations of the world have attempted to formulate a framework by which we all can have our privacy and data rights maintained and sustained. But technology advances and those who choose to violate legitimate promulgations regarding privacy and data protections, some for legitimate national security needs, have made those promulgations ineffective.

Endnotes

1. Standler, Ronald B. "Privacy Law in the USA," 1997, http://www.rbs2.com/privacy.htm

2. Right of Privacy: Personal Autonomy, Cornell University Law School, http://www.law.cornell.edu/wex/index.php/Personal_Autonomy

3. Accurint, Inc. Home Page, http://www.accurint.com and Choicepoint Home page, http://www.choicepoint.com

4. University of Louisville Louis D. Brandeis School of Law, http://www.louisville.edu/library/law/brandeis/privacy.html

5. Browne, Harry. "Does the Constitution Contain a Right to Privacy?" May 9, 2003. http://harrybrowne.org/articles/PrivacyRight.htm

6. "OECD Guidelines," Center for Democracy and Technology. http://www.cdt.org/privacy/guide/basic/oecdguidelines.html

7. Directive 95/46/EC of the European Parliament and of the Council of 24 October 1995 on the protection of individuals with regard to the processing of personal data and on the free movement of such data http://www.cdt.org/privacy/eudirective/EU_Directive_.html and http://www.oecd.org

8. Manolea, Bogdan. "International Framework for Personal Data Protection in Romania." http://www.apti.ro/DataProtection_ro.pdf

9. U.S. Department of Commerce Safe Harbor Homepage, http://www.export.gov/safeharbor/index.html

10. U.S. Department of Commerce Safe Harbor Company List, http://web.ita.doc.gov/safeharbor/shlist.nsf/webPages/safe+harbor+list

11. Montevideo Convention, Wikipedia, http://en.wikipedia.org/wiki/Montevideo_Convention

12. Rosenberg, Matt. "The Number of Countries in the World," About.com: Geography, Mar. 18, 2008. http://geography.about.com/cs/countries/a/numbercountries.htm

13. "League of Nations," Modern World History. http://www.historylearningsite.co.uk/leagueofnations.htm, United Nations Home page, http://www.un.org, Organization for Economic Co-operation and Development Home page, http://www.oecd.org, Council of Europe Home Page, http://www.coe.org.

14. World of Quotes.com http://www.worldofquotes.com/author/Benjamin-Franklin/3/index.html

15. Schweizer P., *Friendly Spies*, New York: Atlantic Monthly Press, 1993, p. 144.

16. Ibid. p. 159.

17. McMillan, Robert. "Sun Puts Pressure on U.S. Encryption Policy," May 20, 1997. http://sunsite.uakom.sk/sunworldonline/swol-05-1997/swol-05-skip.html

18. Galitsky, Alexander. "Who We Are," Billion Minds Foundation Web site. http://www.billionmindsfoundation.org/biography.php?page=Alexander_Galitsky

19. David, Leonard. "Project Echelon: Orbiting Big Brother?" Nov. 21, 2001. Spece.com Web site. http://www.space.com/businesstechnology/technology/echelon_011121-1.html and Wikipedia Web site, http://en.wikipedia.org/wiki/ECHELON

20. Language Computer Corp. Home page http://www.languagecomputer.com and Lymba Corp. Home page, http://www.lymba.com

21. Pike, John. "Lourdes [Cuba] Signal Intelligence (SIGINT) Facility, FAS Intelligence Resource Program," Oct. 17, 2001. http://www.fas.org/irp/imint/c80_04.htm

22. Boyes, Roger. "China Accused of Hacking into the Heart of Merkel's Administration," The Times Online, Aug. 27, 2007. http://www.timesonline.co.uk/tol/news/world/europe/article2332130.ece

23. Spanners, E., and Jeffrey Steinberg. "Israeli Spying in the U.S. Exposé Cracks Cover-up of September 11," Executive Intelligence Review, Dec. 21, 2001. http://www.larouchepub.com/other/2001/2849isr_spies_911.html

24. Ibid.

25. "FBI Says Y2K Software Has Been Tampered With," Reuters, Oct. 1, 1999. http://hv.greenspun.com/bboard/q-and-a-fetch-msg.tcl?msg_id=001Vrb

26. Acohido, Byron. "Theft of Personal Data More Than Triples This Year," *USA Today*, Dec. 9, 2007. http://www.usatoday.com/tech/news/computersecurity/infotheft/2007-12-09-data-theft_N.htm

27. Ruben, Robert. "Preventing Criminal Exploitation of International Trade," International Crime Control Strategy, U.S. Treasury Department, July 23, 1996. http://www.fas.org/irp/offdocs/iccs/iccsvii.html

28. Wikipedia, Shadow Crew description of the U.S. Secret Service's capture of this online criminal organization. http://en.wikipedia.org/wiki/ShadowCrew

29. Jacobsen, Debbie. "Cyber-Crime—A threat to every Internet user," *Ezine*@articles.com. http://ezinearticles.com/?Cyber-Crime—A-Threat-to-Every-Internet-User&id=237999

30. Ibid.

31. Hines, Matt. "TJX Data Heist Confirmed as Largest Ever," *Infoworld*. Mar. 29, 2007. http://www.infoworld.com/article/07/03/29/HNtjxfiling_1.html

32. Chapman, Matt. "UK Government Was Warned on Data Loss," VNUnet.com. Dec. 10, 2007. http://www.vnunet.com/vnunet/news/2205400/uk-government-warned-loss

33. Serjeant, Jill. "'Botmaster' Admits Infecting 250,000 Computers," Reuters, Nov. 9, 2007. http://www.reuters.com/article/domesticNews/idUSN0823938120071110

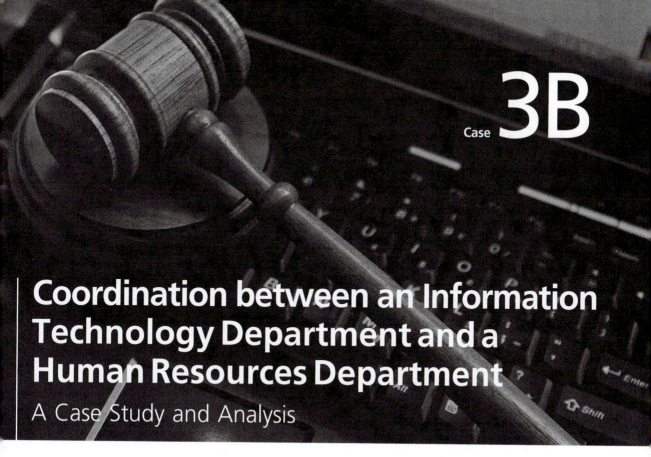

Coordination between an Information Technology Department and a Human Resources Department

A Case Study and Analysis

Jeffrey M. Stanton
School of Information Studies, Syracuse University

Jeffrey Stanton, Ph.D. (University of Connecticut, 1997) is Associate Dean for research and doctoral programs at Syracuse University's School of Information Studies. His research focuses on organizational behavior and technology, with his most recent projects examining how behavior affects information security and privacy in organizations. He is the author with Dr. Kathryn Starn of the book, The Visible Employee: Using Workplace Monitoring and Surveillance to Protect Information Assets Without Compromising Employee Privacy or Trust *(2006, Information Today, ISBN: 0910965749).*

Overview

A medium-sized U.S. engineering company (< 500 full-time employees), referred to in this case study as Cenartech, has a sophisticated information infrastructure that supports engineering, sales, financial, and human resources functions. The information systems infrastructure comprises application and storage servers, wired and wireless networks, email and text messaging services, and a Web presence. A relatively new director of Information Technology figures prominently in this case, as does a more seasoned Human Resources director. Conflict between these two roles provides the primary pedagogical value of this case.

The events described in the case begin with a relatively routine account lock-out reported by an employee. After additional similar events, a review of log files reveals that a variety of username-password combinations was tried from a cluster of computers inside the company. The IT director engages the assistance of the HR director in addressing the problem. The security problem escalates to including tampering with databases and application configurations. Eventually the problem is traced to a rogue employee.

The case presentation follows a chronological progression and is divided into separate phases that you may provide to the students piece by piece or all at once. A bank of discussion questions in the first appendix provides one strategy for starting the conversation in the classroom. Subsequently, an instructor's appendix provides interpretive information that you may find useful in guiding the discussion.

Cenartech Security Case: Part 1

Cenartech is a U.S. engineering company, with approximately 400 employees. The firm makes process-monitoring devices for food manufacturing companies and the pharmaceutical and cosmetics manufacturing industries. Customers know the company as an innovative leader in providing highly accurate products with all the latest features. All Cenartech products contain embedded microprocessors, sensors, and displays. Some products are handheld, while others are installed permanently into manufacturing facilities. After operating in an initial period of about seven years as a start-up company, the firm was sold to and is now privately owned by a European parent company. The firm still operates quasi-independently, has its own management structure, and is responsible for its own day-to-day operations. The parent company sets the strategic direction of Cenartech and obtains the profit from operations.

The firm experienced a rapid period of growth starting three years ago. Since that time, the number of employees has approximately doubled. Initial hiring growth was primarily in engineering, software, and manufacturing departments. Subsequently, additional hiring occurred in organizational support areas: information technology, finance and accounting, technical support, and human resources.

Cenartech now boasts a substantial information technology installation. A fractional DS3 connection to the local exchange carrier provides Internet access for three separate networks that have firewalls between them. One network provides guest wireless access: hosts on this network have access to the Internet and nothing else. A second network exists for financial systems. This network has no authorized wireless access points, and access to the Internet is aggressively filtered and firewalled. The third network is for all other employees and functions, and this network has a wired component as well as wireless access points that require authentication. Internet access on this network is not highly filtered. All authorized computers on this network require a log-in and each employee has their own username and password. All authorized computers in the building have antivirus software. A centralized, open source antispam package exists to pre-filter all email prior to delivery.

Brian Galven is the manager of the IT department at Cenartech and has been with the company for slightly less than two years. Brian is in his late 30s, is of medium height, and dresses casually, favoring flannel shirts, jeans, and sneakers, although he occasionally dons a sport jacket for meetings with outside vendors. His position at Cenartech represents the greatest amount of managerial responsibility that Brian has had, as well as the largest company where he has worked. Prior to Brian's arrival, Cenartech's IT department did not have a manager. Instead, employees working on IT reported to the company's director of finance. The director of finance had also used a number of consultants in the years prior to Brian's arrival to help the company with major IT projects. Within a year of his arrival, Brian had accomplished much to professionalize the company's IT operations and personnel. At the time of the events described in this case, Brian had written a first draft of an IT practices manual that spelled out the different tasks that his staff members had to do, everything from backups to cleaning virus and worm infections from laptops. The manual describes all the necessary steps such that any of the IT people can do a task, even if the person who usually does it calls in sick or goes on vacation. At 12 full-time equivalent employees (FTEs), the IT department is not large enough to have a separate security function, so each IT staff member has some security responsibilities, but Brian does the most, since he has the most knowledge in the security area.

Given his prior work experience as an information security professional, Brian is a strong advocate of the importance of running and analyzing server logs. From the start of his employment with Cenartech he enabled almost every logging option available on the hosts and servers used by the company. Most of his staff members are unfamiliar with security log analysis, so whenever time permits Brian runs analysis on logs, looking for information about the performance of the networks as well as anything out of the ordinary.

Leading up to the events described in this case, Brian had seen repeated failed log-in attempts on a couple of different accounts, but with four or fewer repeats—an insufficient number to cause a lockout. More recently, an employee came into Brian's office complaining that she was having trouble logging in; when Brian investigated, he found that she had been locked out because of five failed log-in attempts. "Did you forget your password?" he asked her. She replied that she didn't think she had, but Brian went ahead and reset her password anyway and he unlocked her account.

After unlocking her account, Brian pored through his security logs, looking for the history of the log-in attempts that had led up to the lockout of the woman's account. When he had correlated some of the log data, he found that failed log-in attempts had come from a workstation in the engineering cluster. All of the recent failed attempts had occurred around lunchtime, and today's lockout was preceded by smaller sets of failed log-ins at lunch hours over the past week. Brian had a hunch that one or more of the product engineers were probably fooling around with the system. Given his background in security, however, Brian was not inclined to ignore the event or wait to see what would happen next. Instead, he decided to report what he had found. Current company policy stated that such incident reports must begin with the human resources department, so Brian made an appointment with the administrative assistant of the vice president of human resources.

James Falkirk is the vice president of human resources for Cenartech. He is a tall man in late middle age, always wears a suit and tie, but speaks in an informal way, and asks people to call him Jim. He was the fifth employee hired into the company when it was a start-up more than 15 years ago; he originally served in the role of general manager at a time when the company used consultants and outside vendors for many of its engineering and fabrication tasks. Jim is a close friend and golf partner of Cenartech's CEO; their association predated the founding of Cenartech. Jim had a modest ownership stake in the firm when it was sold to the German parent company such that he is now financially secure for retirement.

During their meeting, which took about half an hour, Brian explained his findings to Jim. This explanation required substantial effort on Brian's part, as Jim had minimal IT experience and was surprised to learn that Brian kept records of so many different events on the company's networks. Brian persevered, however, and was able to explain the nature of the evidence to Jim as well as the fact that the evidence could not pinpoint a particular individual. The log records showed that the failed log-in attempts came from workstations shared among multiple engineers. Whoever had tried the different username/password combinations had not also used his or her legitimate account information in close time proximity on the same workstations, so it was not even possible to guess which individual had caused the failed log-ins. Jim had difficulty understanding how there was much harm in the failed log-in attempts, and he tended to agree with Brian's tentative hypothesis that it was just an engineering employee simply "fooling around" without malicious intent. Nonetheless, Jim promised to look into the problem: "I'll head on down there and talk to the manager of that group and see what's up with his guys. And I'm sure we'll figure out what's going on, so don't sweat it."

Discussion Questions

1. Given your understanding of the history and status of Cenartech, make some general observations about the firm's security readiness. Is Cenartech at low, moderate, or high risk of a security problem? On what aspects of the description do you base your assessment?

2. What can you say about how security fundamentals were addressed in Cenartech (e.g., issues such as confidentiality, integrity, and availability; authentication and access control; non-repudiation; principle of least privilege, etc.).

3. Compare and contrast the two roles—IT manager and vice president of human resources—in terms of their responsibilities, focus, and goals. Ignore for the moment the particular people involved, just talk about the roles in a general sense.

4. Now think about the two people described in the case, IT manager Brian Galven, and HR VP Jim Falkirk. How are they different?

5. What's your evaluation of Brian's job performance so far?

Cenartech Security Case: Part 2

Following his meeting with the vice president of human resources, Brian returned to his department and turned his attention to important IT projects. At the top of his list, he was setting up a virtual private network (VPN) to help the Cenartech sales staff obtain remote access to client information. The client information resided on databases maintained by the staff in the firm's business office, so the VPN terminated in Cenartech's financial systems network. Brian had to customize the restrictive firewall rules on this network to support the operation of the VPN. With his focus on completing the VPN project on schedule, several weeks went by during which Brian had no time to analyze log files. During this period, he also received no complaints from employees about account lockouts.

Part of the complexity of the VPN project was that the laptops of most members of the sales staff did not have an installed capability for remote management. An IT employee had developed a scripted installation that could run from a CD, but when Brian had sent this to a couple of the salespeople, they had complained that it failed to work. As a result, several of the installation CDs that the IT staffer had created lay unused on a stack on a table in the IT department. Brian had to wait until each member of the sales staff came to the company's headquarters in order to physically access their laptops and install the VPN client.

As Brian began to deploy the VPN clients and send the salespeople back into the field with their updated laptops, he also began to monitor security logs again. He was surprised to find a greater number of incoming VPN connection attempts than he had expected. When he followed up some of the originating IP addresses, he also found that a number of the connections originated from a local cable Internet Service Provider (ISP). He had expected most of the connections from more distant locales, because the salespeople provisioned with the VPN client were all from other regions of the country. Brian ran more log analyses and found that after a brief lull two weeks earlier, that the failed log-in attempts had begun again. Further, he found that while some of the attempted log-ins had again occurred from the engineering cluster around lunchtime, other failed attempts had occurred during the VPN authentication process, mostly after hours, and mostly from IP addresses originating with the local ISP.

Given the recurrence of the original problem, plus the new issues that had arisen with the VPN, Brian requested another meeting with Jim and reported the problems he had seen. This time, Jim got very serious and said, "I'll go back down there to engineering and read them the riot act. We'll definitely get this issue cleaned up. You can leave it to me." Brian felt reassured that Jim was taking the issue more seriously now, and he returned to his projects.

A month went by without incident, but one morning around 7:00 AM, Brian received a frantic call from an accountant whose habit was to arrive at work early. The accountant reported that although she could log in to the network, none of her applications would work. Brian rushed into work and found utter chaos. Several database tables had become corrupted, a large number of files had been deleted, and application configurations had been tampered with. Looking at the datestamps on some of the corrupted files, Brian concluded that much of the damage had occurred late the previous evening. He quickly restored a number of files from backups in order to get key users back up and running. Then he organized his IT staff to get to work on restoring everyone else who had been affected. Fortunately, Brian's attention to standardizing backup procedures and related disaster recovery capabilities meant that his staff had the knowledge and resources to restore almost everything that had been lost and to accomplish this restoration relatively quickly.

The whole process of repairing the damage took about a week, and during this time, Brian collected as much forensic data as he could. Several important findings emerged. First, he found that user accounts existed on some of the financial systems for employees who no longer worked with the firm. Further, these accounts had extensive histories of recent activity from workstations all over the business office. When Brian chatted "off the record" with some of the individuals who worked in the business office (recall that the official policy was that Brian was supposed to address such matters through HR first), he found that many of the employees shared the use of archaic, still-active accounts. When previous employees had left the firm's business office several years ago, they had given their username and password information to their colleagues for the sake of convenience, so that the employees who remained could access the departing person's files and applications. Previously, no one had disabled the user accounts of these departed employees. Now, however, Brian backed up all of the files that remained in these archaic accounts and then he disabled them.

Next, Brian traced the damage to a connection that had occurred through the VPN. The originating IP address showed that the connection was not from a local ISP, nor was it from an ISP in a locale where any of the company's salespeople lived. The account that the attacker had used to disrupt the operations in the business office had used one of the "shared" accounts of a departed employee as mentioned above. Additional analysis of the log files showed that the attacker had used the same archaic account through the VPN in the same timeframe to try to gain access to engineering systems, but the firewalls between the different networks had prevented the attacker from connecting. Related, three weeks earlier the same archaic account had been accessed at lunchtime from within the engineering cluster.

In the aftermath of the attack, Brian met with every member of Cenartech's senior management, and he realized that his job was on the line. He explained everything that he had ascertained about the attacks, and he tried not to sound defensive when describing his existing security measures and what he knew about how they had been circumvented. Brian realized that, with their limited understanding of the technology involved, most of the senior managers seemed to lay blame for the attack on Brian's deployment of the VPN. When Brian met with Jim, and they reviewed the situation together, Jim resolved to interview personally each member of the accounting department and the engineering department to see if anyone had further information that would shed light on the attack.

Discussion Questions

1. Give an analysis of the attack. Given what the case describes, what can you determine about the attacker, his or her motives, and/or the way that the attack was conducted?

2. The goal of the VPN project was to provide remote access to important information for members of the sales staff. Taking into account your analysis of the attack, did the VPN project represent excessive risk for Cenartech?

3. Imagine that you served as a consultant engaged to analyze this case. What would you recommend to the managers at Cenartech for next steps? In other words, how can Cenartech avoid attacks like this one in the future?

4. Taking the previous question into account, what, if any, specific organizational changes would you recommend for:

    a. New technology?

    b. Personnel or staff changes?

    c. Policy or procedural changes?

    d. Other changes?

5. Contrasting the situations in Parts 1 and 2 of the case, has your opinion of Brian's job performance changed?

Cenartech Security Case: Part 3

At the conclusion of their conversation, Brian remembered to ask Jim about the second dialog that Jim had had with the manager of the engineering department. Jim offhandedly said, "Oh, after I chatted again with the manager of that group down there, he caught the guy at it. When all the other folks in his group had gone out to lunch, that guy stuck around and was trying out all kinds of different passwords. So we fired him three weeks ago."

At this revelation, Brian nearly fell out of his chair. Mustering as much calm as he could, he asked Jim why no one had mentioned the firing of the engineer to someone in the IT department so that they could deprovision the fired employee's account access.

Jim said, "You're right, that would have been a good idea, but you know, we've rarely had an employee leave the firm on bad terms, so it's not something that's really come up before."

"But the attack we had last week used an account of an old employee," Brian replied. "One that had apparently left on good terms. So you see how it doesn't matter whether the person is fired or just resigns, we have to know when they leave so that we can deactivate their account."

"Sure, that does make sense," Jim agreed, "but it wouldn't have saved us in this case. The hacker who did this didn't use the account information from the engineer we fired."

Brian then patiently explained to Jim that indeed it might not have prevented the attack, but if they had consistently removed archaic accounts from the company's networks, that the attack might have been avoided. Brian concluded the meeting with several new ideas in his mind about the attack, which he shared a few days later in a one-on-one meeting with the CEO of the company. A few weeks later, a few shake-ups occurred in the management structure of the company, and the CEO issued several new policies that Brian had drafted. One of the new policies pertained to greater coordination between HR and IT, particularly regarding notification of changes in the status of employees—hiring, firing, promotion, etc.

In reflecting on the attack later, Brian believed that the fired engineer was the attacker who caused all the damage. The engineer had apparently used his lunch hour over the past few months to probe the accounts of current and former employees, looking for a username/password combination that would give access to key information systems in the company. The engineer had probably taken a VPN installer disk from the stack on the table in the IT department and installed the VPN on his own system to continue his probing from home or another location on the Internet. Brian believed that the engineer had eventually hit on the correct password for the archaic account at some point either just before or just after he left the company. Brian was unsure of the engineer's original intentions for the account probing, and was unsure as to whether the termination of the engineer's employment had been the trigger for the actual attack. Finally, Brian believed that with records obtained through a legal request to the local ISP that he might obtain enough evidence to bring a criminal case against the engineer, but Cenartech's CEO decided not to pursue that course.

Discussion Questions

1. After examining Brian's analysis of the attack, can you think of any details or issues he may have forgotten?

2. The case states that, "a few shake-ups occurred in the management structure of the company." What "shake-ups" do you believe are likely to have occurred? Given your answer, do you believe this was the right strategy? If you had been the CEO, what personnel actions, if any, would you have taken following the attack?

3. The CEO issued a new policy concerning notification of the IT department when employees joined or left the company. What other policy changes would you recommend, if any?

4. What do you think of the decision not to pursue a legal case against the first engineer? Why do you think the CEO opted not to pursue the case? Was he right? Why or why not?

5. In the aftermath of the attack, what would you tell current employees about the attack? How much detail would you give them? What do you believe their reactions would be?

6. Rewind to the beginning of the case: What should Brian have done differently in order to have prevented the attack? Discuss the challenges he would have met in pursuing your recommended strategy.

7. Now take the previous question from the CEO's perspective: If your primary goal was to help the company succeed, in part by mitigating risks, what might you have done well before the attack to organize the company better?

IT Ethics and Security in an Information Security Certification Exam

Jeffrey P. Landry and J. Harold Pardue
University of South Alabama

Jeffrey P. Landry is a Professor in the School of Computer and Information Sciences at the University of South Alabama, where he teaches courses in information systems strategy and policy, project management, and human computer interaction. Dr. Landry is developing risk assessments of voting systems for federal elections; has conducted risk management for a national, online certification exam; and has published on trust in the IS context, all following a ten-year software industry career.

J. Harold Pardue is a Professor in the School of Computer and Information Sciences at the University of South Alabama, where he teaches courses in n-tier/SOA development, database, and human computer interaction. Dr. Pardue is developing risk assessments of voting systems for federal elections; has acted as chief technology and security officer for a national, online certification exam; and has published in the areas of trust in computing, IS architectures, HCI, and IS education.

Overview

This fictionalized case revolves around the development and deployment of a secure, online certification exam and is constructed from actual events. The project presented numerous security concerns, technical and managerial, as well as ethical and legal issues that put the project, and the professional reputations of its sponsors, at risk. Some of the issues include cheating, inadvertent and intentional release of exam items, defenses against unauthorized access, risk management, confidentiality, and privacy issues related to the information collected on individuals and institutions. Solutions are provided along with critical case questions for students.

Introduction

Professional certificates, such as the CISSP certificate[1] for information security, are credentials highly sought after by professionals seeking greater visibility, opportunities, and jobs. They are useful, too, for employers and job recruiters looking for qualified professionals and for faculty members who want an indicator of whether students are being prepared for professional practice. But certificates are so expensive to obtain that they are out of reach for most students. Enter Gene Hartman, Ph.D. Dr. Hartman, a professor of information systems at Gulf State University, wants to know if Gulf State's four-year information systems degree is adequately preparing students for a career in information security management. He created the iSec-Cert Group, an organization for establishing an information security certification exam targeted at students of four-year college programs in information systems, information technology, or computer science.

This teaching case continues with a description of the organization and its key personnel, and a chronology of events. Security issues are discussed and case questions for students presented. A number of themes are to be recognized as emerging from the case:

1. Professional interaction and collaboration among members of the iSec-Cert team form a basis for understanding how some issues arose as well as how some issues got resolved; information security management cannot be discussed realistically without understanding how these professionals collaborated with one another. This theme is introduced in the first major section of the case, Organizational Context.

2. The process of developing an exam was described. An understanding of the specific domain of developing and administering online exams formed one basis for managing information security at iSec-Cert. These issues are covered in the next major section, Exam Development Process and Security.

3. Additional security risks fall under the category of application level security threats. These are mostly technical threats associated with Internet-based information systems and are covered in the section, Application Security Threats and Countermeasures.

4. Risk management is a critical framework for understanding information security management for the iSec-Cert team. The use of risk management by the iSec-Cert team is covered in the section, Assessing Risks with Less Than a Week to Go.

5. Legal and ethical issues were abundant. Some of these issues are covered in the case's final major section, Ethical and Legal Aspects of Security at iSec-Cert.

Organizational Context

This section provides a background of the organizational context of iSec-Cert, including brief profiles of key people and how their collaboration is relevant to security management.

Organization: The iSec-Cert Group

The original iSec-Cert group consists of three faculty members, described below, who work as a collaborative team of experts to create, administer, and validate a pilot version of an exam.

Products: iSec-Cert Certificate

The certificate is available to students enrolled in four-year programs that cover information security topics. Students must pass the exam, agree to abide by a professional code of ethics, and complete their degree program. The exam is free, but if they qualify by passing, a $150 certificate fee is charged.

Customers: Information Security Educators and Students

The customers are information security students and faculty. Students benefit by obtaining a professional credential. Faculty benefit by gaining a means of program assessment that is useful for accreditation and continuous improvement.

Vision

To create a collaborative group of university educators who, through collegial collaboration, would create a professional certification exam in information security—one that students could afford and universities could use to accredit and improve their information security programs.

Mission

To promote the achievement of excellence in information security education and training through the use of high-quality certification exams.

Competitors

Educational Testing Services (ETS), which offers computer science exams to students and schools, but that currently has no information security exam, is probably the biggest potential competitor, because they are experienced, credible, and well known, and also target the educational market. A number of certification exams aimed at businesses and professionals, such as the aforementioned CISSP and CISM,[2] are direct competitors in information security competencies, but are very high priced and do not compete effectively in the educational market.

Business Strategy

Seek collaborations with university faculty to create a high-quality, secure start-up information security exam, offering this exam free to students and free to universities in the first year, thereafter charging schools an annual fee for services, while increasing the number of participating schools.

Key Personnel

The people described below are key players in the development of the iSec-Cert exam and all contribute to the management of information security. Each key person is listed along with their affiliation, professional role, and areas of specialty. A brief profile is given with an attempt to introduce information security concerns in the case.

Dr. Gene Hartman, Gulf State University, Professor of Information Systems, Founder and Marketing Director

Gene is a "soft skills" IS professor, known as a great people person, a master of interpersonal skills, an extrovert, and avid evangelist of the Covey habits. He is also a creative visionary and risk-seeker. He is the founder of the iSec-Cert group and has a propensity to trust people whom he meets, especially faculty members and students, whom he treats the same. He takes on a marketing role, spending countless hours on his cell phone headset, speaking with faculty contacts.

Dr. Will Sherlock, Gulf State University, Professor of Information Systems; Chief Developer, Application and Data Security

Will is expert at the technical side of IS. He is introverted, efficient and task oriented, and an ethical professional who follows industry best practices. Gene recruited Will as lead implementer of the ambitious, national online certification exam project. Will is a critical person to be involved, because, as a professor who teaches the database and advanced application development courses, he is fluent in the technical competencies needed by the project. He would serve as the chief application developer and be responsible for administering application and database security procedures.

Dr. Janet Jeffries, University of the Midwest, Professor of Information Systems, Project Management, and Exam Security

Janet was a former IT project manager and exam certification director for a professional organization, recruited by Gene at a recent certification conference. Janet is quality-minded and a critical tester and reviewer. She is the team's devil's advocate. Fearing that the project would fail and concerned with technical security issues, she recommends that the exam be paper-based and scored with the bubble sheet, optical scan technology. She loses the debate with Gene over exam format. Instead, Janet is to lead the team in developing security policies for an online exam. Janet prefers a controlling, authoritative management style, one that often alienates other faculty members, who prefer to be more democratic and creatively independent. Janet is very concerned about exam security and insists that stringent security policies be established. She would work closely with Gene and Will to establish security policies.

Collaboration, Trust, and Security

In the fall of 2005, Gene recruits a series of Gulf State graduate students to join him in designing and implementing a prototype test bank database. Gene gives out the DBMS's administrative password to each new recruit. The gesture is a symbol of the trust that Gene likes to establish with each new student brought into Gene's collaborative group. What better way to establish trust than to give out the "keys to the castle"?

In November of 2005, during the forming stages of iSec-Cert, Gene recruits his professorial colleagues, Janet and Will, asking them to collaborate with him and the students working on the project. Will is interested and agrees, but Janet, concerned about quality and security, makes the following recommendations, to which Gene and Will agree:

- Change the DBMS administrative password
- Exclude students from the project
- Provide administrative access only to herself, Will, and the department's network administrator

Gene and Janet argue vociferously over the policy toward student involvement. Janet says that students cannot be trusted to complete and test such a risky system over such a short period of time. She says it would be easier to complete the project with Will than to manage students. Furthermore, since the product is an exam and students stand to gain something by cheating, students cannot be trusted to have access to systems that contain the test questions. Gene, who worked with students on many past IT projects, disagrees, imploring Janet to be more "inclusive." He believes students are helpful and trustworthy, and that it was a worthy goal to involve them. He uses graduate assistants as an example of students selected and hired to teach, assist teachers, and access exams and other sensitive course information. Janet insists on the no-student policy as a precondition of being involved, and Gene relents.

Later, in February, the iSec-Cert group hosts an item-writing workshop attended by 25 faculty members and held at Gulf State University. Their goal is to build up a test bank. Despite agreeing to Janet's "no-student" policy, Gene invites Ralph, a master's student, to the workshop. Janet, surprised and concerned by Ralph's appearance, refuses to grant Ralph access privileges to the iSec-Cert Test Writer, but allows Ralph to submit questions via a paper-based form instead. After the workshop, Will and Janet review Ralph's questions. They read the first 8 of the 25 he submitted, and after deciding none of them were acceptable to use, Janet slides the remaining unread pages off her desk and into the wastebasket.

Review Questions

1. Evaluate the mix of skills and personalities on the iSec-Cert team. Why do you think there is disagreement on security approaches? Do you think this conflict will be good or bad for security management?

2. Is Janet an appropriate choice to lead the iSec-Cert team in security matters? Why or why not?

3. By her attitude and actions toward Ralph, can you infer the security threats that concerned Janet?

4. How could students have been involved while also overcoming Janet's concerns?

5. Identify the threats and countermeasures you would recommend for joint faculty-student projects of this type.

6. Consult the International Information Systems Security Certification Consortium, Inc. (ISC)[2] Code of Ethics,[3] found at https://www.isc2.org/cgi-bin/content.cgi?category=12. Is there anything in the code that can justify Janet's actions toward Ralph's involvement from a professional security ethics standpoint?

Exam Development Process and Security

In order to understand information security issues for an online exam, it is important to examine the process of developing an exam. The following sections describe some of the activities for developing the iSec-Cert exam with security issues arising in the process.

By the end of the item-writing workshop, the iSec-Cert team met to discuss the design and implementation of the exam, and the security policies. They agreed on the following. The most important information asset was the exam questions. A lot of work went into their development, and if they were compromised, the exam scores would be useless. They were not concerned so much with the exam items as intellectual property that was at risk of being acquired by a competitor. They were concerned with students stealing the items and using them systematically, or posting them on the Web in a potentially large cheating ring. Such a breach would probably require a completely new set of questions from a group already tapped of ideas, and invalidate months of prior work. The whole project might collapse.

An early decision without any debate was eliminating the consideration of remote (i.e., at-home) administration of the exam. They agreed that the exam would have to be administered in a highly controlled environment, one with a proctor present at all times, and that the proctor would have to be a faculty member at the school.

Review Questions

1. The iSec-Cert team thought the most important vulnerability was the exam content. Do you agree?

2. Who or what else was vulnerable in this certification project?

3. Is it possible to secure a remote (i.e., non-proctored) certification exam? If so, how? If not, why not?

Creating Organizational Access and Use Policies

The iSec-Cert established security policies around access and use of the exams at the participating universities. They had already begun establishing organizational policies through Gene's interactions with faculty that began a process of relationship and trust building. Many faculty members participating in the project were already his friends and colleagues at other schools, and could be trusted. After making a presentation at an information security conference, additional faculty interesting in giving the exam called or emailed him. In each case, Gene verified that the faculty member was legitimate by double-checking the email address against the published emails on faculty listed on the school's Web site, and he personally phoned the faculty member.

One faculty member from each school was designated as a "faculty contact" and given the highest access privileges, including the role of adding other faculty members at that school. The faculty contact could also decide on roles for the other faculty members at that school. Some of the roles included the activities of verifying students and proctoring exams.

Although the faculty contacts were considered to be legitimate, trustworthy people, very little access to test questions themselves was permitted. The only way a faculty member or faculty contact could be given access to questions is if they signed up to take the exam themselves, or later, join the item writing and review group. Gene did not really expect a rogue faculty member to be a serious concern. Janet was more skeptical and wanted to keep close track of faculty contacts with access to iSec-Cert data.

Review Questions

1. Was the iSec-Cert team too trusting of faculty members?

2. Do you think the access controls and organizational policies provided were adequate steps to prevent unauthorized access to the exam contents? Why or why not?

3. What else could they have done to mitigate the risk of unauthorized access to exam content?

Designing Process Controls—Proctor Policies and Their Enforcement

Considering exam content as the most precious information asset, the biggest process vulnerability was intentional, unauthorized access to exam content. To cope with this threat, proctor policies were created, documented, and distributed to all faculty contacts, and the contacts were given responsibility for educating their proctors.

An important goal of the exam proctoring process was to establish control of the room. There were a number of ways that students could beat the system. The biggest threat was of accidental or intentional access to exam items. A secondary threat was of cheating during the test, where the exam content itself was not compromised.

See Table 3C-1 for a copy of the guidelines provided to exam proctors.

In order for a student to gain access to the questions of an exam, they would have to:

- Register themselves on the log-in page
- Get verified by a faculty member at their chosen school
- Sign up for an exam offered by their school
- Get logged in to a registered exam by the proctor using a secret password

Review Questions

1. Do you think the guidelines for exam proctors are adequate to prevent unauthorized access or cheating? Why or why not?

2. Under what circumstances, if any, do you think a proctor would give out the exam password by, for example, announcing it in class or writing it on the board? What is the likelihood of this occurring? How can these circumstances be mitigated?

3. What about enforcement of proctor policies? What if proctors do not follow policies? How will iSec-Cert know? What should the consequences be for proctors not following policies?

4. How else could iSec-Cert have designed their proctor control processes to avoid the use of a single proctor password?

iSec-Cert Exam Proctor Instructions

1. Register, sign up, and take certification exams at iSec-Cert's Web site: http://isec-cert.org.

2. Students may register with the iSec-Cert by going to the Web address above and clicking "Click here" to register. When registering, students should BE CAREFUL to choose the correct university.

3. We recommend that the proctor have an additional helper on exam day. It is important that the proctor(s) maintain control of the room and assist students rapidly.

4. Students may not use a calculator or any other resources during the exam. You may provide blank scratch paper, but the students must leave the paper in the room after taking the exam. Students should not be allowed to print out questions or use email or chat during the test, and cell phones should be turned off.

5. To begin the exam, the students should log in to the system, using their log-in and password, and then select Start/resume iSec-Cert exam, and pick an exam session from the drop-down list. An error message, "Your registration is not verified. Please contact your university administrator or exam proctor" may appear. If so, then the proctor should log in and verify that student.

6. If the exam session is within 30 minutes of starting, they will be asked for an exam password. This password should have been given to the proctor by the faculty contact at the institution or obtained from the iSec-Cert. DO NOT give this password to the students.

7. Have each student lay a picture ID (school or driver's license) next to their computer so that you can verify that the name/email they have logged in with is their own. At this time, ask them to look away and you type in the password for them.

8. After proctor enters password, student may hit [Proceed—>], which will bring up the Instructions page. The system will not let them begin until the start time of the exam session is reached.

9. There will be extra time (30 minutes) for late log-ins. However, these late log-ins must be registered by the registration deadline, have selected the correct exam session, and be verified in the system by the proctor before the student will be allowed to proceed to the exam. NOTE: Late log-ins are not possible if the student has also missed the registration deadline.

10. The proctors should report suspicious student activity to the iSec-Cert. For example, there should be no keyboard activity during the test. This might indicate email communication or attempts to print or save exam contents. If students close the browser and leave the room during the test, it is possible that they may be able to access the exam on another computer (if they have access to the exam password and there is time remaining). If a proctor suspects that an early quitter may be attempting to cheat, they should report this to us, so that we may check their response log.

If a problem arises, don't hesitate to immediately call an iSec-Cert administrator.

Will Sherlock 555-5802

Janet Jeffries 555-0966

Table 3C-1   Guidelines for a Secure Exam Process

Implementing Safeguards to Support Verification and Proctoring

As Will began the development of the test-taking application, he implemented several security safeguards to support the verification and proctoring processes defined by the group.

First, he agreed to make it extremely difficult for any authorized user to access test questions that could be printed out or downloaded. Will made sure that the only feature in the system that

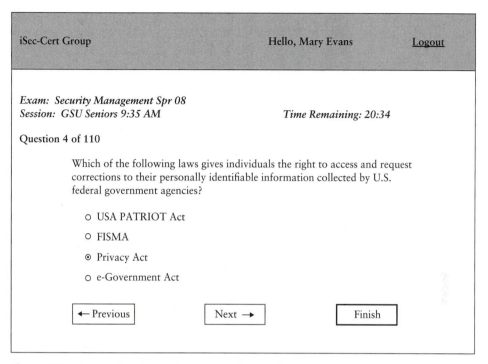

Figure 3C-1 Sample Test Screen for iSec-Certification Exam

Courtesy Course Technology/Cengage Learning

displayed the actual content of a test question was the page that displayed a question for an authorized test taker. See Figure 3C-1. No other features displayed any part of a question, such as a stem or possible answers. For example, Will provided score reports but organized them by topic, and the questions themselves did not appear. Other security safeguards were taken:

- Will disabled caching in the Web browser. Caching creates temporary Internet files that could have enabled unauthorized access to exam questions.

- Will disabled the browser's history buffer that could enable someone to jump back into the middle of an exam that had long since expired.

- Will selected the use of secure socket layers (SSL) technology, which uses encryption to thwart the threat of network packet sniffers.

- Will and Janet decided to randomize the order of questions from one instance of a student's exam to another, to make it nearly impossible for students in the room to cheat by cooperative means, that is, looking at each other's screen or whispering answers.

Review Questions

1. A risk management approach states that security threats and vulnerabilities are related to technology, people, or processes.[4] Consider the complete set of iSec-Cert solutions and identify the remaining issues of concern in each area.

2. In which area do you think iSec-Cert's exam content is most vulnerable: technology, people, or process? Why?

A number of security threats fell under the category of application level threats. These were threats associated with vulnerabilities characteristic of all Internet-based information systems, such as the iSec-Cert examination system. The following section describes some of these threats and countermeasures. These are all technical threats and should be of great interest to students and faculty interested in security issues for the Web-based application development specialists, such as .net programmers. Those readers who are more interested in managerial issues related to information security may choose to skip—without getting lost—to the next major section, entitled Assessing Risks with Less Than a Week to Go, or the final section, entitled Ethical and Legal Aspects of Security at iSec-Cert.

Application Security Threats and Countermeasures

During development, testing, and deployment of the application, a number of application security threats were both anticipated and discovered. Countermeasures for each threat were implemented. The threats ranged in severity from minor to catastrophic. The following threats are a representative sample of those anticipated and encountered.

Connection Pool Leak: Denial of Service Threat

During the testing phase prior to the first release of the software, a pilot exam was given to an undergraduate class of 11 students. Five minutes into the exam period, students began receiving an error message indicating that a connection to the database could not be obtained and the request had timed out. A possible cause was that all pooled connections were in use.

During the pre-pilot testing phase, Will and Janet had successfully completed multiple mock exams and never received this error message. However, the pilot test was the first time the application was used by more than two concurrent exam takers (Will and Janet). After the pilot test, Will replicated the error message and it confirmed that the connection pool was becoming exhausted.

The connection pool became exhausted because each page request for an exam question created a separate connection to the database and these connections were never closed by the application. The default setting for the maximum number of concurrent connections was 100. Although the DBMS will eventually close idle connections, garbage collection is not immediate, so 11 concurrent users very quickly exceeded the default maximum.

The reason the application was not closing the connection was the data object was a connected forward-only cursor (in this case, an ADO.Net data reader) and the data object was passed to a calling method and therefore went out of scope. Once the connected data object was out of scope, there was no means of explicitly closing the connection.

This connection pool leak is a vulnerability that can produce an effect similar to a denial of service attack. Too many connections will exhaust the pool and prevent additional registered takers from making connections. An attacker could even exploit this vulnerability and threaten the system by repeatedly exhausting the connection pool maximum.

The countermeasure for this security threat was to pass data tables instead of connected data objects to the calling method.

3C

Review Questions

1. Would increasing the DBMS's maximum limit for concurrent connections (and adding hardware to support the increased memory demands) be a reasonable countermeasure to this threat? Why or why not?

2. Do a Google search on "connection pool leak." Briefly describe the nature of this threat.

3. Is this threat specific to a certain technology or technology platform (say Microsoft's ADO.Net data reader)?

4. Propose a method for assessing an application's vulnerability to this type of threat.

Multiple Browser Sessions per Exam Taker: Threat of Impersonation

Post-deployment, Will realized that more than one browser session could be open for a given user (exam taker) during an exam. That is, an exam taker could log in to the application multiple times using separate browser sessions. An exam taker could concurrently log in multiple times because the default behavior of a Web application is stateless. Concurrent user log-ins are treated as independent and unrelated events.

The problem with allowing concurrent log-ins is the threat of user impersonation. Specifically, two or more users could conspire to cheat on the exam by exploiting this vulnerability. Several forms of impersonation could be exploited. For example, assume John and Bob are taking an exam at the same time in the same room. In advance, John agrees to help Bob on his exam by periodically logging in as Bob and double-checking answers or providing answers for unanswered questions. Because John was logged in as Bob, the answers given by John will look like Bob's answers.

The countermeasure for this security threat involves removing the stateless behavior of the application. State information about concurrent log-ins must be maintained external to the Web process servicing a given exam taker's session. User log-in information can be stored in a database or Web server memory. When a log-in is attempted, state information is referenced, a concurrent log-in is rejected, and a record of the attempt is logged in an audit file.

Review Questions

1. Suggest another scenario whereby two students could conspire to cheat on an exam by exploiting the threat of user impersonation.

2. Will approached countermeasures to this threat from a strictly application/technology perspective. Are there process or people countermeasures to this threat? Explain.

Layered Security: Passwords as a Single Point of Failure

Passwords often represent a single point of failure in software systems. If a password is compromised, the entire application, system, or network is compromised. This can especially be the case with Web-based systems that connect to databases. If a hacker manages to compromise a Web server hosting a data-connected application, the hacker is also likely to compromise the database as well. Thus, the Web server's credentials can act as a single point of failure.

Will advocated that the exam software be written using a layered approach or a distributed n-tier architecture. The application was developed with four tiers: presentation, business logic, data access, and data. All data operations were implemented behind stored procedures managed by the DBMS at the data tier. No embedded SQL was used in the application.

Will designed the system with multiple authentication mechanisms. Not only did Will require student users to log in with a password, but the Web server also was required to authenticate with the database. Users enter a log-in and password that is checked against a log-in and password stored in the database. In order for the Web server to connect to the database on behalf of the user, the Web application must pass or present a log-in and password to the database.

Will realized that if a hacker compromised the Web server obtaining the credentials used by the Web server to connect to the database, the hacker could then connect to the database independently of the Web server. Once access to the database was achieved, the hacker could execute stored procedures associated with the exam application and thereby gain unauthorized access to the data. The Web server's database credentials (password) represented a single point of failure.

The countermeasure to this threat was to require both the Web server's credentials and a valid user's credentials to successfully execute a stored procedure. That is, although the Web server's user account was given execute permission on a stored procedure, the stored procedure's signature requires, as parameters, a valid user log-in and password for a data operation to commit. A hacker who compromised the Web server could execute a stored procedure, but without a valid user log-in and password the data operation would not commit. That is, no data would be returned by a SELECT statement, or rows inserted by an INSERT operation. In this way, Will reduced the threat of a single point of failure password by essentially requiring two passwords.

Review Questions

1. How effective do you think Will's countermeasure is to the single point of failure threat?

2. How much of an obstacle does Will's countermeasure pose for a hacker?

3. Use Google to research the debate over "embedded SQL versus stored procedures." Based on your research, in terms of security, do you agree with Will's decision to avoid embedded SQL and put all data operations behind stored procedures?

Development versus Production Server: Inadvertent Phishing

3C

Will maintained two working versions of his application: a development version and the production (deployment) version. Both versions were maintained on separate servers. The development server was used as a sandbox to test changes to the application prior to release. Once changes were tested on the development server, the revised application was deployed to the production server. The production server hosted the live version of the exam application.

To speed and simplify testing on the development server, Will often injected test stubs and drivers into the development version of the application or temporarily hardcoded values for variables and addresses. For example, rather than having to repeatedly log-in and traverse through a series of Web pages to get to the Web page to be modified/tested, Will injected a driver that automatically logged him into the system and initialized certain session variables and/or hardcoded logic jumps. An example of a hardcoded logic jump is coding the target for a link to another Web page in the application as a string literal such as "193.234.112.5\ AccountManagement.aspx."

During an especially busy testing cycle, Will received a tech support call from a faculty contact who was at that moment giving the exam; several students were receiving an error message from the system and could not complete their exam. The user reported both the behavior and error message received. Will promised the faculty contact his immediate attention toward a resolution.

Will could not reproduce the error received by the faculty contact's students. Using the debugging tool, he stepped through each and every line of code that could have led to the error message. No errors or anomalous behavior could be detected. Will called the faculty contact back and related that he was logged in as the student and doing exactly the same steps the student had done, and the application was behaving precisely as it should with no error message. The faculty contact, with an increasing tone of frustration, reiterated that he had 35 students trying to take the exam and that it would be difficult to reschedule. Was there anything else Will could investigate? Will queried the faculty contact about browser configurations, etc., but no resolution could be reached. In the end, several students were required to abandon their exam and reschedule.

Will again stepped through each and every line of code but could not discover a cause for the reported behavior. He decided to log in to the system directly, not using the local copy maintained by the Integrated Development Environment (IDE), to test the behavior. The reported error message was eventually reproduced. Thinking that perhaps the production machine and the local copy were not synchronized, he redeployed the changes to the production machine. Will still received the error message.

The error message received by the user represented a type of inadvertent phishing. In this case, after testing a change to the application using the development server, Will neglected to comment out a hardcoded logic jump in a link on a preceding page, that is, a page preceding the page that was throwing the unhandled runtime exception. The student taking the exam clicked on this link and was inadvertently redirected to the version hosted on the development server. The development version contained several incomplete modules and was out of sync with the production version.

Will only realized this redirection when he happened to notice that the IP address changed. He immediately removed the hardcoded value and called the faculty contact back to confirm that the problem was resolved and the exam could be rescheduled. Although initially a tense situation, in the end, Will and the faculty contact were able to laugh about the incident.

Review Questions

1. Briefly describe how Will's problem represents a type of phishing.

2. How might a hacker exploit such a compromised link?

3. Propose a countermeasure for the inadvertent phishing threat created by Will.

Row-Level Audit Tables for Incident Response

Responding to security incidents involves investigating the past. As part of their countermeasures to threats to the integrity of the database, Will and Janet implemented a collection of row-level audit tables. Row-level audit tables maintain historical data about tables in a database. A row's entire life cycle from creation to deletion is documented by maintaining a before and after image of any transactions against that row.

A sample of audit entries for the row having QuestionID 342 is given in Table 3C-2. The ChangeType attribute indicates whether an entry is the before or after image, that is, what the row looked like before or after the transaction. The attribute UserID identifies the user account used to execute the transaction. Row-level audit tables can include a duplicate column or every column in the table audited (which is often called a shadow table), but in the sample in Table 3C-2, only one column is shown, QuestionStem. The attribute QuestionStem contains the text of the question stem as it appeared before and after the transaction.

If a security incident is believed to have occurred, the historical data maintained in the row-level audit table allows Will and Janet to review time-ordered and point-in-time changes to a

LogID	QuestionID	Image Type	TransType	UserID	TimeChanged	QuestionStem
10045	342	AFTER	INSERT	5567	09/12/2007 12:23	Which of the following...
11189	342	BEFORE	UPDATE	4453	10/21/2007 01:30	Which of the following...
11190	342	AFTER	UPDATE	4453	10/21/2007 01:30	Of the following items...
12559	342	BEFORE	UPDATE	5567	01/05/2008 13:54	Of the following items...
12560	342	AFTER	UPDATE	5567	01/05/2008 13:54	Which of the items shown...
Other transactions occurred here...						
15677	342	BEFORE	DELETE	2334	03/7/2008 09:18	Which of the items shown...

Table 3C-2 Sample Row-Level Audit Entries

particular row or collection of rows. In addition, they can identify which user account was used to execute the transaction.

In practice, these audit tables were used to monitor and review concurrent changes made to exam questions by members of the item writing and review group. Janet headed a group of faculty contributors charged with the responsibility of creating, modifying, and deleting exam questions. Without the audit trail provided by the row-level audit table, Janet would have been unable to track and monitor changes to a given exam question. For example, when reviewing questions Janet often found herself wondering, "Was that exam question changed? That bit of wording looks different. Did Fred change that since our last review session or am I just forgetting the changes from the previous session?" The use of the audit table removed such second-guessing.

In a similar way, if a hacker were to gain access to the database and alter exam questions, Will and Janet would be able to both isolate the changes and return the questions to a previous state using a previous before image of the question.

Review Questions

1. How can the use of row-level audit tables as described above meet the reporting requirements of the Sarbanes-Oxley (SOX) Act? (Note: The iSec-Cert group is not subject to SOX requirements; the question is merely academic. For more on SOX, see references.[5,6])

2. Will is storing the audit tables on the same server as the database itself. No copies other than backups of the entire database are preserved. Do you see any possible security vulnerabilities with this practice?

3. Can you describe what happened to Question 342, based on your understanding of the audit log table above, reading from top to bottom?

4. If you were Will, why would you be concerned if user 2334 turned out to be a student at Mountain Valley State who has inexplicably been entered into the system as a faculty member at that school with access rights to "edit questions"?

Implementing Role-Based Security: Question Review Process

When Janet formed the item writing and review group charged with creating, modifying, and deleting exam questions, Will realized that controlling access and protecting the integrity of the exam questions would require close attention to user access privileges. Will would need to control who could create, modify, and delete exam questions and when. For example, which users would have authority to modify a question after the question was placed on an exam? A concern Will had was that faculty members in the item writing and review group might inappropriately alter questions that were already on an exam. What if a faculty contributor changed a question while an exam containing that question was actually in progress?

It was agreed that Will would implement access controls through role-based security. The idea of role-based security is that users can perform certain actions or functionality in a system based on the role they are assigned. A log-in and password grants a user *access* privileges. Roles grant users *authorization* privileges.

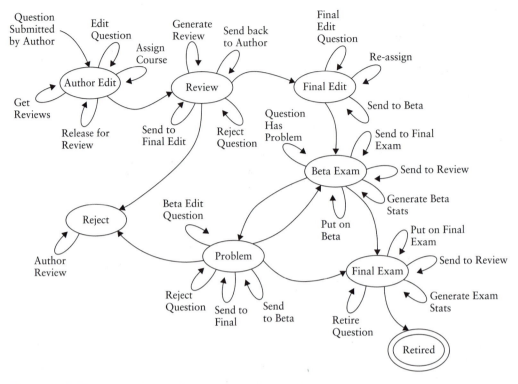

Figure 3C-2 Finite State Machine: Exam Question Review Process

Courtesy Course Technology/Cengage Learning

As a first step in defining roles, Will and Gene developed a finite state machine of the exam question review process. The result of his analysis is depicted in Figure 3C-2. A finite state machine can be used to model the finite number of states a thing can have, transitions between and within states, and actions or activities that can be performed at any given point in time. For role-based security, a finite state machine models points in a process where authorization to perform some action must be granted or denied. For example, in Figure 3C-2, there is a transition labeled "Reject Question." Which user should have authorization to reject a question, the user who created the question, the reviewer, or Janet?

In terms of the application interface, the transitions between and within states become controls on a page. To reject a question, a user clicks a button labeled "Reject Question" on the page that is displaying the question under review. This button is only visible to a user who is a member of the role with authorization to reject questions.

Role-based security is a countermeasure to the security threat of unauthorized access to data and functionality. Roles grant users authorization to view data and perform tasks. For example, the "author" role allows a user to submit and edit questions for review and to read reviews written about the questions they authored. The author role does not have authorization to reject a question or put it on the final exam.

After completing the analysis depicted in Figure 3C-2, Will encoded the authorizations in the programming logic and interface's navigational structure. As the complexity of the transitions in Figure 3C-2 suggest, this was no simple task. Each control on each page and each transition between pages had to be dynamically configured based on the roles of the user currently logged in. The flow of pages had to conform to the transitions defined in Figure 3C-2.

As the deadline for the release of the first major exam loomed near, Janet and her group came under increasing pressure to quickly and efficiently move questions through the process of review, revision, and placement on the exam. Faculty members are very busy individuals with widely varying schedules and commitments. The fine granularity of authorizations encoded into the application meant that at any given point in the process, one user could become a bottleneck for the entire effort. If the only user with authorization to send a question to final edit was unavailable for a few days or a week, the entire process could come to a halt. And it did several times.

At some point the team reached a crisis, and there was a real risk that a completely working system would not be ready by the promised release date. Gene strongly suggested that Will disable role-based security for the question review process and allow anyone in the item writing and review group to have all authorizations. This would allow a single item writer or reviewer to transition a question from creation to placement on the final exam. Will resisted this request and argued that the integrity of the process and the database was more important than meeting the deadline. Gene argued that "the security measures make the interface too complex and the review process too cumbersome; anyway, nothing bad will happen because we trust each other." Will relented and the security measures were disabled. The system was completed by the promised date and no significant security incidents were detected.

Review Questions

1. With whom do you agree on the issue of disabling the security countermeasures? Will or Gene? Why?

2. Briefly discuss how role-based security as described above is a trade-off between ease of use and security.

Assessing Risks with Less Than a Week to Go

Risk management is a fundamental framework for information security management. For the iSec-Cert team, risk management wasn't an activity they performed frequently or even formally. The following section describes a key incident when, in the absence of a formal risk management process, the group realized that it needed to address key risks, or else face the possibility of failure at a critical juncture of the project.

It was a Monday morning and Janet was worried. Under Will's leadership, the security of the iSec-Cert exam system was in good hands, but time was runningout. It was Monday morning. There was less than a week to go before Saturday's pilot test at Midwest. Janet knew from her past industry experience and based on how recent testing had gone that they weren't ready. Two specific concerns were fresh in her mind. First, they still had to find a large group to test the fix to the connection pool leak problem. Second, they were not sure how the exam was going to behave in a different time zone.

When she got to thinking, she began to realize that more and more things could go wrong. If something did go wrong, Janet didn't have any confidence that they would go much better on a second pilot test. She wanted it to go right the first time, or get so close that the second time would be a charm. She certainly didn't want the worst possible things to go wrong—a severe security breach, like the test content getting released into the public—or a complete shutdown of an exam-in-progress. What if that happens? What then? A complete disaster, she thought. With all the testing that needed to be done, and the fact that Will was still coding, Janet was worried. They couldn't push back Saturday's start date, because several schools were on a tight schedule, and it was getting late in the spring semester.

Janet didn't think she was paranoid, but just being a bit negative. She was worried about the risk of failure. Even though there was plenty of work to do before Saturday's kickoff, Janet decided to stop and realistically assess the risk of failure.

She called a meeting with Gene and Will at Satchmo's Coffeehouse, a popular hangout with students and faculty. At the meeting Janet confronted Gene and Will: "Are we ready for Saturday?" With an enthusiastic wave of his fist, Gene responded: "YEEEESSSSSSS!" Will just laughed.

Gene was always the positive thinker of the group, a master of interpersonal skills and motivation, a kind of "wizard" with whom people enjoyed working if for no other reason than feeling good. Janet said, "There is a time for positive thinking, Gene, but this is not it. I don't want us to fail on Saturday, and while I do appreciate your cheerleading, it does nothing for my confidence. It's time for risk management. My question is 'what can possibly go wrong that we need to do something about?'"

Gene, Will, and Janet took turns thinking up things that could go wrong. Not that they thought they would go wrong. They indulged themselves in scenarios of wrongdoing, coming up with about 20 risks, which Janet summarized in a spreadsheet, along with the likelihood and consequence, and associated level of risk. See Table 3C-3, in which the risks are ordered by risk level, from highest (EXTREME) to lowest (LOW).

They then defined risk mitigation and recovery strategies for each risk, starting with the highest priority risks, those at the EXTREME level. It took about three hours. When they were done, they created a work schedule for the rest of the week. It was decided:

- The test questions themselves would undergo one more round of review.
- Software changes could be made up until the last minute, but that one complete system test had to be conducted on Friday night.
- Someone had to be on-call, and the others had to know who was to be on-call, and the phone numbers had to be distributed to all faculty contacts.

One of the threats was that an exam proctor would make a procedural error, resulting in a security breach or a complete failure of an exam session; that is, students cannot take or finish the test and have to leave. A complete failure of this kind is akin to a disaster, in information security terms. The mitigation and recovery strategy involved all of the following:

- Gene would update the proctor guidelines with the cell phone numbers of on-call iSec-Cert personnel, and redistribute the guidelines to all faculty contacts.

Risk	Likelihood	Consequence	Risk Level	Mitigation	Recovery
proctor unable to troubleshoot a problem quickly	LIKELY	CATASTROPHIC	EXTREME	have an iSec-Cert team member "on-call"; publish the on-call schedule for the iSec-Cert team; and list all phone numbers for iSec-Cert and proctors to use (so that all of us can get in touch with one another)	more education and preparation for proctor and on-call iSec-Cert people when they try again
critical failure due to fault in test-taking software	UNLIKELY	CATASTROPHIC	EXTREME	make necessary software changes up to last minute, but also do a last-minute test of whole test scheduling, registration, verification, and test-taking process, with off-campus, too	Will on-call to make a quick fix
GSU network problem shuts down access to server (e.g., domain name server crash)	UNLIKELY	CATASTROPHIC	EXTREME	move to an off-site server, eventually	affected schools must reschedule exam
exam fails to work due to an interoperability issue	POSSIBLE	MAJOR	EXTREME	create a test log-in page for trying out on a machine that will be used to take test	have Will on-call and near computer access for quick adjustments
student discovers exam session password; and can log in off-site to continue exam or call or email the password to someone else	RARE	CATASTROPHIC	HIGH	(a) stress to proctors the importance of not giving out password, and having students turn head while they type it in; (b) have a "no keyboard activity" rule enforced during the test	(a) have proctors report suspicious behavior, like student leaving early in exam after logging in; (b) consider a proctor being able to "turn off" a student's test if they leave without hitting "finish"
time zone confusion	UNLIKELY	MAJOR	HIGH	do an off-site test at an Eastern, Mountain, or Pacific zone school	manipulate server clock to offset
time on server is incorrect	RARE	MAJOR	HIGH	check with network administrator about using atomic clock updates	none

Table 3C-3   iSec-Cert Risk Assessment

Risk	Likelihood	Consequence	Risk Level	Mitigation	Recovery
exam contains spelling, grammar errors, or duplicate questions or questions with >1 correct answer	ALMOST CERTAIN	MINOR	HIGH	perform a last-minute proofread	make changes to questions after first session (Sat.), treating Saturday's session as a pilot, if necessary
students get fatigued; quit test	POSSIBLE	MODERATE	HIGH	have proctor tell students to close browser, take a break, come back, and log them back in	consider shorter test if it's a big problem
system response time is slow	POSSIBLE	MODERATE	HIGH	(a) monitor exam in progress (via database queries and/or cell phone w/ proctor), (b) invest in new server	none
proctor makes a procedural error	POSSIBLE	MODERATE	HIGH	update detailed proctor guidelines; make sure Will and Janet understand them; make sure proctors are registered and have computer access during exam; give proctors the cell phone number of who is on-call	have well-trained support people on-call
students unable to log in to the test	POSSIBLE	MINOR	MODERATE	(a) add a "candidate is not verified" warning when that is the reason for problem; (b) remind proctors to verify candidates	none
students don't get verified in time	POSSIBLE	MINOR	MODERATE	educate proctor in steps of registration and verification	none
students can't get their passwords to log in to their accounts	POSSIBLE	MINOR	MODERATE	verify that emails send out passwords promptly	have students ask proctor, who can check on a student's password; Will, Gene, and Janet are not to take phone calls and give out student passwords over the phone
students can't sign up for exam session	POSSIBLE	MINOR	MODERATE	ask proctor to check to see if student is verified	none

Table 3C-3   Continued

Risk	Likelihood	Consequence	Risk Level	Mitigation	Recovery
figure doesn't show up on a question	RARE	MODERATE	MODERATE	make sure that questions on the test that need a figure, have one defined in the database, and that it shows up in a pre-Saturday beta of real test	make changes to questions after first session (Sat.), treating Saturday's session as a pilot, if necessary
score report not ready for Saturday	UNLIKELY	INSIGNIFICANT	LOW	Will responsible for finishing, testing, debugging, up to last minute	tell students to check back later for scores
browser settings cause anomalies	UNLIKELY	INSIGNIFICANT	LOW	make proctors understand that test software might work differently for different browsers	instruct proctor to ask students to try a different browser or switch machines
too many students sign up, fill up room	UNLIKELY	MINOR	LOW	(a) create IS admin utility to show students signed up in a group; (b) alert proctors to this problem	none

Table 3C-3   Continued

- Janet and Will would review the new proctor guidelines and be on-call during the pilot, with Will agreeing to be within minutes of computer access.
- Will would make sure the proctors were registered and had computer access during the exam.

Before the meeting, Janet wasn't sure if they would be able to identify all the important risks, and that there wouldn't be enough time to do anything about any but the few top-priority threats. But, with the knowledge and experience of the three of them, and working as a team focusing on the task, they were able to be certain that they had identified a comprehensive collection of threats, including the most probable and severe. To their surprise, they were able to come up with risk mitigation and recovery strategies for not just the high-priority threats, but for all of them. They were able to identify some low-effort tactics that could be done within the week's time as well.

Review Questions

1. Was this risk management exercise useful or should the team have just concentrated on testing and debugging up until the last minute?

2. When should this risk management meeting have taken place?

3. How frequently should such an exercise take place during a project? After a system is deployed?

4. Do you think they missed any EXTREME risks?

5. For the risk "students can't get their passwords …" the team decided to allow proctors to access student passwords in order to assist students. What do you think of this response? What new security risk(s) might result from allowing proctors to access student accounts?

Ethical and Legal Aspects of Security at iSec-Cert

The iSec-Cert team was confronted with ethical and legal issues, as well. These issues arose and were addressed at different points in time, and are not covered chronologically, but summarized in this section. One issue was an intellectual property issue—ownership rights to the exam and its questions. Privacy became a big issue when Will pointed out that they were collecting sensitive personal information about students. Reporting data on schools made the team aware of the legal liability that might result, and who is responsible became a key question. Policies needed to be created for students with disabilities. A change in U.S. law that extended daylight savings time created a problem reminiscent of Y2K.

Privacy and Security: Protecting Sensitive Information

After the group initially thought that the unauthorized exam access and loss of reputation were the most serious risks, Will realized that the faculty and students were also at risk. The iSec-Cert group was collecting sensitive information, including social security numbers (SSNs) of students in those cases where schools were still using SSNs for student identification. They were also collecting credit card numbers for applicants who were paying for the certification fees. People were also asked to supply their personal address, phone numbers, and employment history.

There was also a question of how iSec-Cert could use a student's information. Gene, Janet, and Will ironed out a privacy policy. An excerpt from the policy was published on the iSec-Cert Web site and reads:

> Students who register with iSec-Cert are given the following options for granting iSec-Cert privileges for use of their personal information:
>
> - Official business
> - No restrictions
> - Do not use

One of Gene's thesis students, Richard Rose, was working on his study, entitled *The Link Between Professional Certifications and Career Success*. Richard designed a questionnaire to assess career satisfaction, and wanted to give it to past takers of the iSec-Cert exam. Gene enthusiastically asked Janet to supply Richard with an email list of past exam takers.

> "We've got close to 500 of our former students in that database," Gene said, "I want Richard to hit them all."
>
> "Okay, but we've got to see who checked the do not use *option and exclude them," Janet said.

"There you go again," said Gene. *"I know many of these students, and they would be willing to help Richard out."* He was trying to be convincing. *"They are our alumni, and many of them are Richard's friends."*

"That doesn't matter, Gene!" Janet retorted. *"The privacy policy is explicit. Richard's thesis is not official business of the iSec-Cert Group. We can only send his survey to the ones who checked* no restrictions.*"*

It turned out that about 85% of the past takers were in the no restrictions category, and Richard had a healthy sample size anyway.

Review Questions

1. Was Janet correct in her interpretation of the privacy policy or was she making too big a deal?

2. Would there be any negative consequences of sending out the questionnaire to everyone?

3. What other sensitive information might need to be protected (kept private)?

4. How long do you think iSec-Cert should maintain sensitive information?

5. Should iSec-Cert ever consider destroying a student's data?

6. What measures would you take to secure the sensitive information collected?

Intellectual Property: Who Owns the Questions?

The issue of exam ownership became a bit of a dilemma. As faculty members, Gene, Janet, and Will were accustomed to retaining the ownership rights of any material they create for use in a class. For example, if a faculty member changed jobs, moving from one school to another, they would expect to be able to transfer any tests, notes, presentations, or projects they developed and used at their prior institution over to their new school. Of course, they all understood that the iSec-Cert group itself would be the owner of the exam itself, as a traditional form of intellectual property protected by copyright law.

After two years of working on the iSec-Cert project *pro bono*, Janet considered quitting the project. However, she wondered whether she could take some of the questions with her if she did. Could she use them again if she quit? After all, she did work on the project for two years, and some of the questions written were her own. Some of those questions had been ones that Janet used for several semesters in her class—they were not written originally for iSec-Cert.

One day, Janet was under pressure to make up an exam for a project management midterm she was giving in two days. For her exam, she decides to use some of the iSec-Cert questions. She copies the questions from the database, using her own log-in credentials. She uses a combination of questions, including ones she contributed and ones contributed by other professors, mixed in with test questions from the test bank of the course textbook. She doesn't inform the students of the source of all of the questions. She puts them on the test and then administers her paper-based midterm. She goes over the exam with the students, but then collects the exams and does not give them back to the students to permanently keep. Later in the semester, students in Janet's class are among those students taking the iSec-Cert exam.

Review Questions

1. Did Janet do anything unethical by using the iSec-Cert questions on her midterm?

2. Are there any information security concerns posed by Janet's actions? Explain.

3. Who do you think "owns" the exam? Do you think the question authors still own their questions? Does it matter, you think, if the questions were in prior use? Why or why not?

Legal Liabilities—Protecting the Reputation of the Schools

Gene, Janet, and Will had concerns about the effect of the success or failure of the project on their own reputations, but what about their customers—the schools? The schools were concerned about their reputations, and insisted that the names of schools be kept off of the score reports seen by other schools. They didn't want to be represented in the reports by name, next to an aggregate score, or in a list with other schools.

Without much debate and concerned about the legal liabilities of score reporting, Gene, Janet, and Will agreed to keep a university's aggregate scores confidential. Only the school itself could learn of the scores of its students and its aggregate performance. It could have access only to the national aggregate score, not the scores of other individual schools. See Figure 3C-3 for a sample score report.

Protecting the Rights of Disabled Students

One day, a faculty member called up Will to report a problem with a disabled student, Randy. Randy could use his arms but had difficulty with his prosthetic hands. He was unable to complete the test in a timely fashion. The task of clicking on a radio button of a multiple-choice question required the use of a mouse. Randy was proficient at clicking on a keyboard, but using a mouse was very slow and frustrating.

Will gave the faculty member two options. Will would allow extra time for Randy to complete the test, or Randy could be allowed to have someone, such as the proctor, enter his answers for him.

The iSec-Cert Group
Security Management Spr 08

Score Report
East Coast University

Mean score	No. of takers	National mean	National number of takers
56.4	31	51.2	475

Figure 3C-3 Sample Score Report

Courtesy Course Technology/Cengage Learning

Review Questions

1. What do you think of Will's solutions?

2. Does the iSec-Cert exam violate any of Randy's legal rights?

3. Can you think of any alternatives that Will did not consider?

Change in the Law on Daylight Savings Time Affects iSec-Cert

The Energy Policy Act of 2005 extended daylight savings time by four to five weeks, depending on the year. This caused a problem that escaped the iSec-Cert team. Will had forgotten that he had coded an automatic change in daylight savings time with a lookup table. The Energy Policy Act[7] effectively required a change in this table that never occurred. Between March 11—the new start date for DST—and April 1, 2007, the old start date, a school scheduled and attempted to start an iSec-Cert Exam. The result was that the server had not been updated; that is, it had not "sprung ahead." When a school attempted to give an exam at 2 PM, the iSec-Cert server still had it as 1 PM, and a room full of students sat waiting, as the password code did not seem to work. A proctor's call into iSec got Janet and Will scrambling, and they were able to fix the problem that seemed awfully similar to the fears of Y2K.

Review Questions

1. Research the daylight savings time issue and recommend a solution that is more robust to changes in the law.

2. How did the risk management exercise help provide a rapid recovery from failure?

Endnotes

1. ISC2 (2008). *Certified Information Systems Security Professional*. Retrieved August 12, 2008, from https://www.isc2.org/cgi-bin/index.cgi

2. ISACA (2008). *Certified Information Security Manager (CISM) Overview*. Retrieved August 12, 2008, from www.isaca.org/cism

3. Information Systems Security Certification Consortium, Inc. (ISC)[2] (2008). *(ISC)[2] Code of Ethics*. Retrieved August 12, 2008, from https://www.isc2.org/cgi-bin/content.cgi?category=12

4. Herrod, C. (2006). "The Role of Information Security and Its Relationship to Information Technology Risk Management" (p. 53). In M. E. Whitman and H. J. Mattord (Eds.), *Readings and Cases in the Management of Information Security*, Volume I. Boston, MA: Course Technology/Cengage Learning (pp. 45–61).

5. FindLaw (2002). H. R. 3763 (The Sarbanes-Oxley Act 2002). Retrieved December 9, 2008, from http://fl1.findlaw.com/news.findlaw.com/hdocs/docs/gwbush/sarbanesoxley072302.pdf

6. Addison-Hewitt Associates (2006). Sarbanes-Oxley Act 2002: A Guide to the Sarbanes-Oxley Act. Retrieved December 9, 2008, from http://www.soxlaw.com/

7. United States Environmental Protection Agency (2008). PUBLIC LAW 109–58—AUG. 8, 2005: Energy Policy Act of 2005. Retrieved December 9, 2008, from http://www.epa.gov/oust/fedlaws/publ_109-058.pdf

An Etymological View of Ethical Hacking

Michael E. Whitman
Kennesaw State University

Michael Whitman, Ph.D., CISM, CISSP is a Professor of Information Security in the Computer Science and Information Systems Department at Kennesaw State University, Kennesaw, Georgia, where he is also the coordinator of the Bachelor of Science in Information Security and Assurance and the director of the KSU Center for Information Security Education and Awareness (infosec.kennesaw.edu). He and Herbert Mattord are the authors of Principles of Information Security, Management of Information Security, Principles of Incident Response and Disaster Recovery, Readings and Cases in the Management of Information Security, The Guide to Firewall and Network Security: With Intrusion Detection and VPNs, *and* The Hands-On Information Security Lab Manual, *all from Course Technology, Cengage Learning. Dr. Whitman is an active researcher in Information Security, Fair and Responsible Use Policies, Ethical Computing, and Information Systems Research Methods. He currently teaches graduate and undergraduate courses in Information Security. He has published articles in the top journals in his field, including* Information Systems Research, Communications of the ACM, Information and Management, *the* Journal of International Business Studies, *and the* Journal of Computer Information Systems. *He is an active member of the Information Systems Security Association, the Association for Computing Machinery, and the Association for Information Systems. Through his efforts and those of Professor Mattord, his institution has been recognized by the Department of Homeland Security and the National Security Agency as a National Center of Academic Excellence in Information Assurance Education—twice.*

Overview

How we describe something defines it. A specific choice of words can cause irreparable damage to an idea or immortalize it. This paper examines the etymology of "Ethical Hacking." By examining the meaning of the term *ethical hacking* and the ways in which it is used, the field of information security can seek to mitigate some of the notoriety hackers enjoy and avoid slighting the ethical work performed by the discipline.

Introduction

"In the beginning was the Word ..."[1] Words define concepts, and as such can influence perceptions of concepts. How we describe our environment provides definition, scope, and understanding to others. We describe accurately; others can relate and understand. We describe poorly; others can misinterpret, misrepresent, and even negatively influence our environment.

Part of the foundation of the field of information security is the expectation of ethical behavior. Most modern certifications and professional associations in information security, and to a lesser extent, information technology in general, require their members to subscribe to codes of ethics. These canons ("a body of rules, principles, or standards accepted as axiomatic and universally binding in a field of study or art"[2]) provide guidance to the members and associates of an organization. They also represent an agreement between the members and their constituencies to provide ethical ("being in accordance with the rules or standards for right conduct or practice, esp. the standards of a profession"[3]) service. If there is any doubt as to the validity of these ethical codes or to the actual conduct of those who subscribe to them, the entire discipline suffers. One such area gaining notoriety in the field of computing is the concept of the "hacker."

Hacking

When the computer era began, a *hacker* was a term used to describe a computer enthusiast, someone who enjoyed pushing the boundaries of computer technologies, and who frequently had to apply unorthodox techniques to accomplish their desired goals. The term originated in the 1700s as a descriptor of a "person hired to do routine work,"[4] but was soon relegated to describe anyone performing a task for hire, a contractor or freelance agent—most notably associated with writers. In the mid-1950s the term *hacker* was reportedly associated with members of the MIT Tech Model Railroad Club—"one who works like a hack at writing and experimenting with software, one who enjoys computer programming for its own sake."[5] The "purist" perspective on the definition of hacker is shared by many including the contributors of the "New Hacker's Dictionary,"[6] a publication of the MIT Press containing an eclectic collection of jargon and slang related to the field of computing. This document defines a hacker as follows:

1. 'A person who enjoys exploring the details of programmable systems and how to stretch their capabilities, as opposed to most users, who prefer to learn only the minimum necessary.

2. One who programs enthusiastically (even obsessively) or who enjoys programming rather than just theorizing about programming.

3. A person capable of appreciating *hack value.*

4. A person who is good at programming quickly.

5. An expert at a particular program, or one who frequently does work using it or on it; as in "a Unix hacker." [Definitions 1 through 5 are correlated, and people who fit them congregate.]

6. An expert or enthusiast of any kind. One might be an astronomy hacker, for example.

7. One who enjoys the intellectual challenge of creatively overcoming or circumventing limitations.

8. [deprecated] A malicious meddler who tries to discover sensitive information by poking around. Hence, password hacker, network hacker. The correct term for this sense is *cracker.*'[7]

This approach is further supported in the *Internet Users' Glossary*, an informational Request for Comment (RFC) (RFC 1392) published by the Internet Society: "hacker: A person who delights in having an intimate understanding of the internal workings of a system, computers and computer networks in particular. The term is often misused in a pejorative context, where 'cracker' would be the correct term. See also: cracker."[8]

Today, the term has evolved into one with a much more sinister definition. According to the *American Heritage Dictionary*, to hack is

 a. *"Informal* To alter (a computer program)

 b. To gain access to (a computer file or network) illegally or without authorization"[9]

The malevolent association of the term *hacker* is a point of contention of many, even members of the TMRC from whom the term purportedly originated: "Here at TMRC, where the words 'hack' and 'hacker' originated and have been used proudly since the late 1950s, we resent the misapplication of the word to mean the committing of illegal acts. People who do those things are better described by expressions such as 'thieves,' 'password crackers,' or 'computer vandals.' They are certainly not true hackers, as they do not understand the hacker ethic."[10]

The discussion of the "hacker ethic" will be examined shortly. To better understand the popularity of the term *hacker*, and the draw it seems to have on modern culture we must first examine the root of the issue.

The Allure of Notoriety

The problem with hacking isn't merely the fact that some individuals actively seek to gain unauthorized access to others' information assets; rather, the problem is much, much deeper. The problem lies in the inexplicable fascination that society has with the disreputable. This phenomenon is widespread, and one has only to reflect on our own popular culture to find "felonious heroes" like Robin Hood, Jesse James, Al Capone, Bonnie & Clyde, and in more recent popular media, movies like *Thelma and Louise*,[11] *Young Guns*,[12] and *Hitman*[13] as well as TV shows like *The Sopranos*[14] and *Prison Break*,[15] to name a few. We are enthralled by the apparent disregard for authority exhibited by these individuals, many of whom are portrayed as wrongfully accused. Some argue that we live vicariously through those who display no apparent regard for proper behavior, allowing themselves to behave as the whim suits them, rather than by society's bonds. Others seek the public attention afforded those who are reported as "public enemies" and made notorious by the media. Penfold (2003) notes, there is a long-standing history of fascination with criminals and their acts. Early forms included those "outlaw heroes" and "social bandits" who enjoyed considerable public approval (see Hobsbawm, 1959; Kooistra, 1989). Penfold (2003) also suggests that "from the late 19th century these figures increasingly gave way to two new types of celebrated criminality—the criminal celebrity and most recently the celebrity criminal."[16] Whatever the psychological attraction, the end result is that some segments of our society choose to turn a blind eye on certain crimes, most notably in recent generations in the field of computers with the growing notoriety of computer hacking.

Computer hacking in the media is portrayed with a mixed message. Movies like *Ferris Bueller's Day Off*,[17] *WarGames*,[18] and *Hackers*[19] portrayed teenage hackers as misunderstood idols and heroes. Unfortunately this mixed message is being perpetuated into the modern information security society. We as the stoic guardians of the information assets should completely and totally condemn the entire hacker genre and culture. Yet, it appears that we too are drawn in to its illicit allure. Consider the concept of the hacker "hats." In the early days of Western movies, the good guys often wore white hats (e.g., The Lone Ranger), while the bad guys frequently wore black hats. This dichotomy resulted in a distinction between white hat hackers and black hat hackers. If the resulting body of individuals evenly divided themselves in such neat alignments, perhaps this discussion would not be as necessary. In reality it is not a bipolar distribution but more of a continuum, ranging between the white and black hats. In the middle are the "gray hat hackers," a group of individuals who sometimes act ethically and sometimes not. What is not known is when they will choose to behave appropriately and when they will choose not to.

What is interesting about the "gray and black hat" hackers is the inevitable level of "reform" they exhibit once apprehended, or even once they "grow up." The media is fascinated with the reformed hackers like Kevin Mitnick and "Mafiaboy" who now seek to cash in on their notoriety by working the lecture and publishing circuits. While most reputable organizations would not be seduced into hiring such individuals as permanent employees, apparently many are interested in at least hiring them as external consultants, seeking to learn what they know and thus better protect themselves from the "ilk." The problem is they are propagating the very problem they seek to eliminate. Hackers once promoted the concept of "if we're caught, the company will just offer to hire us to show them how we hacked them." This misconception in today's environment can serve to both encourage the gray and black hat hackers to continue the practice of their craft, and further frustrate those they attack.

3D

One case in point was an information security professional's conference in the early 2000s—a unique mix of academic, governmental, and industrial representatives, sponsored by a certain three-letter organization, where the lunch keynote was a self-proclaimed hacker. This hacker took an active part in a discussion of the protection of public infrastructure systems, namely, through his constant proclamation that he could "hack that system in XX minutes." To be fair, this individual went on to become a somewhat respected member of the information security community, but in the late 1990s, he still promoted the renegade persona of the hacker culture. His online bio still provides close ties to well-known hacker cultures, although it now reads more as "a researcher of buffer overflows," even though his online publications were more of the "how to exploit" variety.

The comparison between the "white" and "black" hats even resulted in the establishment of major conventions where good guys and bad guys alike gather to share in this questionable association. According to the Black Hat Conference Web site:

> *About Black Hat*
>
> *The Black Hat Briefings are a series of highly technical information security conferences that bring together thought leaders from all facets of the infosec world—from the corporate and government sectors to academic and even underground researchers. The environment is strictly vendor-neutral and focused on the sharing of practical insights and timely, actionable knowledge. Black Hat remains the best and biggest event of its kind, unique in its ability to define tomorrow's information security landscape …*
>
> *Black Hat Founder and Director Jeff Moss is also the founder of DEFCON, the largest and best-known hacker conference in the world. In 2007, DEFCON celebrated its 15th anniversary. The experience and connections created by 15 years at the intersection of network security and hacker ingenuity is what makes Black Hat the one-of-a-kind conference it is, one where the establishment and the underground are equally at home.*[20]

Note the constant reference to the *underground*—a "secretive organization fighting the established government."[21] Clearly the organizers of this event want to attract hacker-minded individuals and those fascinated with the concept. Those hosting the conference MAY even be affiliated with this "underground" in the past or present. They have realized, however, that the corporate and governmental sectors have one thing that the hacker groups do not—money to attend conferences. The event costs approximately $850—as of its hosting in Japan in 2008, not including hotel and airfare. The average hacker will most likely not attend.

The Ethical Hacker

This brings us to the point of this rant—the ethical hacker. By definition the phrase *ethical hacker* is an oxymoron ("a figure of speech by which a locution produces an incongruous, seemingly self-contradictory effect"[22]). Other definitions of hacker, like those from the *Official (ISC)² Guide to the CISSP CBK* that are couched in terms of ambivalence, provide a mixed message with regard to the term. In the 2007 version of the *Official (ISC)² Guide to the CISSP CBK*, the term is defined differently depending on the domain reviewed—presumably a result of different authorships of each domain's study materials. Under the Information

Security and Risk Management Domain, "a hacker was originally a person who sought to understand computers as thoroughly as possible. Soon hacking came to be associated with phreaking ... which is clearly illegal."[23] The MIT/Stanford "hacker ethic," written by Stephen Levy, attempted to justify the actions of the hacker, stating that "access to computers should be unlimited and total; all information should be free; authority should be mistrusted," further promoting the concepts that hacking "promotes the belief of individual activity over any form of corporate authority or system of ideals."[24] Yet, it is unlikely that Mr. Levy is willing to make his personal financial information "free" to everyone. This manifesto that "information wants to be free" seems to be encouraging an environment designed to promote and encourage illegal activity. According to Young et al. (2007), "The fact that hackers consider their behavior morally right and acceptable to their family and friends in combination with the fact that they believe there is a low likelihood of being arrested, allows them to take risks in the wild Internet frontier."[25]

In the CISSP Operation Security domain of the *Official ISC² Guide to the CISSP CBK*, hacking is described thusly:

> *Malevolent hackers attempt to penetrate systems for fun or profit through the use of self-developed or open-source hacking tools. After a successful penetration, they may introduce other vulnerabilities into the system, such as a backdoor, to provide easier access. Crackers, on the other hand, are focused on breaking security measures within software for their enjoyment or profit. Their activities are primarily conducted to break copyright protection methods incorporated into software packages.*[26]

As is evident by the clarification of *malevolent* hacker, even in the information security community, there is some dissent over the true meaning of hacking; however, it is generally accepted that a hacker is not someone who truly intends to follow the policies, rules, and regulations associated with fair and responsible use of computer resources. According to a study by Young and Zhang, "Akers (1973, p. 7) makes the following statement: 'all behavior that humans are capable of performing is natural, none is intrinsically unnatural or deviant, but only so in relation to social definitions, which may vary by time and place.' One method by which social definitions are shaped is through laws. What constitutes illegal hacking is explicitly defined in U.S. laws and includes any unauthorized infiltration of an organizational or individual's computer system."[27]

Even the revered *Communications of the ACM* hosted a special issue in June 2006 touting "Hacking and Innovation," the perspective that through the advances of this culture, we have learned much about information systems and their security. In the introduction Conti states:

> *Some computer scientists consider it a high honor to be described as a hacker; to others it's a base insult. For many computer scientists, as well as the general public, the word* hacker *has a connotation reflecting the sensationalized stereotype often seen in mainstream media. Objective accounts are rare [1–4]. Perhaps due to this perception, two disjoint, typically mistrustful, technology-focused communities— professional computing and hacking—have emerged. Despite having only infrequent interactions, they are often at odds, ultimately frustrating one another's efforts. As the world increasingly depends on technology, we all must move beyond the semantics and etymology of the word* hacker *[6] to address the true risks and needs of humanity, either through our own research or when we serve as*

technical advisors to legislative and technology policy decision makers. Ultimately, each of our scientific contributions should be weighed on the merit of the related ideas, not on academic credentials, institutional affiliation, or age of the source.[28]

Even with this impassioned call "can't we all just get along?" the fundamental issue remains, society does not permit us to benefit from illegal actions. The same article lumps together a doctor who builds his own equipment (a la the original definition of hacker), and a hacker organization that learns about a new wireless exploit by actually compromising a system. The summary comment "Hacking is more about innovation and less about computer security"[29] really stabs at the heart of the issue—the use of the term *hacking*. Those who insist on hanging on to the original definition—computer enthusiasts—are doing a disservice to those who are trying to educate the public. The public won't make the distinction between hacker and cracker, or between hacker and criminal hacker. To them a hacker is bad news, which brings us to the heart of the dilemma; is it possible to be an ethical hacker?

The problem is further exasperated by those who drift off on the "knowledge is power" tangent, where they misperceive the hacker debate as one of the repression of change and innovation.

> *There is a global culture of people who call themselves computer hackers that is driven by a fundamental belief that information should be free and that the pursuit of knowledge is an essential human right. Most hackers seek to do creative things with technology, but the community is often beset by controversy because it centers on forbidden knowledge; in particular, hackers like to think about how computer security fails. The general public often has difficulty drawing a line between hackers who study computer security as a technical interest and criminals who break into computers and deliberately cause damage. Some observers in the media and the academic community have argued that the sort of information hackers discuss at conferences and in journals should never be shared publicly, saying that knowledge is itself dangerous, irrespective of the motives of the people discussing it.*

> *Controversy involving the hacker community is analogous to new fears being raised about science in general ... Over time, it has become increasingly evident that a broad policy debate about academic freedom is taking form in which the perspective of the hacker community may represent a critical counterweight to overzealous calls for control of the pursuit of knowledge.*[30]

It is easy to see how a straightforward issue with term usage has devolved into a debate of academic freedom. We as a community should not be debating this presumed repression of ideas or innovation, but should attempt to bring light to the irrationality of the promoted notoriety of an illegal activity, fervently being defended and obfuscated by those that revel in it. Outspoken security guru Dan Geer is often quoted and questioned for his opinion on hackers:

> *Dan Geer is suggesting that merchants violate the security of customers they deem as security risks. His argument is, basically, that there are two types of users out there: those who respond "yes" to any request—and therefore are likely to be infected by multiple types of malware doing all sorts of bad things—and those who respond "no" to any request, who are more likely to be safe ... To deal with those [yes] people, Geer says, you should effectively hack their computer. It*

won't be hard, since they're clearly ignorant and open to vulnerabilities—so you just install a rootkit and then you effectively own their machine for the duration of the transaction.

As Kulawiec notes in submitting this: "Maybe he's just kidding, and the sarcasm went right over my (caffeine-starved) brain. I certainly hope so, because otherwise there are so many things wrong with this that I'm struggling to decide which to list first." Indeed, I'm not sure he's kidding either, but the unintended consequences of violating the security of someone's computer, just because you assume they've been violated previously are likely to make things a lot worse ... based on the idea that people are too stupid to cure themselves, and somehow "white hat" hackers can help fix things. ... you're trusting these "good" hackers to do no harm on top of what's been done already, which is unlikely to always be the case.[31]

Penetration Testing

The actions taken by an information security professional to thoroughly test an organization's information assets and their security posture up to and including actually gaining access to the root information by bypassing security controls is not hacking; it is referred to as *penetration testing* (or simply pen testing) or alternatively vulnerability assessment. Most professional information security service organizations offer pen testing and many information security professionals receive training in the craft.

Some will argue that the mindset of the penetration tester is sufficiently different from that of, say, the firewall administrator as to the skills needed to break into a server or network, as opposed to protecting it. They argue that those with the "hacker mentality" have a unique perspective on this activity, whether or not they have acted on their abilities illegally.[32] This begs the question, "Are hackers the only ones who can master these skills?" Is it not possible to undergo professional training, building upon the ingenuity of the human psyche, to be naturally curious to investigate and solve these puzzles? Or must one "walk on the dark side" to gain this knowledge? There are far too many information security professionals tasked with penetration testing to claim that all are "reformed" or "converted" hackers.

The heart of the argument is the distinction between the pen tester and the hacker is really based on the fundamental concept of *authorization*. With authorization ("permission or power granted by an authority; sanction"[33]), the pen tester is able to identify and recommend remediation for faults in the information protection strategy of the organization. They are able to determine the presence of vulnerabilities and exposures and demonstrate the techniques used by hackers to conduct attacks upon them. But at the day's end, the pen tester is responsible for documenting their actions and making recommendations as to the resolution of these flaws in the defense posture. The hacker, being irresponsible, has no expectation of obligation or responsibility, only motives that are dubious at best.

Once we get past the linguistics, as reported by Marcus Ranum, Chief Security Officer of Tenable Network Security, in an interview in 2005: it's really not about what we say, but what we mean:

Truly, the only people who deserve a complete helping of blame are the hackers. Let's not forget that they're the ones doing this to us. They're the ones who are annoying an entire planet. They're the ones who are costing us billions of dollars a year to secure our systems against them. They're the ones who place their desire for fun ahead of everyone on earth's desire for peace and [the] right to privacy.[34]

3D

Conclusions

Some will argue that this reading presents a futile semantic debate, that it's the intent not the title that defines the difference between the white hat and the black hat, the hacker and cracker. Yes, the business world judges harshly on the face value of a professional. To cling to the nefarious title of hacker may make the individual less marketable. In 1998, when @Stake was lauded for hiring a number of the L0pht group, some companies reported "reservations" about engaging @Stake as a consultant. Fortunately or otherwise, the business world can be just as tough as any one hacker group. Symantec bought the @Stake in 2004 and effectively end-of-life'd its products.

In the "Code of the (ISC)^2," (ISC)^2's version of the Hippocratic oath ("... I will prescribe regimens for the good of my patients according to my ability and my judgment and never do harm to anyone ..."[35]) of the information security professional includes the following:

Safety of the commonwealth, duty to our principals, and to each other requires that we adhere, and be seen to adhere, to the highest ethical standards of behavior ...

Code of Ethics Canons:

- *Protect society, the commonwealth, and the infrastructure.*
- *Act honorably, honestly, justly, responsibly, and legally.*
- *Provide diligent and competent service to principals.*
- *Advance and protect the profession.*[36]

The code also calls for information security professionals to: "discourage such behavior as ...:

- *Professional association with non-professionals*
- *Professional recognition of or association with amateurs*
- *Associating or appearing to associate with criminals or criminal behavior"*[37]

The fundamental assertion of this paper is that any group of professionals ("a person who belongs to one of the professions, esp. one of the learned professions; a person who is expert at his or her work"[38]) should be held to higher moral standards than the average employee. Take it for what you will, but information security professionals are expected to be above reproach as the true guardians of the organization's information assets. Any doubt as to our true beliefs, motives, and ethics undermines the efforts of us all. Adopting the juvenile moniker and attitude of "hacker" is a cry for attention, to belong to a group of social outcasts, similar to the "Goth" movements in public schools. Note: You do not see too many "Goths" in corporate America.

Even though an information security professional may not be a member of the (ISC)^2, the fundamental lesson is what is important. Above all else, do no harm.

Endnotes

1. Biblos.com, viewed 10/3/08, from http://bible.cc/john/1-1.htm

2. "Canon," viewed 10/3/08, from http://dictionary.reference.com/browse/canon

3. "Ethical," viewed 10/3/08, from http://dictionary.reference.com/browse/ethical

4. "Hack," viewed 10/3/08, from http://www.etymonline.com/index.php?term=hack

5. Multiple references including http://www.edu-cyberpg.com/Technology/ethics.html

6. http://mitpress.mit.edu/catalog/item/default.asp?ttype=2&tid=3618

7. Jargon Files—Online version of the New Hacker's Dictionary, viewed 10/4/08, from http://catb.org/~esr/jargon/html/H/hacker.html

8. RFC 1392: Hacker, viewed 10/4/08, from http://rfc.net/rfc1392.html

9. http://dictionary.reference.com/search?q=hacking

10. Hackers, TMRC Web site, viewed 10/5/08, from http://tmrc.mit.edu/hackers-ref.html

11. © 1991 MGM

12. © 1998 20th Century Fox

13. © 2007 20th Century Fox

14. © 1999–2007 Home Box Office Television

15. © 2005–2008 Fox Television

16. O'Brien, M., Tzanelli, R., and Yar, M. "Kill-n-Tell (& All That Jazz): The Seductions of Crime in Chicago," *Crime Media Culture* Vol 1(3). 2005. Pp. 243–261.

17. © 1986 Paramount Pictures

18. © 1983 MGM/UA

19. © 1995 MGM

20. http://dictionary.reference.com/browse/underground

21. Ibid.

22. http://dictionary.reference.com/browse/oxymoron

23. Tipton, H. F., and Henry, K. (eds.), *Official (ISC)² Guide to the CISSP CBK*. Boca Raton: Auerbach. 2007.

24. Levy, S., *Hackers: Heroes of the Computer Revolution*, New York: Penguin Putnam. 1984.

25. Young, R., Zhang, L., and Prybutok, V., "Hacking into the Minds of Hackers," *Information Systems Management*, 23(4), Fall 2007, pp. 281–287.

26. Tipton, H. F., and Henry, K. (eds.), *Official (ISC)² Guide to the CISSP CBK*. Boca Raton: Auerbach. 2007.

3D

27. Young, R., and Zhang, L., "Illegal Computer Hacking: An Assessment of Factors That Encourage and Deter the Behavior," *Journal of Information Privacy & Security*, 2007 3(4), pp. 33–52.

28. Conti, G., "Hacking and Innovation: Introduction," *Communication of the ACM*, 2006, 49(6), pp. 32–36.

29. Ibid.

30. Cross, T., "Academic Freedom and the Hacker Ethic," *Communication of the ACM*, 2006, 49(6), pp. 37–40.

31. Masnick, M., "Is it a Good Idea to Violate the Security of Your Customers If They're Security Ignorant?" *Techdirt* www document, viewed 2/1/09, from http://www.techdirt.com/blog.php?tag=dan+geer

32. Schwartz, M., "Should You Hire a Convicted Hacker?" *Information Week* www document, viewed 10/18/08, from http://www.informationweek.com/news/security/cybercrime/showArticle.jhtml?articleID=206902454&pgno=1&queryText=&isPrev=

33. http://dictionary.reference.com/browse/authorization

34. "Ranum, Marcus," viewed 10/3/08, from http://www.edu-cyberpg.com/Technology/ethics.html

35. http://en.wikipedia.org/wiki/Hippocratic_Oath

36. "ISC^2 Code of Ethics," viewed 10/10/08 from https://www.isc2.org/cgi-bin/content.cgi?category=12

37. "ISC^2 Code of Ethics," viewed 10/10/08, from https://www.isc2.org/cgi-bin/content.cgi?category=12

38. http://dictionary.reference.com/browse/professional

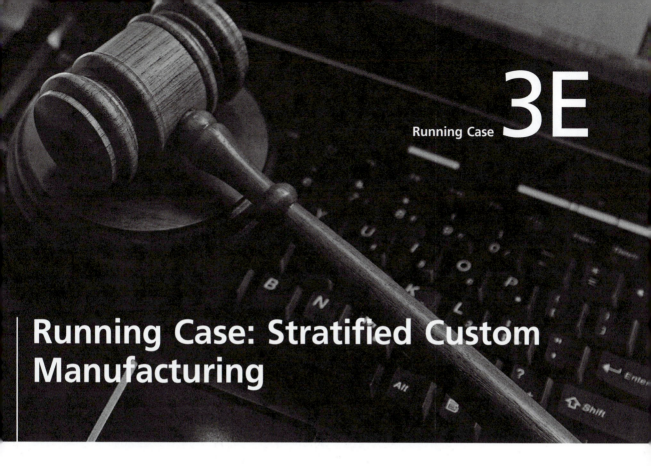

Running Case: Stratified Custom Manufacturing

David MacIntosh, the SCM manager of privacy and compliance and the corporation's Chief Privacy Officer (CPO), was processing his email when the phone rang. "Hello," he said.

He heard, "Hi. Is this David?"

He answered, "Yes, it is. How can I help?"

"This is Sally Skavadale." David recognized the name of the corporation's Director of Human Resources. "We have an issue that has come up we need to discuss. Can we chat?"

David looked at his schedule and saw it was open for at least two hours. "I'm available now."

Sally said, "Earlier today an employee was given a routine exit screening by corporate security." This was a routine part of building security and corporate policy compliance whereby every few minutes an employee leaving the building was chosen at random and had their bags screened to see if any company assets or other proscribed materials were leaving the building. After regular hours, all employees were screened in this way. Sally continued, "One of the managers in the Data Center Operations group was stopped with a large bundle of employee files. They claimed they were working up annual employee reviews, but it is still a clear violation of policy to remove them."

David said, "I see. How can I help in this matter?"

Sally replied, "Part of the procedure we follow is that an incident impact statement has to be prepared so that when the policy violation committee meets, the nature and degree of the infraction can be used to assess a penalty. I am comfortable with the human resources impact, but I would like you to write an assessment of the privacy impact of this incident."

David replied, "Certainly. Can you provide me with an inventory of the documents in question and the policy and practice exemplars of those document types to be sure I see all of the data that was on the forms?"

"No problem," answered Sally. "I will send you what you need along with the draft incident report via InterOffice mail. How long will you need to write up the impact assessment?"

David thought a moment and answered, "No more than two or three days. Will that work?" He hoped it would be okay since otherwise he would need to work later than usual.

Sally answered, "Sure. That's great. I look forward to your report."

They ended the call and David returned to his email. After he deleted the usual flurry of junk mail he had signed up for, including all the magazine-related email and the professional society email and the announcements from all over the company, he came across a new summary email that caught his eye.

> ## DIPLOMA MILL BUSTED BY STATE REGULATORS
>
> CENTERVILLE – State Education Agency officials announced today that Monticello University has been shuttered. Monticello University was a local business that granted undergraduate and graduate degrees to applicants "based on life experience." Regulators have filed an administrative law action to close the business after several complaints had been received by the State Education Agency and by the State Attorney General's Fraud Hotline.

David pondered this note for a minute and then recalled that one of his recent new hires had claimed a degree from Monticello University. "Surely not," he said to himself, but he picked up the phone to call Sally back.

"Sally Skavadale," she answered when she picked up the phone.

"Hi Sally, David here."

"Oh, hi. What's up? Did you need something else for your report? We haven't mailed the packet yet."

"No," said David. "I have another issue that just came up. Did you see the news report about Monticello University being closed down by the State Education Agency?"

"No. That's news to me," she replied.

David continued, "I'm pretty sure one of my staff has an MBA from there. Do you think HR should look into this company-wide?"

"You can count on that," said Sally.

Discussion Questions

1. When an employee removes confidential records from the workplace without permission, without special controls, and against policy, is that a violation of the law?

2. What would you recommend as a punishment for a policy violation involving removal of confidential records for a "harmless" reason like catching up on reading them at home? Would your recommended punishment be different if the violator used them for a different purpose, perhaps using them to perform identity theft?

3. Is it against the law to earn a degree from an unaccredited private college that uses "life experience" to grant diplomas? Is it unethical to pay for and receive such a degree? Is it unethical to use such a degree on an employment application or in a resume?

Risk Management

Part **4**

Objective

The objective for this chapter of the text is an examination of the legal and ethical issues associated with the management of risk in the organization. At its heart, information security management is about risk management, minimizing the probability of a loss, through effective security program operations including understanding the risk environment and organizational exposure to risk.

Contents

A Reading: Cyber Insurance and the Management of IT Security Risk

Tridib Bandyopadhyay

There is no business endeavor with profit motive, yet without attendant risks. Businesses must face risk in their pursuit of return on investment. Risk as opposed to uncertainty is more manageable—often we are able to ascribe an informed mathematical probability on its realization, and assign an expected value of the concomitant loss. The particular type of risk that we discuss here concerns utilization of information assets in businesses and the risks arising thereof—the information security risks or cyber risks.

B   Reading: Rethinking Risk-based Information Security

Herbert J. Mattord

The information security discipline has a common body of knowledge comprised of many facts, techniques, and ways for its practitioners to accomplish the objectives of securing the information assets of the companies by which they are employed. Sometimes these practitioners simply do things the way they have always been done. Perhaps some of the practices need to be reexamined. One that needs attention is the way that risk-based decision making is applied in places that it may not improve the outcomes of the problems being addressed.

C   Case: Video Maze

Patricia Morrison

This case describes the issues associated with a small business entrepreneur who relies on information technology to provide the competitive edge in his video business. Background on the business, business owner, the employees, and technology used are included to create the environment for the exploration of ideas.

D   Running Case

Cyber Insurance and the Management of Information Security Risk

Tridib Bandyopadhyay
Kennesaw State University, Kennesaw

Dr. Tridib Bandyopadhyay is an Assistant Professor at Kennesaw State University. His major research interests are in information security investment issues in the private and public domains. At KSU, Dr. Bandyopadhyay teaches Systems Analysis, E-Business Systems, and Information Security in the BSIS, BSISA, and MSIS programs. Prior to his engagements in the academics, Dr. Bandyopadhyay has worked as an electrical engineer and later as a planning manager in the largest energy-generating company in India.

Overview

There is no business endeavor with profit motive, yet without attendant risks. Businesses must face risk in their pursuit of return on investment. Risk as opposed to uncertainty is more manageable—often we are able to ascribe an informed mathematical probability on its realization, and assign an expected value of the concomitant loss. The particular type of risk that we discuss here concerns utilization of information assets in businesses and the risks arising thereof—the information security risks or cyber risks.

Introduction

Information assets (e.g., computers, servers, PDAs) and the interconnectivity among these assets (LAN, Intranet, and Internet) are integral parts of doing business in today's networked economy. While networked information assets add great value to the business processes, possible abuse/misuse/unuse of such assets and networks do give rise to a substantial amount of information security risks.

There are several options for managing information security risks. At the extremes, a firm could avoid such risks altogether by freeing its business processes from information assets (quite unrealistic), or it could retain all the risks and bear all the probabilistic misfortunes. In reality, firms attempt to mitigate a part or all of the risks, and/or adopt ways to transfer some of the remaining risks to willing parties (the insurer). The mitigation of information security risk is generally achieved through the layered regimes of prevention (e.g., firewall) and detection (e.g., IDS, Honey Nets) to minimize threats, and providing for the measures for loss/damage control (e.g., incidence response, disaster recovery, and business continuity planning). Among others, the transfer of the risks could be achieved through financial instruments, formally known as cyber insurance contracts. Cyber insurance provides indemnity for losses on information assets: which could arise out of the unuse (e.g., DoS), abuse (e.g., unauthorized access), misuse (e.g., identity theft), third-party loss (e.g., customers' personally identifiable information), and losses from cyber extortion. Cyber insurance is a new concept in the management of information security risks, and although IT security managers express increasing interest in these instruments (Ernst and Young Survey, 2007), the cyber insurance market is still in a nascent stage of development. In what follows, we introduce the readers to the basics of insurance economics, integrate such prudence in the information risk domain, and then briefly discuss the products, providers, and utilization of cyber insurance as an integral part of the organizational IT risk management program.

The following pages in this chapter have been divided into several sections. Section 2 presents the economic concepts of cyber insurance and section 3 discusses the needs of organizations that translate to the demand for cyber insurance. Section 4 presents the involved decisions in cyber insurance. Section 5 provides a discussion on the major cyber insurance carriers and the cyber insurance products that are available in the market, and explains how IT Managers could effectively integrate these products in their information risk management programs and initiatives. Section 6 provides an outlook for the cyber insurance industry including some concluding remarks.

The Economics of Cyber Insurance

The insurer is in the insurance market because of profit motive, but the prospect (insured) firm's motivation arises out of risk aversion. Because the future is uncertain, the prospect firm faces potential variability in its wealth—a risk.[1] The insurance market offers instruments with which a risk-averse firm could transfer their risk to the insurer firms, whose business model aggregates and averages the risks (law of large numbers) to manageable proportions.[2]

Suppose that if there is no data theft, the net wealth of the prospect firm would be $10 million, but if the future turns out to be adverse (for example, a hacker steals sensitive data), the net wealth of the firm could be only $2 million. Moreover, this adverse outcome could be so debilitating that the firm may be forced out of business! Assume that the firm could buy cyber insurance from the insurer who would pay the shortfall of wealth (10 – 2 = $8 million) in the event of data theft, but only when an upfront premium is paid. In one hypothetical scenario, the prospect firm may pay $4 million as the premium, and in the event of data theft, the insurer could pay an indemnity of $8 million. Note that this arrangement would ensure that in either of the outcomes of the future, the prospect firm would be left with a net wealth of $6 million. More interestingly though, we see that the firm has successfully managed the variability of its future wealth but paid $4 million to achieve this. In other words, the firm has transferred its information risk of data theft for a premium of $4 million to a willing party, the insurer. The insurer is willing to take the risk so long there is no expected loss from it (when we assume perfect competition, the zero profit situation is the outcome*), or when it has issued many such contracts, and has moderated its risk exposure on the whole. However, the prospect firm cannot bear this risk because of possible threat of business closure in cause of data theft (and no insurance). In other words, the insurance contract may have equal monetary value to the contracting parties, but the insured firm likely derives higher utility out of it because of its inherent risk aversion. The cyber insurance market exists for this fundamental reason.[3]

We need to look more closely at the hypothetical scenario that we had utilized for the insurance premium in the last paragraph. We had implicitly assumed that the future outcomes were equally probable. In that scenario, the insured firm faced a 50% probability of data theft, which is equivalent to exposing the insurer to a 50% probability for the indemnity payment of $8 million. That also explains the premium of $4 million. Clearly, a pertinent question here is that of the likelihood of the occurrence of the data theft.

Suppose that there is only 25% probability that there will be a data theft, such that the expected wealth of the firm is now $8 million (0.75 × 10 + 0.25 × 2). Note that the only difference from the earlier scenario is that of the altered expectation of the data theft, which, however, alters the expected indemnity payout that the insurer faces: only $2 million (25% of 8 million). In the new scenario, the prospect firm could pay $2 million in an upfront premium (a certain payment) for which the insurer would be ready to pay an indemnity of $8 million in the probabilistic event of data theft.

Three concepts are noteworthy here:

1. The insured firm trades the uncertainty of outcomes for an assurance of certainty, and pays for it up front.
2. The insurer balances its risk (which is really the expected large indemnity payments) over the large numbers of insurance contracts that it sells.
3. The probability of ruin is instrumental in determining the premium that is required in the arrangement.

The example scenarios suggest that as the probability of the occurrence of data theft decreases, the insured firm is required to pay even lower levels of the premium. This is a standard observation in insurance, and makes good sense. There is one last thing to remember here. In order to ensure that an insurance contract may not be utilized to gamble up the losses

---

*The cyber insurance market is far away from perfect competition, and an arbitrary loading factor should be assumed on the premium in general.

and shore in higher indemnity, regulators impose strict provisions for penalty in case an insured firm indulges in such fraudulent actions.

Let us look closely at the probability and loss aspects of the future event.[4] Who decides how probable the data theft is, or how much loss it incurs? The interests of the contracting parties are diagonally opposite here. The prospect firm is interested to exhibit that there is a small probability of data theft and lower eventual loss, because these variables reduce the premium. On the other hand, for any underestimation of the probability or the magnitude of loss, the insurer loses money through higher than expected indemnity payout. It is important to realize that the prospect firm knows and understands its own systems much better than the insurer (information asymmetry), yet has no obvious incentive to be truthful. Because the information asymmetry works against the interest of the insurer, objective estimations of the probability and the magnitude of loss from data theft through truthful revelation are imperative in the process. Two measures are commonplace in the cyber insurance market today:

1. The prospect firm is required to submit self-assessment paperwork, which essentially reveals the assets, processes, and procedures of IT security management of the firm and

2. The prospect firm is audited by a third party for an independent analysis, which tends to compensate for the lack of technical prowess of the insurer.

Finally, these assessment and analysis reports are consolidated, and the two parties arrive at the agreed "probability" and "loss" from data theft for the prospect firm, which then go into structuring the cyber insurance contract. When the prospect firm can exhibit technical, procedural, and policy controls in place, a better sense of data assurance prevails, and a lower probability of data theft is evident. On the other hand, when the prospect firm exhibits that adequate planning and provisioning have gone into the measures toward incidence response, disaster recovery, and business continuity management, a lower magnitude of loss from eventual compromise of the network is apparent. It is important to realize that the magnitude of loss from abuse/unuse/misuse of information assets is intrinsically difficult to estimate because these assets are often utilized across multiple lines of business and used by multiple departments, giving rise to interaction effects. Finally, all these pre-contract investigations and analyses raise the contract writing costs of cyber insurance substantially, which of course is passed on to the insured firm.

Stepping aside, let us look closely at the prospect firms as a group in general. The firms that employ a high amount of controls against data theft and operationalize security-savvy policies and procedures face lower probability of data theft and a lower amount of losses from a realized breach. This is also the type of firm that would likely exhibit lower propensity for cyber insurance products than those who face a higher probability of data theft or higher losses, or both. However, the insurer is more interested in selling a cyber insurance contract to the first type of firm rather than the second. In other words, like other insurance markets, the cyber insurance market is prone to adverse selection as well. As a result, firms that find cyber insurance more attractive are less likely to receive coverage, while the insurer is hard pressed to differentiate between the good and bad risks. In the cyber insurance market, firms space themselves in a wide spectrum of this variability, and the insurers are compelled to run third-party audits and restrict themselves in writing private contracts (especially for larger coverage) rather than offering canned products, which could otherwise lower contract-writing costs substantially.

Once the initial IT security health of the prospect firm is assessed and the contract is written, the insured firm enjoys the assurance of certainty in future outcomes, but is now prone to lose vigilance on the control and policy strengths, which in the first place earned the cyber insurance contract, or lowered the premium (or both)! This is known as moral hazard, and mechanisms are designed and integrated to cyber insurance contracts to counter the effect. For example, an insurer may require the insured firm to regularly monitor and update the IDS system during the contract period, and report the same as an indication that there are no obvious lacks in its measures. On top of the above, deductible clauses are often applied to a cyber insurance contract to make sure that a part of loss is borne by the insured party, encouraging the insured firm to keep security breaches to the minimum. As such, the effect of a deductible on the performance of cyber insurance contracts is broad based. A higher deductible results in lower amount of up-front premium, which often increases the salability of a cyber insurance contract. Also, a deductible plays an indirect role in reducing the number of claims, and limits the origination and disbursement costs that are associated with indemnity payouts. Larger cyber insurance contracts could also feature caps on the liability that the insurer accepts. This is particularly important in case of IT risks, because the business impact of losses is not yet fully understood, and regulations on data and information repositories are not quite developed yet.

The Need for Cyber Insurance

There are several reasons why cyber insurance has its place in the management of IT security risks.[5] First, the technological controls lag hacker innovation. Second, even if the technological controls could catch up to the rate of the hackers' nefarious innovations, the advantage of effort still would lie with the hackers' community even for the remaining vulnerabilities in a system. While the defender of a system is required to know all the vulnerabilities of the system and also be able to protect them with absolute certainty, the hacker needs to find only one small subset of these vulnerabilities to unleash a massive attack. Third, modern software systems rely, at least in part, on post-release user testing and feedback (competitive pressures often force the provider to release the software before the bulk of its vulnerabilities are known or understood in a lab setting). As a result, even if the defender could implement all the latest technological controls (though cost may be prohibitive), residual IT security risks could still remain in the IT system.[6] Finally, IT risks are increasingly being differentiated from the way the insurance industry deals more traditional risks. This is primarily because we have not fully resolved the debate whether information assets could be treated as tangible property. Consider the case where the insured company maintains an online discussion board, and some outsider discussants post defamatory or racially discriminatory messages. The insurers have exhibited resistance/refusal to cover such incidents under the general liability insurances that the firm might possess. Similarly, the insurers of traditional insurance products have consistently refused to identify potential liabilities arising from a chat room as equivalent to those from the activities in a physical room of the insured premise (e.g., how lawyers' risks are redefined may be found at http://www.brunswickcompanies.com/pl-cyber-liability-insurance.html). Essentially, in many occasions, the insured firms find themselves frustrated between the way they interpret the standard insurance contracts and the way the providers of insurance prefer to exclude information assets from them. As a result, in more recent liability insurances, property damage excludes computer data from the definition of tangible property. Amendments like these have created gaps in the coverage of the firms, creating the need for insurance products specifically designed for cyber losses. Liability clauses affected by such gaps are inadvertent distribution of malice (e.g., virus), unauthorized use of company information (e.g., meta tagging or deep linking of Web resources), intellectual property infringement/distortion (e.g., Web content and graphics), and loss of privacy issues, to name a few. Moreover, there are certain risks that are new and characteristic of IT assets only, yet pose significant potential losses to firms (e.g., DDoS, cyber extortion, etc.).

Clearly, there is a need for specialized insurance products that could help manage the residual risks remaining after the technological controls are placed, or for those risks now falling through the cracks of interpretation from traditional insurance contracts.

The Fundamental Decisions in Cyber Insurance

Technology alone cannot mitigate all the IT risks, meaning that the firm must manage some residual risk; and second, budgetary considerations rarely provide for all the countermeasures, meaning that the firm must accept and live with some amount of unmitigated IT risks. It is between these two considerations that the utilization of cyber insurance products falls: a standard pattern tends to emerge as a firm contemplates how to manage its information risks. The firm attempts to transfer that part of the risks it may neither control in a cost-effective fashion with current technologies nor can accept (and live with) yet avoid potential catastrophic outcomes. The transfer of this part of the risk is achieved through the vehicle of cyber insurance.

In what follows, we briefly describe an elegant framework for utilization of cyber insurance products in the management of IT security risk provided by Gordon et al. in their 2003 CACM article.[7]

Their model framework suggests that a firm first needs to assess its risks that arise out of the abuse/unuse/misuse of data and information assets. Integral in this are the creation and ranking of threat-vulnerability pairs in an appropriate scale of "severity." The threat-vulnerability pairs, which contribute to the highest proportion of security risks, are then subjected to technology controls (e.g., firewall, encryption technologies, etc.), as long the process remains cost effective. The residual risks, which still remain after all these technological controls are already in place, are then addressed with the help of cyber insurance products. Subsequently, the firm must create a maintenance regime that can tune the technological controls and readjust the cyber insurance coverage on a regular basis to take care of the exposures from new threats and vulnerabilities for times to come.

In the same work, Gordon et al. also provide a four-step decision process that could operationalize the above framework into an organization specific implementation. They suggest that a firm should

1. Audit all its information resources vis-à-vis the threats and vulnerabilities that could affect those resources, and assess the dollar value of the total exposure.

2. Check the existing coverage from all existing insurance contracts. (This process would likely point out the gaps in coverage that we have already discussed in an earlier section.)

3. Research and investigate cyber insurance providers and their products with special consideration to exclusion and mandatory observation clauses.

4. Select only those contracts that complement the firm-specific IT risk scenario as managed with the help of technological and other organizational controls together.

4A

The Providers and Their Cyber Insurance Products

We begin with a discussion on the specific types of coverage that the cyber insurance products provide. First-party coverage refers to losses that accrue directly at the insured firm. These are the losses that the insured firm suffers when data, information, or network assets become unavailable for use in their business processes. For example, first-party cyber insurance contracts could cover losses arising out of business interruption caused by accidental data loss, or a network failure because of an attack by hackers. Other contracts in this category could provide for the expenses associated with the recovery of data after a breach or accident. One popular category of cyber products here relates to criminal extortion, especially from threats of DDoS attacks. E-commerce and other pure presence firms, which must depend on their bandwidth to ensure a steady flow of revenue, are often the victims of DDoS attacks, and may find this type of cyber insurance products quite helpful in their IT security management programs.

Cyber insurance products are also available for third-party cyber losses. Such losses relate to those liability issues that typically inflict the firm in an indirect fashion. For example, in case a firm loses customer data, it could become responsible for restitution of the financial loss that the customer suffers from the resulting identity theft. Cyber contracts could cover such third-party losses and provide the compensation on behalf of the insured firm. Third-party contracts also exist for liabilities in media usage (e.g., Web publishing, Web chat, email copyright, etc.) or for other Internet liabilities when the computers or other network resources of a firm are unwittingly utilized in a botnet to stage cyber attacks on other firms.[8]

As the utilization of information and network assets exploded over the last decade in terms of penetration and intensity of use, cyber insurance providers have also attempted to provide products that are either more focused or provide higher coverage. As part of their focused strategy, providers of cyber insurance are also offering market specific cyber insurance products. For example, Ace USA now offers products that apply to the financial services industry only.

One aspect of cyber insurance contract that has shown definite maturity is the IT risk assessment process, which is often a prerequisite for a cyber insurance contract. (Many major insurance carriers now provide managed assessment service along with possible cyber insurance contracts.) This process could include administration of self-assessment questionnaires as well as on-site audits as deemed fit for the case in hand. Elaborate self-assessment questionnaires could require documentation for several of the following:*

1. Enterprise-specific, issue-specific, technical, and organizational policies, their governance and management;
2. Physical security measures of information assets and networks, physical and biometric access controls, building security and third-party managed services;

*One detailed questionnaire for a cyber insurance module for network security can be accessed from AIG at http://www.aig.com/Network-Security-and-Privacy-Insurance-(AIG-netAdvantage)_20_2141.html under the heading of *Network Security Self Assessment.*

3. Configurations, rules, procedures, and maintenance schedules for operating systems of all network nodes and routers;

4. Business continuity planning including incident response, disaster recovery with backup and recovery programs and histories;

5. Security Education, Training and Awareness (SETA) policies and program details; and

6. Specifics of vulnerability monitoring and software patch management in the IT security maintenance program.

The major providers of cyber insurance today are AIG, Ace, AON, Chubb, CNA, Lloyd's, St. Paul Travelers, and Zurich. The coverage for cyber property and theft in these insurance products include destruction of data or software, recovery from virus attacks, data loss, business interruption, DoS, cyber extortion, and terrorist attacks while the liability provisions include those of media injury, copyright, and network security issues (the Betterly report, June 2006).

The major players in cyber insurance offer a fairly exhaustive set of choices, a vast improvement over the first-generation cyber insurances of a decade ago. In reality, the cyber insurance products are now differentiated in the way they are bundled. For example, AIG offers an array of products selectively grouped across individual coverage options. AIG's NetAdvantage line of products is indeed a set of bundled products, each offering different combinations of risk mitigation capabilities (Figure 4A-1). Competitors of AIG have responded similarly in the individual coverage; cross-differentiated bundles are now offered by the major insurance providers. Unlike the first cyber insurance products that focused on first-party losses, cyber insurance products now cater to the emerging need of third-party liability insurance. As we have discussed before, one major reason for much emphasis on cyber liability is the fact that the data assets are increasingly being considered as a special type of assets as against the usual physical assets. This has caused the liabilities from data assets not being covered by the standard business liability insurances.

The premiums for cyber insurance can vary depending on the type and size of business, the intensity of information goods and assets in the firm's business processes, the extent of policy and technological controls, and on other existing cyber insurance coverage. A typical cyber insurance premium could fall from 0.5% to 6% of coverage for a million dollar coverage (for coverage details, see an article by Mollie Niel, *Protecting your assets with cyber insurance* at   http://smallbusinessreview.com/technology/Protect_Your_Assets_With_Cyber_Insurance/). Unlike more conventional products, the cyber insurance products do not have a high volume of sales, and still do not benefit from the economies of scale. The cost of writing cyber insurance is still high, and there is much subjectivity in the process of evaluation of cyber risk.

The Outlook for Cyber Insurance

Early estimations of cyber insurance in the beginning of the 1990s were high.[9] Although cyber insurance products have come a long way, especially compared to the first-generation hacker insurance products offered in the early 1990s, such expectation of market size has not been realized. The market, by popular estimates, is still below the billion dollar mark in premium revenue. The reasons for such lackluster growth of cyber insurance markets have been

4A

AIG CYBER INSURANCE (BUNDLED) PRODUCTS REVEAL DIFFERENTIATION STRATEGY							
Coverage/Net Advantage Product (NA)	NA	NA Professional	NA Commercial	NA Liability	NA Property	NA Security	NA Complete
Cov-1	–		Yes	Yes	–	Yes	Yes
Cov-2	Yes	Yes	Yes	Yes	–	Yes	Yes
Cov-3	–	Yes	–	Yes	–	–	Yes
Cov-4	–	–	–	–	Yes	Yes	Yes
Cov-5	–	–	–	–	Yes	Yes	Yes
Cov-6	–	–	Yes	Yes	Yes	Yes	Yes
Cov-7	–	–	–	–	Yes	Yes	Yes
Cov-8	–	–	Yes	Yes	Yes	Yes	Yes
Cov-9	Yes	Yes	Yes	Yes	Yes	Yes	Yes
Cov-10	–	–	–	–	Yes	Yes	Yes
Cov-11	–	–	–	–	Yes	Yes	Yes
Cov-12	Yes	Yes	Yes	Yes	–	Yes	Yes
Cov-13	–	–	Yes	Yes	–	Yes	Yes

List of Coverage: 1) Network Security Liability, 2) Web Content Liability, 3) Internet Professional Liability, 4) Network Business Interruption, 5) Information Asst Coverage, 6) Identity Theft, 7) Extra Expense, 8) Cyber Extortion, 9) Cyber Terrorism, 10) Criminal Reward Fund, 11) Crisis Communication Fund, 12) Punitive, Exemplary and Multiple Damages, 13) Physical Theft of Data on Hardware/Firmware

Figure 4A-1 Net Advantage Line of Bundled Products from AIG[10]

(Source: Majuca, R. P., Yurcik, W., Kesan, J. P., The Evolution of Cyberinsurance, 2006, http://arxiv.org/ftp/cs/papers/0601/0601020.pdf)

explained from several angles. Our inability to accurately and objectively calculate losses from information assets is possibly the most accepted reason. Other possible reasons are the accounting difficulties of losses, the dearth of actuarial data, and the inexperience of IT managers in utilization of insurance in their cyber risk management programs. The lack of acceptance/use of cyber insurance products has affected the economy of scale that the insurance industry enjoys in other standard products: thus, contract-writing costs are high on an individual cyber insurance contract, and products are generally perceived to be expensive.

There is no denying of the fact that insurance can play an important role in the management of cyber risks in today's businesses (http://www.cl.cam.ac.uk/~rja14/econws/53.pdf). As a matter of fact, in the brick-and-mortar side of the economy, insurance industry drives the security and safety industries in a big way. Thus, it appears natural for one to expect that the same could happen to the cyber security industry. However, before that, the risks that unuse/ misuse/abuse of data, information, and network assets pose to the general business processes are required to be understood, and then integrated in the organizational risk management programs. IT managers are technologically oriented and skilled, while the organizational risk managers share different philosophies in the way they look at the organizational risks in general. Unless these two groups of managers share a common process of assessment of cyber risk, and address them in a unified fashion, the real impetus for the growth of the cyber insurance products could remain elusive.

References

Borch, K. *The Mathematical Theory of Insurance*. Lexington Press, USA. 1974.

Institute for Catastrophic Loss Reduction. *Cyber-Incident Risk in Canada and the Role of Insurance*. April 2004. Canada. (http://www.iclr.org/pdf/Cyber-incident%20Risk%20Final%20Report_April%202004.pdf)

Endnotes

1. Anderson, R. *Why Information Security Is Hard—An Economic Perspective*. 2001. (http://www.ftp.cl.cam.ac.uk/ftp/users/rja14/econ.pdf)

2. Borch, K. *Economics of Insurance*. North Holland Publishing Company. 1990.

3. Betterley, R. S. "CyberRisk Market Survey 2006," *The Betterley Report*, June 2006.

4. Mossin, J., and Smith, T. "Aspects of Rational Insurance Purchasing." *Journal of Political Economy*. July/August, Vol. 76, 1968.

5. Kesan, J. P., Majuca, R. P., and Yurcik, W. J. *Cyberinsurance as a Market-Based Solution to the Problem of Cyber Security—A Case Study*. 2005. (http://infosecon.net/workshop/pdf/42.pdf)

6. Ogut, H., Menon, N., and Raghunathan, S. *Cyber Insurance and IT Security Investment: Impact of Interdependent Risk*. 2005. (http://infosecon.net/workshop/pdf/56.pdf)

7. Gordon, L. A., Loeb, P. M., and Sohail, T. "A Framework for Using Insurance for Cyber Risk Management." *Communications of the ACM*, Vol. 46, No. 3, 2003.

8. *New Liability Forms and Media, Tech, and E-Business Risks*. 2004. Rossi, M. A. Insurance Law Group. (http://www.irmi.com/expert/Articles/2004/Rossi05.aspx)

9. Bohme, R. *Cyber-Insurance Revisited*. 2005. (http://infosecon.net/workshop/pdf/15.pdf)

10. Majuca, R. P., Yurcik, W., and Kesan, J. P. *The Evolution of Cyberinsurance*. 2006. (http://arxiv.org/ftp/cs/papers/0601/0601020.pdf)

Rethinking Risk-based Information Security

Herbert J. Mattord
Kennesaw State University

Herbert Mattord, MBA, CISM, CISSP completed 24 years of IT industry experience as an application developer, database administrator, project manager, and information security practitioner in 2002. He is currently an Assistant Professor of Information Security, on the faculty at Kennesaw State University. He and Michael Whitman are the authors of Principles of Information Security, Management of Information Security, Principles of Incident Response and Disaster Recovery, Readings and Cases in the Management of Information Security, The Guide to Firewall and Network Security: With Intrusion Detection and VPNs, *and* The Hands-On Information Security Lab Manual *all from Cengage Course Technology. During his career as an IT practitioner, he has been an adjunct professor at Kennesaw State University; Southern Polytechnic State University in Marietta, Georgia; Austin Community College in Austin, Texas; and Texas State University: San Marcos. He currently teaches undergraduate courses in Information Security. He is the coordinator for the department's Certificate in Information Security and Assurance, and is also an active member of the Information Systems Security Association and the Association for Computing Machinery. He was formerly the Manager of Corporate Information Technology Security at Georgia-Pacific Corporation, where much of the practical knowledge found in this and his earlier textbook was acquired. Herb is currently an ABD Doctoral Candidate, pursuing a Ph.D. in Information Systems at Nova Southeastern University.*

Overview

The information security discipline has a common body of knowledge comprised of many facts, techniques, and ways for its practitioners to accomplish the objectives of securing the information assets of the companies by which they are employed. Sometimes these practitioners simply do things the way they have always been done. Perhaps some of the practices need to be reexamined. One that needs attention is the way that risk-based decision making is applied in places that it may not improve the outcomes of the problems being addressed.

Rethinking Risk-based Information Security

When insurance underwriters or financial industry risk managers use the risk assessment processes developed for their industries, they have access to sources of empirical data designed and collected specifically for their needs. In those settings, the measured data are accurate, complete, and applicable. The risk assessment processes implemented by insurance and financial experts have evolved to use empirical data in ways that assure organizations the results are as accurate and as complete as possible, and that the decisions they support will consistently add value to their risk control objectives. The risk assessment processes used by IT and information security (InfoSec) risk management do not work as well. The processes for risk assessment used in IT and InfoSec are either taken wholesale from these or other disciplines, and the empirical data that is available is either inadequate or nonexistent. For example, there are currently few generally accepted data sources a security manager can use to determine the average costs incurred when an attacker breaks into his or her database. But the casualty underwriter can find the average percentage value lost when a particular type of business experiences a burglary. As another example, an InfoSec project manager cannot get an accurate predictor for the frequency of a successful Web server attack. However, a financial service risk manager can access the current projections for default on the loans in a specific portfolio of loans being considered for purchase. Current practices in IT risk assessment draw on risk assessment techniques borrowed from the insurance and other industries. These quantitative methods use estimates of the inputs used for expected-loss formulae. As those in the fields of IT and InfoSec who rely on these processes are finding, this approach is not sustainable in the long term as it lacks the reliable inputs needed to have accurate forecasts.

Why then do IT and InfoSec practitioners continue to assess risk? In most cases it is done to validate a risk control strategy or to justify the expense of a risk control regime. The current relationship between business enablement and information security results in the ongoing need for such validation and justification. When each unit of an organization's limited resources are consumed, whether that resource is human, or it is economic capital, or it is a time-to-market consideration, current circumstance requires a business case be made. The dominant practice at this time is to express a risk-based assessment in the trappings of a cost-benefit analysis using the best tools at hand. This is not often an adequate response.

4B

One noted authority in the area of information security (Parker, 2006) has proposed an alternative approach. In his article "Making the Case for Replacing Risk-based Security," Parker proposes that a three-pronged approach can replace the current reliance on risk-based justification. These three elements are: due diligence in following accepted practices, compliance with laws and regulations that increasingly apply to commercial use of information technology, and a philosophy of business enablement. In addition to Parker's perspective, there are other alternatives to the dominant approach described in the literature that encompass the use of a philosophy of due care and compliance to laws and standards implemented in ways to enable business functionality.

This paper describes some of the deficiencies in the risk-based methodology currently in widespread use within the field of IT risk assessment. It will then describe how alternative approaches, such as Parker's, can work. Evidence to support this discussion has been drawn from a survey, designed and administered to begin measuring how practitioners use current techniques and how they feel about the use of alternatives as identified by Parker. While this survey shows that those sampled are very much still focused on the traditional quantitative approach, there is concern enough about the continued viability of the traditional approaches to make these practitioners more open to new methods for justifying risk control strategies and information systems control regimes.

We've Always Done It That Way

The current approach to risk assessment used in InfoSec and IT for strategic, project, and control justification is based on recommended practices. These practices, ranging from the *Generally Accepted Information Security Practices* (GAISP) to ISACA's *COBIT* and extending to the *Common Body of Knowledge* from ISC^2, are built around frameworks similar to NIST's Loss Expectancy model (Stoneburner, Goguen, & Feringa, 2002). This type of model is used to provide validation when an organization justifies decisions to expend resources for programs that control operational risk for information technology (IT) systems. This paradigm for risk-based assessment of information technology security controls has a variety of appellations, and, for the purposes of this discussion, is labeled the Threat-Vulnerability-Asset (TVA) paradigm.

This approach assesses risk by first identifying information assets (the A in TVA). Each of these assets is then assigned an asset value. Each asset, usually starting with those of highest assigned value, is then examined to discern possible threats (the T in TVA). At the intersection of each asset-threat pair, an assessment of the vulnerabilities that that asset faces for that threat source is undertaken (being the V in TVA). At these intersection points, the TVA cells are then assigned a likelihood of occurrence and a loss estimate in the event of occurrence. Then aggregating by asset, the value of the asset is multiplied by the likelihood of a loss for each credible vulnerability and then multiplied again by the loss forecast for that eventuality. This aggregate value is used to forecast a value called the *annualized loss expectancy* (ALE). The ALE is intended to be used to quantify expectation of loss as compared to other similar forecasts. When placed into rank order, it will do a credible job of estimating, in a single value, a combination of factors to reveal which assets need protection most urgently and from which threats.

One weakness of the TVA approach, beyond the lack of quality sources of empirical data, is that the values do not translate well to the operational world of business, and may not offer business managers the necessary accuracy or reliability needed to make risk-based decisions. Each of the values used in this additive process is fraught with its own inaccuracies and limitations. In other industries, asset values are typically assessed using market replacement value or book value (acquisition cost less depreciation). There is less consensus about how the valuation of information assets should be assessed compared to the value of buildings or financial instruments. The values used for likelihood of attacks are often created from whole cloth, based on the expectations of subject matter experts and shaped by current events and perceived probabilities rather than measured experiences from significant populations. The estimates of losses that may be experienced are also usually based on what-if scenarios and come from best-case/worst-case/likely case forecasts. When the inaccuracies of most ALE calculations are considered, the chances are the values will not provide the users what they need to make operational decisions beyond that of comparing one asset's risk to another's.

These types of deficiencies in TVA have been noted by Smithson and Simkins (2005), Straub and Welke (1998), and Peltier (2005), to name but a few. But few alternatives have been widely considered; most writing in the field strives to make incremental improvements in processes and in estimating practices. The ongoing research and development of variations on TVA, variously named and modeled, have evolved for many years (Vorster & Labuschagne, 2005). Among the widely used variants are those mentioned by Parker, OCTAVE, FRAP, FAIR, and the Hoo model (2005, p. 9). A complete list of approaches that have been developed to operationalize the approach of identifying information assets, assessing asset value, predicting loss estimates, forecasting attack probability, and frequency of occurrence are too numerous to catalog here. The approaches have been discussed and compared by some, such as Vorster and Labuschagne (2005). New approaches have been developed that synthesize new variants from among others such as the work done by Bandyopadhyay and Mykytyn (1999).

The systematic application of mathematically rigorous approaches has been proposed by Hoo (Geer, Hoo, & Jacquith 2003), Mohammed and Noureddine (2003), and others. Other approaches that follow a more qualitative model, less driven by calculation, are also in use. These include recommendations to adopt clustering approaches like that of Kothheimer and Coffin (2003) and Seify (2006).

Best Practices May Not Always Be Best

Current models of justifying IT risk use practices borrowed from the insurance and financial sectors that calculate loss estimates based on inputs of rich and reliable data sources. IT risk assessment practices are based on these practices but do not have the benefit of the robust, reliable, and rich data sources for likelihood of critical events and asset valuation. For instance, if insurance industry actuaries want to justify the premium for a hazard insurance policy, they can access a large pool of empirically derived data to determine both the probability and the scale of the losses over the term of the policy. On the other hand, an InfoSec project manager has no such pool of data to determine the likelihood of the next Web server defacement nor can the losses from network denial of service attack be predicted.

As practitioners apply the models emerging from the TVA paradigm, they have noted deficiencies. Parker (2006) points out that many methods used to rationalize the risk estimates drawn from egregiously weak estimating regimes result in climates like "the emperor's new clothes" (p. 7). He goes further to state that results from the TVA paradigm in current practice "have faded away when the high cost, easily disputable results, and changing environment" come into play (p. 7). Others have also questioned the method of solving complex formulae based on highly subjective estimates in order to make risk-based predictions (Smithson & Simkins, 2005; Straub & Welke, 1998). And, as Parker noted, "No study has ever been published to demonstrate the validity of information security risk assessment, measurement and control based on real experience" (2006, p. 7).

The Information Systems Security Association (ISSA), which is an international group of information security practitioners, promotes a set of recommended practices called the Generally Accepted Information Security Principles (GAISP). Currently in its third version, GAISP is an evolving statement of what those who practice information security believe should be part of the practice of the discipline. "GAISP correctly assumes that the generally accepted concept of security is that it is driven by risk" (Parker, 2006, p. 7). The problem, as noted by Parker, is that GAISP does not note that the risk of loss from well-documented sources must be handled differently from the risk of loss from those sources that are less well known or less able to be accurately forecast. The methods used to assess the risk and then plan and build controls for expected losses from a well-defined risk, such as that from viruses or worms, may have to be different from those used to assess and plan for the risks from less certain sources, such as data spills of confidential data.

If Not The Old Way, Which Way?

If risk assessment is not the answer to justify information security actions, an alternative is needed (Parker, 2006, p. 9). The alternative Parker proposes is based on a combination of due diligence, compliance, and a philosophy of business enablement.

Due Diligence

Due diligence, performing the level of preparation that is expected and that is reasonable and customary, can be used to justify information security risk controls. By comparing the internal state of readiness in an organization to what has been done at other, well-known and well-regarded organizations, a case can be made to management that certain risk control measures are needed to improve information security. When this case is endorsed by the organization's decision-making bodies, management can then accept that the costs of such measures are also customary in their industry and thus justified. While simple due diligence is done without regard to the quality of the results at the source organizations, it can lead to mediocrity. But, if the sources for comparison are chosen with a concern for outcomes, it can lead to the spread of those approaches and control systems that achieve desirable results.

The due diligence approach can also be considered to be in effect when organizations choose to follow voluntary standards or choose to follow laws, regulations, or compulsory standards from other industries or settings that do not apply to them. For instance, if a private manufacturing company chooses to adopt the control systems recommended by the Sarbanes-Oxley Act, which do not apply to them by law, they are following a form of due diligence.

Compliance

Many organizations implement strategic approaches and control regimes that are imposed on them by laws, regulations, and/or compulsory standards. As more organizations find themselves bound by these requirements, management finds ways to implement the mandates they contain. Recent years have seen several instances when a "fire-drill" mentality sets in and needed resources, including human resources, are brought to bear to meet this kind of compliance requirement. Discussions have been held about how this diversion of resources may have led to suboptimum project selection, with organizations funding compliance projects to the detriment of other projects that may have been more effective in reducing risk. While that is true, the mandated projects were usually successful in responding to the need for compliance.

Business Enablement

Security is a requirement for many business processes. In the best organizations, security is planned into IT projects from the inception. When a case is made that a security strategy or control regime is essential to meet competitive forces and in order to assure marketplace success, management is more likely to make sure necessary resources are planned into the project.

Other Ways

In addition to the initiative from Parker, in recent years, several researchers have begun to identify alternative approaches to risk assessment that do not rely on the TVA paradigm. From incremental revision through synthesis (Bandyopadhyay et al., 1999) to broad and far-reaching changes in approach. The ideas of those departing, more or less, from TVA include the DDCE model proposed by Parker (2006), using standards in general (Iachello, 2003), using specific standards such as ISO/IEC 17799 (Sanchez et al., 2006), or use of the provisions of the Sarbanes-Oxley Act (Spears & Cole, 2006). Two recent books on this topic also propose elements of a new approach: one by Loch, Meyer, and Pich (2006) that is focused on project management risk topics and the other by Tarantino (2006) that explores the use of legislative and standards compliance in a more systematic and applied way.

Practitioners Are Ready

In order to assess whether or not the IT risk management practitioners of the world are ready to move toward the DDCE model, a formal survey was conducted from October 2006 to January 2007. The instrument was designed to collect opinion assessment using a simple rating scale (5-point Likert) and was administered to a convenience sample of 57 IT risk managers solicited from personal mailing lists and professional association memberships (ISSA and ISACA chapters).

Survey Respondents

Partial responses were collected from 52 respondents, with 5 respondents removing themselves from consideration when asked if they were responsible for all or part of the IT risk management function at their organization. All told, 35 respondents provided answers through to the end of the questionnaire.

Most respondents in the sampled group are employed by medium to large organizations. The largest group of respondents (34%) were from organizations with from 101 to 1,000 employees and/or contractors, and only a few (16%) were from smaller organizations with 100 or fewer employees and/or contractors. The largest type of organization represented in the sample was the For-Profit group at 83%. This was followed by 8% in Government, and 2% working with Non-Profit organizations. The remainder (4%) indicated they worked at an Educational institution, but did not declare if public or private. The 47 respondents who provided an Industry sector replied with one of 15 categories. The largest single group (21%) replied they were employed in the High-Tech sector. The next largest group (13%) noted they were in the Education sector. The third largest group (9%) were in the Banking and Investment sector. All others reported they were in Aerospace/Defense, Chemical, Consulting, Consumer Products, Government, Healthcare, Insurance and Finance, Media, Retail, Telecommunications, or the Utility sectors.

Given the relatively small sample group, it was determined to limit the survey analysis to the sample group as a whole since subgroups were not large enough to be statistically significant. Hopefully, later research can collect sufficient data to perform industry- and size-based comparisons of these practices.

A Survey of Current Practices

After collecting the baseline demographic data, the survey used three questions to probe the degree to which the responding practitioner used estimation in the risk management process. The first of these questions asked the degree to which estimates, rather than empirically derived values, are used for asset valuation. While no one responded that they use estimation to completely derive asset values, 75% noted that they use estimates somewhat (39%) or to a large degree (36%). This is a significant point since this demonstrates that only 25% of current IT risk managers sampled do not use estimates (7%) or only use them to a small degree (18%) to derive asset values.

When it comes to estimating in the prediction of the likelihood of a loss event, the numbers bear out even more of a reliance on estimation. Only one person responded that they use estimation to completely derive likelihood (2%). However, a significant group (85%) noted that they use estimates somewhat (21%) or to a large degree (64%). This is noteworthy since this demonstrates that only 13.6% of current IT risk managers sampled do not use estimates (4.5%) or only use them to a small degree (9.1%) to derive loss event likelihood.

The final question in the estimating sequence showed that few practitioners used estimation to jump straight to the key fact used for risk assessment, annualized loss expectancy (ALE), and this bears out the assumption that current practitioners rely on estimating the factors of the ALE calculation but do not estimate ALE itself by using estimation as often. Only one respondent (2%) relies completely on estimating of ALE directly. Other respondents are almost evenly distributed in their use of estimating ALE with 23% avoiding ALE estimates completely, 23% using ALE estimates to a small degree, 27% using estimates somewhat, and 25% using them to a large degree. The conclusion that we can draw from this is that many practitioners will estimate components of their ALE calculations, whereas few actually estimate the final ALE value.

The next four questions of the survey probe the source of estimate data as to its nature (qualitative vs. quantitative) and where it is derived from (internal or external) and how much reliance is placed on these sources of data. This line of inquiry begins by asking about whether facts used for subjective assessment (qualitative data) come from inside or outside the respondents' own organization. Responses from 38 practitioners who claimed to use qualitative data sources show that an average of approximately 64% of the data is sourced from inside their own organization and 36% comes from outside the respondents' own organization.

With regard to the ratio of qualitative (subjective) data being used as compared to quantitative (objective) data being used, 38 people responded to the question. They indicated that 53% of the data used for risk management program decision making comes from quantitative or objective sources and 47% of the data is sourced from qualitative or subjective sources. This is an interesting measurement, since the most widely held belief is that metrics programs, designed to collect objective, quantitative data should drive InfoSec and risk management programs, whenever possible. It seems, based on these responses, it is only possible slightly more than half the time.

The third and fourth questions in the sourcing series ask to what degree the respondent relies on qualitative criteria that come from outside and inside their own organizations. Converting the responses from the Likert scale to a mean value shows that external sources are relied on at a level of 2.98 (with 1 being Not at All, and 5 being Completely) and internal sources are relied on at a level of 3.53. Internally derived subjective data is more reliable to practitioners than that which is externally derived. When it comes to sources of qualitative data, the opinion of the survey respondents indicates that not only is more data collected from inside the respondents' own organization, it is more reliable to them as well.

The next sequence of questions was developed to collect the opinion of the respondents as to how much they and their organizations have already integrated the processes of legal/regulatory compliance, compulsory industry standards compliance, and voluntary industry standards compliance into their risk management programs. In the first case, most (74%) respondents agree that their current IT risk management approach relies on being compliant with laws and regulations imposed by governments (20% *Completely* and 54% *To a Large Degree*). Only 26% replied that they were not at all or only somewhat reliant on legal compliance (2% *Not at All*, 8% *To a Small Degree*, and 15% *Somewhat*).

The survey participants were asked to list, in descending order of importance, up to five laws and/or regulations having the biggest impact on risk management procedures. Using a weighted-factor analysis, three laws were seen as the most significant: the Sarbanes-Oxley Act of 2002 (SOX), the Gramm-Leach-Bliley Act (often abbreviated to GLBA and also known as the Financial Services Modernization Act of 1999), and the Health Insurance Portability and Accountability Act of 1996 (HIPAA). Collectively, SOX received 30% of the weighted-average response, while GLBA and HIPAA received 22% and 17%, respectively. When looking at number of times mentioned, SOX was identified by 18 of 29 respondents, GLBA and HIPAA were listed by 9 and 6, respectively. All of the other 14 laws and regulations offered collectively represented 31% of the weighted response.

When it comes to compulsory standards, only one respondent said their risk management approach is *Completely* reliant on compulsory standards. Over half (53%) are *To a Large Degree* reliant on compulsory standards. Roughly 17% are *To a Small Degree* or *Not at All* reliant on compulsory standards. The third question in this series of reliance attempted to gauge the respondent's reliance on voluntary standards. Interestingly, it was answered in a way that came to nearly the same aggregate response (3.225 mean response for compulsory standards and 3.275 for voluntary standards) but with differing component answers: the *Not At All* response showing only one respondent for voluntary standards, whereas there were six for that choice for the compulsory standards.

When asked which standards had the most impact on their risk management procedures, respondents' answers clustered around three responses. First, the *Information*

Questions	Responses					
	1 Not at all	2 To a small degree	3 Somewhat	4 To a large degree	5 Completely	Mean
Due Diligence	0	1	11	23	0	3.63
Compliance	1	3	11	17	2	3.47
Enabling Business Requirements	9	1	16	18	0	3.49

Table 4B-1 Responses to Questions On Alternative Approaches

technology—Security techniques—Code of practice for information security management (ISO17799) received 22% of the weighted-average response and was listed by 5 of 20 respondents. Next, the Payment Card Industry Data Security Standard (PCI-DSS) received 19% of the weighted-average response and was listed by 6 of 20 respondents. Finally, the Control Objectives for Information and related Technology (COBIT) received 13% of the weighted response and was listed by 4 of 20 respondents. All other standards noted made up 46% of the weighted response and was spread over 16 other standards.

Respondents' Opinion on Alternatives

The final sequence of questions in the survey was intended to gauge the opinion of the respondent on how well the techniques of due diligence, compliance, and business enablement would be received as an alternative mechanism for IT risk assessment. Each question was to be answered in a Likert scale with the options of *Not at All*, *To a Small Degree*, *Somewhat*, *To a Large Degree*, and *Completely*. The results are shown in Table 4B-1.

Based on these responses, respondents think that due diligence has some chance of meeting the needs in the area of IT risk management, with most of them (23% or 66%) replying that it would meet their needs to a large degree and a near unanimous perception (97%) that it will at least *Somewhat* meet their needs. The responses to the other two questions were not as positive as the first, but by and large showed that these alternatives offer some opportunity to improve the risk assessment process for respondents.

While this survey was limited to a relatively small convenience sample, it does show indications that those practitioners surveyed by and large follow the current recommended practices of using the TVA approach for risk assessment practices and that they may be open to alternatives for improvements in the methods used for these activities.

Conclusion

A review of some of the literature and the results of a preliminary survey seem to reinforce the conclusions drawn by Parker. Risk assessment practices used today to justify that risk-reducing strategies and controls are currently broadly implemented by practitioners using the TVA approach. This approach is known to be imperfect and, while work to make it more effective has gone on for many years, there are still opportunities for improvements.

The direction to be taken for these improvements needs to be considered: Should the industry continue to rely on risk-based techniques for validation of strategies and controls or is something else needed?

Two fruitful avenues for future research are: first, to explore both the satisfaction of practitioners with the current quantitative tools and data sources as well as the accuracy of these current tools as predictors for loss estimates, and second, to explore how the proposal made by Parker for due diligence, compliance, and business enablement can be fully defined, well articulated, and then operationalized for the community of IT risk managers.

Given that the primary means used to validate and justify information security strategies and control programs is based on providing reliable estimates of risk, a fundamental shift in the core paradigm of that validation and justification process will have far-reaching consequences. Those who use these procedures in practice as well as those who teach information security need to remain informed about this possible shift in the practices for such a critical element of the discipline, else future generations of practitioners will be poorly equipped for the change in how risk assessment and risk management are accomplished in coming years.

References

Bandyopadhyay, K., Mykytyn, P. P., & Mykytyn, K. (1999). A framework for integrated risk management in information technology. *Management Decision*, 37(5).

Geer, D., Hoo, K., & Jaquith, A. (2003). Information security: Why the future belongs to the Quants. *IEEE Security & Privacy*, 1(4), 24–32.

Iachello, G. (2003). *Protecting personal data: Can IT security management standards help?* Paper presented at the 19th Annual Computer Security Applications Conference (ACSAC 2003).

Kotheimer, C. J., & Coffin, B. (2003). How to justify business continuity management. *Risk Management*, 50(5), 30–34.

Loch, C., Meyer, A. D., & Pich, M. T. (2006). *Managing the unknown: A new approach to managing high uncertainty and risk in projects*. Hoboken, NJ: John Wiley.

Mohamed, H., & Noureddine, B. (2003). *Algebraic specification of network security risk management*. Paper presented at the Proceedings of the 2003 ACM workshop on Formal methods in security engineering.

Parker, D. B. (2006). Making the case for replacing risk-based security. *The ISSA Journal*. 6–9.

Peltier, T. R. (2005). *Information security risk analysis* (2nd ed.). Boca Raton: Auerbach Publications.

Sanchez, L., Villafranca, D., Fernandez-Medina, E., & Piattini, M. (2006). *Practical approach of a secure management system based on ISO/IEC 17799*. Paper presented at the First International Conference on Availability, Reliability and Security (ARES 2006).

Seify, M. (2006). *New method for risk management in CRM security management*. Paper presented at the Third International Conference on Information Technology: New Generations (ITNG 2006).

4B

Smithson, C., & Simkins, B. J. (2005). Does risk management add value? A survey of the evidence. *Journal of Applied Corporate Finance, 17*(3), 8–17.

Spears, J., & Cole, R. (2006). *A preliminary investigation of the impact of the Sarbanes-Oxley Act on information security.* Paper presented at the Proceedings of the 39th Annual Hawaii International Conference on System Sciences (HICSS 2006) Track 9.

Stoneburner, G., Goguen, A., & Feringa, A. (2002). *Risk management guide for information technology systems: Recommendations of the National Institute of Standards and Technology.* Retrieved from http://csrc.nist.gov/publications/nistpubs/800-30/sp800-30.pdf

Straub, D. W., & Welke, R. J. (1998). Coping with systems risk: Security planning models for management decision making (Vol. 22, pp. 441–469): Society for Information Management and The Management Information Systems Research Center.

Tarantino, A. (2006). *Manager's guide to compliance: Sarbanes-Oxley, COSO, ERM, COBIT, IFRS, BASEL II, OMB A-123, ASX 10, OECD principles, Turnbull guidance, best practices, and case studies.* Hoboken, NJ: John Wiley & Sons.

Vorster, A., & Labuschagne, L. (2005). *A framework for comparing different information security risk analysis methodologies.* Paper presented at the Proceedings of the 2005 annual research conference of the South African institute of computer scientists and information technologists on IT research in developing countries, White River, South Africa.

Video Maze*

Patricia Morrison
Financial & Information Management, Shannon School of Business,
Cape Breton University, Sydney, Nova Scotia, Canada

Patricia Morrison is an instructor in IT, Financial, and Information Management, Shannon School of Business, Cape Breton University. She received a diploma in Information Technology and a Bachelor of Business Administration from CBU and a Master of Business Administration from City University. She is an I.S.P. designate of C.I.P.S. She is the recipient of the CBU President's Award for the pursuit of common purpose.

Overview

This case describes the issues associated with a small business entrepreneur who relies on information technology to provide the competitive edge in his video business. Background on

---

*This case was written by Patricia Morrison, Shannon School of Business, Cape Breton University, Sydney, Nova Scotia, Canada. The case was prepared for a class assignment utilizing materials from referenced sites including Microsoft, HP, ICTC, RCMP, and Central Queensland University. The case itself is fictitious but demonstrates a series of considerations required in reviewing a security situation. It is intended as a basis for classroom discussion and is not intended to represent either correct or incorrect handling of administration issues. The author recognizes the contributions of colleagues Dr. Sherry Finney, Joanne Pyke, Ben Pickles, Parker MacDonald.

the business, business owner, the employees, and technology used are included to create the environment for the exploration of ideas.

Introduction

On a cold day in January, Richard Maze sat in his favorite café with a regular cup of coffee and the morning newspaper. The front page headline caught his eye; it read "Information stolen, business being sued." Immediately, Richard looked to see what business had been compromised. He thought to himself—it can't be a small-sized business like Video Maze; it must be a multinational company for there to be so much hype. Upon further review, however, Richard was amazed to see the company in question was very similar to his own both in size and structure. Although the business was similar in structure, the function differed. All of these things set Richard to thinking—what do I have in place for my business? Next year I am planning to expand operations by adding another location in a city 20 miles away. Will my current system setup carry over to the new location? Can I interface the two systems and operate my computer services at a cost savings?

With these questions in mind, Richard set out to determine how to more efficiently run his business, while at the same time protect it from the range of new problems in security and operations associated with the continuously changing IT sector.

Business Background

Video Maze opened in the downtown area of the heavily populated city of Millville, by Richard Maze in 2005. Video Maze later registered the business name as DVD Video Maze, and as the new title indicated, both DVDs and videos were for sale or rental. The video/DVD business had been the primary operation, but a variety of amenities available from the coffee bar made the video selection a pleasure for customers rather than a task. Customers could sit at one of the 10 PCs and view movie choices by searching the online database with key words or favorite titles rather than walk the perimeter of the store trying to read empty video cases. Not only could the choices be viewed in the store, but they could be viewed in the comfort of the customer's home. Customers could send an email to the shop to make or confirm a movie reservation instead of doing it through the Web page. At pickup, employees requested the customer's reservation code to call up their record for processing. At this point, the exchange was made, the customer got the DVD or video, and the employee received the payment, which was entered into the system.

The coffee bar menu included tea/coffee, cappuccino, pop, juice, and water. Snacks included chips, bars, nachos, and other confectionary items. The goal was to make refreshments and snacks available to customers while using the computers, or to take home with them, for a reasonable price.

Customers could use the computers to check their email and browse the Internet and, therefore, receive an added benefit to their DVD Video Maze experience. Convenience, ease of

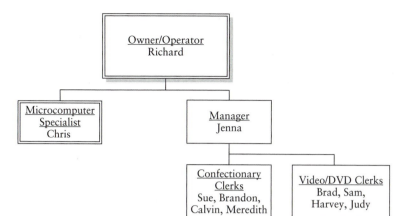

Figure 4C-1 Organization Chart

Courtesy Course Technology/Cengage Learning

use, and availability of the computers, which otherwise would be unused, lent more value to the social aspect of the business.

The impact of information technology on this business has yielded high returns in the past. Competitors were gradually shifting to online booking and soon it would be the industry norm. Future growth would depend on the efficiencies of the information system within the business.

Management and Staffing at Video Maze

The organizational structure was comprised of the owner/operator (Richard), the manager (Jenna), the techy (Chris), the video/DVD clerks (Brad, Sam, Harvey, Judy), and the confectionary clerks (Sue, Brandon, Calvin, and Meredith). See Figure 4C-1.

Each employee was permitted full access to the computer network for personal use during slow periods in the day. Richard tried to stress, however, that business operations were the first priority.

Richard's educational background focused on the Arts. His entrepreneurial spirit was sparked from an urgency to experiment with the unknown adventures of business. When it came to technology, Richard admitted he was afraid of it. Richard relied heavily on the expertise provided by Chris. Richard had decided to offer Chris a challenge if Chris would agree to manage all IT-related areas for both the current and new business operations. If Chris accepted the challenge, he would receive a raise in pay.

Chris was self-taught and easy-going. His interest and excitement over processing power had traditionally caused him to exceed his hardware budget unnecessarily. Chris had been with the business a long time and reassured Richard that he stayed current with the changing IT industry.

The video/DVD clerks ranged in experience levels for data entry and transaction processing. The transactions were processed in the DVD/video computer system. The coffee bar clerks provided the customer with the product and received the payment, thereby completing the transaction. The cash transactions were entered into the database as they occurred.

Hardware Specifications

The hardware configuration was a very important component of the business operations. Richard knew that the Ethernet network consisted of a bank of 10 PCs wired (cat 5e) in a star topology. Chris had prepared a network diagram and store layout as well as system hardware specifications for the servers, computers, and printers. This information is provided later in Figures 4C-2 and 4C-3 in the section called "Supplemental Information."

Windows® 2003 was installed on the operational server. The other server, which was set up to mirror the operational server, was housed in the basement in the area that had a foundation. Chris was pleased with his planning and boasted of the online, up-to-date, current backup, which was ready to be used at any time. He figured this scenario was better than using CDs, DVDs, or tapes because it eliminated storage problems. Chris strongly believed that tape media was at risk of damage in a damp basement.

Software Specifications

Windows® 2003 comes with a default setup and Chris installed it with only one change. He created, read/write access for all DVD Video Maze employees, and a multi-user customer log-in "video" with the password "maze." Chris left inactive accounts from past years installed for testing on the system.

Chris had set up each of the PC workstations to perform standard functions for the customers, which included the search and selection of titles from the DVD/video database, the option to view the clips of the titles and to reserve the title from the computer bank in-house or from home. The software used for this was Microsoft Access® database interfaced with a Web page form. The Web page was located on the main server. The fees for Internet access were monthly. The PCs had a browser installed to access the Internet via the local ISP. Chris felt that some of the software bundled with the PCs at the time of purchase were not necessary and, therefore, did not install them. See the following section of supplemental information for a complete list of the bundled software. Norton Security software was resident on all systems but was not active.

Any user/customer could log in to a PC, modify or save any kind of files to the hard drive, anywhere on the network except for Chris's. Chris set himself up as administrator on the server and used administrator access rights only to clear log files accruing on the server. If he could have figured out how to stop log files from being created, he would put an end to them.

The cash systems accessed the database to view the customer's selection and ultimately processed the transaction and updated the inventory table. The interface to interact with the Microsoft Access® database and perform cash register functions was developed years ago by

4C

an old friend of Chris's. Additional staff information such as scheduled shifts and employee records were also a part of the same Microsoft Access® database.

Chris designed the business database in Microsoft Access® 2007. The database had multiple tables and multiple keys. The key for the tables associated with the customer was the customer number. The key associated with the timesheets and payroll information was the employee number. Chris used remote software to log in and fix problems from home or elsewhere.

Chris figured all customers knew their customer number so it made a perfect key for entering transactions. As a precaution, Chris printed a list of all customers and their associated numbers just in case a customer forgot their number. The video/DVD clerks found this a nuisance at peak times and often relied on guesses to put customer numbers in. Chris set up the same scenario for employee numbers.

Some of the fields from Chris's notes included:

Customer_Number	Member_Number	Emp_id
First_Name	Status	Emp_rate
Last_Name	Discount_rate	Emp phone
Address	Member_fee	Emp_SIN
Telephone	Date_joined	Emp_Fname
Customer_balance		Emp_Lname
	Confectionary_code	Emp_number
Video code	Confectionary_desc	Emp_Address
Video description	Confectionary_price	Emp_Tax_rate
Video availability		Emp_hours
Video reserved	Transaction_id	Emp_YTD
Video rate		Emp_ded1
Video rental price		Emp_ded2
		Emp_ded3
		Emp_ded4
DVD code		Emp_ded5
DVD description		Emp_shift
DVD availability		
DVD reserved		
DVD rate		
DVD rental price		

When the field naming system had been devised, Chris had told Richard that he jotted down the fields quickly and might be missing some information but "it wasn't a concern" because anyone could get the idea of what the labels represented.

Business Operations

Richard noted that one of his employees always sat at the computer farthest away from everyone. He never seemed to share his Internet search results with anyone and was consciously monitoring anyone who sat at that same computer. Richard asked Chris if there was any chance that Brad could be using the computer inappropriately and if he would be legally obligated and possibly have his computer equipment confiscated. Chris did not know the answer to Richard's question.

Some of the employees had received complaints from customers. Some customers said it took forever to access the DVD/Video Maze Web page, and when they did get into the system, it took a long time to process their selection. Chris told the clerks the system was like anything else: it has good days and bad days and there was nothing to be concerned about. He said the backup server was online and ready to go if the main server crashed.

As for business reporting, every couple of months Chris met with Richard to discuss improvements for the computer aspects of the operation. Each time, Chris spoke in technical language emphasizing the need for replacement or for upgrades to the existing systems. Richard, unfamiliar with the lingo, invested additional dollars trying to stay on top of the technology wave. Chris believed speed was what the customers wanted when searching the database and insisted that hardware was the way to go. Chris believed the computer bank should be upgraded constantly.

Chris reassured Richard that the business expansion discussed earlier was simple. He said the new operation required onsite hardware the same as the current site and another ISP connection. All transactions and business processing could be processed at the main site (current site).

With respect to working hours, Chris logged many hours of work and ultimately received a paycheck greater than anyone else working at Video Maze, including Richard. Richard felt this was fair considering his lack of knowledge when it came to IT.

Chris's time was usually devoted to removing files from the system hard drives. Chris has asked Richard to approve specifications to upgrade all the hard drives. Chris felt the upgrade would pay for itself by reducing the number of hours he spent cleaning the hard drives.

Employees were permitted to check their email account during break time. Several months ago, during one of Chris's breaks, he noted an email from a friend in the industry, which included an attachment about server disaster guidelines (see the Windows 2000 Server Disaster Recovery Guidelines in the section of Supplemental Information later in this case). Chris felt he didn't have the time to read it now but put it in his "to do" pile. He figured it was outdated anyway. He never did seem to get the time to read emails like this and others.

The Situation and Alternatives

After his eye-opening experience while having coffee that January morning, Richard decided that he would contact Chris, his PC specialist, to discuss the current system. During their conversation, Chris firmly stated the system was secure and that there was no way business information could be compromised. Chris refused to even consider the possibility of risk and told Richard he did not have the time to "fool around" with unimportant tasks such as an assessment on a system he knew by heart. Chris did agree, however, to give Richard permission to pass on his notes on the system and setup to someone else, if Richard really felt it was necessary to have an assessment conducted.

After the discussion with Chris, Richard decided to contact his good friend Paul, who was an IT instructor at the local university. Paul suggested having a group of his competent students investigate and observe the business operation with the intent of producing a threat and risk assessment document. A time was set up for Richard to speak with the class, and once the meeting was over, Richard felt he had been well received by the Systems Security, Audit, and Control class. He also felt assured that the students would meet the challenge. Richard passed the business information on to the students. He was, however, unable to answer any additional questions other than the information provided by Chris by way of his notes and his own knowledge.

Conclusion

It was now several weeks since Richard had given the students the details, and in that time Richard was doing a lot of thinking. A threat and risk assessment might answer the security question, but not the business expansion question and vice versa. Is the business system secure? Is the business system scalable to accommodate a second business at a different location? Is Richard responsible for the security of his customers' information? Is Richard responsible for the actions of his employees in the workplace? Are there any inefficiencies in the system or the business that could be corrected? He looked forward to receiving the students' response, and he hoped their analysis would shed light on some of these important questions.

Student Assignment

More and more organizations are performing threat and risk assessments in order to formulate safeguards and identify vulnerabilities for their business assets, systems, and information. Use the Guidelines for Computer Security to complete a Threat and Risk Assessment for the owner of Video Maze.

The guidelines can be found at CQU, by A. C. Lynn Zelmer, PhD at http://www.cqu.edu.au/ documents/compsec/guidelines/cqu_seca1.html or Appendix C of the *Security Information Publication 5, Guide to Threat and Risk Assessment for Information Technology*, November 1994 at http://www.rcmp.ca /tsb/pubs/it_sec/g2-001_e.pdf

Supplemental Information

Network Diagram 2

Appendix A

Network diagram

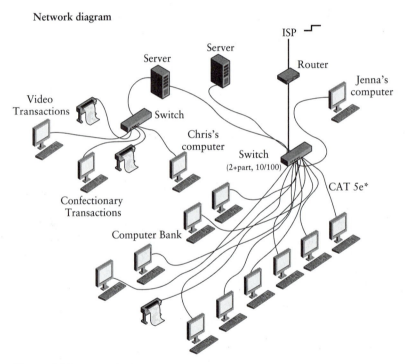

Figure 4C-2 Network Diagram

*Courtesy Course Technology/Cengage Learning

Store Layout

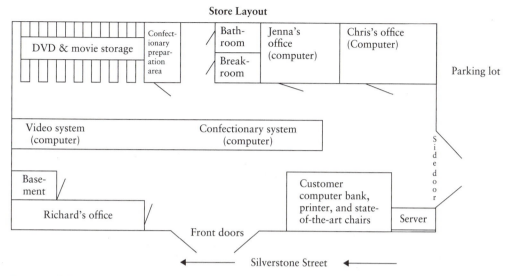

Figure 4C-3 Store Layout

Courtesy Course Technology/Cengage Learning

Specifications (Servers)

ProLiant ML110 G5

Processor type—Intel® Xeon® 3065 Dual Core Processor 2.33 GHz

Processor speed—2.33 GHz

Number of processors—1 processor

Processor core available—Dual

Processor front side bus—1333 MHz Front Side Bus

Internal cache—1 × 4 MB Level 2 cache

Standard memory—1 GB (1 × 1 GB) Standard Memory

Memory slots—4 DIMM slots

Standard memory—1 GB (1 × 1 GB) Standard Memory

Memory type—PC2-6400 unbuffered DDR2 ECC 800 MHz

Internal drives—72 GB SAS Non Hot Plug Hard Drive

Hard disk drive speed—15,000 rpm

Hard disk controller—HP SC40Ge Host Bus Adapter with RAID 0, 1, 1 + 0 support

Optical drives—16x SATA DVD-ROM

Internal mass storage—Maximum 1.8 TB (4 × 450 GB) SAS

Chassis type—Micro ATX Tower

Chipset—Intel® 3200 Chipset

Network interface—Embedded NC105i PCI Express Gigabit Ethernet Server Adapter

External I/O ports—Parallel - 0; Serial - 1; Pointing Device (Mouse, PS2) - 1; Graphics - 1; Keyboard (PS2) - 1; USB - 8 total (4 rear, 2 front panel, 2 internal (one for USB Tape connectivity)); Network RJ-45 (Ethernet) - 1; Management: HP ProLiant G5 Lights-Out 100c Remote Management port (Optional)

Expansion slots—Slot 1: PCI 32-bit/33MHz at 3.3V; Slot 2: PCI-Express x8 connector with x1 link; Slot 3: PCI-Express x8 connector with x1 link; Slot 4: PCI-Express X8 connector with x8 link

Power supply type—365 watts power supply

Power requirements—90 to 132 VAC, 180 to 264 VAC; 47 to 63 Hz

Compatible operating systems—Microsoft® Windows® Server 2003 Web edition; Microsoft® Windows® Server 2003 Standard Edition (x86 and x64); Microsoft® Windows® Server 2003 Enterprise Edition (x86 and x64); Microsoft® Windows® 2003 Small Business Edition; Microsoft® Windows® Server 2003 R2 Standard Edition (x86 and x64); Microsoft® Windows® Server 2003 R2 Enterprise Edition (x86 and x64); Microsoft® Windows® Small Business Server 2003 R2; Microsoft® Windows® Server 2008 Web Edition; Microsoft® Windows® Server 2008 Standard Edition (x86 and x64); Microsoft® Windows® Server 2008 Enterprise Edition (x86 and x64); Microsoft® Windows® Server 2008 Small Business Edition (x86 and x64); Red Hat Enterprise Linux; SUSE Linux Enterprise Server; Netware

Product dimensions (W × D × H)—17.5 × 42.6 × 36.7 cm

Product weight—10.8 kg

Compliance industry standards—ACPI V3.0a Compliant; PCI 2.3 Compliant; PXE Support; WOL Support; IPMI 2.0 compliance

Security management—Power-on password; Setup password; USB lock

Service & support features—1 year Parts, 1 year Labor, 1 year on-site support http://h10010.www1.hp.com/wwpc/me/en/sm/WF06b/15351-15351-241434-3328424-3328424-3577708-3632987.html, February 16, 2009

Specifications (PCs)

HP Compaq dc5800 Business PC Series

System: Microsoft® Windows® XP Professional Version 2002 Service Pack 3

Computer: Intel(R) Core (TM)2 DUO CPU E8400 @ 3.00 GHz 2.99 GHz 2.98 GB of RAM

Physical Address Extension

Details

- Computer—ACPI Multiprocessor PC
- Disk Drives—Generic—Compact Flash USB Device, MS/MS-Pro USB Device, SD/MMC USB Device, SM/xD Picture USB Device
- Display Adapters—Intel(R) Q33 Express Chipset Family
- DVD/CD-ROM Drives—HL-DT-ST DVD RAM GH15L
- Floppy Disk Controllers—Standard floppy disk controller
- IDE ATA/ATAPI Controllers—(2) Primary IDE Channels, (2) Secondary IDE Channels, (2) Standard Dual Channel PCI IDE Controllers
- Keyboard—Standard 101/102-Key or Microsoft Natural PS/2 Keyboard
- Mouse—PS/2 compatible mouse
- Monitor—(2) Plug and Play
- Network Adapters—Intel® 82566DM-2 Gigabit Network Connection
- Ports—Communications Port (COM1)
- Processors—Intel® Core2™ DUO CPU E8400 @ 3.00 GHz
- Sound, Video, and Game controllers—Audio codecs, Legacy Audio Drivers, Legacy Video Capture Devices, Media Control Devices, SoundMAX Integrated Digital HD Audio
- Storage Volumes—(4) generic volumes
- System Devices—ACPI Fixed Feature Button, ACPI Power Button, Advanced Programmable interrupt controller, Direct Memory Access Controller, High Precision event timer, Infineon Trust Platform Module, Intel® 82801 PCI bridge–244E, Intel® Management Engine Interface, ISA PNP Read Data Port, Microcode Update Device, Microsoft ACPI-Compliant System, System Management BIOS Driver, UAA Bus Driver for High Definition Audio, Windows Management Interface for ACPI, (3) Motherboard Resources, Numeric data processor, PCI Bus, PCI Standard host CPU bridge, PCI Standard ISA bridge, (2) PCI Standard PCI-to-PCI bridge, Plug and Play Software Device Enumerator, Programmable Interrupt controller, System Board, System CMOS/real time clock, System speaker, System timer, Terminal Server Device Redirector
- Universal Serial Bus Controllers—(8) Standard Enhanced PCI to USB Host Controller, USB Mass Storage Device, USB Printing Support, (8) USB Root Hub

Software

Preinstalled Software—Microsoft® Windows® XP Pro Service Pak 3, Adaptec Easy CD Creator, Compaq Knowledge Center, Symantec Norton Antivirus, Microsoft® Money 2008, Microsoft® Windows® Media Player 11, Microsoft® Works 8.0, Selective QuickRestore

Internet/Online—Microsoft® Internet Explorer 7, America Online 6.0, Microsoft® Encarta® Online Deluxe (1 year free subscription)

Software on CD—My Presario, Learning More CD, Recovery CD, Symantec Norton Internet Security 2008, Adaptec Easy CD Creator

http://h10025.www1.hp.com/ewfrf/wc/genericDocument?docname=c00009363&cc=us&dl-c=en&lc=en&jumpid=reg_R1002_USEN

Specifications—Printers

HP LaserJet 9050 Printer series

Black: Up to 50 ppm

Resolution: 600 × 600 dpi [with HP FastRes 1200 and Resolution Enhancement technology (REt)]

Paper trays: up to 4 input tray(s)

Paper input capacity: Up to 3100 sheets

Monthly volume: Up to 300,000 pages

High-performance, high-volume, 11 × 17 black-and-white network printer with automatic two-sided printing.

http://h10010.www1.hp.com/wwpc/us/en/sm/WF25a/18972-18972-3328059-14638-3328068-410000.html

Note: HP site used for all hardware specifications.

Planning Guidelines

Windows 2000 Server Disaster Recovery Guidelines

The quantity of data being stored on computer networks has increased exponentially over the last decade. This data explosion shows no signs of slowing down. In addition, the number of users supported continues to increase, as does the complexity of network systems. In this constantly growing and changing environment, the information technology community must maintain mission-critical applications, prevent excessive downtime, and manage increasing business dependence on computer systems.

System administrators must protect their networks from both data loss and machine failure. This effort encompasses both routine procedures performed on an ongoing basis and nonroutine steps taken to prevent or recover from unexpected disasters.

Some of the potential causes of failure include:

- Hard disk subsystem failure
- Power failure
- Systems software failure
- Accidental or malicious use of deletion or modification commands

- Destructive viruses
- Natural disasters (fire, flood, earthquake, and so on)
- Theft or sabotage

After outlining a strategy for developing disaster prevention and recovery procedures and listing new or enhanced Microsoft Windows 2000 file system, data storage, and System State features, this paper introduces the improved Windows 2000 Backup utility and provides guidelines for administrators for recovery of machines running Windows 2000 Server. The discussion includes restoring server services and how to verify the successful restoration of distributed services.

The intended audience for this paper is an administrator with experience in backing up and restoring complex systems, who is also familiar with Windows 2000, its Active Directory™ service, and related features such as Active Directory replication, the system volume (Sysvol), and the File Replication Service (FRS).

Windows 2000 Server Disaster Recovery Guidelines, White Paper, Pg 1, http://www.microsoft.com/windows2000/docs/recovery.doc

References

Dean, T., (2006) *Networking: Network+ guide to Networks* (4th ed.). Boston: Course Technology, Cengage Learning.

Find Articles, Available URL: *http://findarticles.com/p/articles/mi_m0WUB/is_2000_April_24/ai_61634901/print*, Accessed June 12, 2007.

Guidelines for Computer Security at CQU, A. C. Lynn Zelmer, Available URL: http://www.cqu.edu.au/documents/compsec/guidelines/cqu_seca1.html, Accessed May 30, 2007.

HP Compaq dc5800 Business PC Series, © Copyright 2008 Hewlett-Packard Development Company, L.P.,4AA1-9521ENUC Rev. 1, June 2008, Available URL: h10010.www1.hp.com/wwpc/pscmisc/vac/us/product_pdfs/dc5800_data_sheet.pdf -, Accessed February 16, 2009.

Hewlett Packard Website, Software, Available URL: http://h10025.www1.hp.com/ewfrf/wc/genericDocument?docname=c00009363&cc=us&dlc=en&lc=en&jumpid=reg_R1002_USEN, Accessed May 30, 2007.

Hewlett Packard Website, Servers, Available URL: http://h10010.www1.hp.com/wwpc/me/en/sm/WF06b/15351-15351-241434-3328424-3328424-3577708-3632987.html, February 16, 2009.

Hewlett Packard Website, Printer, Available URL: http://h10010.www1.hp.com/wwpc/us/en/sm/WF25a/18972-18972-3328059-14638-3328068-410000.html, Accessed May 30, 2007.

Information and Communciations Technology Council, Current Snapshot of the Canadian ICT Labour Market, March 2007, Branham Group Inc., Available

URL: http://www.ictc-ctic.ca/uploadedFiles/Labour_Market_Intelligence/Snapshot%20Current%20State.pdf, Accessed June 12, 2007.

Microsoft Company, Windows 2000 Server Disaster Recovery Guidelines, Available URL: http://www.microsoft.com/windows2000/docs/recovery.doc, Accessed May 30, 2007.

Security Information Publication 5, Guide to Threat and Risk Assessment for Information Technology, Available URL: http://www.rcmp.ca/tsb/pubs/it_sec/g2-001_e.pdf, Accessed May 30, 2007.

Reynolds, G., (2007). *Ethics in information technology*. Boston: Course Technology, Cengage Learning.

Whitman, M. E., & Mattord, H. J. (2008). *Management of Information Security* (2nd ed.). Boston: Course Technology, Cengage Learning.

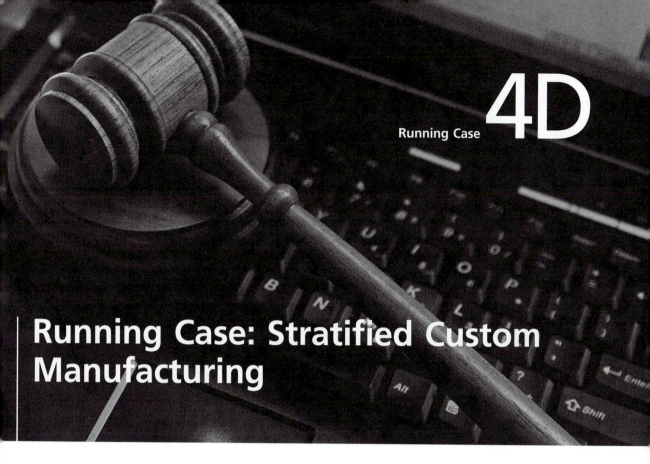

Running Case: Stratified Custom Manufacturing

Drew Cubbins was not happy as he left the meeting. He often found himself in a bad mood after any meeting that involved attorneys. This event was no exception.

SCM faced a civil suit from one of its business partners who claimed they were the victim of a cyber attack launched from yet another of SCM's business partners. The firm initiating the suit was Bullard Enterprises, a subassembly parts supplier. The third party, Caldwell Supply, was the firm that was first completely compromised or *pwned*[1] by the attackers and then whose systems and networks were used by the attackers to launch a second, more lucrative attack against Bullard Enterprises.

Bullard Enterprises was suing SCM under the theory of downstream liability, claiming SCM should have enforced more stringent controls on the shared wide area network used by SCM and its various business partners. SCM had published a set of network-recommended practices for its vendor interconnection network, but these standards were only loosely enforced and no one could ever recall a potential business partner being denied access to the network for a failure to comply with the recommendations.

Drew had just finished a meeting with his own lawyers in which they were attempting to craft a strategy for their defense in this suit. He was pretty sure they were going to lose the suit and pay substantial damages to Bullard.

Now, his thoughts were on what to do with the vendor network and how to make it more secure without incurring too much in the way of expenses for that effort. It would no doubt require the buy-in from every one of the major suppliers and money and resources from

SCM. He considered his options and then came to the conclusion that Takio Sumi, the CIO of SCM, would have to take point on this project.

Discussion Questions

1. Given the facts you have seen regarding this lawsuit, is SCM really going to face any liability? What do you base that opinion on?

2. Regardless of the legal outcome, do you think that SCM has had an ethical lapse in how it has created and operated its vendor network?

3. Pretend you are listening in on the meeting with Drew Cubbins and Takio Sumi. What would be the main points of the conversation?

Endnotes

1. "In hacker jargon, pwn means to compromise or control, specifically another computer (server or PC), web site, gateway device, or application. It is synonymous with one of the definitions of hacking or cracking." Naone, Erica (November 2008). "The Flaw at the Heart of the Internet", *Technology Review* **111** (6): 62–67.

Part 5

Management of Security Technology

Objective

The objective for this chapter of the text is an examination of the legal and ethical issues associated with the management of security technologies. While information security is a management problem—dealing with human issues, it does have some technological solutions. By better understanding the specification, implementation, and management of these technologies, as well as the human factors associated with technology management, the organization can hope to better integrate the technologies into its security profile.

Contents

Standard is defined as "a level of quality." Standards provide the following benefits: interoperability, security, and quality. There are many organizations responsible for the standardization of certain cryptography functions and algorithms, such as industrial standardization organizations, international standardization organizations, and national standardization organizations. The cryptography standards normally are for specific applications, such as federal agents, banking, communications, and Internet use. This chapter presents many standards and covers most of the cryptography general fields, such as symmetric, asymmetric, and key managements. The chapter focuses on "most used cryptography standardization." There are many standards not presented in this chapter as well, such as non-reputation, authorization, key agreements protocols, email encryption, and others; this is because these standards are beyond the theme of this chapter. This chapter provides guidelines for management in cryptography standards in the market; it does not provide great technical and mathematical details for algorithms, however. For each type of algorithm, the chapter starts by explaining the standard organizations, then looks at each algorithm as a general description, and finally lists or explains the standards that cover the algorithm.

B   Reading: Cyber Terrorism: Impacts, Vulnerabilities, and U.S. Policy

Tridib Bandyopadhyay

Terrorism is one major problem that plagues our world today. The memories of the bombings in the London subway (2005) and the Madrid commuter train (2004) are vivid in our memory. The attack of the World Trade Towers in September 2001 has fundamentally changed the way we look at our lives. Unlike the religious extremism that has dominated the recent terrorism scenarios in the new millennium, the twentieth century saw much diverse extremism: the independence struggles of colonies, the ethnic clashes, and the revolutionary left/right wing separatist movements—all have had the dubious distinctions of being terrorism.

C   Case: Advanced Topologies, Inc.

Michael Whitman and Herbert Mattord

Network security is an important topic and skill set for the Information Security professional. This case explores the broader topic of network security and exposes the reader to some of the challenges facing networks that operate on the increasingly hostile Internet. It will look at information security in general, the basics of network security as well as looking at packet filtering, Virtual Private Networks, and a variety of related topics.

D   Reading: Web Applications: Vulnerabilities and Remediation

Shankar Babu Chebrolu and Vinay K. Bansal

With the rapid growth of Internet, security vulnerabilities in Web applications have become more prominent. The lack of data type safety checks—input validation and output sanitization—leads to buffer overflows, code injection attacks (e.g., SQL injection), Cross-site scripting (XSS), and Cross-site request forgery (CSRF). Attackers have exploited Web applications and launched malware and worms to execute malicious code outside the browser on users' machines, leaving unsuspecting users unaware that an attack has occurred.

E   Reading: Managing Secure Database Systems

Li Yang

This chapter is a guide on managing secure database systems via bridging information security regulation and policies with implementation of database security and audit.

F   Running Case

Reading **5A**

Cryptography Algorithms Standards: Guidelines for Management

Wasim A. Al-Hamdani
Information Security Laboratory, Division of Computer and
Technical Sciences, Kentucky State University

Wasim A. Al-Hamdani is an Associate Professor of cryptography and information security at Kentucky State University (KSU). He plays a leading role at KSU in developing the Information Assurance Master Program and Information Security Bachelor degree. Al-Hamdani was at the University of Technology in Baghdad from 1985 to 1999. He has published six textbooks and more than 53 papers dealing with computer science and cryptography and has contributed six chapters in research books.

Overview

Standard is defined as "a level of quality."[1] Standards provide the following benefits: interoperability, security, and quality. There are many organizations responsible for the standardization of certain cryptography functions and algorithms, such as industrial standardization organizations, international standardization organizations, and national standardization organizations. The cryptography standards normally are for specific applications, such as federal agents, banking, communications, and Internet use. This chapter presents many standards and covers most of the cryptography general fields, such as symmetric, asymmetric, and key

115

managements. The chapter focuses on "most used cryptography standardization." There are many standards not presented in this chapter as well, such as non-reputation, authorization, key agreements protocols, email encryption, and others; this is because these standards are beyond the theme of this chapter. This chapter provides guidelines for management in cryptography standards in the market; it does not provide great technical and mathematical details for algorithms, however. For each type of algorithm, the chapter starts by explaining the standard organizations, then looks at each algorithm as a general description, and finally lists or explains the standards that cover the algorithm.

Introduction

Standard is defined as "a level of quality,"[2] "an accepted example of something against which others are judged or measured,"[3] and "a reference point against which other things can be evaluated."[4] "Standard," in general, "can designate ... any measure by which one judges a thing as authentic, good, or adequate. ... Standard applies to any authoritative rule, principle, or measure used to determine the quantity, weight, or extent, or esp. the value, quality, level, or degree of a thing" (*The American Heritage Dictionary of the English Language*, 1969).[5]

The term *standard*, or *technical standard*, as mentioned in the National Technology Transfer and Advancement Act (NTTAA), includes: "Common and repeated use of rules, conditions, guidelines or characteristics for products or related processes and production methods, and related management systems practices. The definition of terms; classification of components; delineation of procedures; specification of dimensions, materials, performance, designs, or operations; measurement of quality and quantity in describing materials, processes, products, systems, services, or practices; test methods and sampling procedures; or descriptions of fit and measurements of size or strength."[6]

A *standard* means level of quality, and applying standards to a product or service means assigning level of assurance in which a customer could trust the product. Many organizations assign level of assurance and guarantee of functionality to increase the level of consumer trust. Standards may also be classified by the user group, such as company, government, international, industry, or education standards. Standards may be classified according to specific requirements, such as design and performance requirement (for example, NSA Suite B Cryptography). For assistance in identifying specific standards, indexes of organizations are listed in NIST National Center for Standards and Certification Information (NCSCI).[7]

A de facto standard is "a standard (formal or informal) that has achieved a dominant and accepted position. It is usually a product, process, system, or technical standard that has achieved status informally by public acceptance, market forces,"[8] and has persisted by tradition. *De facto* is a Latin expression that means "concerning the fact" or "in practice" but not ordained by law. It is commonly used in contrast to de jure (which means "by law") when referring to matters of law, governance, or technique (such as standards) that are found in the common experience as created or developed without or contrary to a regulation. When discussing a legal situation, de jure designates what the law says, while de facto designates action of what happens in practice. It is analogous and similar to the expressions "for all intents and purposes" or "in fact."

From an industry and end user prospective, standards are very important; national and an international standard benefits everyone in many ways. These benefits include: elimination of duplication of effort in the creation process, standards compliance will be eased, and the elimination of duplicate but different standards (national or regional standards that are the same but different). The standard creates a level of assurance and guarantee in a product, procedure, or process that the product has satisfied the requirement of a previously (formally) agreed specification, operation, or procedure. The standards are usually creating high levels of trust in a product that has great impact on economy and marketing a product.

Benefits of Standards

"Standards are important because they define common practices, methods, and measures/ metrics. Therefore, standards raise the reliability and efficiency of products and ensure that the products are produced with a degree of quality. Standards provide solutions that have been accepted by a wide community and evaluated by experts. By using standards, organizations can reduce costs. Standards provide the following benefits: interoperability, security and quality."[9]

Many NIST standards and recommendations contain related tests and specify the conformance requirements. The conformance tests validate the NIST standard or recommendation. Some standards provide a common form of reference as in NIST Special Publication 800-21.[10]

There are many cryptography algorithms. Some are still on the research table, others have been proven as best practices and are widely used, and still others are adopted as the standard. There are three types of standardization organizations.

- National standardization organizations: *National Institute of Standards and Technology (NIST), American National Standards Institute (ANSI),* and *British Standards Institute (BSI)*

- International standardization organizations: *International Organization for Standardization (ISO), International Electrotechnical Commission (IEC),* and *International Telecommunication Union (ITU)*

- Industrial standardization organizations: *Institute of Electrical and Electronics Engineers (IEEE), Public-Key Cryptography Standards (PKCSs), Internet Engineering Task Force (IETF), Standards for Efficient Cryptography Group (SECG), Third Generation Partnership Project (3GPP),* and *European Telecommunications Standard Institute (ETSI)*

A cryptography standard is the "level of algorithm quality in which an algorithm that's been proved theoretically and practically is strong and can stand different attacks for years." Some algorithms need special procedures to satisfy the standard and it should be clarified that certain standardized techniques are known to be weak unless used with care and such guidance is also typically present in the standard itself.

The chapter will cover the standards listed below:

- Symmetric algorithms (Block cipher standards)
- Asymmetric standards
- Cryptography hash standards
- Digital signature standards

- Public-key infrastructure (PKI) standards
- Key management standards

Each algorithm will be covered in terms of:

- General definition
- Standards

Standards Organizations[11]

Standards organizations can be classified in different ways: geographically, by areas of interest, by type of industry, or by areas of professional practice.

Regional Standards Organizations

Regional standards bodies include such organizations as CEN, the European Committee for Standardization; CENELEC, the European Committee for Electrotechnical Standardization (created in 1973); the European Telecommunications Standards Institute (ETSI)[12] (an independent, not-for-profit standardization organization of the telecommunications industry [equipment makers and network operators] in Europe); the IRMM (International Measurement Evaluation Programme) in Europe; the Pacific Area Standards Congress (PASC); the Pan American Standards Commission (COPANT); and the African Organization for Standardization (ARSO). Regional standards bodies typically do not have a history of developing technical cryptographic standards and most of their work is concerning economical and combined resources to balance the activities of other global economic powers.

National Standardization Organizations

Many countries have their own national standardization bodies. These bodies may produce standards of their own, and may also be part of, and contribute to, the work of international standardization bodies. National standardization bodies that contribute to the ISO standardization body are known as ISO member bodies. Examples include ISO members—Brazil (ABNT); American National Standards Institute (ANSI); DIBt (Deutsches Institut für Bautechnik); BSI British Standards, which is the UK's National Standards Body (NSB); and others.

American National Standards Institute (ANSI)[13]

ANSI facilitates the development of American National Standards (ANS) by accrediting the procedures of standards-developing organizations (SDOs). These groups work cooperatively to develop voluntary national consensus standards. Accreditation by ANSI signifies that the procedures used by the standards body in connection with the development of American National Standards meet the Institute's essential requirements for openness, balance, consensus, and due process. ANSI's mission is to enhance both the global competitiveness of U.S. business and the U.S. quality of life by promoting and facilitating voluntary consensus standards and conformity assessment systems, as well as safeguarding their integrity; the U.S. member body is ISO. ANSI is also responsible for developing standards of its own.

It does this by accrediting other bodies with the task of studying and creating standards on ANSI's behalf. Within the area of cryptography, the ANSI X9 organization is probably the most prolific of the ANSI-accredited standardization bodies. X9 is responsible for developing, publishing, and promoting standards for the financial services sector and works closely with the International Organization for Standardization's TC68 committee.

National Institute of Standards and Technology (NIST)[14]

NIST is the federal standardization agency within the U.S. Commerce Department's technology; it has developed a variety of security standards, most notably the Advanced Encryption Standard (AES). NIST's output takes the form of federal information processing standards (FIPS).

NIST carries out its mission in four cooperative programs; these are:

- Conducting research that advances the nation's technology infrastructure and is needed by U.S. industry to continually improve products and services;

- The Baldrige National Quality Program, which promotes performance excellence among U.S. manufacturers, service companies, educational institutions, health care providers, and nonprofit organizations and conducts outreach programs and manages the annual Malcolm Baldrige National Quality Award, which recognizes performance excellence and quality achievement;

- The Hollings Manufacturing Extension Partnership, a nationwide network of local centers offering technical and business assistance to smaller manufacturers; and

- The Technology Innovation Program, which is planned to provide cost-shared awards to industry, universities, and consortia for research on potentially revolutionary technologies that address critical national and societal needs. (Note: This is a newly created program that has been authorized by Congress.)

British Standards Institute (BSI)[15]

British Standards develops standards and standardization solutions to meet the needs of business and society. BSI is recognized by the UK government as the National Standards Body (NSB) for the United Kingdom. It develops, publishes, and markets standards and related information products. Additionally, the NSB works with businesses, consumers, and governments to represent UK interests and facilitate the production of European and international standards. It also produces a series of standards of its own, although it does not have a history of developing technical cryptographic standards. BSI has nevertheless produced several influential standards on management techniques, including the two-part BS 7799 standard on information security management.

International Standardization Organizations

International Organization for Standardization (ISO)[16] The ISO is the world's largest developer and publisher of international standards. ISO is a network of the national standards institutes of 157 countries, one member per country, with a central secretariat in Geneva, Switzerland, that coordinates the system. ISO is a nongovernmental organization that forms a bridge between the public and private sectors. On the one hand,

many of its member institutes are part of the governmental structure of their countries, or are mandated by their government. On the other hand, other members have their roots uniquely in the private sector, having been set up by national partnerships of industry associations.[17]

ISO standards are developed by technical committees (subcommittees or project committees) comprised of experts from the industrial, technical, and business sectors that have asked for the standards and subsequently put them to use. These experts may be joined by representatives of government agencies, testing laboratories, consumer associations, nongovernmental organizations, and academic circles.

Proposals to establish new technical committees are submitted to all ISO national member bodies, who may opt to be participating (P), observer (O), or non-members of the committee. The secretariat (i.e., the body providing the administrative support to the work of the committee) is allocated by the Technical Management Board (reports to the ISO Council), usually to the ISO member body that made the proposal. The secretariat is responsible for nominating an individual to act as chair of the technical committee. The chair is formally appointed by the Technical Management Board.

The standardization work of the ISO is completed by a number of different technical committees (TCs), each concerned with a wide subject area. The technical committees further distribute the work to a series of subcommittees (SCs), which, in turn, distribute the work to various working groups (WGs). Work on cryptographic standards within the ISO is primarily conducted by two technical committees: TC68 and JTC1. The ISO/IEC Joint Technical ISO standards are numbered and are referred to by their standard number. For example, ISO 8730 is the ISO standard that details the requirements that a message authentication code must satisfy if it is to be used in the financial sector. Standards that have been split into multiple parts are referred to by their standard number and part number. For example, ISO 8731-1 is the first part of ISO 8731 and contains the specifications of a particular message authentication code algorithm. Standards that are published jointly by ISO and the IEC through the joint technical committee are referred to as ISO/IEC standards.[18]

International Telecommunication Union (ITU)

The International Telecommunication Union is an international organization established to regulate international radio and telecommunications. Its main tasks include standardization, allocation of the radio spectrum, and organizing interconnection arrangements between different countries to allow international phone calls.

The International Telecommunication Union (ITU), is an agency of the United Nations (UN)[19] whose purpose is to coordinate telecommunication operations and services throughout the world. The International Telegraph Union was founded in 1865 and is the oldest existing international organization. ITU headquarters are in Geneva, Switzerland.

The ITU consists of three sectors:

- Radio Communication (ITU-R)—ensures optimal, fair, and rational use of the radio frequency (RF) spectrum
- Telecommunication Standardization (ITU-T)—formulates recommendations for standardizing telecommunication operations worldwide

- Telecommunication Development (ITU-D)—assists countries in developing and maintaining internal communication operations

5A

The ITU sets and publishes regulations and standards relevant to electronic communication and broadcasting technologies of all kinds, including radio, television, satellite, telephone, and the Internet. The organization conducts working parties, study groups, and meetings to address current and future issues and to resolve disputes. The ITU organizes and holds an exhibition and forum known as the Global TELECOM every four years.

International Electrotechnical Commission (IEC)[20] The IEC produces standards for all electrical and electronic technologies. Its main standardization effort in cryptography and security-related issues is achieved through the joint technical committee it has formed with ISO, JTC1.

Industry Standardization Organizations

Internet Engineering Task Force (IETF)[21] The Internet Engineering Task Force (IETF) is a large open international community of networks, vendors, operators, designers, and researchers concerned with the evolution of the Internet architecture and operation of the Internet. The IETF mission statement is documented in IETF RFC 3935.[22]

The work of the IETF is done in its working groups, organized by topic into several areas (e.g., security, transport, routing, etc.). Most of the work is handled via mailing lists. The IETF holds meetings three times per year. "The IETF working groups are grouped into areas, and managed by area directors, or ADs. The ADs are members of the Internet Engineering Steering Group (IESG). Providing architectural oversight is the Internet Architecture Board (IAB). The IAB also adjudicates appeals when someone complains that the IESG has failed. The IAB and IESG are chartered by the Internet Society (ISOC) for these purposes. The general area director also serves as the chair of the IESG and of the IETF, and is an ex-officio member of the IAB."[23]

The Internet Assigned Numbers Authority (IANA) is the central coordinator for the assignment of unique parameter values for Internet protocols. The IANA is chartered by the Internet Society (ISOC) to act as the clearinghouse to assign and coordinate the use of numerous Internet protocol parameters.

Internet Research Task Force (IRTF)[24] "The Internet Research Task Force (IRTF) is the sister organization to the IETF. The IRTF works on topics related to Internet protocols, applications, architecture, and technology. Its research groups are expected to have the stable long-term (with respect to the lifetime of the research group) membership needed to promote the development of research collaboration and teamwork in exploring research issues. Participation is by individual contributors, rather than by representatives of organizations. The IRTF research groups' guidelines and procedures are described more fully in IETF RFC 2014."[25]

Institute of Electrical and Electronics Engineers (IEEE) "The IEEE is an association of engineers that seeks to promote and share information in technical, electrical, and electronic engineering. Besides producing standards, it also hosts conferences and publishes books and journals. Membership is open to all professional electrical and electronic engineers. The Standards Association (IEEE-SA) has strategic relationships with the IEC, ISO, and the ITU and satisfies all Standards Developing Organizations (SDOs) requirements set by the World Trade Organization, offering more paths to international standardization. Examples are P1363 Standard Specifications for Public Key and P1363.1 Standard Specification for Public-Key Cryptographic Techniques Based on Hard Problems over Lattices."[26]

European Telecommunications Standard Institute (ETSI)

The ETSI, an independent collection of businesses with a mutual interest in developing standards for telecommunications, is one of the organizational partners that coordinate the 3GPP project.

Third Generation Partnership Project (3GPP)

"The 3rd Generation Partnership Project (3GPP) is a collaboration agreement that was established in December 1998. The collaboration agreement brings together a number of telecommunications standards bodies, which are known as **organizational partners**. The current organizational partners are ARIB, CCSA, ETSI, ATIS, TTA, and TTC. The establishment of 3GPP was formalized in December 1998 by the signing of the 'The 3rd Generation Partnership Project Agreement.'"[27]

The original scope: "to produce globally applicable technical specifications and technical reports for a 3rd Generation Mobile System based on evolved GSM core networks and the radio access technologies that they support (i.e., Universal Terrestrial Radio Access [UTRA], both Frequency Division Duplex [FDD] and Time Division Duplex [TDD] modes)."[28]

A permanent project support group, called the Mobile Competence Centre (MCC), has been established to ensure the efficient day-to-day running of 3GPP. The MCC is based at the ETSI headquarters in Sophia Antipolis, France.

The Standards for Efficient Cryptography Group (SECG)[29]

The Standards for Efficient Cryptography Group (SECG), an industry consortium, was founded in 1998 to develop commercial standards that facilitate the adoption of efficient cryptography algorithms and their usage across a wide range of computing platforms. Members include leading technology companies and key industry players in the information security industry. The group exists to develop commercial standards for efficient and interoperable cryptography based on elliptic curve cryptography (ECC).

RSA Laboratories Public-Key Cryptography Standards (PKCSs)[30]

The Public-Key Cryptography Standards are produced by RSA Laboratories in cooperation with secure systems developers worldwide for the deployment of public-key cryptography. First published in 1991 as a result of meetings with a small group of early adopters of public-key technology, the PKCS documents have become widely referenced and implemented. Contributions from the PKCS series have become part of many formal and de facto standards, including ANSI X9 documents, PKIX, SET, S/MIME, and SSL.

Cryptography[31]

The word *cryptography* means "secret writing." Some define *cryptography* as the "study of mathematical techniques." *Cryptography* is a function that transfers *Plaintext* (P_t) into *Ciphertext* (C_t), and decryption is the inverse function that transfers *Ciphertext* into *Plaintext*. The goals of cryptography are privacy or confidentiality, data integrity, authentication, and nonrepudiation.

A **Crypto** system could be classified generally as **"unkeyed"** (key is not required for encryption and decryption) based algorithms and **"keyed"** (key is required) based. **Unkeyed** base can be classified further to **"hash functions"** (a method of turning data into a [relatively] small number that may serve as a digital "fingerprint" of the data) or **"pseudorandom generator"** (an algorithm that generates a sequence of numbers that approximate the properties of random numbers). **Keyed** base is classified into **"symmetric"** key (**"secret key"**) (which uses identical keys for encryption and decryption) and **"asymmetric"** (**"public key"**) (the key for encryption and decryption are not identical). **Symmetric** algorithms are classified into **"block cipher"** (encryption and decryption accomplished on fixed size of plaintext/ciphertext called block of bits), **"stream ciphers"** (encryption and decryptions are accomplished on sequence of bits one bit at a time), **"digital signatures"** (an electronic signature that can be used to authenticate the identity of the sender of a message or the signer of a document), **hash functions, pseudorandom generator, "identification"** (identifying something; map a known entity to unknown entity to make it known), and **"authentications"** (who or what it claims to be). **Asymmetric** algorithms are classified into **digital signatures, identification,** and **authentications.**

The **symmetric** could be classified as **"conventional"** or **"classical"** and **"modern"** algorithms. The **classical** are classified into **"transposition"** and **"substitution"**; another type of cryptography is called the **"hybrid,"** which combines symmetric and asymmetric to form hybrid ciphers.

Attacks on crypto system are **"passive attacks"** (called **"traffic analysis"** in which the intruder eavesdrops but does not modify the message stream) and **"active attack"** (intruder modifies [deletes, replays] the message). There are many different attacks, such as ciphertext-only attack, known-plaintext attack, chosen-plaintext attack, adaptive chosen-plaintext attack, chosen-ciphertext attack, adaptive chosen-ciphertext attack, and birthday attack.

The Need for Cryptography

Information security means keeping data safe from unauthorized access. The best defense is physical security (placing the machine to be protected behind physical walls). Nevertheless, physical security is not always an option because of:

- Cost
- Efficiency
- Multifactor consideration
- The need of some level of logical control

A number of mechanisms are commonly employed to achieve this:

- Controlling access to the computer system or media. For instance, through "log-on" authentication (e.g., via passwords)
- Employing an access control mechanism (such as profiling)
- Restricting physical access (e.g., keeping media locked away or preventing access to the computer itself)

This problem can be broken down into five requirements that must be addressed:

1. Confidentiality: assuring that private data remain private.
2. Authentication: assuring the identity of all parties attempting access.
3. Authorization: assuring that a certain party attempting to perform a function has the permissions to do so.

4. Data Integrity: assuring that an object is not altered illegally.

5. Non-Repudiation: assuring against a party denying a data or a communication that was initiated by them.[32]

For confidentiality, cryptography is used to protect data whether stored or passed through on network, and is also used to secure the process of authenticating different parties attempting any function on the system.

When an entity wishes to be granted access (for some function) to the system, they must present "something" that proves they indeed are who they say they are; the "something" is known as "credentials." Additional measures must be taken to ensure that these credentials are used only by their rightful owner. The most classic credential is passwords. Passwords are encrypted to protect against illegal usage.

"Authorization is a level built on top of authentication in the sense that the entity is authenticated by presenting the credentials required (passwords, smart cards, etc.). After the credentials are accepted, the authorization process is started to ensure that the requesting entity has the permissions to perform the functions needed."[33] Data integrity and Non-Repudiation are achieved by means of digital signature.

Cryptographic Algorithm Validation Program (CAVP)[34]

The Computer Security Division at NIST maintains a number of cryptographic standards, and coordinates algorithm validation tests suites for many of those standards. The Cryptographic Algorithm Validation Program (CAVP) encompasses validation testing for FIPS-approved and NIST-recommended cryptographic algorithms. Cryptographic algorithm validation is a prerequisite to the Cryptographic Module Validation Program (CMVP). CAVP was established by NIST and the Communications Security Establishment Canada (CSEC) in July 1995. All of the tests under CAVP are handled by third-party laboratories that are accredited as Cryptographic Module Testing (CMT) laboratories by the National Voluntary Laboratory Accreditation Program (NVLAP). Vendors interested in validation testing of their algorithm implementation may select any of the accredited laboratories. CAVP currently has algorithm validation testing for the following cryptographic algorithm: symmetric algorithm.

FIPS 197: Advanced Encryption Standard (AES). FIPS 197 specifies the AES algorithm.

FIPS 46-3 and FIPS 81: Data Encryption Standard (DES) and DES Modes of Operation.

FIPS 46-3 specifies the DES and Triple DES algorithms.

FIPS 185: Escrowed Encryption Standard (EES), which specifies the Skipjack algorithm.

Symmetric Algorithms (Block Algorithms Family Standards)

Data Encryption Standard (DES) encrypts a message into block, then maps n-bit plaintext to n-bit ciphertext, where n is the block size, defined as in equation $C_t = E(k, P_t)$, $P_t = D(k, C_t)$. A block ciphers system is evaluated according to: key size, block size, security level, complexity, data expansion, and error propagation. DES is used for the protection of unclassified computer data and it is not approved for protection of national security classified information.

5A

DES applies a 56-bit key to each 64-bit block of data. The process involves 16 rounds with two major processes: key and plaintext.

The cipher became a FIPS standard (NBS FIPS Pub. 46) and later an ANSI standard (ANSI X3.92). It has been widely adopted, most notably in the banking industry where almost all the cryptography used is based in some way on DES. On May 9, 2005, the NIST withdrew FIPS 46-3.[35]

Triple DES

Triple-DES (3DES) is a 64-bit block cipher with 168-bit key and 48 rounds, 2^{56} times stronger than DES, and uses three times as many resources to perform the encryption/decryption process compared to DES. These could be as:

DES-EEE3—three different keys

DES-EDE3—three different keys

DES-EEE2—two different keys

DES-EDE2—two different keys

The Triple Data Encryption Algorithm (TDEA)[36] is an approved cryptographic algorithm as required by FIPS 140-2, *Security Requirements for Cryptographic Modules*. TDEA specifies both the DEA cryptographic engine employed by TDEA and the TDEA algorithm itself.

Advanced Encryption Standard (AES)

AES ("Rijndael") is designed to use simple byte operations. The key size and the block size may be 128 bits, 192 bits, or 256 bits with a variable number of rounds. The rounds are:

- 9 if both the block and the key are 128 bits long.
- 11 if either the block or the key is 192 bits long, and neither of them is longer than that.
- 13 if either the block or the key is 256 bits long.

The total number of round-key bits is equal to block length multiplied by the number of rounds plus 1 (e.g., for a block length of 128 bits and 10 rounds, $128 \times (10 + 1) = 1408$ round-key bits are needed). The AES standard (NIST FIPS Pub. 197) was published in 2002.[37] The algorithm is adopted for the Internet community through the use of RFC: 3394 ("Advanced Encryption Standard (AES) Key Wrap Algorithm").[38]

IETF RFC has many document focuses of integrating AES with other Internet and network application such as the IETF RFC numbers: 3268, 3394, 3537, 3565, 3566, 3602, 3664, 3826, 3826, 3853, 3962, 4434, 4615, 4494, 4493, 4615, 5288, 5289, 3268.[39]

- Cryptographic Message Syntax
- IPSec
- Internet Key Exchange (IKE) Protocol
- IPSec Encapsulating Security Payload (ESP)
- Simple Network Management Protocol (SNMP) User-based Security Model
- S/MIME
- AES-CMAC Algorithm
- Kerberos 5

- The AES-CMAC-96 Algorithm
- AES-CMAC-PRF-128
- Galois Counter Mode (GCM) Cipher Suites for TLS
- Transport Layer Security (TLS)

ISO/IEC 18033-3:2005[40] specifies block ciphers. A block cipher is a symmetric encipherment system with the property that the encryption algorithm operates on a block of plaintext (i.e., a string of bits of a defined length) to yield a block of ciphertext. ISO/IEC 18033-3:2005 specifies the following algorithms.

- 64-bit block ciphers: TDEA, MISTY1, CAST-128
- 128-bit block ciphers: AES, Camellia, SEED

AES is used for other applications and specified with ISO as ISO 26429-6:2008. "This defines the syntax of encrypted digital cinema non-interleaved material exchange format (MXF) frame-wrapped track files and specifies a matching reference decryption model. It uses the advanced encryption standard (AES) cipher algorithm for essence encryption and, optionally, the HMAC-SHA1 algorithm for essence integrity. The digital cinema track file format is designed to carry digital cinema essence for distribution to exhibition sites and is specified in the sound and picture track file specification."[41]

ISO 26429-6:2008 "assumes that the cryptographic keys necessary to decrypt and verify the integrity of encrypted track files will be available upon demand. More precisely, it does not specify the fashion with which cryptographic keys and usage rights are managed across digital cinema distribution and exhibition environments."[42]

In addition, ISO 26429-6:2008 does not address the use of watermarking, fingerprinting, or other security techniques to provide additional protection.

Stream Cipher

One time pad system (vernam cipher) is defined as $C_{ti} = P_{ti} \oplus K_i$ for $i = 1, 2, 3, 4, \ldots n$ where $P_{t1}, P_{t2}, P_{t3}, \ldots P_{tn}$ plaintext bits, $k_1, k_2, k_3, \ldots k_n$ key bits, $C_{t1}, C_{t2}, C_{t3}, \ldots C_{tn}$ ciphertext bits, and $\oplus$ is the XOR function. The decryption is defined by $P_{ti} = C_{ti} \oplus K_i$ for $i = 1, 2, 3, 4$. Synchronous stream cipher is one in which the key stream is generated independently of the plaintext/ciphertext. Self-synchronizing or asynchronous stream cipher is one in which the key stream is generated as a function of the key and a fixed number of previous ciphertext bits. When ciphertext bits are deleted or inserted, it will cause a fixed number of plaintext characters to be unrecoverable.

There have not been many attempts to standardize stream ciphers. There are two major reasons for this.

- Secure stream ciphers are notoriously difficult to design. Speed is a major factor in the design of stream ciphers, and
- Designers often find it hard to produce ciphers that are both secure and fast.

The second reason is that many stream ciphers that are commonly used have not been released into the public domain. Many owners prefer to keep stream ciphers to encrypt

GSM mobile telephone communications. For confidentiality, GSM standardized the use of three stream ciphers: A5/1, A5/2, and A5/3. The descriptions of A5/1 and A5/2 were never released to the public, yet in both cases the algorithms were reverse-engineered from their implementations and the schemes subsequently broken.

RC4 is a stream cipher designed by Rivest for RSA Data Security. "RC4" is a variable key-size stream cipher with byte-oriented operations. The algorithm is based on the use of a random permutation. Analysis shows that the period of the cipher is overwhelmingly likely to be greater than 10^{100}. Eight to 16 machine operations are required per output byte, and the cipher can be expected to run very quickly in software. Independent analysts have scrutinized the algorithm and it is considered secure."[43]

RC4 is used for file encryption in products such as RSA SecurPC. It is also used for secure communications, as in the encryption of traffic to and from secure Web sites using the SSL protocol. IETF RFC 4757 specifies the use of RC4 with HMAC Kerberos, Microsoft Windows. RC4 is most commonly used to protect Internet traffic using the SSL (Secure Sockets Layer) protocol and Wired Equivalent Privacy (WEP).[44]

Block Cipher Mode of Operation

A block cipher mode is an algorithm that features the use of a symmetric key-block cipher algorithm to provide an information service, such as confidentiality or authentication. NIST has approved eight modes of the approved block ciphers in a series of special publications; there are "five confidentiality modes (ECB, CBC, OFB, CFB, and CTR), one authentication mode (CMAC), and two combined modes for confidentiality and authentication (CCM and GCM)."[45] NIST has proposed to approve an additional confidentiality mode, XTS-AES, by reference to IEEE STD 1619-2007.

First Part: Five Confidentiality Modes

"In NIST Special Publication 800-38A, five confidentiality modes are specified for use with any approved block cipher, such as the AES algorithm."[46] The modes are updated versions of the ECB, CBC, CFB, and OFB modes that are specified in FIPS Pub. 81 (to work with DES); in addition, SP 800-38A specifies the CTR mode. The NIST has developed a proposal to extend the domain of the CBC mode with a version of "ciphertext stealing."[47]

Second Part: An Authentication Mode

The CMAC authentication mode is specified in Special Publication 800-38B "for use with any approved block cipher."[48] CMAC stands for cipher-based message authentication code (MAC), analogous to HMAC, the hash-based MAC algorithm.[49]

Third Part: An Authenticated Encryption Mode

Special Publication 800-38C specifies "the CCM mode of the AES algorithm. CCM combines the counter mode for confidentiality with the cipher block chaining technique for authentication."[50] The specification is intended to be compatible with the use of CCM within a draft amendment to the IEEE 802.11 standard for wireless local area networks.[51]

Fourth Part: A High-Throughput Authenticated Encryption Mode

Special Publication 800-38D specifies: "the Galois/Counter Mode (GCM) of the AES algorithm. GCM combines the counter mode for confidentiality with an authentication mechanism that is based on a universal hash function."[52] GCM was designed to facilitate high-throughput hardware implementations; software optimizations are also possible, if certain lookup tables can be precomputed from the key and stored in memory.[53]

In the future, "NIST intends to recommend at least one additional mode: the AES Key Wrap (AESKW). AESKW is intended for the authenticated encryption (wrapping) of specialized data, such as cryptographic keys, without using a nonce for distribution or storage. AESKW invokes the block cipher about 12 times per block of data. The design provides security properties that may be desired for high assurance applications; the trade-off is relatively inefficient performance compared to other modes."[54]

Asymmetric Algorithms (Public Key)

Public key is a one-way function. A one-way function is easy to compute $f(x)$ from x but computation of x from $f(x)$ should be hard for the crypto attacker. The legal receiver should have a *trapdoor* available.

RSA

Publicly described in 1977, the RSA is widely used in electronic commerce protocols. It uses three parts: key generation, encryption, and decryption. *Key generation*: Primes p and q such that $n = pq$ and $\phi = (p - 1)(q - 1)$. Select e with $1 < e < \phi$ and $gcd\ (e, \phi) = 1$. (In other words, e is relatively prime to ϕ), then find d with $1 < d < \phi$ with $ed \equiv 1 \pmod{\phi}$; *Encryption*: $C_t = P_t^e$ mod n; and *Decryption*: $P_t = C_t^d$ mod n. Some RSA in practice used with digital signatures included PGP: Pretty Good Privacy and Secure Sockets Client.

Elliptic Curve

Elliptic curves are mathematical constructions from number theory and algebraic geometry, which in recent years have found numerous applications in cryptography. An elliptic curve can be defined over any field (e.g., real, rational, complex). Elliptic curves can provide versions of public key methods that, in some cases, are faster and use smaller keys, while providing an equivalent level of security. Their advantage comes from using a different kind of mathematical group for public key arithmetic.

Elliptic Curves over Real Numbers

They are named because they are described by cubic equations. In general, cubic equations for elliptic curves take the form $y^2 + axy + by = x^3 + cx^2 + dx + e$ where a, b, c, d and e are real numbers and x and y take on values in the real numbers. It is sufficient to be limited to equations of the form $y^2 = x^3 + ax + b$ (Cubic). Also included in the definition is a single element denoted O and called the *point at infinity* or the *zero point*, which to plot such a curve, we need to compute $y = \sqrt{x^3 + ax + b}$ for given values of a and b; thus, the plot consists of positive and negative values of y for each value of x.

RSA Laboratories

"Public-Key Cryptography Standards (PKCS) are specifications produced by RSA Laboratories in cooperation with secure systems developers worldwide for the purpose of accelerating the deployment of public-key cryptography. First published in 1991 as a result of meetings with a small group of early adopters of public-key technology, the PKCS documents have become widely referenced and implemented. Contributions from the PKCS series have become part of many formal and de facto standards, including ANSI X9 documents, PKIX, SET, S/MIME, and SSL."[55]

5A

PKCS #1: RSA Cryptography Standard

PKCS #3: Diffie-Hellman Key Agreement Standard

PKCS #5: Password-Based Cryptography Standard

PKCS #6: Extended-Certificate Syntax Standard

PKCS #7: Cryptographic Message Syntax Standard

PKCS #8: Private-Key Information Syntax Standard

PKCS #9: Selected Attribute Types

PKCS #10: Certification Request Syntax Standard

PKCS #11: Cryptographic Token Interface Standard

PKCS #12: Personal Information Exchange Syntax Standard

PKCS #13: Elliptic Curve Cryptography Standard

PKCS #15: Cryptographic Token Information Format Standard

RSA-PKCS standards were not the only industrial encryption standards produced, but they were one of the most successful. Another industry standard was published by the Standards in Efficient Cryptography Group (SECG) including: Certicom, VeriSign, and NIST. This group was primarily focused on standardizing the use of elliptic curves in asymmetric cryptography.

Standard Specifications for Public Key Cryptography

The standards document IEEE 1363-2000: "Standard Specifications for Public Key Cryptography has been adopted as a standard by the IEEE. From the contents of the IEEE P1363 Standard, there are three families of cryptographic functions, according to the underlying computationally difficult problem:

- Discrete logarithm in the group of remainders modulo a prime (DL)
- Discrete logarithm in the group of points on an elliptic curve over a finite field (EC)
- Integer factorization (IF)"[56]

DL standards include the following algorithms:

- Diffie-Hellman key agreement allowing up to two key pairs from each party
- Menezes-Qu-Vanstone key agreement, which requires two key pairs from each party
- DSA Signatures, with SHA-1 and RIPEMD-160 as hash functions
- Nyberg-Rueppel Signatures with appendix, with SHA-1 and RIPEMD-160 as hash functions

EC standards mirror the DL family; the only significant difference is the change in the underlying group. For the IF family, the standard will include the following algorithms:

- RSA encryption with Optimal Asymmetric Encryption Padding (OAEP)
- RSA signature with appendix using a hash function and ANSI X9.31 padding of the hash value
- Rabin-Williams (even exponent) equivalents of the above RSA signatures

The publications are:

IEEE 1363: Standard Specifications for Public Key Cryptography

IEEE 1363a: Standard Specifications for Public Key Cryptography, Amendment 1: Additional Techniques

IEEE P1363.1: Standard Specification for Public Key Cryptographic, Techniques Based on Hard Problems over Lattices

IEEE P1363.2: Standard Specification for Password-Based Public Key, Cryptographic Techniques

IEEE P1363.3: Identity-Based Public Key Cryptography Using Pairings

In addition, RSA standard work for the use of elliptic curve, the IETF RFC,[57] has different works, which are:

- RFC 3278: Use of Elliptic Curve Cryptography (ECC) Algorithms in Cryptographic Message Syntax (CMS). S. Blake-Wilson, D. Brown, P. Lambert. April 2002.
- IRFC 4050: Using the Elliptic Curve Signature Algorithm (ECDSA) for XML Digital Signatures. S. Blake-Wilson, G. Karlinger, T. Kobayashi, Y. Wang. April 2005.
- RFC 4492: Elliptic Curve Cryptography (ECC) Cipher Suites for Transport Layer Security (TLS). S. Blake-Wilson, N. Bolyard, V. Gupta, C. Hawk, B. Moeller. May 2006. (Updated by RFC5246)
- RFC 4754: IKE and IKEv2 Authentication Using the Elliptic Curve Digitalm Signature Algorithm (ECDSA). D. Fu, J. Solinas. January 2007. (Status: PROPOSED STANDARD)
- RFC 5289: TLS Elliptic Curve Cipher Suites with SHA-256/384 and AES Galois Counter Mode (GCM). E. Rescorla. August 2008.

The International Organization for Standardization (ISO) has issued the following relevant standards:

ISO 15946 (Information technology—Security techniques—Cryptographic techniques based on elliptic curves) is a standard series comprising several parts. The following parts are of interest:

- Part 1 (General)
- Part 2 (Digital signatures)
- Part 3 (Key establishment)
- Part 4 (Digital signatures giving message recovery)

The other use of elliptic curve is digital signature, key management, and key agreement wireless transport layer security. The standards that cover this are:

- ANSI X9.62, Public Key Cryptography for the Financial Services Industry: The Elliptic Curve Digital Signature Algorithm (ECDSA), approved January 1999.

- ANSI X9.63, Public Key Cryptography for the Financial Services Industry: Key Agreement and Key Transport Using Elliptic Curve Cryptography, Working Draft ver. 1999, 1, 8.

- SEC1 of Certicom Research, Elliptic Curve Cryptography, v1.0 (2000, 9, 20).

- SEC2 of Certicom Research, Recommended Elliptic Curve Cryptography Domain Parameters, v1.0 (2000).

- GEC2, Test Vectors for SEC1 ver. 0.3 (1999, 9, 29).

- FIPS 186-2 of NIST, included DSA and ECDSA, 2000, 1, 27.

- ECC Cipher Suites for TLS, TLS WG draft, March 2001.

- Additional ECC Groups For IKE, IPSec WG draft, March 2001.

- Use of ECC Algorithms in CMS, S/MIME WG draft, May 2001.

- Algorithms and Identifiers for the Internet X.509 Public Key Infrastructure Certificate and CRL Profile, PKIX WG draft, July 2001.

- Wireless Transport Layer Security Specification, approved version (WAP 2.0), WAP Forum, (2001).[58]

There are some newer fields, such as hyperelliptic curves, that are still in the research environment and have not been practically proven.

Cryptographic Hash Functions

A hash function takes a message of any length as input and produces a fixed-length string as output and is referred to as a message digest or a digital fingerprint. A cryptographic hash function is a hash function with certain additional security properties to make it suitable for use in various information security applications, such as authentication and message integrity. Encryptions may be either by using a public key or private key algorithm. Encryption of digest prevents an active attacker from modifying the message and recalculating its checksum accordingly. Hash functions have the following two properties: compression and ease of computation.

There are major two types of hash functions: *modification detection codes* (MDCs) (also known as *manipulation detection codes* or *message integrity codes* [MICs]) and *message authentication codes* (MACs). The purpose of MDC is *hash* with *additional* properties. MDCs are a subclass of unkeyed hash functions and there are two types (*one-way hash functions* [OWHFs] and *collision resistant hash functions* [CRHFs]). Finding any two inputs having the same hash value is difficult. The purpose of a MAC is that it is *without additional* mechanisms. The differences between the *key hash function* and *unkeyed hash function* is based on further properties, which are pre-image resistance, second pre-image resistance, and collision resistance.

Cryptography Hash Function

Characteristics:

- **Models**: Iterated, serial, and parallel.
- **Flow**: If either h_1 or h_2 is a collision resistant, then $h(x) = h_1(x) \parallel h_2(x)$
- **Data Representation**: Different data representations (e.g., ASCII vs. EBCDIC) must be converted to a common format before computing hash values.
- **Padding and Length Blocks**: Extra bits appended before hashing,

Unkeyed Cryptography Hash Functions (MDCs) There are three categories for MDCs: customized, based on block ciphers, and based on modular arithmetic. Customized are those that are specifically designed "from scratch" for the explicit purpose of hashing, with optimized performance in mind.

Cryptography Hash Functions Based on Modular Arithmetic The basic idea is mod m arithmetic as the basis of the function. A major factor with this type is to meet the required security level, and a significant disadvantage is speed.

Hash Standards

The Federal Information Processing Standard 180-2, Secure Hash Standard, specifies algorithms for computing five cryptographic hash functions—SHA-1, SHA-224, SHA-256, SHA-384, and SHA-512. FIPS 180-2 was issued in August 2002, superseding FIPS 180-1.

In recent years, serious attacks have been published against SHA-1. In response, NIST held two public workshops to assess the status of its approved hash functions and to solicit public input on its cryptographic hash function policy and standard. As a result of these workshops, NIST has decided to develop one or more additional hash functions through a public competition, similar to the development process of the Advanced Encryption Standard (AES). NIST has proposed a tentative timeline for the competition, and also published a policy on the use of the current hash functions.

NIST issued draft minimum acceptability requirements, submission requirements, and evaluation criteria for candidate hash algorithms in January 2007[59] for public comments; the comment period ended on April 27, 2007. Based on the public feedback, NIST has revised the requirements and evaluation criteria and issued a call for a "New Cryptographic Hash Algorithm (SHA-3)" family, on November 2, 2007.[60]

The RSA[61] has MD2, MD4, and MD5 developed by Rivest. They are meant for digital signature applications where a large message has to be "compressed" in a secure manner before being signed with the private key. All three algorithms take a message of arbitrary length and produce a 128-bit message digest. While the structures of these algorithms are somewhat similar, the design of MD2 is quite different from that of MD4 and MD5. MD2 was optimized for eight-bit machines, whereas MD4 and MD5 were aimed at 32-bit machines. Descriptions and source codes for the three algorithms can be found as:

- RFC 1319: The MD2 Message-Digest Algorithm, B. Kaliski. April 1992.
- RFC 1320: The MD4 Message-Digest Algorithm, R. Rivest. April 1992.
- RFC 1321: The MD5 Message-Digest Algorithm, R. Rivest. April 1992.

5A

- RFC 3174: The U.S. Secure Hash Algorithm 1 (SHA1). D. Eastlake 3rd, P. Jones. September 2001.[62]

ISO works are:

- ISO/IEC 10118-1[63](general information about hash functions)
- ISO/IEC 10118-2[64] (hash functions using an *n*-bit block cipher)
- ISO/IEC 10118-4[65] (hash functions using modular arithmetic)

SO/IEC 10118-3:2004[66] specifies the following seven dedicated hash functions (i.e., specially designed hash-functions):

- Hash function (RIPEMD-160) in Clause 7 provides hash codes of lengths up to 160 bits;
- Hash function (RIPEMD-128) in Clause 8 provides hash codes of lengths up to 128 bits;
- Hash function (SHA-1) in Clause 9 provides hash codes of lengths up to 160 bits;
- Hash function (SHA-256) in Clause 10 provides hash codes of lengths up to 256 bits;
- Hash function (SHA-512) in Clause 11 provides hash codes of lengths up to 512 bits;
- Hash function (SHA-384) in Clause 12 provides hash codes of a fixed length, 384 bits; and
- Hash function (WHIRLPOOL) in Clause 13 provides hash codes of lengths up to 512 bits.

For each of these dedicated hash functions, ISO/IEC 10118-3:2004 specifies a round function that consists of a sequence of sub-functions, a padding method, initializing values, parameters, constants, and an object identifier as normative information, and also specifies several computation examples as informative information.

Message Authentication Codes (Macs)

"MACs are used to protect the integrity of transmitted or stored data (*data integrity*) and to provide evidence regarding the origin of data (*data origin authentication*). A MAC algorithm takes as input the data string to be protected and a secret key, and gives as output a short, fixed-length string called the MAC. This MAC is then stored or sent with the message to be protected. An entity that receives a transmitted message or recovers a stored message can then check the MAC to determine that it must have been sent by someone who knows the secret key (*origin authentication*) and that it has not been modified (*data integrity*)."[67]

As specified in ISO/IEC 9797-1,[68] the following two properties must hold for a MAC algorithm:

- Computing a MAC from a message and a secret key must be straightforward (*usability*).
- Finding a MAC for a given message without authorized access to the secret key must be infeasible, even if the attacker has access to the correct MACs for a number of other messages, including some that may be chosen by the attacker (*security*).

An amendment to ISO/IEC 9797-1 is ISO/IEC 9797-2:2002[69] in the HMAC scheme; MAC algorithm 2 from ISI/IEC 9797-2 is of the second type (i.e., it uses the hash function as a "black box"). We let h denote the hash function that has been chosen to be used to build the MAC algorithm. ISO/IEC 9797-2 requires that the hash function be chosen from among those standardized in ISO/IEC 10118-3.

ISO/IEC 9797-2:2002 specifies three MAC algorithms that use a secret key and a hash function (or its round function) with an n-bit result to calculate an m-bit MAC. These mechanisms can be used as data integrity mechanisms to verify that data has not been altered in an unauthorized manner. The strength of the data integrity mechanism and message authentication mechanism is dependent on the length (in bits) k and secrecy of the key, on the length (in bits) n of a hash code produced by the hash function, on the strength of the hash function, on the length (in bits) m of the MAC, and on the specific mechanism.

Three mechanisms specified in ISO/IEC 9797-2:2002 are based on the dedicated hash functions specified in ISO/IEC 10118-3. The first mechanism specified in ISO/IEC 9797-2:2002 is commonly known as MDx-MAC. It calls the complete hash function once, but it makes a small modification to the round function by adding a key to the additive constants in the round function. The second mechanism specified in ISO/IEC 9797-2:2002 is commonly known as HMAC. It calls the complete hash function twice. The third mechanism specified in ISO/IEC 9797-2:2002 is a variant of MDx-MAC that takes as input only short strings (at most 256 bits). It offers a higher performance for applications that work with short input strings only.

An HMAC[70] function is used by the message sender to produce a value (the MAC) that is formed by condensing the secret key and the message input. The MAC is typically sent to the message receiver along with the message. The receiver computes the MAC on the received message using the same key and HMAC function as was used by the sender, and compares the result computed with the received MAC. If the two values match, the message has been correctly received and the receiver is assured that the sender is a member of the community of users that share the key.

The HMAC specification in this standard is a generalization of HMAC as specified in Internet RFC 2104, *HMAC, Keyed-Hashing for Message Authentication*, and ANSI X9.71, *Keyed Hash Message Authentication Code*. Message authentications have standards for banking applications, such as:

- ANSI X9.9[71]
- ANSI X9.19[72]
- ANSI X9.71[73]
- American Bankers Association, ANSI X9 TG–24[74]
- ISO 8730: 1986, Banking Requirements for Message Authentication[75]
- ISO 8731–1: 1987, Banking Approved Algorithm for Message Authentication—Part 1 and Part 2[76]

NIST Special Publication 800-38B, The RMAC,[77] and NIST-SP 800-107[78] are a recommendation for Applications Using Approved Hash Algorithms and Authentication Mode.

The RFC have many reports that cover cryptography hash functions with different technology. These are:

- RFC 2104 HMAC: Keyed-Hashing for Message Authentication. H. Krawczyk, M. Bellare, R. Canetti. February 1997.

- RFC 2803 Digest Values for DOM (DOMHASH). H. Maruyama, K. Tamura, N. Uramoto. April 2000.

- RFC 3174 US Secure Hash Algorithm 1 (SHA1). D. Eastlake 3rd, P. Jones. September 2001. (Updated by RFC4634).

- RFC 3537 Wrapping a Hashed Message Authentication Code (HMAC) Key with a Triple-Data Encryption Standard (DES) Key or an Advanced Encryption Standard (AES) Key. J. Schaad, R. Housley. May 2003.

- RFC 3874 A 224-bit One-way Hash Function: SHA-224, R. Housley. September 2004.

- RFC 4418 UMAC: Message Authentication Code Using Universal Hashing. T Krovetz, Ed. March 2006.

- RFC 4418 UMAC: Message Authentication Code Using Universal Hashing. T. Krovetz, Ed. March 2006.

- RFC 4814 Hash and Stuffing: Overlooked Factors in Network Device Benchmarking. D. Newman, T. Player. March 2007.

- RFC 4843 An IPv6 Prefix for Overlay Routable Cryptographic Hash Identifiers (ORCHID). P. Nikander, J. Laganier, F. Dupont. April 2007.

- RFC 4894 Use of Hash Algorithms in Internet Key Exchange (IKE) and IPSec. P. Hoffman. May 2007.

- RFC 4982 Support for Multiple Hash Algorithms in Cryptographically Generated Addresses (CGAs). M. Bagnulo, J. Arkko. July 2007.

- RFC 5155 DNS Security (DNSSEC) Hashed Authenticated Denial of Existence. B. Laurie, G. Sisson, R. Arends, D. Blacka. March 2008.[79]

Digital Signature

Digital Signature (*electronic signature*)

The process has three parts: key generation, signature, and verification. There are other terms that come in association with digital signature, such as *digital certificates* (DC). This certificate includes (*certificate authority* [CA]), the date of validity of the certificate, certificate signer/provider, sites/hosts, code signer/provider, cross-certification, personal, file, key recovery, and PKCS #12.

How Does It Work?

Hash Function (Signature Information) = Hash Value

Asymmetric Function (Key, Digital Signature) = Decrypted Signature

Digital Signature = (key, Asymmetric Function (Hash Value = Hash Function(M)))

The second part with each digital signature is the verification.

$$\text{Equal} \begin{cases} \text{Hash Function (Signature Information)} = \text{Hash Value} \\ \text{Asymmetric Function (Key, Digital Signature)} = \text{Decrypted Signature} \end{cases}$$

FIPS 186 is the digital signature. Its components include:

- FIPS-186, the first version of the official DSA specification
- FIPS-186, change notice No.1, the first change notice to the first version of the specification
- FIPS-186-1, the first revision to the official DSA specification
- FIPS-186-2, the second revision to the official DSA specification (including the first change notice to this revision)
- FIPS-186-3, draft for the third revision to the official DSA specification

The guidance document SP 800-25Oct 2000[80] was developed by the Federal Public Key Infrastructure Steering Committee to assist federal agencies that are considering the use of public key technology for digital signatures or authentication over open networks such as the Internet. This includes communications with other federal or nonfederal entities, such as members of the public, private firms, citizen groups, and state and local governments. Most public key technology applications for digital signatures provide for user authentication as well. However, public key technology can be used for user authentication only without digital signatures. Standards such as X.509 Version 3 (International Telecommunication Union Recommendation X.509 [03/00]—Information technology—Open systems interconnection—The directory: public-key and attribute certificate frameworks) provide for that functionality.

American National Standards Institute ANSI X9.30[81] is the United States financial industry standard for digital signatures based on the federal Digital Signature Algorithm (DSA), and ANSI X9.31[82] is the counterpart standard for digital signatures based on the RSA algorithm and covers both the manual and automated management of keying material using both asymmetric and symmetric key cryptography for the wholesale financial services industry. ANSI X9.30 requires the SHA-1 hash algorithm encryption; ANSI X9.31 requires the MDC-2 hash algorithm. A related document, X9.57,[83] covers certificate management encryption.

RSA signing function can be found in ISO/IEC 9796-2 information technology—Security techniques—Digital signature schemes giving message recovery—Part 2: Integer factorization based mechanisms.[84]

ISO/IEC 9796-3: 2006 specifies digital signature mechanisms giving partial or total message recovery aiming at reducing storage and transmission overhead; it specifies mechanisms based on the discrete logarithm problem of a finite field or an elliptic curve over a finite field. ISO/IEC 9796-3:2006 defines types of redundancy: natural redundancy, added redundancy, or both, and gives the general model for digital signatures partial or total message recovery aiming at reducing storage and transmission overhead.[85]

U.S. and the EU legislations recognize the need for a digital signature to be demonstrated using a public key and both the ESIGN Act and the EU directive 1999/93/EC state the requirements that a certificate of authority (CA) must satisfy in order to be considered secure. The IETF has produced a profile for qualified certificates for use on the Internet IETF RFC 3039.[86]

Other ISO documents are: ISO/IEC 14888-1: 1998, ISO/IEC 14888-2: 1999.[87] There are many documents with RFC concerning digital signature with TCP MD5, LDAP Control, RSA, XML, and DNS (IETF RFC 2385, 2649, 2792, 2802, 2807, 2931)[88] and only one document covers elliptic curve digital signature with XML, which is IETF RFC 4050.[89]

Public Key Infrastructure (PKI)

PKI is the infrastructure necessary to support the distribution of public keys to the entity that needs to use them. The distribution achieved to ensure the recipient of a public key can be sure of its integrity and authenticity. A PKI can be made up of a variety of different elements depending on the technology and organizational structure used to distribute and guarantee the correctness of public keys. The most common form of PKI is one based on the generation and distribution of public key certificates.

PKI is an arrangement that binds public keys with respective user identities by means of a certificate of authority (CA). The user identity must be unique for each CA. The binding is established through the registration and issuance process, which may be carried out by software at a CA, or under human supervision. The PKI role that assures this binding is called the registration authority (RA). For each user, the user identity, the public key, their binding, validity conditions, and other attributes are made hard to defend in public key certificates issued by the CA.

Entity of PKI is:

- Certification authority: generating public key certificates according to defined certification practice statement, and such certificate policy;

- Registration authorities (RAs): verifying the identities of individuals requesting the generation of a certificate by a CA;

- Certificate repositories: store and make available public key certificates; and

- Certificate status servers: provide online information (on request) regarding the current status of a certificate.

A PKI has many uses and applications. As discussed later in this article, a PKI enables the basic security services for such varied systems as:

- SSL, IPSec, and HTTPS for communication and transactional security

- S/MIME and PGP for email security

- SET for value exchange

- Identrus for B2B

Public Key Infrastructures—U.S. Federal PKI

Federal PKI NIST plays a leading role in the deployment of the Federal PKI, serving as leading the development, evaluation, and maintenance of certificate policies for the Federal PKI. The Federal PKI architecture features the Federal Bridge Certification Authority (FBCA), which supports interoperability among PKI domains with disparate policies in a peer-to-peer fashion, and the Common Policy Root CA, which manages a hierarchical PKI.

FPKI Architecture The FBCA issues certificates to the Principal CA of a PKI domain after the Federal PKI Policy Authority:

- Determines which FBCA levels of assurance are satisfied by the policies supported in that PKI domain;

- Determines that the PKI domain fulfills its responsibilities under those policies; and
- Establishes a legal agreement between the FBCA and the PKI domain.

Hierarchical Federal PKI The Common Policy Root CA operates under the Common Policy Framework, which specifies three policies with a relatively uniform level of assurance. The Common Policy Root CA issues a certificate to a secondary CA operated by or on behalf of a federal agency after determining that the CA's operations satisfies the requirements of the Common Policy.

SP 800-32 "Feb 2001 developed to assist agency. It is intended to provide an overview of PKI functions and their applications. Additional documentation will be required to fully analyze the costs and benefits of PKI systems for agency use, and to develop plans for their implementation. The document provides a starting point and references to more comprehensive publications."[90]

AS 4539.1.3-1999 "ANSI Information technology—Public Key Authentication Framework (PKAF)—General—X.509 supported algorithms profile is a document that specifies hash, digital signature, encryption and key-exchange algorithms, and the format for the keys that these algorithms use."[91]

ANSI X9.55:1997 "specifies extensions to the definitions of public-key certificates and certificate revocation lists in Public Key Cryptography for the Financial Services Industry."[92]

Public Key Infrastructures—Other PKI

ISO 21188:2006 "sets out a framework of requirements to manage a PKI through certificate policies and certification practice statements and to enable the use of public key certificates in the financial services industry. It also defines control objectives and supporting procedures to manage risks."[93]

ISO 20828:2006 "establishes a uniform practice for the issuing and management of security certificates for use in Public Key Infrastructure applications. Assuming that all entities, intending to set up a secure data exchange to other entities based on private and public keys, are able to provide their own certificate, the certificate management scheme guarantees that the entities get all additional information needed to establish trust to other entities, from a single source in a simple and unified format."[94]

ISO 17090-1:2008 "defines the basic concepts underlying use of digital certificates in health care and provides a scheme of interoperability requirements to establish a digital certificate-enabled secure communication of health information. It also identifies the major stakeholders who are communicating health-related information, as well as the main security services required for health communication where digital certificates may be required."[95]

ISO 17090-2:2008 "specifies the certificate profiles required to interchange health care information within a single organization, between different organizations and across jurisdictional boundaries."[96]

ISO 17090-3:2008 "guidelines for certificate management issues involved in deploying digital certificates in health care."[97] It specifies a structure and minimum requirements for certificate policies, as well as a structure for associated certification practice statements. This document also identifies the principles needed in a health care security policy for cross-border communication and defines the minimum levels of security required.

Most of RFC concerning public key infrastructure (PKI) for the period of 1999–2008 work is relating to X.509 as a standard for public key infrastructure (PKI); however, some of the work focused on Key Exchange Algorithm (KEA), Keys in Internet X.509, IPSec, and LDAPv2. The list of RFC is (IRTF 2008):

- RFC 2459 Internet X.509 Public Key Infrastructure Certificate and CRL Profile. R. Housley, W. Ford, W. Polk, D. Solo. January 1999.

- RFC 2510 Internet X.509 Public Key Infrastructure Certificate Management Protocols. C. Adams, S. Farrell. March 1999.

- RFC 2527 Internet X.509 Public Key Infrastructure Certificate Policy and Certification Practices Framework. S. Chokhani, W. Ford. March 1999.

- RFC 2528 Internet X.509 Public Key Infrastructure Representation of Key Exchange Algorithm (KEA) Keys in Internet X.509 Public Key Infrastructure Certificates. R. Housley, W. Polk. March 1999.

- RFC 2559 Internet X.509 Public Key Infrastructure Operational Protocols—LDAPv2. S. Boeyen, T. Howes, P. Richard. April 1999.

- RFC 2560 X.509 Internet Public Key Infrastructure Online Certificate Status Protocol—OCSP. M. Myers, R. Ankney, A. Malpani, S. Galperin, C. Adams. June 1999.

- 2585 Internet X.509 Public Key Infrastructure Operational Protocols: FTP and HTTP. R. Housley, P. Hoffman. May 1999.

- RFC 2587 Internet X.509 Public Key Infrastructure LDAPv2 Schema. S. Boeyen, T. Howes, P. Richard. June 1999.

- RFC 3029 Internet X.509 Public Key Infrastructure Data Validation and Certification Server Protocols. C. Adams, P. Sylvester, M. Zolotarev, R. Zuccherato. February 2001.

- RFC 3039 Internet X.509 Public Key Infrastructure Qualified Certificates Profile. S. Santesson, W. Polk, P. Barzin, M. Nystrom. January 2001.

- IETF RFC 3161 Internet X.509 Public Key Infrastructure Time-Stamp Protocol (TSP). C. Adams, P. Cain, D. Pinkas, R. Zuccherato. August 2001.

- 3280 Internet X.509 Public Key Infrastructure Certificate and Certificate Revocation List (CRL) Profile. R. Housley, W. Polk, W. Ford, D. Solo. April 2002.

- RFC 3647 Internet X.509 Public Key Infrastructure Certificate Policy and Certification Practices Framework. S. Chokhani, W. Ford, R. Sabett, C. Merrill, S. Wu. November 2003.

- RFC 3709 Internet X.509 Public Key Infrastructure: Logotypes in X.509 Certificates. S. Santesson, R. Housley, T. Freeman. February 2004.

- RFC 3739 Internet X.509 Public Key Infrastructure: Qualified Certificates Profile. S. Santesson, M. Nystrom, T. Polk. March 2004.

- RFC 3820 Internet X.509 Public Key Infrastructure (PKI) Proxy Certificate Profile. S. Tuecke, V. Welch, D. Engert, L. Pearlman, M. Thompson. June 2004.

- RFC 4043 Internet X.509 Public Key Infrastructure Permanent Identifier. D. Pinkas, T. Gindin. May 2005.

- RFC 4055 Additional Algorithms and Identifiers for RSA Cryptography for use in the Internet X.509 Public Key Infrastructure Certificate and Certificate Revocation List (CRL) Profile. J. Schaad, B. Kaliski, R. Housley. June 2005.

- RFC 4059 Internet X.509 Public Key Infrastructure Warranty Certificate Extension. D. Linsenbardt, S. Pontius, A. Sturgeon. May 2005.

- RFC 4158 Internet X.509 Public Key Infrastructure: Certification Path Building. M. Cooper, Y. Dzambasow, P. Hesse, S. Joseph, R. Nicholas. September 2005.

- RFC 4210 Internet X.509 Public Key Infrastructure Certificate Management Protocol (CMP). C. Adams, S. Farrell, T. Kause, T. Mononen. September 2005.

- RFC 4211 Internet X.509 Public Key Infrastructure Certificate Request Message Format (CRMF). J. Schaad. September 2005.

- IETF RFC 4325 Internet X.509 Public Key Infrastructure Authority Information Access Certificate Revocation List (CRL) Extension, S. Santesson, R. Housley. December 2005.

- RFC 4386 Internet X.509 Public Key Infrastructure Repository Locator Service. S. Boeyen, P. Hallam-Baker. February 2006.

- RFC 4387 Internet X.509 Public Key Infrastructure Operational Protocols: Certificate Store Access via HTTP. P. Gutmann, Ed. February 2006.

- RFC 4491 Using the GOST R 34.10-94, GOST R 34.10-2001, and GOST R 34.11-94 Algorithms with the Internet X.509 Public Key Infrastructure Certificate and CRL Profile. S. Leontiev, Ed., D. Shefanovski, Ed. May 2006.

- RFC 4683 Internet X.509 Public Key Infrastructure Subject Identification Method (SIM). J. Park, J. Lee, H. Lee, S. Park, T. Polk, October 2006.

- RFC 4985 Internet X.509 Public Key Infrastructure Subject Alternative Name for Expression of Service Name. S. Santesson. August 2007.

- RFC 5217 Memorandum for Multi-Domain Public Key Infrastructure Interoperability. M. Shimaoka, Ed., N. Hastings, R. Nielsen. July 2008.

- RFC 5280 Internet X.509 Public Key Infrastructure Certificate and Certificate Revocation List (CRL) Profile. D. Cooper, S. Santesson, S. Farrell, S. Boeyen, R. Housley, W. Polk. May 2008.

Key Management Framework

Three bodies have worked extensively on key management issues:[98] ANSI X9, ISO TC68, and ISO/IEC JTC1. ISO/IEC JTC1 have published a three-part general purpose standard on key management: ISO/ IEC 11770.

The first part is developing a key management framework, and many of the concepts of key management as early as 1985 ANSI published its first standards on this subject: ANSI X9.17 (first published in 1985) and ANSI X9.24[99] (first published in 1992). Both deal with key management issues for financial institutions. ANSI X9.17 defines procedures for the manual and automated management of keying materials and contains a number of options. Systems built to conform to all options of ANSI X9.17[100] are likely to be complex and expensive.

5A

ANSI X9.24 deals with key management issues between retail devices, such as between point-of-sale devices and the banking establishments that control the ANSI X9.17, which specifically targeted the use of single-length DES keys; ANSI X9.17 was withdrawn in 1999. On the other hand, the third edition of ANSI X9.24 deals with symmetric key management and only standardizes those techniques that utilize symmetric cryptography. It does not explicitly develop a key management framework, but rather implies one by placing strict rules on the way keys can be used and manipulated. Both of these standards have played an influential role in development of the key management standards published by the ISO banking technical committee, TC68. This committee has published several standards that include (mostly implicit) key management frameworks for banking. The most relevant of these are ISO 8732 (which is based on ANSI X9.17) and ISO 11568 (which is a multipart standard based on ANSI X9.24). The implied framework of these standards is essentially the same as the framework for ANSI NIST, SP 800-57 Mar 2007[101] Recommendation for Key Management SP800-57-Part 1. This document has been developed by the National Institute of Standards and Technology (NIST) in furtherance of its statutory responsibilities under the Federal Information Security Management Act (FISMA) of 2002, Public Law 107-347. It consists of three parts. Part 1 provides general guidance and best practices for the management of cryptographic keying material. Part 2 provides guidance on policy and security planning requirements for U.S. government agencies. Finally, Part 3 provides guidance when using the cryptographic features of current systems. This recommendation does not address implementation details for cryptographic modules that may be used to achieve the security requirements identified. These details are addressed in FIPS140-2 and the derived test requirements (available at http://csrc.nist.gov/cryptval/).

ISO/IEC 11770-1[102] standardizes a general model for the key life cycle. In this model, keys exist in one of seven different *key states: Pending active, Active, Generation, Activation, Deactivation, Reactivation,* and *Destruction.* This model provides a general working framework to talk about the different states that a key may be in, and what happens when a key moves between states.

ISO/IEC 11770-2:2008[103] specifies a series of 13 mechanisms for establishing shared secret keys using symmetric cryptography. These mechanisms address three different environments for the establishment of shared secret keys: point-to-point key establishment schemes, mechanisms using a Key Distribution Centre (KDC), and techniques that use a Key Translation Centre (KTC). ISO/IEC 11770-2:2008 describes the content of messages that carry keying material or are necessary to set up the conditions under which the keying material can be established. This second edition is a technically revised version of the first edition: Mechanism 12, and has been modified to address identified security shortcomings.[104]

ISO/IEC 11770-3:2008 defines key management mechanisms based on asymmetric cryptography. It specifically addresses the use of asymmetric techniques to achieve the following goals:

- Establish a shared secret key for a symmetric cryptographic technique between two entities A and B by key agreement.
- Establish a shared secret key for a symmetric cryptographic technique between two entities A and B by key transport.
- Make an entity's public key available to other entities by key transport.

Some of the mechanisms of ISO/IEC 11770-3:2008 are based on the corresponding authentication mechanisms in ISO/IEC 9798-3. ISO/IEC 11770-3:2008 does not cover aspects of key management such as key lifecycle management, mechanisms to generate or validate asymmetric key pairs, mechanisms to store, archive, delete, destroy keys, etc. ISO/IEC 11770-3:2008 does not explicitly cover the distribution of an entity's private key (of an asymmetric key pair) from a trusted third party to a requesting entity; the key transport mechanisms described can be used to achieve this. A private key can in all cases be distributed with these mechanisms where an existing, noncompromised key already exists. However, in practice the distribution of private keys is usually a manual process that relies on technological means like smart cards, etc.

ISO/IEC 11770-4: 2006[105] defines key establishment mechanisms based on weak secrets. It specifies cryptographic techniques specifically designed to establish one or more secret keys based on a weak secret derived from a memorized password, while preventing off-line brute-force attacks associated with the weak secret. More specifically, these mechanisms are designed to achieve one of the following three goals.

The RFC provides many documents to cover:

- Group Key Management Protocol (GKMP) Specification
- KEY Management API
- Internet Security Association and Key Management Protocol
- Session-Key Management Protocol
- Guidelines for Cryptographic Key Management

And these documents are (IETF, Internet Engineering Task Force [IETF] 2008):

- RFC 2093 Group Key Management Protocol (GKMP) Specification, H. Harney, C. Muckenhirn, July 1997.
- RFC 2094 Group Key Management Protocol (GKMP) Architecture, H. Harney, C. Muckenhirn, July 1997.
- RFC 2367 PF_KEY Key Management API, Version 2, D. McDonald, C. Metz, B. Phan, July 1998.
- IRFC 2408 Internet Security Association and Key Management Protocol (ISAKMP), D. Maughan, M. Schertler, M. Schneider, J. Turner, November 1998.
- RFC 2522 Photuris: Session-Key Management Protocol, P. Karn, W. Simpson, March 1999.
- RFC 2627 Key Management for Multicast: Issues and Architectures, D. Wallner, E. Harder, R. Agee, June 1999.
- RFC 2786 Diffie-Helman USM Key Management Information Base and Textual Convention, M. St. Johns, March 2000.
- RFC 4046 Multicast Security (MSEC) Group Key Management Architecture, M. Baugher, R. Canetti, L. Dondeti, F. Lindholm, April 2005
- RFC 4107 Guidelines for Cryptographic Key Management, S. Bellovin, R. Housley, June 2005.
- RFC 4535 GSAKMP: Group Secure Association Key Management Protocol, H. Harney, U. Meth, A. Colegrove, G. Gross, June 2006.

- RFC 4567 Key Management Extensions for Session Description Protocol (SDP) and Real Time Streaming Protocol (RTSP), J. Arkko, F. Lindholm, M. Naslund, K. Norrman, E. Carrara, July 2006.
- RFC 4962 Guidance for Authentication, Authorization, and Accounting (AAA) Key Management, R. Housley, B. Aboba., July 2007.
- RFC 5169 Handover Key Management and Re-Authentication Problem Statement, T. Clancy, M. Nakhjiri, V. Narayanan, L. Dondeti, March 2008.
- RFC 5247 Extensible Authentication Protocol (EAP) Key Management Framework, B. Aboba, D. Simon, P. Eronen, August 2008.
- RFC 5275 CMS Symmetric Key Management and Distribution, S. Turner, June 2008.

5A

Conclusion

This chapter presents cryptography standards such as symmetric standards, asymmetric, and key managements. The chapter focuses on "most used cryptography standardization." The chapter provides guidelines for management in cryptography standards in the market; it does not provide great technical and mathematical details for algorithms, however.

The chapter began by defining standards and recognizing standard organizations dealing with cryptography. Then it presented very short cryptography algorithm definitions and their applications.

There are many standards not presented in this chapter such as non-reputation, authorization, key agreements protocols, email encryption, and others; this is because these standards are beyond the theme of this chapter.

Bibliography

(ANSI), American National Standards Institute. *American National Standards Institute (ANSI).* 2008. Can be retrieved from http://www.ansi.org/about_ansi/introduction/.

3GPP. *The 3rd Generation Partnership Project (3GPP).* Can be retrieved from http://www.3gpp.org/About/about.htm.

Al-Hamdani, Wasim A. "Chapter XI: Cryptography for Information Security." In *USA Handbook of Research on Information Security and Assurance*, by Jatinder Gupta and Sushil K Sharma, 122–136. IGI, 2008.

Allman, E., J. Callas, M. Delany, M. Libbey, and J. Fen. "IETF RFC 4871 DomainKeys Identified Mail (DKIM) Signatures." IETF RFC 4871 can be retrieved from http://www.ietf.org/, May 2007.

Alvestrand, H. A Mission Statement for the IETF Request for Comments: 3935, October 2004.

ANSI. *American Bankers Association, ANSI X9 TG–24, Technical Guideline: Managing Risk and Migration Planning: Withdrawal of ANSI X9.9, Financial Institution*

Message Authentication Codes (MAC) Wholesale, 1999. ANSI X9 TG–24–1999 can be retrieved from http://www.ansi.org/, ANSI, 1999.

ANSI. *American National Standards Institute (ANSI): Accredited Standards Committee X9.9—Financial Services, Financial Institution Message Authentication.* ANSI X9.9–1986 (Revised) can be retrieved from http://www.ansi.org/, ANSI, April 1986.

ANSI. *American National Standards Institute (ANSI): Accredited Standards Committee X9 —Financial Services, ANSI X9.19, Financial Institution Retail Message Authentication,.* ANSI X9.19:1986 can be retrieved from http://www.ansi.org/, ANSI, August 1986.

ANSI. *American National Standards Institute (ANSI): Accredited Standards Committee X9 —Financial Services, ANSI X9.71, Keyed Hash Message Authentication Code.* ANSI X9.71–2000 can be retrieved from http://www.ansi.org/, ANSI, 2000.

ANSI. *American National Standards Institute (ANSI): Retail Financial Services Symmetric Key Management—Part 2: Using Asymmetric Techniques for the Distribution of Symmetric Keys.* ANSI X9.24-2:2006 can be retrieved from http://www.ansi.org/, ANSI, 2006.

ANSI. *ANSI X9.30-1:1997 American National Standards Institute Public Key Cryptography Using Irreversible Algorithms—Part 1: The Digital Signature Algorithm (DSA).* ANSI X9.30-1:1997 can be retrieved from http://www.ansi.org/, ANSI, 1977.

ANSI. *ANSI X9.31:1998 American National Standards Institute Digital Signatures Using Reversible Public Key Cryptography for the Financial Services Industry (rDSA).* ANSI X9.31:1998 can be retrieved from http://www.ansi.org/, ANSI, 1998.

ANSI. *ANSI X9.55:1997 American National Standards Institute, Public Key Cryptography for the Financial Services Industry: Extensions to Public Key Certificates and Certificate Revocation Lists.* ANSI X9.55:1997 can be retrieved from http://www.ansi.org/, ANSI, 1997.

ANSI. *ANSI X9.57:1997 American National Standards Institute Public Key Cryptography for the Financial Services Industry: Certificate Management.* ANSI X9.57:1997 can be retrieved from http://www.ansi.org/, ANSI, 1997.

ANSI. *AS 4539.1.3-1999 American National Standards Institute, Information Technology— Public Key Authentication Framework (PKAF)—General—X.509 supported algorithms profile.* AS 4539.1.3-1999 can be retrieved from http://www.ansi.org/, ANSI, 1999.

Barker, Elaine B., William C. Barker, and Annabelle Lee. "Guideline for Implementing Cryptography in the Federal Government." NIST Special Publication 800-21, 2005.

Barker, William C. "Recommendation for the Triple Data Encryption Algorithm (TDEA) Block Cipher Revised." NIST Special Publication 800-67 Version 1.1, 19 May 2008.

Bellovin, S., and A. Zinin. "IETF RFC 4278 Standards Maturity Variance Regarding the TCP MD5 Signature Option (RFC 2385) and the BGP-4 Specification." IETF RFC 4278 can be retrieved from http://www.ietf.org/, January 2000.

Blake-Wilson, S., G. Karlinger, T. Kobayashi, and Y. Wang. "IETF RFC 4050 Using the Elliptic Curve Signature Algorithm (ECDSA) for XML Digital Signatures." IETF RFC 4050 can be retrieved from http://www.ietf.org/, April 2005.

Boyer, J., M. Hughes, and J. Reagle. "IETF RFC 3653 XML-Signature XPath Filter 2.0." IETF RFC 3653 can be retrieved from http://www.ietf.org/, December 2000.

Branstad, Dennis (ed.). "Computer Security and the Data Encryption Standard Edited by Dennis Branstad." NIST Special Publication 500, 1978.

BSI. *BSI British Standards Institution.* 2008. Can be retrieved from http://www.bsi-global.com.

Cambridge. *Cambridge Advanced Learner's Dictionary.* Cambridge: Cambridge University Press, 2008.

Dang, Quynh. "DRAFT NIST Special Publication 800-107 Recommendation for Applications Using Approved Hash Algorithms." NIST Special Publication 800-107, July 2008.

Davidson, K., and Y. Kawatsura. "IETF RFC 2802 Digital Signatures for the v1.0 Internet Open Trading Protocol (IOTP)." IETF RFC 2802 can be retrieved from http://www.ietf.org/, April 2000.

Dent, Alexander W., and Chris J. Mitchell. *User's Guide to Cryptography and Standards.* Artech House, 2005.

Dictionary, Free. *The Free Dictionary.* 2008. Can be retrieved from http://www.thefreedictionary.com/standard.

Dworkin, Morris. "National Institute of Standards and Technology (NIST), NIST Special Publication 800-38B, Draft Recommendation for Block Cipher Modes of Operation: The RMAC." NIST Special Publication 800-38B, 2004.

Eastlake, D. "IETF RFC 2931 DNS Request and Transaction Signatures (SIG(0)s)." IETF RFC 2931 can be retrieved from http://www.ietf.org/, September 2000.

Eastlake 3rd, D., J. Reagle, and D. Solo. "IETF RFC 3275 (Extensible Markup Language) XML-Signature Syntax and Processing." IETF RFC 3275, March 2002.

Eastlake 3rd, D., J. Reagle, and D. Solo. "IETF RFC 3075 XML-Signature Syntax and Processing." IETF RFC 3075 can be retrieved from http://www.ietf.org/, March 2001.

Federal Register. *Announcing Approval of the Withdrawal of Federal Information.* Announcing Approval of the Withdrawal of Federal Information [Docket No. 040602169–5002–02]: Department of Commerce, National Institute of Standards and Technology, Thursday, May 19, 2005, Vol. 70, No. 96.

Federal Register. Department of Commerce, National Institute of Standards and Technology, *Announcing the Development of New Hash Algorithm(s) for the Revision of Federal Information Processing Standard (FIPS) 180-2, Secure Hash Standard.* [Docket No. 061213336–6336–01], Federal Register, 2007.

Federal Register. Department of Commerce, National Institute of Standards and Technology, *Announcing Request for Candidate Algorithm Nominations for a New*

Cryptographic Hash Algorithm (SHA–3) Family. [Docket No. 070911510–7512–01], Federal Register, 2007.

FIPS. "Federal Information Processing Standards Publication—The Keyed-Hash Message Authentication Code (HMAC)." FIPS PUB 198-1, July 2008.

FIPS-197. *Announcing the Advanced Encryption Standard (AES).* Federal Information Processing Standards Publication, November 26, 2001.

Fu, D., and J. Solinas. "IETF RFC 4754 IKE and IKEv2 Authentication Using the Elliptic Curve Digital Signature Algorithm (ECDSA)." D. Fu, J. Solinas. January 2007. IETF RFC 4754 can be retrieved from http://www.ietf.org/, January 2007.

Greenblatt, B., and P. Richard. "IETF RFC 2649 An LDAP Control and Schema for Holding Operation Signatures." IETF RFC 2649 can be retrieved from http://www.ietf.org/, August 1999.

Heffernan, A. "IETF RFC 2385 Protection of BGP Sessions via the TCP MD5 Signature Option." IETF RFC 2385 can be retrieved from http://www.ietf.org/, August 1998.

IEC. *IEC International Electrotechnical Commission.* 2008. Can be retrieved from http://www.iec.ch/.

IEEE. *The IEEE P1363 project Home Page.* Can be retrieved from http://grouper.ieee.org/groups/1363/.

IEEE Standard Association. 2008. Can be retrieved from http://standards.ieee.org/.

IETF. *Internet Engineering Task Force (IETF).* 2008. Can be retrieved from http://www.ietf.org/.

RFC site. 2008. Can be retrieved from http://www.ietf.org/iesg/1rfc_index.txt.

IRTF. *Internet Research Task Force (IRTF).* 2008. Can be retrieved from http://www.irtf.org/.

ISO. "International Organization for Standardization ISO/IEC 9797-1:1999 Information technology—Security techniques—Message Authentication Codes (MACs)—Part 1: Mechanisms using a block cipher." ISO/IEC 9797-1:1999, 1999.

ISO. "International Organization for Standardization, ISO 8731–1:1987, Banking Approved Algorithm for Message Authentication—Part 1: DEA, 1987." ISO 8731–1:1987, 1987.

ISO. "International Organization for Standardization, ISO 8731–2: 1992, Banking Approved Algorithm for Message Authentication—Part 2: Message Authenticator Algorithm, 2nd ed., 1992." ISO 8731–2:1992, 1992.

ISO. "International Organization for Standardization, ISO/IEC 10118–1, Information Technology—Security Techniques—Hash-Functions—Part 1: General, 2nd ed." ISO, 2000.

ISO. "International Organization for Standardization, ISO/IEC 10118–2, Information Technology—Security Techniques—Hash-Functions—Part 2: Hash-Functions Using a non-Bit Block Cipher, 2nd ed." 2000.

ISO. "International Organization for Standardization, ISO/IEC 10118–3, Information Technology—Security Techniques—Hash-Functions—Part 3: Dedicated Hash-Functions." ISO, 2003.

ISO. "International Organization for Standardization, ISO/IEC 10118–4, Information Technology—Security Techniques—Hash-Functions—Part 4: Hash-Functions Using Modular Arithmetic." ISO, 1998.

ISO. "International Organization for Standardization, ISO/IEC 14888-1:1998, Information Technology—Security Techniques—Digital Signatures with Appendix—Part 1: General." ISO/IEC 14888-1:1998, 1998.

ISO. "International Organization for Standardization, ISO/IEC 14888-2:1999, Information Technology—Security Techniques—Digital Signatures with Appendix—Part 2: Identity-Based Mechanisms." ISO/IEC 14888-2:1999, 1999.

ISO. "International Organization for Standardization, ISO/IEC 9796-2:2002, Information Technology—Security Techniques—Digital Signature Schemes Giving Message Recovery—Part 2: Integer Factorization Based Mechanisms, 2nd ed." ISO/IEC 9796-2:2002, 2002.

ISO. "International Organization for Standardization, ISO/IEC 9796-3:2000, Information Technology—Security Techniques—Digital Signature Schemes Giving Message Recovery—Part 3: Discrete Logarithm Based Mechanisms." ISO/IEC 9796-3:2000, 2000.

ISO. "International Organization for Standardization, ISO/IEC 9796-3:2006, Information Technology—Security Techniques—Digital Signature Schemes Giving Message Recovery—Part 3: Discrete Logarithm Based Mechanisms." ISO/IEC 9796-3:2006, 2006.

ISO. "International Organization for Standardization, Road Vehicles Extended Data Link Security." ISO 15764:2004, 2004.

ISO. "International Organization for Standardization,ISO 8730:1986, Banking Requirements for Message Authentication, 2nd ed." ISO 8730:1986, 1990.

ISO. *ISO (International Organization for Standardization).* 2008. Can be retrieved from http://www.iso.org/iso/about.htm.

ISO. "ISO 17090-1:2008 Health Informatics—Public Key Infrastructure—Part 1: Overview of Digital Certificate Services." ISO 17090-1:2008, 2008.

ISO. "ISO 17090-2:2008 Health Informatics—Public Key Infrastructure—Part 2: Certificate Profile." ISO 17090-2:2008, 2008.

ISO. "ISO 17090-3:2008 Health Informatics—Public Key Infrastructure—Part 3: Policy Management of Certification Authority." ISO 17090-3:2008, 2008.

ISO. "ISO 20828:2006 Road Vehicles—Security Certificate Management." ISO 20828:2006, 2006.

ISO. "ISO/IEC 11770-2:2008 Information Technology—Security Techniques—Key Management—Part 2: Mechanisms Using Symmetric Techniques." ISO/IEC 11770-2:2008 can be retrieved from http://www.iso.org/, ISO, 2008.

ISO. "ISO/IEC 11770-3:2008 Information Technology—Security Techniques—Key Management—Part 3: Mechanisms Using Asymmetric Techniques." Can be retrieved from http://www.ansi.org/, ISO, 2008.

ISO. "ISO/IEC 11770-4:2006 Information Technology—Security Techniques—Key Management—Part 4: Mechanisms Based on Weak Secrets." Can be retrieved from http://www.ansi.org/, 2006.

ISO. "ISO/IEC 18033-3:2005 Information Technology—Security Techniques—Encryption Algorithms." Can be retrived from http://www.iso.org/, 2005.

ISO. "ISO/IEC 9797-2:2002 International Organization for Standardization Information Technology—Security Techniques—Message Authentication Codes (MACs)—Part 2: Mechanisms Using a Dedicated Hash-Function." ISO/IEC 9797-2:2002.

ISO. "Public Key Infrastructure for Financial Services—Practices and Policy Framework." ISO 21188:2006, 2006.

Jaganathan, K., L. Zhu, and J. Brezak. *RFC 4757 The RC4-HMAC Kerberos Encryption Types Used by Microsoft Windos.* Can be retrieved from http://www.ietf.org/, ietf, December 2006.

Kuhn, D. Richard, Vincent C. Hu, W. Timothy Polk, and Shu-Jen Chang. *Introduction to Public Key Technology and the Federal PKI Infrastructure.* NIST SP-800 32, NIST, 2001.

Leech, M. *"IETF RFC 3562 Key Management Considerations for the TCP MD5 Signature Option."* IETF RFC 3562, July 2003.

M. Blaze, J. Ioannidis, and A. Keromytis. *"IETF RFC 2792 DSA and RSA Key and Signature Encoding for the KeyNote Trust Management System."* IETF RFC 2792 can be retrieved from http://www.ietf.org/, March 2000.

NIST. *Block Cipher Modes.* 2008. Can be retrieved from http://csrc.nist.gov/groups/ST/toolkit/BCM/index.html.

NIST. "Computer Security and the Data Encrytion Standard Edited by Dennis Branstad." NIST Special Publications 500, 1978.

NIST. *Cryptographic Algorithm Validation Program.* Can be retrieved from http://csrc.nist.gov/groups/STM/cavp/index.html, 2008.

NIST. "FIPS PUB 81: DES Modes of Operation." National Institute of Standards and Technology (NIST), Federal Information Processing, 1980.

NIST. "National Institute of Standards and Technology (NIST), NIST Special Publication 800-38B, Draft Recommendation for Block Cipher Modes of Operation: The RMAC." NIST Special Publication 800-38B, 2003.

NIST. *NIST The National Institute of Standards Technology.* Can be retrieved from http://www.nist.gov/, 2008.

NIST. *NIST- SP 800-25 Oct 2000, Federal Agency Use of Public Key Technology for Digital Signatures and Authentication.* http://csrc.nist.gov/, NIST, 2000.

NIST. *NIST Special Publication 800-57 Recommendation for Key Management—Part 1: General.* NIST-Sp-800-57-1 can be retrievd from http://csrc.nist.gov/publications/PubsSPs.html, NISt, March 2007.

Pinkas, D., J. Ross, and N. Pope. "IETF RFC 3126 Electronic Signature Formats For Long Term Electronic Signatures." IETF RFC 3126 can be retrieved from http://www.ietf.org/, September 2000.

Pinkas, D., J. Ross, and N. Pope. "IETF RFC 3126 Electronic Signature Formats for Long Term Electronic Signatures." IETF RFC 3126 can be retrieved from http://www.ietf.org/, September 2001.

Pinkas, D., N. Pope, and J. Ross, and "IETF RFC 5126 CMS Advanced Electronic Signatures (CAdES)." IETF RFC 5126 can be retrieved from http://www.ietf.org/, March 2008.

Reagle, J. "IETF RFC 2807 XML Signature Requirements." IETF RFC 2807 can be retrieved from http://www.ietf.org/, July 2000.

RSA. *Public-Key Cryptography Standards (PKCS), Standard Initiatives.* 2008. Can be retrieved from http://www.rsa.com/rsalabs/node.asp?id=2124.

RSA. *RSA, Crypto FA, Question 3.6.6 What Are MD2, MD4, and MD5?* Can be retrieved from http://www.rsa.com/r, 2008.

RSALab. *Crypto FAQ Q3.6.3 What Is RC4?* Can be retreved from http://www.rsa.com, 2008.

RSALab. "RSA Lab, Public-Key Cryptography Standards (PKCS)." Can be retrieved from http://www.rsa.com/, 2008.

Santesson, S., W. Polk, P. Barzin, and M. Nystrom. "Internet X.509 Public Key Infrastructure Qualified Certificates Profile." IETF RFC 3039 can be retrieved from http://www.ietf.org/, January 2001.

Schaad, J. "IETF RFC 4056 Use of the RSASSA-PSS Signature Algorithm in Cryptographic Message Syntax (CMS)." IETF RFC 4056:2005.

Schaad, J., and R. Housley. "Advanced Encryption Standard (AES) Key Wrap Algorithm." IETF RFC: 3394, September 2002.

SecurityTechNet.com. *Elliptic Curve Cryptography.* Can be retrieved from http://cnscenter.future.co.kr/.

The European Telecommunications Standards Institute (ETSI). Can be retrieved from http://en.wikipedia.org/wiki/ETSI.

Weis., B. "IETF RFC 4359 The Use of RSA/SHA-1 Signatures within Encapsulating Security Payload (ESP) and Authentication Header (AH)." IETF RFC 4359 can be retrieved from http://www.ietf.org/, January 2006.

Whatis.com. The Leading IT Encyclopedia and Learning Center. 2008. Can be retrieved from http://whatis.techtarget.com/.

wikipedia. *Standards Organization.* Can be retrieved from http://en.wikipedia.org/wiki/Standards_organization.

wikipedia. *The 3rd Generation Partnership Project (3GPP)*. 2008. Can be retrieved from http://en.wikipedia.org/wiki/3GPP.

X9.17, ANSI. "ANSI X9.17 American National Standards Institute, ANSI X9.17: Financial Institution Key Management, 1995." ANSI X9.17:1995.

Endnotes

1. *Cambridge Advanced Learner's Dictionary* (Cambridge University Press, 2008), 3.

2. Ibid.

3. *The Free Dictionary* can be retrieved from http://www.thefreedictionary.com/standard

4. Ibid.

5. Felix E. Hirsch, *Introduction: Why Do We Need Standards?* http://www.ideals.uiuc.edu/handle/2142/6674

6. Standards.gov

7. NIST reference service for information on standards and technical regulations (http://ts.nist.gov/) National Center for Standards and Certification Information (NCSCI)

   • NSSN: A National Resource for Global Standards (http://www.nssn.org/)

   • Global distributor of technical standards, codes, specifications, and related documents (http://global.ihs.com/)

   • Worldwide provider of engineering standards and databases (http://www.ili-info.com/)

   • Library of Congress Science, Technology and Business Division maintains an extensive collection of U.S., (http://www.loc.gov/)

   • The American National Standards Institute (ANSI) provides information on nearly 100,000 standards and purchasing discounts to GSA customers (http://webstore.ansi.org/)

8. wikipedia.org

9. Elaine B. Barker, William C. Barker, and Annabelle Lee, NIST Special Publication 800-21, "Guideline for Implementing Cryptography in the Federal Government."

10. Ibid.

11. Standards organization can be retrieved from http://en.wikipedia.org/wiki/Standards_organization

12. The European Telecommunications Standards Institute (ETSI) http://en.wikipedia.org/wiki/ETSI

13. American National Standards Institute (ANSI) can be retrieved from http://www.ansi.org/

14. NIST, The National Institute of Standards Technology can be retrieved from http://www.nist.gov/

15. British Standards Institution (BSI) can be retrieved from http://www.bsi-global.com/

16. International Organization for Standardization (ISO) can be retrieved from http://www.iso.org/

17. The Free Dictionary.

18. Alexander W. Dent and Chris J. Mitchell, *User's Guide to Cryptography and Standards*, Artech House 2005.

19. Whatis.com, "The Leading IT Encyclopedia and Learning Center" can be retrieved from http://whatis.techtarget.com/

20. IEC International Electrotechnical Commission can be retrieved from http://www.iec.ch/

21. Internet Engineering Task Force (IETF) can be retrieved from http://www.ietf.org/

22. H. Alvestrand, "A Mission Statement for the IETF," RFC: 3935 October 2004.

23. International Organization for Standardization.

24. Internet Research Task Force (IRTF) can be retrieved from http://www.irtf.org/

25. Ibid.

26. Dent and Mitchell, *User's Guide to Cryptography and Standards*.

27. Ibid.

28. The 3rd Generation Partnership Project (3GPP) can be retrieved from http://www.3gpp.org/About/about.htm

29. Standards for Efficient Cryptography Group (SECG) can be retrieved from http://www.secg.org/

30. Public-Key Cryptography Standards (PKCS), Standard Initiatives, can be retrieved from http://www.rsa.com/

31. Wasim A Al-Hamdani, Chapter XI: "Cryptography for Information Security, USA Handbook of Research on Information Security and Assurance," Ed. Jatinder N. D. Gupta and Sushil K. Sharma.

32. Network Security Center, "NetSec" 2001. Can be retrieved from http://www.netsec.org.sa/cryptography.htm

33. Ibid.

34. NIST, Cryptographic Algorithm Validation Program. Can be retrieved from http://csrc.nist.gov/

35. Federal Register /Vol. 70, No. 96 /Thursday, May 19, 2005 /Notices Department of Commerce, National Institute of Standards and Technology.

36. William C. Barker, Recommendation for the Triple Data Encryption Algorithm (TDEA) Block Cipher Revised, 19 May 2008.

37. Federal Information Processing Standards Publication 197 Announcing the Advanced Encryption Standard (AES), November 26, 2001.

38. J. Schaad and R. Housley, Advanced Encryption Standard (AES) Key Wrap Algorithm Request for Comments: 3394.

39. RFC site can be retrieved from http://www.ietf.org/iesg/1rfc_index.txt

40. ISO/IEC 18033-3:2005 Information technology—Security techniques—Encryption algorithms http://www.iso.org/iso/

41. ISO 26429-6:2008 Digital cinema (D-cinema) packaging—Part 6: MXF track file essence encryption can be retrieved from http://www.iso.org/

42. Ibid.

43. RSA Laboratory, What is RC4? Can be retrieved from http://www.rsa.com/

44. Ibid.

45. Network Security Center.

46. Block Cipher Modes, Current Modes. Can be retrieved from http://csrc.nist.gov/groups/ST/toolkit/BCM/current_modes.html

47. In cryptography, ciphertext stealing (CTS) is a general method of using a block cipher mode of operation that allows for processing of messages that are not evenly divisible into blocks without resulting in any expansion of the ciphertext, at the cost of slightly increased complexity.

48. Block Cipher Modes, Current Modes.

49. Morris Dworkin, Recommendation for Block Cipher Modes of Operation: The CMAC Mode for Authentication. NIST Special Publication 800-38B.

50. Block Cipher Modes, Current Modes.

51. Dworkin, Recommendation for Block Cipher Modes of Operation.

52. Block Cipher Modes, Current Modes.

53. Dworkin, Recommendation for Block Cipher Modes of Operation.

54. Block Cipher Modes, Current Modes.

55. RSA Lab, Public-Key Cryptography Standards (PKCS) can be retrieved from http://www.rsa.com/

56. IEEE, The IEEE P1363 project Home Page, can be retrieved from http://grouper.ieee.org/groups/1363/

57. RFC.

58. Elliptic Curve Cryptography can be retrieved from http://cnscenter.future.co.kr/

59. Federal Register /Vol. 72, No. 14 /Tuesday, January 23, 2007 /Notices; Department of Commerce, National Institute of Standards and Technology [Docket No. 061213336–6336–01], Announcing the Development of New Hash Algorithm(s) for the Revision of Federal Information Processing Standard (FIPS) 180–2, Secure Hash Standard.

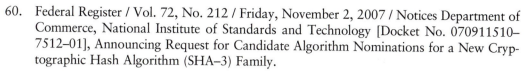

60. Federal Register / Vol. 72, No. 212 / Friday, November 2, 2007 / Notices Department of Commerce, National Institute of Standards and Technology [Docket No. 070911510–7512–01], Announcing Request for Candidate Algorithm Nominations for a New Cryptographic Hash Algorithm (SHA–3) Family.

61. RSA, Crypto FA, question 3.6.6 What are MD2, MD4, and MD5?

62. RFC.

63. International Organization for Standardization, ISO/IEC 10118–1, Information Technology—Security Techniques—Hash-Functions—Part 1: General, 2nd ed., 2000.

64. International Organization for Standardization, ISO/IEC 10118–2, Information Technology—Security Techniques—Hash-Functions—Part 2: Hash-Functions Using an n-Bit Block Cipher, 2nd ed., 2000.

65. International Organization for Standardization, ISO/IEC 10118–4, Information Technology—Security Techniques—Hash-Functions—Part 4: Hash-Functions Using Modular Arithmetic, 1998.

66. International Organization for Standardization, ISO/IEC 10118–3, Information Technology—Security Techniques—Hash-Functions—Part 3: Dedicated Hash- Functions, 2nd edition, 2003.

67. Block Cipher Mode, Current Modes.

68. ISO/IEC 9797-1:1999 Information Technology—Security Techniques—Message Authentication Codes (MACs)—Part 1: Mechanisms Using a Block Cipher.

69. ISO/IEC 9797-2:2002 Information Technology—Security Techniques—Message Authentication Codes (MACs)—Part 2: Mechanisms Using a Dedicated Hash-Function.

70. FIPS PUB 198-1, Federal Information Processing Standards Publication: The Keyed-Hash Message Authentication Code (HMAC), July 2008.

71. Accredited Standards Committee X9—Financial Services, ANSI X9.9–1986 (Revised), Financial Institution Message Authentication (Wholesale), April 1986.

72. Accredited Standards Committee X9—Financial Services, ANSI X9.19, Financial Institution Retail Message Authentication, August 1986.

73. Accredited Standards Committee X9—Financial Services, ANSI X9.71–2000, Keyed-Hash Message Authentication Code, 2000.

74. American Bankers Association, ANSI X9 TG–24–1999, Technical Guideline: Managing Risk and Migration Planning: Withdrawal of ANSI X9.9, Financial Institution Message Authentication Codes (MAC) Wholesale, 1999.

75. International Organization for Standardization, ISO 8730:1986, Banking Requirements for Message Authentication (Wholesale), 2nd ed., 1990.

76. International Organization for Standardization, ISO 8731–1:1987, Banking Approved Algorithm for Message Authentication—Part 1: DEA, 1987. International Organization for Standardization, ISO 8731–2:1992, Banking Approved Algorithm for Message Authentication—Part 2: Message Authenticator Algorithm, 2nd ed., 1992.

77. National Institute of Standards and Technology (NIST), NIST Special Publication 800-38B, Draft Recommendation for Block Cipher Modes of Operation: The RMAC.

78. Quynh Dang, DRAFT NIST Special Publication 800-107 Recommendation for Applications Using Approved Hash Algorithms, July 2008.

79. RFC.

80. SP 800-25 Oct 2000 Federal Agency Use of Public Key Technology for Digital Signatures and Authentication, http://csrc.nist.gov/

81. ANSI X9.30-1:1997 American National Standards Institute Public Key Cryptography Using Irreversible Algorithms—Part 1: The Digital Signature Algorithm (DSA).

82. ANSI X9.31:1998 American National Standards Institute Digital Signatures Using Reversible Public Key Cryptography for the Financial Services Industry (rDSA).

83. ANSI X9.57:1997 American National Standards Institute Public Key Cryptography for the Financial Services Industry: Certificate Management.

84. International Organization for Standardization, ISO/IEC 9796-2:2002, Information Technology—Security Techniques—Digital Signature Schemes Giving Message Recovery—Part 2: Integer Factorization Based Mechanisms, 2nd ed., 2002. International Organization for Standardization, ISO/IEC 9796-3:2000, Information Technology—Security Techniques—Digital Signature Schemes Giving Message Recovery—Part 3: Discrete Logarithm Based Mechanisms, 2000. International Organization for Standardization, ISO/IEC 9796-3:2000, Information Technology—Security Techniques—Digital Signature Schemes Giving Message Recovery—Part 3: Discrete Logarithm Based Mechanisms, 2000.

85. International Organization for Standardization, ISO/IEC 9796-3:2006 Information Technology—Security Techniques—Digital Signature Schemes Giving Message Recovery—Part 3: Discrete Logarithm Based Mechanisms.

86. Internet X.509 Public Key Infrastructure Qualified Certificates Profile. S. Santesson, W. Polk, P. Barzin, M. Nystrom. January 2001.

87. International Organization for Standardization, ISO/IEC 14888-1:1998, Information Technology—Security Techniques—Digital Signatures with Appendix—Part 1: General, 1998. International Organization for Standardization, ISO/IEC 14888-2:1999, Information Technology—Security Techniques—Digital Signatures with Appendix—Part 2: Identity-Based Mechanisms, 1999. International Organization for Standardization, ISO/IEC 14888-2:1999, Information Technology—Security Techniques—Digital Signatures with Appendix—Part 2: Identity-Based Mechanisms, 1999.

88. Internet Engineering Task Force (IETF), 2008 can be retrieved from http://www.ietf.org/

89. RFC 4050 Using the Elliptic Curve Signature Algorithm (ECDSA) for XML Digital Signatures. S. Blake-Wilson, G. Karlinger, T. Kobayashi, Y. Wang. April 2005.

90. SP 800-32 Feb 2001, Introduction to Public Key Technology and the Federal PKI Infrastructure.

91. AS 4539.1.3-1999, American National Standards Institute, Information Technology—Public Key Authentication Framework (PKAF)—General—X.509 supported algorithms profile.

92. ANSI X9.55:1997, American National Standards Institute, Public Key Cryptography for the Financial Services Industry: Extensions to Public Key Certificates and Certificate Revocation Lists.

93. ISO 21188:2006, Public Key Infrastructure for Financial Services—Practices and Policy Framework.

94. ISO 20828:2006, Road Vehicles—Security Certificate Management.

95. ISO 17090-1:2008, Health Informatics—Public Key Infrastructure—Part 1: Overview of Digital Certificate Services.

96. ISO 17090-2:2008, Health Informatics—Public Key Infrastructure—Part 2: Certificate Profile.

97. ISO 17090-3:2008, Health Informatics—Public Key Infrastructure—Part 3: Policy Management of Certification Authority.

98. Dent and Mitchell, User's Guide to Cryptology and Standards.

99. ANSI X9.24-2:2006, American National Standards Institute (ANSI): Retail Financial Services Symmetric Key Management—Part 2: Using Asymmetric Techniques for the Distribution of Symmetric Keys. Can be retrieved from http://www.ansi.org/

100. ANSI X9.17 American National Standards Institute, ANSI X9.17: Financial Institution Key Management (Wholesale), 1995. can be retrieved from http://www.ansi.org/

101. NIST, SP 800-57 Mar 2007, Recommendation for Key Management sp800-57-Part 1. Can be retrieved from http://csrc.nist.gov/

102. ISO/IEC 11770-1:1996 Information Technology—Security Techniques—Key Management—Part 1: Framework. Can be retrieved from http://www.iso.org/

103. ISO/IEC 11770-2:2008 Information Technology—Security Techniques—Key Management—Part 2: Mechanisms Using Symmetric Techniques. Can be retrieved from http://www.iso.org/

104. ISO/IEC 11770-3:2008, Information Technology—Security Techniques—Key Management—Part 3: Mechanisms Using Asymmetric Techniques. Can be retrieved from http://www.ansi.org/

105. ISO/IEC 11770-4:2006, Information Technology—Security Techniques—Key Management—Part 4: Mechanisms Based on Weak Secrets. Can be retrieved from http://www.ansi.org/

Reading 5B

Cyber Terrorism: Impacts, Vulnerabilities, and U.S. Policy

Tridib Bandyopadhyay
Kennesaw State University

Dr. Tridib Bandyopadhyay is an Assistant Professor at Kennesaw State University. His major research interests are in information security investment issues in the private and public domains. At KSU, Dr. Bandyopadhyay teaches Systems Analysis, E-Business Systems, and Information Security in the BSIS, BSISA, and MSIS programs. Prior to his engagements in the academics, Dr. Bandyopadhyay has worked as an electrical engineer and later as a planning manager in the largest energy-generating company in India.

Overview

Terrorism is one major problem that plagues our world today. The memories of the bombings in the London subway (2005) and the Madrid commuter train (2004) are vivid in our memory. The attack of the World Trade Towers in September 2001 has fundamentally changed the way we look at our lives. Unlike the religious extremism that has dominated the recent terrorism scenarios in the new millennium, the twentieth century saw much diverse extremism: the independence struggles of colonies, the ethnic clashes, and the revolutionary left/right wing separatist movements—all have had the dubious distinctions of being terrorism.

Introduction

While the reasons and rationales behind the terrorist movements could vary widely, there is one striking similarity in their immediate goals. The terrorists, by their acts and activities, attempt to create the maximum psychological impact among the general population.[1] The largely imbalanced set of resources (in comparison to their adversaries, mostly the institutional forces) compels the terrorists to be in constant lookout for innovative ways of attack, which are not only cost effective but could also provide adequate anonymity and avoid easy detection. This is where the networked economy of the twenty-first century offers an important avenue for attack—enter the age of cyber terrorism!

In what follows, we first define the concept of terrorism as it potentially impacts our economy (second section), before we qualify and explain the nuances of *cyber* terrorism (third section). Thereafter we discuss the vulnerabilities from cyber terrorism (fourth section) and present the general appreciation of the problem as evidenced in our federal policies (fifth section). Finally, we close the chapter with a reality check of the problem and some concluding thoughts.

Terrorism

The USA Patriot Act, 2001, defines terrorism as the "activities that (*A*) involve acts dangerous to human life that are a violation of the criminal laws of the U.S. or of any state, that (*B*) appear to be intended (*i*) to intimidate or coerce a civilian population, (*ii*) to influence the policy of a government by intimidation or coercion, or (*iii*) to affect the conduct of a government by mass destruction, assassination, or kidnapping, and (*C*) occur primarily within the territorial jurisdiction of the U.S." Note that the high points of this definition include intentional intimidation and coercion of civilians and governments, as well as the mass disruption of business, life, and livelihood. The UK Terrorism Act of 2000 additionally notes the purposes of such acts: "...purpose of advancing a political, religious or ideological cause."

The relatively small numerical toll of terrorism on human lives barely signifies the overall impact of terrorism on nations, states, and their economies and societies. As a matter of fact, many of our daily activities, including driving automobiles, regularly expose us to much higher risks of harm than the overall risks of terrorism![2] The immediate purpose of the acts of terrorism is, however, to draw attention of the common people to their cause, often through gory and ghastly acts, and with the ultimate intention to exert indirect pressure on the authorities. This explains why terrorists seek high-visibility acts and attempt to create high psychological effect. Nevertheless, the long-term effects of terrorism are profound and multifaceted.

First, terrorist attacks destroy a country's wealth much like what happened with the 9/11 attack on the twin trade towers at New York. Frequent terrorist attack on crude oil pipelines or important trade routes is another example in this category. The attacked countries/establishments are often forced to replenish such economic wealth and bear the immediate effects of supply/demand distortions. For example, a nuclear attack on New York could cost our economy 3% of its productive capability with attendant increase in economic uncertainty and attrition in public confidence.[3]

Second, terrorism induces uncertainty in the economy and the society in general. This then alters individual consumption of goods and services, and changes the patterns and weights of savings and investments of households and firms. Terrorism also has immense impact on the financial climate; the 9/11 attack caused much turmoil and volatility in our financial systems and adjusted many of the indices of our economy. Social changes in terms of demographic shifts and altered job preferences are also important to consider here.

Third, a climate of terrorism affects the risk perceptions of external investors. This decreases foreign direct investments (FDI) and affects macroeconomic growth.

Fourth, constant danger of terrorism forces a country to become insulated from the outer world, restricting cross-border trades as well as the flows of the technological/managerial innovations. Economic, cultural, and social gains from international tourism suffer greatly as well.

Fifth, a general climate of fear discourages innovation in the native firms, promotes conservatism, and affects long-term growth.

Finally, acts of terrorism force governments/authorities to impose costly security measures and implement security controls/products at the expense of resources, which otherwise could have been utilized for productive purposes.

Cyber Terrorism

Defining *cyber terrorism* is not without problems. Some consider cyber terrorism as a subset of cyber crime where perpetrators are motivated by political agendas or are against sovereign countries. For example, Dorothy Denning[4] defines cyber terrorism as "the convergence of cyberspace and terrorism. It refers to unlawful attacks and threats of attack against computers, networks, and the information stored therein when done to intimidate or coerce a government or its people in furtherance of political or social objectives...."

The definition from the Federal Emergency Management Agency (FEMA) looks at the target as well as the goals of such attacks, "unlawful attacks and threats of attack against computers, networks, and the information stored therein when done to intimidate or coerce a government or its people in furtherance of political or social objectives."

On the other hand, Pollitt[5] defines cyber terrorism as "the premeditated, politically motivated attack against information, computer systems, computer programs, and data which result in violence against noncombatant targets by sub-national groups or clandestine agents."

The definition of cyber terrorism is not limited to the targets as computer nodes or information assets. As we observe, the generally accepted commonalities in the definition of *cyber terrorism* are rather the facts that they are motivated by (eventual) political reasons, perpetrated by subnational or foreign groups, targeted against the assets of sovereign nations and geared toward creating highly visible, gory or catastrophic events that are able to create large-scale psychological effect utilizing an attack that, in any part of its inception, enablement, enactment, propagation, and/or effect include the cyber space, information assets, the Internet, and the computers and communication assets and networks of the interconnected world.

Technology Engagement and Capability Hierarchy in Cyber Terrorism

The threats of cyber terrorism have been identified long before the recent (9/11) and more widespread realization and awakening toward the terrorism threats that we face here in the United States. The U.S. federal government started to analyze the cyber terrorism threats as early as in the mid-1990s. In 1996, John Deutch, the then-director of the Central Intelligence

Agency (CIA), in a statement before the Permanent Subcommittee on Investigations, the U.S. Senate Governmental Affairs Committee, deposited the following: "International terrorist groups clearly have the capability to attack the information infrastructure of the United States, even if they use relatively simple means. Since the possibilities for attacks are not difficult to imagine, I am concerned about the potential for such attacks in the future. The methods used could range from such traditional terrorist methods as a bomb—directed in this instance against, say, a telephone switching or other communications node—to electronic means of attack. The latter methods could rely on paid hackers. The ability to launch an attack, however, is likely to be within the capabilities of a number of terrorist groups, which themselves have increasingly used the Internet and other modern means for their own communications."

Likewise, in a later date, while defining *cyber terrorism* and the threats that we face from cyber terrorism, the then FBI Director Louis Freeh, in his statement before the U.S. Senate Committee on Appropriations, Armed Services, and Select Committee on Intelligence, May 10, 2001, reiterated threats of cyber terrorism that John Deutch pointed out in 2000, yet categorically added the possibility of cyber terrorism as it could affect our infrastructural facilities, "The FBI believes cyber-terrorism, the use of cyber-tools to shut down, degrade, or deny critical national infrastructures, such as energy, transportation, communications, or government services, for the purpose of coercing or intimidating a government or civilian population, is clearly an emerging threat for which it must develop prevention, deterrence, and response capabilities."

A sense of comparative escalation to higher degree and more intense exposure of our economy to the threats of cyber terrorism are evident from the above. The same is evident in the new interest among the researchers of terrorism as they attempt to define and juxtapose the technology capabilities, interconnectivity of the networked world, and the threats of terrorism facing sovereign countries. The Center for the Study of Terrorism and Irregular Warfare, Monterey, CA, in their 1999 whitepaper "Cyberterror, Prospects and Implications," attempts to provide a sense of the progression of the capabilities of the cyber terrorists through the following set of definitions and a hierarchy of capabilities:

- *Cyberterror support*: Include capabilities to use information systems to support, augment, or enhance other terrorist acts, but may not have own capability to inflict terror.

- *Simple-Unstructured*: Include capabilities for one or more of the following but does not have the capacity to analyze target or advance learning capabilities:
  - Execute basic hacking and disruption, and
  - Utilize hacking tools independently that have been created by others

- *Advanced-Structured*: Include capabilities for:
  - Target analysis
  - Attacks against multiple systems or networks, including sequential attacks
  - Modification of hacking tools.
  - Assimilation of new knowledge (technologies) and dissemination through training

- *Complex-Coordinated*: Include capabilities for:

  - Coordinated attacks leading to mass disruption.

  - Creation of attack tools.

  - Analyze vulnerabilities and penetrate defenses.

  - Target analysis.

  - Build and maintain strong command and control structure.

  - Unleash simultaneous attacks.

  - High learning capacity to acquire and assimilate latest technology, and diffuse such knowledge through training programs.

  - Utilize indoctrination to enhance all the above capabilities.

In the working paper *Cyberterrorism: Hype and Reality*, Conway[6] has distinguished between the use, misuse, and abuse of the technological capabilities from the perspective of the goal orientation of the user and provided a contrasting set of definitions for users, hackers, hacktivists, crackers, and cyber terrorists (Table 5B-1). Further expanding on the types and goals of attacks, Ballard Hornik, and McKenzie present an attack typology (categories of attack) of the cyber terrorists in their paper *Technological Facilitation of Terrorism: Definitional, Legal and Policy Issues.*[7] In this work, they define and differentiate between information attacks, infrastructure attacks, technological facilitation, and fund raising as the most prominent categories in cyber terrorism (Table 5B-2).

However, scholars and researchers have differed in their focus and detail in the way they have attempted to identify and isolate the varied usage of the Internet for cyber terrorist purposes. Conway (2005) in another work, *Terrorist Use of the Internet and Fighting Back*,[8] compares four prominent works to present the whole spectrum of possible use of the Internet for terrorist purposes (Table 5B-3). In the article, *The Networking of Terror in the Information Age*,[9] Zanini and Edwards have critically analyzed the relative merits and demerits of

Action	Definition	Source	Example
Use	Using the Internet to facilitate the expression of ideas and communication(s)	Internet users	Emails, mailing lists, newsgroups, websites
Misuse	Using the Internet to disrupt or compromise Web sites or infrastructure	Hackers, Hacktivists	Denial-of-Service (DoS) attacks
Offensive use	Using the Internet to cause damage or engage in theft	Crackers	Stealing data (e.g., credit card details)
Cyber terrorism	An attack carried out by terrorists via the Internet that results in violence against persons or severe economic damage	Terrorists	A terrorist group using the Internet to carry out a major assault on the New York Stock Exchange

Table 5B-1 **Typology of Cyber Activism and Cyber Attacks**

Source: Conway, M. (www.ir.dcu.ie/501/02/cybert_hype_reality_2007.doc)

Category	Definition and Explanation
Information attacks	Cyber terrorist attacks focused on altering or destroying the content of electronic files, computer systems, or the various materials therein.
Infrastructure attacks	Cyber terrorist attacks designed to disrupt or destroy the actual hardware, operating platform, or programming in a computerized environment.
Technological facilitation	Use of cyber communications to send plans for terrorist attacks, incite attacks, or otherwise facilitate traditional terrorism or cyber terrorism.
Fund raising and promotion	Use of the Internet to raise funds for a violent political cause to advance an organization supportive of violent political action, or to promote an alternative ideology that is violent in orientation.

Table 5B-2   Cyber Incident Typology

Source: Ballard et al., American Behavioral Scientist, *2002*

Authors	Furnell and & Warren (1999)	Cohen (2002)	Thomas (2003)	Weimann (2004a)
Uses	– Propaganda & Publicity – Fundraising – Information Dissemination – Secure Communications	– Planning – Finance – Coordination and Operations – Political Action – Propaganda	– Profiling – Propaganda Anonymous /Covert Communication – Generating "Cyberfear" – Finance – Command & Control – Mobilization & Recruitment – Information Gathering – Mitigation of Risk – Theft/Manipulation of Data – Offensive Use – Misinformation	– Psychological Warfare – Publicity & Propaganda – Data Mining – Fundraising – Recruitment & Mobilization – Networking – Sharing Information – Planning & Coordination

Table 5B-3   Terrorist Use of the Internet

Source: Conway, M., Terrorist 'Use' of the Internet and Fighting Back, *2005*

the cyber enablement of terrorism. They argue that the new (cyber) enablement and the networked world do not offer unblemished advantage to the terrorists. The cyber terrorists, by the utilization of open source and pervasive technologies of the Internet, also expose them to a different set of detection and identification methodologies and capabilities that the institutional authorities are able to master and operationalize (Table 5B-4).

Vulnerability from Cyber Terrorism

In general, *vulnerability* can be defined as the fallibility of a system at one or more suscepti-ble points. However, depending on the field of concern, very many versions of the definition of *vulnerability* exist. Because cyber terrorism is in the interface of attack against the sover-eignty of a nation through or directed at the nation's computer systems, the definition from

5B

IT use	Facilitating	Mitigating
Organizational	• Enables dispersed activities with reasonable secrecy, anonymity • Helps maintain a loose and flexible network • Lessens need for state sponsorship	• Susceptibility to wire and wireless tapping • Digitally stored information can be easily retrievable unless well protected • Cannot by itself energize a network; common ideology and direct contact still essential
Offensive	• Generally lower entry costs • Eradication of national boundaries • Physically safer • Spillover benefits for recruitment and fund-raising	• Current bombing techniques already effective • Significant technical hurdles for disruptive and destructive IO • Unique computer security risks impose recurring costs

Table 5B-4   Benefits and Drawbacks of IT Use for Netwar Terrorists

Source: Zanini et al., Rand Research Publication, Document #MR-1382-OSD

both the military as well as the computer security areas are pertinent here. The U.S. military defines *vulnerability* as "The susceptibility of a nation or military force to any action by any means through which its war potential or combat effectiveness may be reduced or its will to fight diminished,"[10] whereas in computer security, the term *vulnerability* could be defined as "a security exposure in an operating system or other system software or application software component."[11] The vulnerability to cyber terrorism in this chapter refers to the susceptibility of a nation's assets, interests, and (its) subjects' livelihood, from a motivated and/or directed attack, which is vectored though the Internet-worked computing and communication networks of today. Ozeren argues that the vulnerabilities to cyber terrorism stem from technical, legal, cultural, and political reasons and circumstances as explained in the following bullet points:[12]

- **Technological Aspect of Vulnerability:** The increased dependence of a nation and its infrastructure on the information systems is the underlying premise for technical vulnerability to cyber terrorism. The infrastructure sectors today utilize commercially available off-the-shelf software (COTS), as well as popular operating systems in building their information assets and networks. Thus, the native vulnerabilities of these commercial systems also get embedded in the strategic infrastructure systems. In certain infrastructure sectors, communication networks and computing assets mesh with the manufacturing/production processes through Supervisory Control and Data Access (SCADA) type applications and systems (e.g., energy sector). This exposes a direct level cyber terrorism vulnerability to critical infrastructural facilities. In general, the computing and telecommunication networks are now highly connected across the globe; thus, the threats to the systems of a nation are much interconnected. Major General James D. Bryan, U.S. Army, Commander, Joint Task Force—Computer Network Operations, U.S. Strategic Command and Vice Director, Defense Information Systems Agency, in his deposition before the House Armed Services Subcommittee on Terrorism, Unconventional Threats and Capabilities stated, "The battlespace of the cyber war consists of the globally interconnected grid of complex information networks...."[13] As a result, it is now possible that the vulnerability could be compromised from anywhere in the world. On the other hand, this also makes it possible that a breach/compromise to a critical system could now propagate to more interconnected systems, giving rise to the interdependent (and more difficult) nature of vulnerability to cyber terrorism. Such interdependent vulnerability is further exacerbated by the rapid adoption of Web technologies and services (open standards of the Internet technologies) in the infrastructure sector. Knowing that we transact a huge amount of wealth over the interconnected data networks and that a large part of our intellectual capabilities and physical properties are now accessible through interconnected networks, technical vulnerability to cyber terrorism is quite stupendous.

In order to reduce our technological vulnerability toward cyber terrorism, several actions could be taken: taking more than one action generally adds to the relative impregnability of our assets and systems. We may isolate our critical resources from direct access through interconnected networks. This is specifically important for some of our infrastructural and intellectual assets. For example, infrastructure firms may like to use proprietary protocols to effectively isolate control systems of physical infrastructural operations, or isolate intellectual property, especially proprietary processes that could run from systems that are not at all accessible from outside networks. When such isolation is impossible, creating a DMZ (demilitarized zone) between the outer world (untrusted network) and the trusted network through use of proxy servers is helpful. This then creates a first line of defense against cyber terrorists. Even when such defense is in place, it is often recommended to utilize encryption technologies while storing and communicating sensitive information. Although algorithms of popular encryption technologies are common knowledge, intelligent deployment and management of encryption keys effectively lowers the probability of code breakage and/or add time and resource requirement for code breakage and thus increases the probability of detection. Lastly, adding the capabilities of detection generally increases the deterrence aspect of a cyber attack and is helpful in general.

- **Legal and Control Aspect of the Vulnerability**: Vulnerabilities to cyber terrorism also arise in the areas of law, governance, practices, and provisions among the countries in the world. The very first problem arises from the fact that many countries do not have any appropriate laws that can define and fix responsibilities for behaviors that amount to cyber terrorism. Once this is the case, the authorities of these countries lack legal authorities to pursue or punish cyber terrorists. In still some other countries, either legal provisions are minimal or resources are meagerly allocated, making it difficult to combat such problems. Because the essence of combating cyber terrorism lies in the countries' technological capabilities to detect such machinations, even when some legal provisions may exist, many economically and technologically disadvantaged nations find it very difficult to combat the vulnerabilities in their systems to cyber terrorism. Yet in another level, a second-degree legal vulnerability to cyber terrorism arises from the disparity of the legal provisions across the nations. "While the international legal system contains some rules for allocation of prescriptive jurisdiction, these rules are unclear and incomplete."[14] Absence of a common set of laws and legal provisions makes it very hard to address the vulnerability of cyber terrorism in a global/cross-national level. Because vulnerability to cyber terrorism can be exploited through interconnected networks/economies of today's world, the need to realize a common set of standard laws and prosecution provisions is truly critical. Somewhat intuitively though, countries that are more industrialized and economically developed

5B

are also the ones who are better equipped with legal provisions, albeit they remain more vulnerable to cyber terrorism in general.[15]

As apparent, addressing legal vulnerability to cyber terrorism is not only a national but an international issue. First, we need legal provisions that can clearly define a cyber attack as it involves computing and communicating assets as the subjects, conduits, and/or objects of such attacks, and we need such provisions in every nation that effectively joins the Internet-worked map of this world. Second, we need parity of these legal provisions to make mis-interpretation of these laws improbable/unlikely. Third, we need legal provisions of cyber terrorism to be exercised through the Interpol as we have similar abilities for other criminal activities. Finally, awareness and training programs across law enforcement agencies all over the world must also include the above understandings such that proper appreciation of the vulnerabilities to cyber terrorism can be ensured across the globe.

- **Cultural Aspects of Vulnerability**: In order to achieve an adequate level of protection against cyber terrorism, it is imperative that both the government as well as the private sector work toward minimizing the technical and other vulnerabilities in today's interconnected systems. While the elected governments tend to look at cyber security as an economic (security) product, and are influenced by the general apprehension of the citizens, the same may not be true for the private sector. Where profit motive and stakeholder wealth maximization are the primary goals, it is as such difficult for the private sector to justify budget allocation for remediation of vulnerability to cyber terrorism. That we have not seen any large-scale incident of cyber terrorism till now and that the corporate responsibilities in this regard are not clearly understood at the decision makers' end are also major debilitating factors. A section of the business leaders argue that the real possibilities of large-scale cyber terrorism are extremely unlikely, and they do not see economic justification for allocation of funds and resources toward cyber terrorism vulnerability management programs.

Recognizing that truly global mindsets and pervasive alliances are required to combat the multifaceted vulnerabilities of cyber terrorism that threatens the networked world of today, a new global initiative to combat cyber terrorism, the International Multilateral Partnership Against Cyber Terrorism (IMPACT), was announced in May 2008. The organization is headquartered in Cyberjaya, Malaysia, and aims to create an international platform that could fight cyber terrorism by bringing together private companies, governments, and academics from around the world. IMPACT believes that "An isolated cyber attack can have global consequences, and therefore, governments and businesses alike have an interest to work together to ensure protection against cyber terrorism. IMPACT recognizes that private companies have a particularly critical role in fighting cyber terrorism because professionals are often at the forefront of current information technology (IT) research and development. Most importantly, the private sector could benefit from increased network security and deeper insight into government priorities, trends, and needs...."[16]

- **Political Aspects of Vulnerability**: As we have already discussed, "terrorism" stems from political reasons, aspirations, and circumstances. Thus, a system's vulnerability to cyber terrorism bears implications of political agenda of the perpetrators against the owners of the system. A country's vulnerability to cyber terrorism depends on the country's relative position in the world's power game, its multilateral relationships, and overall actions and influences on other economies and sociopolitical groups. The influence and prominence that the United States enjoys globally also become the reason why groups of population in lands and countries far distant could be affected (in a real or perceived sense) by the U.S. decisions in the international social, political, and economic arenas. Because terrorists in the eye of country-X could be the religious fighters in the eye of the citizens of country-Y, the political aspect of vulnerability to cyber terrorism is itself a tricky issue to consider.

Cyber Terrorism and U.S. National Policy

The United States is one of the forerunners in proactive planning for securing cyber space as well as creating a strategic comprehensive cyber vulnerability management program that cuts across the public and private sectors. The Commission on Critical Infrastructure Protection (PCCIP) in 1996 was charged to assess the vulnerabilities of the infrastructure sector viz. energy (electrical power, and oil and gas distribution and storage), civic services (water supply and transportation) telecommunications, banking and finance, and the government services. Through a Presidential Directive, the general policymaking and overseeing bodies in the federal government for counterterrorism measures were established, which included responsibilities to ensure protection, and response capabilities of the computer-based systems that were fast becoming integrated in the business processes of our economy. The above efforts culminated in the publication of *The National Strategy to Secure Cyberspace* by the federal government, which is described as "an implementing component of the *National Strategy for Homeland Security* and is complemented by a *National Strategy for the Physical Protection of Critical Infrastructures and Key Assets....*"[17]

The National Strategy to Secure Cyber Space delineates three strategic objectives that should guide our priorities:[18]

1. *Preventing cyber attacks against critical infrastructures,*
2. *Reducing vulnerability to cyber attacks*, and
3. *Minimizing both damage and recovery time from cyber attacks when such eventualities are realized.*

Under those strategic objectives, this document provides five (5) national cyberspace security priorities, which, in turn, include detailed action points for each of these priorities. In what follows, we provide a brief précis of these action points in the priorities:

1. *A National Cyberspace Security Response System*
   a. Creation of a single point of contact between government and industry
   b. Installation of intelligence network and warning systems
   c. Raise cyber awareness, cooperation in information dissemination, and ensure better preparedness among private and public sectors

2. *A National Cyberspace Security Threat and Vulnerability Reduction Program*
   a. Improve information sharing and investigative coordination within the enforcement communities, and develop a National Threat Assessment Program
   b. Enhance security of Distributed Control Systems/Supervisory Control and Data Acquisition Systems in infrastructure sector

5B

    c. Facilitate communication between research communities to a ensure steady stream of emerging security technologies

3. *A National Cyberspace Security Awareness and Training Program*

    a. Evaluation of the security of large enterprise networks that may impact the security of the nation's critical infrastructures

    b. Implement training programs for cyber security professionals in the United States, and facilitate graduate, postdoctoral, and faculty development programs

    c. Build foundations for the development of security certification programs

4. *Securing Governments' Cyberspace*

    a. Install systems that can continuously check for unauthorized connections/access to federal networks

    b. Provide encouragement and support for IT security programs in state and local government departments and agencies

5. *National Security and International Cyberspace Security Cooperation*

    a. Improve ability to quickly attribute sources of attacks and take effective response

    b. Develop capabilities to prevent cyber attacks reaching infrastructures systems

    c. Encourage APEC, EU, and OAS to form a committee for cyber security

    d. Ensure that North America is a "Safe Cyber Zone" by identifying and securing critical common networks in United States, Canada, and Mexico

While actions stipulated in *The National Strategy to Secure Cyber Space* are implemented on a continued basis, newer system vulnerabilities and cyber exploits emerge in regular intervals as well. One major concern in this area has been the criminalization of cyber attacks, further complicated by the distributed nature of the attacks (DDoS) on the information networks. The CRS report for Congress, "Botnets, Cybercrime, and Cyberterrorism: Vulnerabilities and Policy Issues for Congress," which is one of the latest documents that addresses the cyber terrorism issues in the global policy perspective, provides an update of the states of affairs in cyber crime and cyber terrorism in the following words: "Cybercrime is becoming more organized and established as a transnational business. High technology online skills are now available for rent to a variety of customers, possibly including nation states, or individuals and groups that could secretly represent terrorist groups.... Cybercriminals have reportedly made alliances with drug traffickers in Afghanistan, the Middle East, and elsewhere where profitable illegal activities are used to support terrorist groups. In addition, designs for cybercrime botnets are becoming more sophisticated, and future botnet architectures may be more resistant to computer security countermeasures...."[19]

Following several cyber security incidents in 2006–07, the Center for Strategic and Information Studies (CSIS) Commission on cyber security for the 44th presidency was formed in late 2007.[20] The commission was charged to assess the existing plans and strategies for combating cyber terrorism, and advise improvement avenues to the administration. The commission released its findings including its recommendations in December 2008. This report delineates the very latest state of affairs in the security measures against cyber terrorism. We will conclude this section with an abridged synopsis of the findings and the recommendations of the commission (Table 5B-5):

Findings	Recommendations
1. Cyber security is now a major national security problem for the United States	1. Create a comprehensive national security strategy for cyber space • Diplomatic, Intelligence , Military and Economic (DIME), including law enforcement
2. Decisions and actions must respect privacy and civil liberties	2. Lead from the White House • Create a new office for cyber space in the executive office of the President
3. Only a comprehensive National Security strategy that embraces both the domestic and international aspects of cyber security will make the United States more secure	3. Reinvent the public-private partnership • Emphasis on building trust, and focus on operational activities
	4. Regulate cyber space • Voluntary action is not enough
	5. Authenticate digital identities • Privacy and civil liberties must be protected at the core
	6. Modernize authorities • US laws need to be rewritten in view of the interconnected world of today
	7. Use acquisition policies to improve security • Create guidelines for secure products and procure only secure products and services
	8. Build capabilities • Provide federal support for focused research, education, training, development in cyber security
	9. Do not start over • Begin with the advances already made by CNCI (Comprehensive National Security Initiative)

Table 5B-5 **Summary Findings and Recommendations of the CSIS Commission, 2008**

Source: http://www.csis.org/media/csis/pubs/081208_securingcyberspace_44.pdf

Reality Checks and Concluding Remarks

Although information systems are attacked regularly (more recently for financial gains or other criminal motives) or the fact that highly sensitized hypothetical scenarios of cyber terrorism often feature in popular media, there is no recorded event of cyber terrorism attack on critical infrastructure of United States as yet. There are some who think that cyber terrorism is quite possible and is within the capabilities of some of the terrorist groups in this world, while others argue that cyber terrorism is not possible in any large scale. As of today, most experts believe that the terrorists are neither capable nor contemplating to unleash large-scale cyber attacks of major proportion on any national infrastructure. For instance, Jim Lewis, in his 2002 report for the Center for Strategic and International Studies *Assessing the Risks of Cyberterrorism, Cyber War, and Other Cyber Threats*, opines that the nation's infrastructures are more robust than what the early analysts assumed them to be. He also points out to the fact that the infrastructure sector regularly deals with system failures of various natures as well as from myriad sources (the systems are as such capable to absorb partial failure with redundancy and other design features) such that a cyber attack would be unlikely to inflict a very high level of damage to our infrastructure.

In reality, only a fraction of a percent of the hackers who employ exploits over the Internet or other interconnected networks are actually sophisticated enough to launch any serious cyber attacks. Apart from this, the requirement of high technical capabilities, strong motivation, brazen recalcitrance, low fear of apprehension and complete apathy to physical/social consequences are simultaneously required in a perpetrator before a successful cyber terrorist activity could take place. Even when all of these are present and there is availability of funds and other resources, it would still be quite difficult to access/destroy very sensitive information retained by the FBI, CIA, or the Pentagon; or control the physical assets like the nuclear reactors because of what is known as the *air-gapping* policy, which effectively isolates these critical resources from all interconnected networks, including the Internet.

Can our air traffic or the interconnected train systems, or our gas or power line and other connected systems be jeopardized by cyber terrorists, should they desire to do so? In order to launch a successful large-scale attack on these systems, cyber terrorists would require added knowledge and sophistication of these engineering systems on top of all the other cyber skills that we had discussed in the last paragraph, making such possibilities even more unlikely. However, if cyber terrorists could recruit disgruntled insiders or ex-hires to fill the skill and knowledge gap, theoretically, such possibilities of exploit could exist. In 2002, the Australian police investigated an insider's[21] attempt to use the Internet to release a huge amount of raw sewage in the coastal waters. Although this created a health/ecological scare for some time, even this would not possibly qualify as a disaster because such leakages may not remain undetected for a long time! As we have already argued, the critical infrastructure systems are purposely designed and built with high redundancies and localization schemes, and the personnel are trained and prepared to combat disasters from natural (e.g., hurricane) or system failures (e.g., cascading energy failure). It is not easily comprehensible how a new threat vectored through the Internet could destabilize the system and personnel preparedness so substantially as to create widespread devastation in the effectual damages. The joint war game simulation exercise "Digital Pearl Harbor" of 2002 also demonstrated that only sporadic damages on the Internet were realistically possible and that too when hundreds of millions of dollars and years of preparation time are allowed to a very large group of the sophisticated technologists.

There is another level of difficulty in our assessment and address of the threat of cyber terrorism; the reality and science fiction often face each other. Bendrath points out, "Sometimes it is hard to tell what is science and what is fiction.... Even renowned cyber-war theoreticians like John Arquilla have not hesitated to publish thrilling cyber-terror scenarios for the general audience. But these works are not only made for entertainment. They produce certain visions of the future and of the threats and risks looming there."[22]

Although we have argued that cyber terrorism attacks are highly improbable in recent times, there is an important aspect of the equation that we must appreciate in the right perspective and with enough seriousness. Such eventualities of cyber terrorism could generate fear psychosis in the minds of the citizens. Research in social sciences suggests when outcomes of a disaster or attack on public life and property are vivid, gory, or evoke memory that is strong in terms of effect, we are prone to assign higher than actual probability for a realization of the event.[23] For example, a terrorist attack leading to large-scale loss of life and property (like that of 9/11) causes us to ascribe a higher probability of such acts of terrorism, higher than what a rational analysis of the situation/scenario in hand could justify. Social researchers call this phenomenon *probability neglect*. Doomsday prognostics, media hype, science fictions, etc. paint these possible events in a vivid fashion, which, in turn, can bolster probability neglect. Such probability neglect, on a mass scale, can have far-reaching effect. For example, among others, this could give rise to a general need for higher protection to obviate such events. Such needs, in turn, translate to demand for stricter regulation and/or higher government/corporate spending to mitigate such risks. Finally, through elected representatives, popular probability neglect may eventually cause higher than optimal investment/regulation in the mitigation of risks of cyber terrorism. Thus, although in reality we may face only a miniscule threat from cyber terrorism, it is appropriate that we assess the impact of cyber terrorism not only from the damage of our assets and systems, but also from the larger socioeconomic impacts.

References

Ballard, J. D., Hornik, J. G., and McKenzie, D. (2002). "Technological Facilitation of Terrorism: Definitional, Legal and Policy Issues." *American Behavioral Scientist*, 45 (6), 989–1016.

Bandyopadhyay, T., and Mattord, H. R. 2008. *Defending Cyber Terrorism—A Game Theoretic Approach.* Proceedings of the American Conference on Information Systems, Toronto, Canada.

Becker, G. S., and Rubinstein, Y. 2004. *Fear and the Response to Terrorism: An Economic Analysis.* www.ilr.cornell.edu/international/events/upload/BeckerrubinsteinPaper.pdf

Bendrath, R. 2003. "The American Cyber-Angst and the Real World: Any Link?" in Robert Latham (Ed.), *Bombs and Bandwidth: The Emerging Relationship between Information Technology and Security.* New York: New Press, 49.

Cohen, F. 2002. "Terrorism and Cyberspace." *Network Security*, Vol. 5.

Conway, M. 2003. *Cybercortical Warfare, the Case of hizbollah.org.* Paper prepared for presentation at the European Consortium for Political Research (ECPR) Joint Sessions of Workshops, Edinburgh, UK, 28 March–2 April, 2003. http://www2.scedu.unibo.it/roversi/SocioNet/Conway.pdf

Conway, M. 2005. *Terrorist Use of the Internet and Fighting Back.* Paper prepared for presentation at the conference *Cybersafety: Safety and Security in a Networked World: Balancing Cyber-Rights and Responsibilities.* Oxford Internet Institute (OII), Oxford University, UK, 8–10 September 2005.

Conway, M. 2007. *Cyberterrorism: Hype and Reality.* Working paper, Dublin City University. www.ir.dcu.ie/501/02/cybert_hype_reality_2007.doc

Definition of *Vulnerability. PC Magazine.* http://www.pcmag.com/encyclopedia_term/0,2542,t=vulnerability&i=54160,00.asp#

Deutch, J. 1996. Statement before the US Senate Governmental Affairs Committee (Permanent Subcommittee on Investigations), June 25. http://www.nswc.navy.mil/ISSEC/Docs/Ref/InTheNews/fullciatext.html

Denning, D. *Cyberterrorism*. August 24, 2000. Prepublication version. http://www.cs.georgetown.edu/~denning/infosec/cyberterror-GD.doc

Denning, D. 2001. "Activism, Hactivism, and Cyberterrorism: The Internet as a Tool for Influencing Foreign Policy," in John Arquilla and David Ronfeldt, eds., *Networks and Netwars*, Rand Publications, USA (document # MR-1382-OSD).

Denning, D. 2001. *Is Cyber War Next?* Social Science Research Council. http://www.ssrc.org/sept11/essays/denning.htm

Department of Defense. *Dictionary of Military and Associated Terms*. http://jdeis.cornerstoneindustry.com/jdeis/dictionary/qsDictionaryPortlet.jsp?group=dod

Department of Homeland Security. *Document Overview of the National Strategy to Secure Cyberspace*. http://www.dhs.gov/xprevprot/programs/editorial_0329.shtm

Frey, B. S., Leuchinger, S., and Stutger, A. 2007. "Calculating Tragedy: Assessing The Costs of Terrorism." *Journal of Economic Surveys*, 21(1)

Lenain P., Bonturi M., and Koen V. 2002. *The Economic Consequences of Terrorism*. OECD Working Paper No. 334. JT 00129726

Nelson, B., Choi, R., Iacobuccci, M., Mitchell, M., and Gagnon, G. Bill. *Cyberterror, Prospects and Implications*. 1999 Whitepaper. Center for the Study of Irregular Warfare, Monterey, CA. http://www.dtic.mil/cgi-bin/GetTRDoc?AD=ADA393147&Location=U2&doc=GetTRDoc.pdf

Ozeren, S. 2005. *Global Response to Cyberterrorism and Cybercrime: A Matrix for International Cooperation and Vulnerability assessment*. Published dissertation for the degree of Doctor of Philosophy, University of North Texas,. http://digital.library.unt.edu/permalink/meta-dc-4847:1

Pollitt, M., M. 1997. *A Cyberterrorism: Fact or Fancy?* Proceedings of the 20th National Information Systems Security Conference, pp. 285–289.

Securing Cyberspace for the 44th Presidency: A Report of the CSIS Commission on Cybersecurity for the 44th Presidency. Center for Strategic and International Studies (CSIS), Washington, DC December 2008 http://www.csis.org/media/csis/pubs/081208_securingcyberspace_44.pdf

Soo Hoo, K., Goodman, S., and Greenberg L. 1997. "Information Technology and Terrorism Threat." *Survival* 39(3).

Sunstein, C. R. 2003. "Terrorism and Probability Neglect." *Journal of Risk and Uncertainty* 26(2-3), 121–136.

The National Strategy to Secure Cyberspace. February 2003 http://www.dhs.gov/xlibrary/assets/National_Cyberspace_Strategy.pdf

Trachtman, J., P. *Global Cyberterrorism, Jurisdiction, and International Organization*. 2004. SSRN Working paper. http://ssrn.com/abstract=566361 or DOI: 10.2139/ssrn.566361

Viscusi, W. K., and Zeckhauser, R. J. 2003. "Sacrificing Civil Liberties to Reduce Terrorism Risks." *Journal of Risk and Uncertainty* 26(2-3), 99–120.

5B

Wilson, C. 2007. *Botnets, Cybercrime, and Cyberterrorism: Vulnerabilities and Policy Issues for Congress*. Congressional Research Service (CRS) report (Order Code RL32114) http://www.fas.org/sgp/crs/terror/RL32114.pdf

Zanini, M., and Edwards, S. J. A."The Networking of Terror in the Information Age," in John Arquilla and David Ronfeldt, eds., *Networks and Netwars*, Rand Publications, USA (document # MR-1382-OSD).

Zeichner Risk Assessment. *Newsletter*. Vol. 1, No. 30, May 30, 2008 http://www.zra.com/docs/ZRA_Newsletters/ZRA_053008.pdf

http://www.fema.gov/pdf/onp/toolkit_app_d.pdf

http://www.nswc.navy.mil/ISSEC/Docs/Ref/InTheNews/fullciatext.html

http://www.dod.mil/dodgc/olc/docs/test03-07-24Bryan.doc

Endnotes

1. C. R. Sunstein, "Terrorism and Probability Neglect," *Journal of Risk and Uncertainty* 26, no. 2-3 (2003), 121–136

2. The Bureau of Transportation Statistics reports over 41,000 motor vehicle fatalities in USA alone in 2006: (http://www.bts.gov/publications/national_transportation_statistics/html/table_02_18.html

3. P. Lenain, M. Bonturi, and V. Koen, *The Economic Consequences of Terrorism*. OECD Working Paper No. 334. JT 00129726.

4. D. Denning, "Activism, Hacktivism, and Cyberterrorism: The Internet as a Tool for Influencing Foreign Policy," in John Arquilla and David Ronfeldt, eds., *Networks and Netwars*, Rand Publications, 2001 (document #MR-1382-OSD).

5. M. Pollitt, *A Cyberterrorism: Fact or Fancy?* Proceedings of the 20th National Information Systems Security Conference, pp. 285–289.

6. M. Conway, *Cyberterrorism: Hype and Reality*. Working paper, Dublin City University. www.ir.dcu.ie/501/02/cybert_hype_reality_2007.doc

7. J. D. Ballard, J. G. Hornik, and D. McKenzie, "Technological Facilitation of Terrorism: Definitional, Legal and Policy Issues," *American Behavioral Scientist*, 45, no. 6 (2002), 989–1016.

8. M. Conway, *Terrorist 'Use' of the Internet and Fighting Back*. Paper prepared for presentation at the conference *Cybersafety: Safety and Security in a Networked World: Balancing Cyber-Rights and Responsibilities,* Oxford Internet Institute (OII), Oxford University, UK, 8–10 September 2005.

9. M. Zanini and S. J. A. Edwards, "The Networking of Terror in the Information Age," in John Arquilla and David Ronfeldt, eds., *Networks and Netwars*, Rand Publications, USA (document # MR-1382-OSD).

10. Department of Defense, *Dictionary of Military and Associated Terms*. http://jdeis.cornerstoneindustry.com/jdeis/dictionary/qsDictionaryPortlet.jsp?group=dod

11. *PC   Magazine.*   http://www.pcmag.com/encyclopedia_term/0,2542,t=vulnerability&i= 54160,00.asp#

12. S. Ozeren, *Global Response to Cyberterrorism and Cybercrime: A Matrix for International Cooperation and Vulnerability Assessment.* Published dissertation for the degree of Doctor of Philosophy, University of North Texas, 2005. http://digital.library.unt.edu/ permalink/meta-dc-4847:1.

13. Testimony of Major General James D. Bryan, U.S. Army, before the House Armed Services Subcommittee on Terrorism, Unconventional Threats and Capabilities, Washington, D.C., July 24, 2003.

14. J. P. Trachtman, *Global Response to Cyberterrorism and Cybercrime: A Matrix for International Cooperation and Vulnerability assessment.* Published dissertation for the degree of Doctor of Philosophy, University of North Texas, 2004. http://digital.library .unt.edu/permalink/meta-dc-4847:1.

15. Conway, *Terrorist Use of the Internet and Fighting Back.*

16. Zeichner Risk Assessment, *Newsletter*, 1, no. 30 (May 30, 2008). http://www.zra.com /docs/ZRA_Newsletters/ZRA_053008.pdf

17. Department of Homeland Security, *Document Overview of the National Strategy to Secure Cyberspace.* http://www.dhs.gov/xprevprot/programs/editorial_0329.shtm

18. Department of Homeland Security, *Document Overview of the National Strategy to Secure Cyberspace.* http://www.dhs.gov/xlibrary/assets/National_Cyberspace_Strategy.pdf

19. CRS report for Congress, "Botnets, Cybercrime, and Cyberterrorism: Vulnerabilities and Policy Issues for Congress," November 2007, Order Code RL-32114.

20. *Securing Cyberspace for the 44th Presidency: A Report of the CSIS Commission on cybersecurity for the 44th Presidency*, Center for Strategic and International Studies (CSIS), Washington, DC. December 2008. http://www.csis.org/media/csis/pubs /081208_securingcyberspace_44.pdf

21. The man had earlier worked for the company that designed the sewage treatment plant.

22. R. Bendrath, "The American Cyber-Angst and the Real World: Any Link?" in Robert Latham (Ed.), *Bombs and Bandwidth: The Emerging Relationship between Information Technology and Security*, New York: New Press (2003), 49.

23. Sunstein, "Terrorism and Probability Neglect."

Advanced Topologies, Inc.

Michael Whitman and Herbert Mattord

An Introduction to Information Security

Matthias Paul looked up from his monitor to glance at the clock hanging on the wall. It was 4:15 AM and he had almost four hours to go before his shift was over. From the start of his shift Matthias had been processing new account setup requests for one of the companies serviced by his employer, Advanced Topologies, Inc. Every hour he took a short break to check the logs from the client's network.

Matthias was not exactly sure he knew what he was looking for, but he thought it was a good idea to stay aware of what was happening on the client's network. Matthias had only been on the job at ATI for a few weeks and did not consider himself a critical member of the watch team for this client. Mostly he did semi-clerical tasks, like setting up new users and verifying the deactivation of the client's former employees.

"Matt."

Matthias looked up to see his supervisor, Alfonso Agostino.

"Yes, Al, what's up?"

Al looked at Matthias over his glasses and said, "I just got the word that your training plan was approved by Human Resources. You start your classes next week. Your first class will be three days on the basics of information security at the corporate training center."

"Great!" said Matthias. "But why do I need information security training? Wasn't I hired to be a network administrator?"

Al responded, "Sure, but how can you do your job as a netadmin if you don't know the company security policies and practices? The class spends two days covering basic concepts of security, and one day reviewing our company polices. Everyone in an IT-related position takes this class. You'll get more advanced networking training over the next few months—eventually we plan to send you out for some advanced network security training, to fill in any gaps in your college classes on these subjects."

Matthias nodded. "OK. I'll be there."

Matthias was back on the job Friday night at midnight. He had been out of the data center during his three days at the training center. He was a little sleepy, since he had attended the training during the day shift and now he was back for third shift.

Al walked up and said, "Hi Matt, how was the class?"

Matthias replied, "Pretty good, I guess. I really liked the stuff about the ways that systems get attacked, but I thought the threat stuff was kind of boring."

Al said, "I suppose it can seem that way, but you have to try to figure out how the information about threats can affect our work and how we do our jobs."

Questions

1. Which threat would be most likely to impact Matthias and Al in their jobs as network administrators at ATI?

2. List at least two threats you did not mention that might be encountered by a network administrator.

3. For each of the three threats you listed, list and describe two attacks that could come from these threats.

An Introduction to Networking

Eliana was visiting her alma mater, recruiting network administrators for her company, Advanced Topologies, Inc. The career services group at the school had contacted the Human Resources group at ATI about a month ago, and invited them to participate in this information technology job fair. Now Eliana stood in front of the ATI company information board, ready to screen applicants.

She greeted the first student. "Hello, I'm Eliana. I'm the supervisor of network operations at ATI. Are you interested in our company?"

The student said, "Yes, what kinds of jobs do you have?"

Eliana replied, "We're looking for graduates who are interested in network operations and, eventually, network design."

"Oh, too bad," said the young woman. "Database management and design is my area of interest."

Eliana agreed to take her résumé to the HR department, though she didn't think ATI was hiring in that area.

The next student who approached held out his hand for a business card. "Are you interested?" she asked.

"Sure," he replied. "What are you willing to pay?"

Eliana hid her surprise. Maybe things were different in college recruiting than they used to be. She said, "That depends; how much experience do you have with computer networks?"

Eliana waited for the student's reply.

He said, "Well, I've had some coursework in networking, and I've used networks a lot in several classes, including one on network defense. I wouldn't call myself a network expert, but I'm well-grounded in the theory and am willing to learn."

Eliana smiled back at the student's infectious grin and said, "Well, if you have the basic skills we need, we would make a competitive offer, and we are willing to train. It sounds like you might fit, so let me have a copy of your résumé."

Questions

1. Do you think this student is a good choice for ATI in today's employment market?

2. How else could the student have explained his networking background to Eliana?

3. Did the student come across too strongly, bringing up salary from the beginning?

Security Policies, Standards, and Planning

Matthias was ready to apply the firewall scripts to protect the servers belonging to ATI's clients. The Linen Planet had hired ATI to design, configure, and operate the network and defenses used to implement the electronic commerce startup's business plan. Matthias had a text file with more than 300 scripted instructions that had to be added to the firewall.

Since this change would affect the client's entire network, it was being tested in tonight's third-shift change-window, a time-slot during which network technicians could interrupt the normal operation of the network for a short time. Even though Matthias had only recently become involved in this project, it had been under development for several weeks, and the activities planned for tonight had been approved by the change control committees at Linen Planet and at ATI.

The plan was for Matthias to update the firewall command interface and be ready to commit the new rules at 2:30 AM. He had already made the connection and edited the file, and he was waiting to commit the new rules so the quality assurance testing team could spend an hour furiously testing the new configuration. At the first sign of a test failure, they would tell Matthias to back out the changes and reset the firewall to its original configuration.

He had a few minutes to wait, and Al sat down next to him to monitor the event.

Matthias said, "Hi, Al. I have a question."

Al looked over his arm at the monitor to review Matthias's work. Seeing it was all in order and that the commit time was still a few minutes away, he said, "OK. Shoot."

Matthias pointed at the work order with the attached script of complex firewall rules and said, "Who writes these rules, and how do they know what the rules should do?"

Al looked at him and said, "One word—policy."

"Huh," said Matthias. "What does that mean?"

"Well," said Al, "every company has a set of policies that lets everyone know what they can and can't do with the company network. *Linen Planet* has an enterprise policy and a network usage policy that specify how they manage their network. Also, they have certain technical control systems in place, like intrusion detection systems that need to operate on their network. Our engineers take all of these factors into account and write rules that they hope will make it all work."

"Oh," said Matthias. "Well, it's time to commit these rules."

He pressed the Enter button on his keyboard.

Matthias and Al watched the monitor for a few more minutes. The firewall at *Linen Planet* seemed to be running just fine.

Al stood up and went on to his next task, and Matthias also moved on to his next task. After an hour, he picked up the phone and called the number for the QA team.

"Hello, QA Test Team, Debbie speaking."

"Hi, Debbie," said Matthias. "What's the word on the Linen Planet firewall project?"

"Oh, we just finished," said Debbie. "We're good to go. The new rules can stay in place."

Matthias said, "OK. We won't roll back. Thanks for the info."

Debbie replied, "OK. I'll put a note on the test log. Thanks for your help."

They both hung up the phone. As Al walked across the room, Matthias called out to him, "Is it always this easy?"

Al shook his head. "Not hardly, you must be having beginner's luck."

Questions

1. What are some of the things that might have gone wrong in the test?
2. If the test had failed, what do you think the rollback plan would have entailed?

Finding Network Vulnerabilities

The elevator chimed as it opened and Virginia Burnett, who worked at the ATI reception area on the 14th floor, straightened a little in her chair. A tall dark-haired man dressed in coveralls and carrying a large toolbox walked off the elevator and then around Virginia's desk with a confident stride.

"Can I help you?" asked Virginia, smiling.

He walked a few more steps until he was almost past her desk.

Virginia raised her voice a little. "Stop! What do you want?"

He stopped. "Yes. Hi. My name is Greg Reiner; I'm a contractor working for building maintenance. Someone reported a water leak in the break room."

"Can I see your photo ID and maintenance work order, please?" asked Virginia.

The man turned toward her and sank his hand into his front pocket. It came out empty. Then he looked at the clipboard he was carrying. "Well, it looks like I left them in the van."

He smiled and said, "Surely you can see that I'm no thief, though."

Virginia said tightly, "I don't know anything about a leak, and in any case, ATI has very strict policies about who can come and go in our offices. I really need your credentials before I can allow you through. I'll be right here when you get back."

The man looked exasperated. "Well, I would hate for your attitude about my badge to cause property damage—that leak isn't going to stop itself, so I'm sure you can make an exception." He started to walk toward the office area.

Virginia got the man's attention by shouting, "Stop!" When he turned around, she said, "Sir, unless you leave this floor immediately, I will call security. Please get your badge and work order, and then you can do your job. I'm just doing mine."

He said, "Obviously, this is getting us nowhere." He turned on his heel and left.

Questions

1. Without knowing the ATI policy on visitors, do you think Virginia handled this situation correctly?

2. What do you think she should do now?

Firewall Planning and Design

Matthias was grinning when he entered the conference room. Earlier in the week he had been given his first design assignment. A new client had hired ATI to build a network for them, and as part of his training, Matthias was going to work with the design team to plan the new client's network. This meeting was the kickoff for the project.

Matthias was eager to meet with the experienced network engineers from ATI. He had already begun to consider the options for this new client. Would they need to use a proxy server? Would they have to provide a reverse proxy? Would the firewall need to use a state table?

Austin Tuck, a network engineer and the project manager, came into the meeting room next. He didn't greet Matthias, and sat at the head of the table and started collating handouts for the meeting. The rest of the attendees came as a group and all of them sat down. It was obvious they all knew each other quite well.

Austin called them to order and began, "Hi everyone. Let me introduce our trainee. This is Matthias Paul. He is a third-shift network admin who is training for network security design. He'll be joining us for the project, which is why we'll always meet at 8:30 in the morning—he meets with us after his regular shift."

Austin continued, "Let's handle the rest of the introductions first."

The woman to Austin's left said, "Hi Matthias, my name is Keesha Williams. I'm the security engineer for this project. I work for Andy Ying, the manager of the security consulting group."

The man to her left said, "Hello. I'm Jeff Noak, security architect."

The next person to the left said, "My name is Kaz, and I'm the senior network architect."

Andy said, "OK. That's it for introductions. Here's the initial design packet and the customer specs. I think this is a 'number 3' with a volume rating of 4. Please check out my specs and let me know what you think. I have it set for first reading at change control this Thursday."

Andy stood up and said, "Thanks everyone."

Everyone but Andy and Matthias left the room.

Matthias asked, "Andy, what happened? We spent more time on introductions than on the project work. Did I miss something?"

Andy said, "Nope. That's just the way it works. In fact, the project kick-off didn't require a face-to-face meeting; we probably could have done this one by email. There are only so many ways you can set up a network, and when you have set up and secured a hundred or so like we have in the past two years, it goes pretty quick."

Matthias nodded. Then he said, "But I was hoping to learn something from this, and that meeting didn't really give me anything except a few new names and faces and a packet of papers."

Andy said, "That should be a start. Every one of the people you met today really knows their stuff and will be ready to help you understand the proposed design."

Questions

1. Make a list of the meeting attendees and describe what role you think each would play in a more elaborate network design project.

2. For each of the meeting attendees, list one or two questions that Matthias could ask about the proposed system design.

Packet Filtering

Kiara Spring was bored. She was a smart seventh grader who made excellent grades and enjoyed a variety of after-school activities. Since her parents worked late quite often and her older brothers were usually out, she spent a lot of time on her own, in front of her computer.

Kiara had made a discovery at school that day. When she was in the guidance office to pick up her course-planning packet for next year's classes, she saw a Post-it note on the secretary's desk. She had a pretty good memory, and after she left the office, she made a note of the Web address, the username, and the password that were written on the sticky note.

Kiara just wanted to see if she could connect to the school system and see her own records—she had no desire to change anything, since she had good grades, but getting into the system seemed like a fun and challenging thing to do. She had watched the guidance office secretary use this program on several occasions. The same screen opened up for her now. She typed in the username and password she had written down.

Instead of a screen allowing her to pick out a student record to view, a window opened that said "OFF NETWORK ACCESS ATTEMPTED—PLEASE USE DISTRICT APPROVED VPN FOR CONNECTION." About five seconds later, the browser program on her computer was automatically redirected to the school district's home page.

Kiara's attempt to hack the school district was over before it had really started.

A few days after her attempt to connect to the school system, Kiara was back in the guidance office. She noticed the secretary was not her usual happy self. The sticky note with all the connection information was gone. Trying to be her normal, friendly self, Kiara asked the secretary, "Why so glum, Ms. Simpson?"

Ms. Simpson answered, "It seems somebody tried to access the school district mainframe from the Internet and they used my username. I got in trouble for failure to properly secure my log-in credentials and had to go take a special security awareness class yesterday. My manager is really upset with me, and I'm worried about keeping my job."

Kiara said, "I'm sorry, Ms. Simpson. Do they know who did it?"

Ms. Simpson said, "They didn't really tell me, except they said something about firewalls and audit logs and some kind of investigation."

Kiara left the office quickly.

Questions

1. What kind of packet filtering rule might have been set up to detect Kiara's hacking attempt?

2. Is it possible Kiara will be found out from this hacking attempt? Is it likely?

Working with Proxy Servers and Application-Level Firewalls

Ron Hall was dreaming of his next vacation. He had been working for Andy Ying, the manager of the security consulting group, on a very demanding project for nearly six months. Today he finally finished the work and had a few minutes to surf the Web to plan his upcoming trip to New Zealand.

Ron knew that ATI did not allow indiscriminate Web surfing and that they used a proxy server to ensure compliance with this policy, but he felt he had earned this treat and believed that Andy would have no problems with a little recreational Web surfing. Besides, it was almost 5:00 and nearly time to go home.

Google was allowed by the proxy server, so Ron went there to start his search. He typed in "new zealand vacation spots." Faster than he could blink, the giant search engine Google came back with a list of relevant links. The first entry looked promising: "New Zealand Tourism Online: New Zealand Travel Guide." But the second one looked even better: "New Zealand Pictures." He clicked that URL.

No pictures opened up. No green valleys. No coral reefs. No gorgeous mountains. Just a plain white screen with black letters that read:

ACCESS PROHIBITED—CONTACT PROXY SERVER ADMINISTRATOR FOR INSTRUCTIONS ON HOW TO ACCESS THE REQUESTED CONTENT.

Ron was not surprised, but he had hoped. He clicked the "Back" button and tried the next link. He got the same message. He tried three or four more times and then realized he was not getting any pictures today.

Ron got to his desk a little early the next morning. He turned on his PC and went to get a cup of coffee while it booted up. When he got back he opened his email program. In the list of new email was a note from the network security group. He opened the message and saw it had been addressed to him and to Andy Ying, his boss. It also had a CC to the HR department. The message said:

> Recently, your account was used to access Web content that has not been approved for use inside ATI. We are asking you to explain your actions to your supervisor.
>
> You are encouraged to enroll in a class on appropriate use of the Internet at ATI at your earliest convenience.
>
> Until you complete the class or your supervisor contacts this office, your network privileges have been suspended. If this access attempt was for legitimate business purposes, please have your supervisor notify us at once so that this Web location can be added to the ATI approved Web locations list.

What a hassle. Ron did not look forward to his conversation with Andy.

Questions

1. Does the ATI policy on Web usage seem harsh to you? Why or why not?

2. Do you think Ron was justified in his actions?

3. How should Andy react to this situation if Ron is known to be a reliable and a diligent employee?

Firewall Configuration and Administration

It was a nondescript building, in an area full of nondescript buildings. It was featureless on the outside and even though it was larger than 20,000 square feet, it seldom had more than 15 people in it. Its hard-working air-conditioning system blew a plume of heat exhaust that could be detected by thermal imaging cameras in orbit.

Inside this structure was a room, a big room, which was filled with rack upon rack of quietly humming equipment. Some of the machines processed electricity to make it more reliable. Some of the machines were hooked to the exterior air-conditioning compressors to maintain a stable temperature of 21.5 degrees Celsius.

In one rack was a computer. This computer was configured to run as a firewall. It was as much like its neighboring firewalls as its designers could make it. The company that owned this equipment, ATI, tried to keep all of the systems that performed a given function as much alike as possible. Standardized hardware and standardized software was the mantra at ATI. This specific computer had been running without pause for 116 days, since it was last rebooted as part of a scheduled maintenance routine. A few weeks ago, the firewall rule set was updated during a routine change window. The testing of that update seemed to show the revised rules were correct, but somehow, something went wrong.

One of the rules was meant to allow customers of Linen Planet, a Web-based business, to make secure connections to the commerce server, and then, a reverse proxy connection would connect to the Web server behind the firewall, in the protected network leased by Linen Planet from ATI. This was what the firewall engineer had written. This is what was typed into the script file that was applied by Matthias Paul. These were the rules tested by Debbie Masters. This was exactly what everyone wanted to result from the change control process so carefully set up by ATI to keep Linen Planet in business. Too bad it didn't work.

The rule that "allowed" the reverse-proxy connection was written to forward both secured and nonsecured (ports 80 and 443) packets to the application server inside Linen Planet's network. Unfortunately one of the network administrators made a last-minute bug fix that caused the secure Web server to have a different address than the firewall rule set expected. The port 80 rule still worked, but when a customer linked to the HTTPS service, the rule that handled port 443 pointed to the wrong server. The folks at Linen Planet were only now starting to hear from customers that could not connect. Even worse, some of those customers abandoned their online shopping carts, and moved on to one of their competitors.

Questions

1. How could ATI make sure glitches like this do not catch them unawares in the future?

2. How should the owners of the business Linen Planet protect themselves from losing business in cases like this?

Encryption and Firewalls

Padma Santhanam, the CTO of Linen Planet, was commuting to work her usual way—riding the train from the suburban station near her home to her office in a commercial business area across town. As she turned the page of the morning paper, her cell phone rang. She looked at the caller ID and saw it was her assistant, David Kalb.

"Hello, David. What's up?"

"Hi, Padma. Crisis here as usual. Our customer service rep at ATI is on the other line. He says you have to log in to the work order system and approve the change request ASAP or they'll miss the next change window for the new version of our online credit application."

Padma said, "OK. I'll be in the office in 25 minutes or so. The train just left Broadmore station."

"He says they can't wait that long. You were supposed to do this day before yesterday, and somehow it got overlooked. They say they need it now or we'll lose a week waiting for the next change window."

Padma sighed. Then she said, "OK. I want you to browse the work order Web site, you know the one we use at linenplanet.biz/wo, and log in for me. You can approve the change order and we won't miss the window. I'll change my password when I get there. My username is papa, sierra, alpha, november, tango, alpha. Got that?"

David said "Got it. Password?"

Looking both ways first, Padma lowered her voice some and said, "Romeo, lima, eight, four, bang, zulu, india, victor, dollar sign."

David repeated it back. He said, "OK, I am logged on now and just approved the work order. I'll tell our rep we're good to go."

"Thanks, David."

In the row behind Padma, Maris Heath closed her pocket notepad and clicked her ballpoint pen closed. Smiling, she hefted her laptop bag and stood up to exit the train at the next station, which she knew sat right next to an Internet cafe.

Maris opened her laptop and connected her browser to the Linen Planet Web server. The firewall asked for her username and password. She flipped open her notepad and punched in the data she had written down while eavesdropping on Padma's cell phone call. Her browser connected in no time. She noticed that the security icon was showing at the bottom of her browser window. The encryption between her browser and the server was now in place. At least no other hackers could watch her while she put a back door into Linen Planet's Web servers.

5C

She would spend several hours over the next few days scouting out the network and planning her raid. It looked like she would be able to buy that new game system sooner than she had planned.

Questions

1. Was the firewall and Web server used by Linen Planet providing encryption services? If so, what kind of protection was in place?

2. How could the access to Linen Planet's Web server have been better secured?

Authenticating Users

Niki Simpson was in the conference room waiting for the training session to begin. She was at the session because her user account credentials had been used by an unidentified attacker, attempting to access the school computer system. She had been an employee of the local school district for 12 years, and this was her first formal training in information security.

Three hours and thirty minutes later, Niki closed her workbook. The trainer said, "And that concludes the basic information security training session for school district employees. Are there any questions?"

Niki raised her hand. When the trainer acknowledged her, she said, "OK. I understand that the district policy is to have a twelve-character password of nonsense syllables that are changed by the system every 30 days. I also understand we are not supposed to write the new passwords down on anything. Any suggestions on how I am supposed to remember this password?"

The trainer said, "I really can't say. I suppose you'll just have to memorize the new password before you clear the screen when it is assigned to you."

Niki's mouth dropped open. She said to the trainer, "That's easy for you to say, but I think I'm going to have a hard time with that."

The day after her remedial security class, Niki got a call at her office from the help desk. The technician on the other end said that her account had been reset and she could log on again and her temporary password would be her employee ID number and then the last 4 digits of her social security number. A short while later, she was ready to try to connect to the system for the first time in a week—her access had been suspended until she took the training class.

She turned on her computer, and after it had booted, she entered her username and password as instructed. The next screen that opened said that her password had been reset. It displayed her new password as a series of twelve letters, numbers, and special characters, and then provided a brief mnemonic nonsense phrase. She saw:

HA YU M2 KA Y! I7

Hello All, You're Unhappy, Me Too, Keep Apples, Yes Bang, It's Seven

Niki looked at the "helpful" nonsense phrase and just shook her head. She was going to get another one of these every month! She reached for her yellow sticky notes and started writing down her new password.

Questions

1. Does the school district's password policy seem to be effective, considering the needs of the employees affected?

2. How would you suggest the district IT department adjust its password approach?

3. Consider how your recommendations might improve or degrade compliance with the policy. How would your suggestions alter the strength of the passwords?

Setting Up a Virtual Private Network

Constantine "Connie" Dimitrios opened his tent flap to watch the sun rise over the gentle slopes of the Virginia countryside. He had been hiking for four days on this leg of his ongoing quest to hike the roughly 2,175 miles of the Appalachian trail. He had begun his adventure in the summer of his junior year in college, but did not have the time to complete it in one go.

He listened carefully and could only hear a few birds in the nearby brush and, after a few minutes, the drone of an airplane high overhead and the dull growl of traffic on the interstate. He was considering whether to have a dry breakfast or to get started making coffee when the shrill ring of his cell phone sounded, evaporating the morning calm like an air-raid siren.

"Hello," he said, not bothering to conceal his irritation.

"Dr. Dimitrios," began a voice. "This is Debbie Masters from the QA team at ATI. I am working as part of an incident team that was formed 36 hours ago. It seems the intrusion system is not working, and no one here is able to make any progress. We worked this as long as we could without calling you, but we're out of options, and Ms. Johnson said to get you on the problem."

Connie was not surprised. He had pretty much rewritten the implementation of the commercial IDS that was in place when he took over that department eight years ago. It was good, but nothing was perfect.

"OK," he said. "I'll get online as soon as possible."

Connie now shifted his planning from coffee to finding a secure online link, as quickly as possible. It would take him 18 hours to get to the office if he left this minute. His cell phone couldn't provide enough bandwidth, and in any case couldn't provide a secure connection.

He pulled out his GPS map and saw that there was a Starbucks in the next valley, about a 30 minutes' hike from where he stood. He began breaking camp immediately.

Connie walked into Starbucks and ordered a Venti drip coffee. He found a table that could reach a power outlet and started his laptop. He started the VPN client software and authenticated using his user ID, his PIN, and the numbers from his cryptographic security token.

Once a secure connection was in place, he ran the remote desktop software, and it was as if he were sitting in his office. He plugged in his headset and ran the virtual meeting software.

He saw that there was a standing conference for the incident team. He clicked into the meeting.

Questions

1. Are Connie's communications, which are being carried over a public network, going to be safe?

2. What kind of authentication do you think is being used by this VPN?

3. Describe the VPN configuration Connie is using.

Contingency Planning

It was Friday night. All the employees had long since left for the day, except for a select group of senior staff who were crowded around the conference table with binders open and index cards in hand. Hedda Linn, who was facilitating the meeting, turned to Al Agostino, who was the acting incident manager for this meeting, and said, "It's your turn."

Al looked at the next index card in his deck. The two words made him grimace: "Power out."

Hedda asked, "How widespread and for how long?"

"Beats me," Al replied. "That's all I know."

Al flipped through his tattered copy of the disaster recovery plan, finally settling on a page. He looked for the communications coordinator, Jeffrey Noak. Jeffrey, a more experienced security architect, was responsible for all communications during this disaster recovery practice session.

"Okay, Jeff," he said. "Please call the power company and ask how widespread the outage is."

Jeff, who was reading the same binder page as Al, looked up. "Okay, I'll let you know as soon as I have an answer. Anything else?"

"Just a minute." As Al looked for the next step, Tana Stainforth, the second shift supervisor, said, "We've got about 45 minutes of battery time, but the generators need to be manually started. I'm going to need power to maintain network operations."

"Right!" Al said. He turned to Meredith Isaacs, who represented the building management company that leased space to ATI. "Can you get a team to the generator and get it going?"

Meredith said, "Okay. I'm on it. We already turned on the heaters. It takes 10 to 15 minutes from a cold start, and in this weather it's a very cold start. We need five to seven more minutes before we can crank the motor, and three to four minutes after that we can generate power."

Everyone at the table laughed. The weather outside was 92 degrees and humid, but the disaster scenario they were rehearsing was a massive snowstorm impacting operations.

"How long will the generators run?" Al asked.

Meredith flipped a page in her binder and replied, "Days. If we have to, we can siphon gas from employee vehicles! With the reserve tank, supplemented by gas from employee vehicles, we have plenty of fuel, provided the generator doesn't break down."

"Whew! That's a relief." Al smiled as he leaned back in his seat. "OK, what's our next step?" He glanced over at Hedda.

Hedda said, "Good job everybody. Al, flip the next card."

Review the scenario above, and then consider these questions:

1. In the scenario, the group was practicing for a snow emergency. What other incident cards would you expect to see in addition to power outage?

2. For each of the incident cards you listed, what would be the proper response?

3. How often should an organization rehearse its contingency plans?

4. Who should coordinate rehearsal of the contingency plans? Why is that the appropriate person?

5. What degree of cross-training among the various roles in the plans is most effective?

6. Identify the advantages and disadvantages of such a cross-training plan. What trade-offs do you think exist between extensive and minimal cross-training?

7. Notice that the corporate CIO and CEO were not at this rehearsal. Do you think it is important that the CIO, or even the CEO, participate in this kind of readiness exercise? Why or why not?

8. How can you make progress in contingency planning in the face of resistance from upper management?

Intrusion Detection and Prevention Systems

Matthias Paul, at the end of his graveyard shift, was reviewing and finalizing the automated intrusion event recognition report for one of ATI's many customers, the Springdale Independent School District (SISD), for whom ATI provided hosting services and limited intrusion prevention services. SISD had its own in-house information security group, but the work of screening the automated intrusion detection and prevention system had been outsourced to ATI.

Matthias opened up the intrusion event resolution application. The system correlated all of the various system logs and event recordings from the many services that ATI provided to SISD. As he worked his way through the false alarms, he came across a log entry from a Web server indicating that an external network location had tried to connect to the intranet-based student records application. The system had refused entry. Since Matthias knew that SISD allowed only remote access to student records using a VPN connection with two-factor authorization, he thought he would look at the log files from the VPN concentrator, and also at the log from the VPN authentication server.

The logs showed that the user who had tried to connect to the student records system had not attempted to set up a VPN connection. Either someone was trying to hack the system, or an authorized user had forgotten all of their training about security policy and remote access.

Matthias looked at the connection attempt and found the TCP/IP address of the person who had tried to access the student records system. It was registered to a pool of addresses used by the biggest Internet service provider (ISP) in the city where SISD was located. It would take a court order to get access to the detailed ISP records to find out who had tried to access the system. On the other hand, it was easy to identify the user account that had been used to attempt access.

Matthias mumbled, "Hmmm … looks like a user just forgot to follow the rules."

He pulled up the screen in the intrusion event resolution system to escalate the event from a candidate incident to an actual incident. He provided all of the facts he had discovered and then moved on to the next item. He knew someone would be getting an unpleasant contact from the SISD security group in the near future.

Review the earlier scenario titled "Packet Filtering," which describes the events that led to the IDPS alert that Matthias deals with in the opening scenario of this chapter. Review also the earlier scenario "Authenticating Users," which describes the consequences of Niki Simpson's habit of posting her password on sticky notes.

Questions

1. What type of IDPS system is ATI using for this contract?

2. Was this event the result of a honeypot or honeynet? Why or why not?

3. How realistic do you think this case is? Can and do events like this happen in real networked applications?

Digital Forensics

It was a few minutes before 5:00 PM on one of the worst Fridays that Mary Lewis, senior storage administrator for ATI, had ever experienced. The rumors of downsizing had been circulating for some time, and that afternoon three of her colleagues had been called to meet with Human Resources, and were then escorted out of the building by the corporate security team. Her team had been understaffed for the past year; she was still juggling work and on-call schedules to accommodate its reduced size when the phone rang.

"Mary, this is Delmar in Eastern Operations. The server support crew says that the engineering programs are aborting left and right—something about drives not being available. They say each server is fine; can you take a look?" She sighed as she hung up; it was always a storage area network (SAN) problem until she proved it wasn't.

She pointed her Web browser at the Eastern Operations server SAN switch and determined that the disks were hosted on disk array Charlie. She connected her computer to the management console for array Charlie and immediately saw that something was terribly wrong—the disks assigned to the Eastern Operations server had been deleted.

Mary faced a serious situation—had the disks been deleted accidentally, or was it a retaliatory act by one of the dismissed storage administrators? How would she collect the information that would enable ATI to pursue legal action if it was sabotage? In other words, Mary had just found herself in the midst of a forensic investigation.

Mary resisted the temptation to try to recover the disks. Destroying critical business information is a serious matter, and ATI and its customers might want to prosecute if it could be shown that the fired staff members were responsible. She sat back down at her desk and began sketching out a fault tree that identified the ways the data might have been deleted. She quickly identified two main branches: human error and malicious intent.

Since the management applications used to create and delete storage devices log each action on the central log server, if an authorized user had accidentally deleted the devices, Mary knew there should be a record of it.

She thought further down the malicious intent branch and developed two scenarios:

- The fired administrators used their credentials to delete the devices.
- The fired administrators set up a "logic bomb" to delete the devices if they were terminated.

Since the administrators were escorted from the building immediately upon termination, they would have had to access the network remotely in order to delete the devices manually. The VPN server logs and the authentication server would have recorded any access by the administrators after they were removed from the building. Also, the management application logs would trace the deletions to the terminated administrators' credentials. A logic bomb could have been concealed in many places, but Mary concluded the most likely location would be on the workstations assigned to the administrators.

Questions

1. What information should Mary collect first to support her investigation?

2. What forensic methods and processes will Mary have to use on the log servers and the administrators' workstations?

3. Can you think of other places Mary might look for relevant information?

Web Applications: Vulnerabilities and Remediation

Shankar Babu Chebrolu and Vinay Bansal
Cisco Systems

Shankar Babu Chebrolu, PhD(Cand), CISSP, GSEC, is an IT architect responsible for securing Web-based applications in Customer Value Chain Management at Cisco Systems, working closely with Cisco Supply Chain partners, Customers, Application Service Providers, Solution Vendors, Functional IT teams, and Corporate Security Programs Organization. Shankar is currently pursuing a PhD in Information Technology at Capella University and holds a Master's Degree in Computer Science & Engineering from Indian Institute of Technology (IIT), Mumbai, India. His research interests include information security management, cloud computing, IT effectiveness and strategic alignment with business.

Vinay K. Bansal CISSP, CISA, works as a senior security architect in Cisco System's Corporate Security Programs Office. He is the lead architect for Cisco's "Web and Application Security Architecture Team." Vinay has 17+ years of industry experience in successfully leading; architecting and implementing IT-based solutions with focus on security/Internet/e-commerce applications. Vinay worked at various Fortune 500 companies including Cisco, IBM, Nokia, Experian, and Plessey Telecom (UK). Vinay holds a Master's Degree in Computer Science from Duke University.

Overview

With the rapid growth of Internet, security vulnerabilities in Web applications have become more prominent. The lack of data type safety checks—input validation and output sanitization—leads to buffer overflows, code injection attacks (e.g., SQL injection), Cross-site scripting (XSS), and Cross-site request forgery (CSRF). Attackers have exploited Web applications and launched malware and worms to execute malicious code outside the browser on users' machines, leaving unsuspecting users unaware that an attack has occurred.[1]

Introduction

A new threat to Web users is the presence of malware residing in cached Web pages on servers, including those used by popular search engines, social networking Web sites, and news portals.[2] Web applications that allow users to upload content, code scriptlets, or both, carry additional risk; hence, they are popular targets for hackers. Web applications are also pushing the boundaries of browser security models largely because developers designed the models without anticipating the widespread use of the browser as a next generation platform to run applications.[3]

The arrival of Web 2.0 technologies, such as Asynchronous JavaScript and XML (AJAX) and mashups, which allow composing HTML content from different sources within the browser at runtime, further complicated the security posture of Web applications.[4] AJAX security depends on the reliability of the provider's content, whereas mashups connect dynamically to Web sites not necessarily under the provider's control; therefore, content providers should always validate content and secure their servers, which they do not necessarily do.[5]

The ubiquitous data access nature of the Web 2.0 world creates additional security challenges as users expect data to be accessible from any device, anywhere. As smart phones become a platform for accessing Web 2.0 applications, the encryption of voice, video, and data communications originating and terminating on those mobile devices is essential. It is no longer sufficient to approach enterprise security focused solely on the network layer and perimeter controls. Perimeter controls with devices like firewalls, Intrusion Prevention Systems (IPS), and Intrusion Detection Systems (IDS) are important; however, application security controls are becoming equally or even more important as enterprise borders are fading away, creating a borderless enterprise.

Web 2.0 technologies provide a better user experience with productivity advantages; therefore, these technologies are becoming standard even on high data sensitivity Web sites such as banking, financial, government, and enterprise applications, which inherently require additional security controls. Maturing Web 2.0 technologies and globalization policies will challenge the future landscape of security and privacy standards.[6]

Why Web Applications Are Targeted

Internet security threats continue to evolve as hackers attempt to stay ahead of security defenses that are being applied at the application and network layers. A growing number of hackers have shifted their focus from regular network attacks and email viruses to Web-based attacks, which form easy targets and present significant business risks. "Around 75%

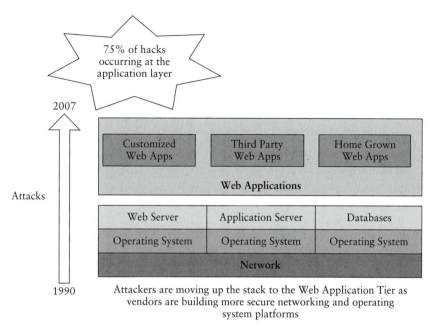

Figure 5D-1 Increasing Application Attacks

Source: Gartner Research

of Web attacks are now occurring at the application layer," says John Pescatore, vice president and research fellow at Gartner Research.

New attack vectors are using trusted Web sites to install malware to compromise users' privacy and identity.[7] Existing security defense mechanisms such as browser same-origin policy and URL filtering do not expect malicious content to arrive from trusted origins, hence they do not protect against such attacks. Previously, attackers have used storage servers to distribute malware, which puts Web 2.0 services at risk because they frequently include a massive amount of storage. Essentially, with additional complexity in the architectures of Web 2.0 applications due to a service-oriented and distributed nature, it makes it very hard to describe an overall system. The complexity being security's enemy, more likely those security vulnerabilities remain undetected in Web 2.0 applications.[8] For example, a back-end service or sub-system might depend on input or data validation that should happen earlier in the overall processing of an end-to-end system. Sometimes unexpected changes in mutually trusted subsystems may open up security issues in an end-to-end system process. It would be ideal to conduct data validation at all processing stages; however, it is rarely done.

Architects and developers need to closely inspect and understand how objects interact and behave at runtime within the browser. There are toolkits and frameworks available for Web application development that are effective at stopping cross-site scripting and injection attacks in Web applications. A combination of changes in the runtime enforcement within browsers and the adoption of secure development frameworks can achieve significantly more secure Web applications without placing the burden of additional code defenses on the developer.[9]

Web Application Security Principles

There are fundamental security principles that IT professionals should always follow when designing, developing, and implementing applications. These principles have remained consistent even as the underlying application development languages and deployment strategies continued to evolve. Programming languages for Web application development have moved from C/C++ to Java/Javascript. Similarly, application deployment strategies have changed from mainframes to client-server computing to Web-based deployments.

Build Defense in Depth

Application security is only as strong as its weakest link; therefore, security should be build at multiple tiers of an application like medieval castles, which had strong external walls, multiple internal walls, and restricted entrance gates at multiple points. Web application developers should incorporate security at the network, host, operating system, and database layers and around shared services such as messaging and Web services.

Multi-tier Web application architecture is a good example of defensive security. Common multi-tier Web architecture has three application tiers—the external Web tier, the middle application tier, and the internal database tier. The external Web tier is exposed directly to the Internet; therefore, the Web server host should be hardened and configured to demilitarized zone (DMZ) standards. The Web server should terminate the HTTP/S request and then interpret and forward it to the middle tier, where the application server should authenticate the request and apply business logic. Databases should run on the third tier (innermost) and should be accessible only by the second tier (application) for data read/write operations.

Strong Authentication and Authorization

Applications should use strong authentication and authorization frameworks.[10] Authentication is the first gate of entry to an application and it checks the user identity. Applications should enforce strong passwords at the point of initial log-in. Authorization controls the access or privileges of an authenticated user. Authorization is different from authentication and should not be confused. Two different authenticated (logged in) users can have different privileges (authorizations) within an application. Many application flaws are due to weak implementation of authorization controls, which allows an attacker with lower privilege access to escalate its privileges.

The HTTP protocol in a Web application inherently does not maintain any state or session for the user. After a user is authenticated, the Web application uses a unique session identifier (cookie) for subsequent Web requests. It is important to maintain high entropy for the session identifier to ensure it is not predictable and remains encrypted to minimize tampering. A short session timeout minimizes the probability of replaying the session identifier.

Identify Trust Boundaries and Validate Requests

Applications commonly have multiple integration points with other applications, middleware services, and back-end databases. It is important to identify all the integration points and establish trust boundaries and security zones. Any communication with the lower-trusted component should require a higher level of validation. For example, in a Web application the communication with the back-end database server is more trusted (innermost security zone) than the communication with the client browser (external security zone). That is why it is important to validate the requests and parameters received from the client browser (input validation). The same validation rigor is not required while receiving data from the more trusted back-end database server.

Minimize the Attack Surface

More exposed functionality means more potential points for an attacker to exploit. Applications should expose only the required services and functionality from the external tier. Unnecessary application functionality should not be exposed, and ideally, it should be disabled. Enterprises increasingly use third-party commercial, off-the-shelf (COTS) applications to run their businesses instead of developing them in-house. Most of these third-party COTS applications come with a lot more features than required, which should be disabled for security reasons. Similarly, a Web 2.0 application that uses AJAX exposes functionality through APIs. Thus, some Web 2.0 applications increase the attack surface. To minimize the risks, each exposed API must be reviewed for security vulnerabilities and be secured by proper authentication/authorization controls.

Principle of the Least Privilege

All the services and application components should run in the least-required privilege on the underlying operating system. This principle aligns with the multi-tier defense. For example, a Web server should run with the least-required privilege user rather than root or superuser. If the Web server were compromised, the attacker would only have access as the low-privilege user rather than gaining full, or root access. Similarly, an application that uses a back-end database should be designed to use a limited privilege database account with database access limited to only required tables rather than an account with full database access (sysadmin). It helps to minimize the exposure during an SQL injection attack, where the loss is limited to the tables/data specific to an application rather than everything within a database.

Security Is a Process Not a Product

Security threats change constantly. An application solution known to be secure today may become insecure in the future because of newly discovered vulnerabilities. For example, Data Encryption Standard (DES) was a known, secure encryption algorithm that became an industry standard; however, now it can be easily broken with the computation power available today. It has since been replaced by 3DES (triple DES) as the acceptable encryption standard. Similarly, application and IT vendors continue to find vulnerabilities in their previously shipped products and issue security patches. Security should be an ongoing process rather than a product—periodic assessments of the application, patch maintenance, and monitoring and log analysis should all be part of the application security process.

Web Applications' Security Vulnerabilities

There are several common security vulnerabilities found in Web applications, the most dangerous among them being cross-site scripting (XSS) and SQL Injection. Fortunately, developers can remediate both of these vulnerabilities with proper input validation and output sanitization at the Web server or appserver side. Client-side validation (using JavaScript) alone will not help because hackers tend to bypass client-side validations by using browser options or other free and commercial tools like Web scarab to launch attacks on Web applications running on the server side directly.

There are three types of cross-site scripting issues: reflected, stored, and Document Object Model based, the former being the most common and easiest to exploit. Reflected type refers to the vulnerability where a script code (e.g., JavaScript) within user-provided input is executed and the results are reflected directly back to the user. Stored type refers to the vulnerability where a script code is stored in a persistent data store such as a database or a file system. When a victim accesses the Web page, that script code will be executed and the results of that script could be sent via email (like session information) to the attacker or embedded within the dynamic Web page of the victim. These kinds of attacks are common with Web 2.0 applications such as blogs and discussion forums. In DOM-based cross-site scripting, the Web application's JavaScript code and variables are manipulated to launch an attack.

If a user's input in a Web application is passed directly to an SQL string, which is part of the application code, without input data validation, then the Web application is vulnerable to SQL Injection. If Web applications are vulnerable to SQL Injection, attackers can insert simple SQL or database specific commands to access unauthorized data, or worse, make unauthorized data modifications in the database. This vulnerability can be remediated with proper input validation or by using parameterized SQL queries.

The top ten Web application vulnerabilities including those aforementioned can be found at the OWASP website.[11]

Application Security Defense Strategies

The five pillars of application security defense strategies can help build a solid foundation for an application security program. This application defense strategy is based on years of

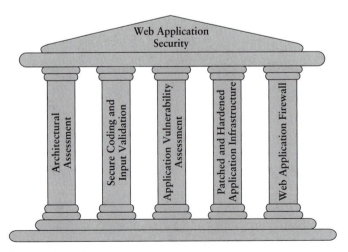

Figure 5D-2 Pillars of Web Application Security

Courtesy Course Technology/Cengage Learning

experience by the authors in designing and maintaining the security of hundreds of Web applications in multiple, large enterprises. Each of these pillars plays a strategic role to help keep the applications and Web infrastructures secure.

Architectural Assessment

Conducting an architectural assessment is the most important step to build a secure Web application infrastructure. It is performed at an early design phase and includes a security review of the application and its components. An individual outside of the application development team should conduct the security assessment to help ensure the separation of duties and to receive a non-biased perspective on security controls. Security controls within an application should be based on the exposure risks to the application and the sensitivity of data it handles. Applications that handle sensitive data require more rigid security controls to help maintain the confidentiality, integrity, and availability (CIA) of the data.

The scope of the architectural assessment is to review all of the application components and to ensure that the integration and data flow between the various application components is secure. Applications should use standard, well-known protocols rather than proprietary protocols. Similarly, the use of standard, well-known encryption algorithms are preferred over proprietary encryption.

Applications should establish a multi-tier defense by running services and components in different security zones. For example, an Internet facing application should run the Web and application server components in the DMZ, while the database component that is responsible for persistence storage of data should run in an internal protected security zone. The protocols and the data flow between the components in different security zones should be mutually authenticated. Application infrastructure should enforce strong authentication and authorization mechanisms for users. Generally, an enterprise business uses a shared Web infrastructure to run multiple applications. Security assessments should ensure that a new application does not lower the security posture of existing applications in the shared infrastructure and proper logical segmentation between applications is present.

Secure Coding and Input Validation

Application developers should receive proper training to help them understand the secure coding practices. Time and resources invested in providing security awareness training to developers has a very high return on investment (ROI) to help keep the applications secure. It is most economical to identify and remove the application flaws as early in the Software Development Life Cycle (SDLC) process as possible. If application developers understand the importance of doing input validation in their code, it helps to minimize the security vulnerabilities.[12]

Along with the strong coding practices, application developers should also be taught general security principles discussed previously, such as using strong authentication and authorization frameworks and leveraging right encryption mechanisms. They also need to understand the importance of security zones and trust boundaries between the application components and integration points. For example, integration with an internal database has trust that is more inherent and needs fewer security controls as compared to an integration with an external Web service that requires additional security controls.

Application Vulnerability Assessment

Application Vulnerability Assessment tests the application for potential security flaws before the attackers find them. Generally, the assessment is completed before the application is deployed to production. It ensures that the application developers remediate all the potential vulnerabilities and functional flaws and perform regression testing before deployment. Vulnerability assessment is also called negative testing or testing the "misuse" cases.[13] A misuse case is actually a use case that tests the system from the hostile actor's perspective.[14] Vulnerability assessment should be tied to the QA or testing phase of the application SDLC.

Vulnerability assessment tools are broadly categorized into two groups: penetration testing tools and static code analyzers. Penetration testing tools work against a running application and try to exploit it using well-known attack vectors such as SQL injection, cross-site scripting, and privilege escalations.[15] Penetration testing does black box testing of the application and is closer to how an actual attacker will try to exploit the application. Static code analysis uses white box testing methodology by analyzing the source code and/or binaries of an application to identify all the entry and end points.[16] It ensures that all the input received at these entry points is validated before it is processed by the application.[17] The lack of input validation and output sanitization are responsible for numerous application vulnerabilities.[18]

Patched and Hardened Application Infrastructure

Application hardening is a process to configure all components of an application securely. It includes ensuring that the latest security patches have been executed for the operating system, servers, or services (e.g., Web servers, application servers, and databases), and the application. It also involves disabling default passwords and shutting down unnecessary functionality, modules, and services. Application hardening ensures that attackers are not able to use publicly known vulnerabilities or back doors to get unauthorized access into the application.

The security posture of an application and its components continually changes as new flaws are discovered. Application vendors periodically release security patches to remediate these flaws. It is also important to ensure that the application infrastructure is running the latest supported versions of the application and its components. Many legacy applications pose security risks due to unsupported, non-patched application components.

As part of the hardening, the exposed surface area is reduced by restricting access to the admin interface and disabling unnecessary functionality. Most of the application components come with more functionality—bells and whistles—than is required. Default test accounts should be locked and the default passwords should be changed to use strong passwords.

Web Application Firewall

Web Application Firewalls (WAFs) are an important component of operational defense in a Web infrastructure. A WAF sits in front of the Web server and can detect and stop most of the common attacks from reaching the Web application. The WAF works at Layer 7 and can detect and defend against Web application attacks. Traditional network firewalls run at the network layer, layers 3–4, and have limited capability to defend against application attacks that occur at the higher layers.

After an Internet-facing Web application is live and in production, it may receive continual attack attempts from automated scripts. Attacks will often consist of well-known Web application exploits. It is similar to a thief canvassing a neighborhood and knocking on a door to see if it is open or loose.

WAF is also a useful tool for virtual patching of the Web applications.[19] Many times, there may be known vulnerabilities in the Web applications and it may not be feasible to fix it immediately; therefore, virtual patching is a way to set up custom rules within WAF to detect and prevent the known exploits from reaching the application, thus allowing the vulnerable application to still run securely behind a WAF. WAF also provides detailed application logs to the monitoring team, which are useful during incident handling.

Conclusion

A threat to Web applications is a reality; as they become easy targets and present significant business risks, attackers will continue to search for exploits. The security and privacy standards landscape will further be challenged by the maturing Web 2.0 technologies and globalization policies. Web application security assurance is a gap today and cannot be ignored. Security principles such as defense in depth, strong authentication and authorization, identifying trust boundaries, minimizing the attack surface, and the principle of least privilege help to reduce vulnerabilities. Finally, the five pillars of Web application defense strategies provide a solid foundation for an enterprise application security program. By incorporating these five pillars into an organization's SDLC, the security posture of Web applications can be improved.

References

Alexander, I. (2003). "Misuse Cases: Use Cases with Hostile Intent." *IEEE Software*, 20(1), 58–66. Retrieved from IEEE database.

Barnett, R. C. (2007). Virtual Patching During Incident Response: United Nations Defacement. Message posted to http://www.modsecurity.org/blog/archives/2007/08/virtual_patchin.html

Damodaran, M. (2006). "Secure Software Development Using Use Cases and Misuse Cases." *Issues in Information Systems*. 150–154. Retrieved from http://www.iacis.org/iis/2006_iis/PDFs/Damodaran.pdf

Davidson, M. A., and Yoran, E. (2007). Enterprise security for Web 2.0. *IEEE Computer*, 40(11), 117–119. Retrieved from IEEE database.

Farrell, S. (2008). "Security Boundaries." *IEEE Internet Computing*, 12(1), 93–96. 10.1109/MIC.2008.19

Howard, M., LeBlanc, D., and Viega, J. (2005). *19 Deadly Sins of Software Security*. New York: McGraw-Hill.

Hsu, F. (n.d.). *Input Validation of Client-Server Web Applications through Static Analysis*. Retrieved October 31, 2008, from http://seclab.cs.rice.edu/w2sp/2007/papers/paper-210-z_9464.pdf

Huseby, S. H. (2004). *Innocent Code: A Security Wake-Up Call for Web Programmers.* Wiley.

Keukelaere, F. D., Bhola, S., Steiner, M., Chari, S., and Yoshihama, S. (2008). "SMash: Secure Component Model for Cross-Domain Mashups on Unmodified Browsers." *Proceedings of the 17th International Conference on World Wide Web.* 535–544. Retrieved from ACM database.

Landau, S. (2008). "Security and Privacy Landscape in Emerging Technologies." *IEEE Security & Privacy,* 6(4), 74–77. doi:10.1109/MSP.2008.95

Lawton, G. (2007). "Web 2.0 Creates Security Challenges." *IEEE Computer,* 40(10), 13–16. Retrieved from IEEE database.

Livshits, B. (2006). *Improving Software Security with Precise Static and Runtime Analysis* (Doctoral dissertation, Stanford University, 2006). Retrieved from http://suif.stanford.edu/~livshits/papers/pdf/thesis.pdf

Livshits, B., & Erlingsson, U. (2007). "Using Web Application Construction Frameworks to Protect Against Code Injection Attacks." *PLAS'07: Proceedings of the 2007 Workshop on Programming Languages and Analysis for Security,* 95–104. Retrieved from ACM Digital Library Database.

Nichols, E. A., and Peterson, G. (2007). "A Metrics Framework to Drive Application Security Improvement." *IEEE Security & Privacy,* 5(2), 88–91. doi:10.1109/MSP.2007.26

OWASP Principles. (2008). *Category: Principle.* Retrieved October 31, 2008, from http://www.owasp.org/index.php/Category:Principle

OWASP Top Ten. (2007). *Top Ten Project.* Retrieved January 13, 2009, from http://www.owasp.org/index.php/Top_10_2007

Rabinovitch, E. (2007). "Protect Your Users Against the Latest Web-based Threat: Malicious Code on Caching Servers." *IEEE Communications Magazine,* 45(3), 20–22. 10.1109/MCOM.2007.344569

Endnotes

1. G. Lawton, Web 2.0 creates security challenges. *IEEE Computer, 40,* no. 10(2007): 13–16. Retrieved from IEEE database.

2. E. Rabinovitch, "Protect Your Users Against the Latest Web-based Threat: Malicious Code on Caching Servers," *IEEE Communications Magazine, 45,* no. 3(2007): 20–22. 10.1109/MCOM.2007.344569

3. F. D. Keukelaere, S. Bhola, M. Steiner, S. Chari, and S. Yoshihama, "SMash: Secure Component Model for Cross-Domain Mashups on Unmodified Browsers," *Proceedings of the 17th International Conference on World Wide Web* (2008), 535–544. Retrieved from ACM database.

4. B. Livshits and U. Erlingsson, "Using Web Application Construction Frameworks to Protect against Code Injection Attacks," *PLAS'07: Proceedings of the 2007 Workshop*

on Programming Languages and Analysis for Security (2007), 95–104. Retrieved from ACM Digital Library Database.

5. Lawton, "Web 2.0 Creates Security Challenges."

6. S. Landau. "Security and Privacy Landscape in Emerging Technologies," *IEEE Security & Privacy, 6*, no. 4(2008): 74–77. doi:10.1109/MSP.2008.95

7. Rabinovitch, "Protect Your Users Against the Latest Web-based Threat."

8. S. Farrell, "Security Boundaries," *IEEE Internet Computing, 12*, no. 1(2008): 93–96. 10.1109/MIC.2008.19

9. Livshits and Erlingsson, "Using Web Application Construction Frameworks."

10. M. Howard, D. LeBlanc, and J. Viega, *19 Deadly Sins of Software Security*. New York: McGraw-Hill, 2005.

11. OWASP Top Ten, *Top Ten Project*, 2007. Retrieved January 13, 2009, from http://www.owasp.org/index.php/Top_10_2007

12. S. H. Huseby, *Innocent Code: A Security Wake-Up Call for Web Programmers*, 2004. New York: John Wiley & Sons.

13. M. Damodaran, "Secure Software Development Using Use Cases and Misuse Cases," *Issues in Information Systems* (2006): 150–154. Retrieved from http://www.iacis.org/iis /2006_iis/PDFs/Damodaran.pdf

14. I. Alexander, "Misuse Cases: Use Cases with Hostile Intent," *IEEE Software, 20*, no. 1(2003): 58–66. Retrieved from IEEE database.

15. OWASP Principles, *Category: Principle* (2008). Retrieved October 31, 2008, from http://www.owasp.org/index.php/Category:Principle

16. F. Hsu, "Input Validation of Client-server Web Applications Through Static Analysis," 2007. Retrieved October 31, 2008, from http://seclab.cs.rice.edu/w2sp/2007/papers/paper-210-z_9464.pdf

17. B. Livshits, *Improving Software Security with Precise Static and Runtime Analysis* (Doctoral dissertation, Stanford University, 2006). Retrieved from http://suif.stanford.edu/~livshits/papers/pdf/thesis.pdf

18. OWASP Top Ten, *Top Ten Project*, 2007. Retrieved January 13, 2009, from http://www.owasp.org/index.php/Top_10_2007

19. R. C. Barnett, "Virtual Patching During Incident Response: United Nations Defacement. Message posted to http://www.modsecurity.org/blog/archives/2007/08/virtual_patchin .html

Reading 5E

Managing Secure Database Systems

Li Yang
Department of Computer Science and Engineering,
University of Tennessee at Chattanooga

Dr. Li Yang is an Assistant Professor in the Department of Computer Science and Electrical Engineering at the University of Tennessee at Chattanooga. Her research interests include network and information security, databases, and engineering techniques for complex software system design. She authored papers on these areas in refereed journals, conferences, and symposiums. She is a member of the Association for Computing Machinery (ACM).

Overview

This chapter is a guide on managing secure database systems via bridging information security regulation and policies with implementation of database security and audit.

Introduction

Database security issues are often a matter of incorrect configuration, and the fact that the database implements a rich security model does not mean that it is secure. The security model may not be used or may not be used correctly. There are several examples of database security violations that made the headlines. In 2001, information from almost 100,000 credit cards was stolen after an attack on Bibliofind, a division of Amazon.com that trades rare and out-of-print books. In March 2001, the FBI reported that almost 50 bank and retail Web sites were attacked and compromised by Russian and Ukrainian hackers. In October 2004 a hacker compromised a database containing sensitive information on more than 1.4 million California residents. The breach occurred on August 1 but was not detected until the end of the month.[1]

Emerging electronic commerce and business have significantly changed our daily life. We shop from online retailers, pay credit card balances and utility bills from online banking, etc. Moreover, besides minimizing stocking time, businesses use software to manage relationships with their customers. While e-commerce has certainly added many indirect users on the database, e-business has had a much bigger impact on security (or the lack of it). The addition of functionality in new technologies means more bugs can be exploited by hackers, and many of the leading vendor databases have been plagued with bug-related vulnerabilities. Corporate crimes, frauds, and weak accounting practices endanger client interests; as a result regulators enforce regulations on security management and IT auditing. To avoid financial or criminal penalties associated with noncompliance of regulations such as Sarbanes-Oxley, GLBA, and HIPAA, it is important for businesses to manage secure database systems. Therefore, it is imperative that information professionals obtain the expertise and knowledge to invest in the security of their databases.

Best Practices of Hardening Database Environment

Hardening is a process by which you make your database more secure and is sometimes referred to as locking down the database. When we harden our database environment, we remove vulnerabilities that result from careless configuration options and can even compensate for vulnerabilities that are caused by vendor bugs. Although it is not possible to fix these bugs, we can form an environment in which those bugs cannot be exploited. The essence of this process involves three main principles. The first involves locking down access to important resources that can be misused—maliciously or by mistake. The second involves disabling functions that are not required for our implementation, which can by misused by their very existence. The third principle is that of least privileges (i.e., giving every user, task, and process the minimal set of privileges required to fulfill their role).

SQL Server, as one of the most functionally rich databases, has suffered from a lot of exploits and attacks. Fortunately, Microsoft is investing a lot to improve security of SQL Server platforms. There are numerous resources and large community help to secure the SQL Server environment. Hardening an SQL Server environment includes applying all service packs and hot fixes to both the operating system and SQL Server, using a low-privilege user account for the SQL Server service, deleting setup files that may contain plain text and sensitive configuration information, and removing all sample users and sample databases. All the passwords and roles assigned to users should be reviewed periodically. Network libraries that are not used should be removed because an SQL Server can be accessed through several network libraries. Procedures that are available to PUBLIC should be checked and limited. An excellent resource for *hardening SQL Server* is available from www.sqlsecurity.com. MySQL is an open-source database platform whose source code can be accessed by hackers, which means hackers can figure out weaknesses and exploits from its source code. The best practices of *hardening MySQL* are available in the Apendix. Oracle is one of the most well-documented database environments and many hardening scripts are available on the Internet, for instance, Pete Finnigan's checklist at www.petefinnigan.com/orasec.htm. Best practices of *hardening a DB2 environment* are also available in the Appendix.

After the database environment is hardened, the database needs to be periodically checked to make sure that it is still locked down and no new misconfigurations have been introduced. Such continuous efforts can be automated with a set of tools. For example, the Microsoft Baseline Security Analyzer (MBSA) is a tool that scans one or more Windows systems for common security misconfigurations. MBSA can check members of the *sysadmin* group, restrictions of *cmdexec* rights, SQL Server local account passwords, directory access, registry key security, and so on.

Patching is one of the most important and fundamental techniques in hardening database environments because it defends you against threats that are launched against known problems. Several Web sites track security vulnerabilities, alerts, and advisories, including vulnerabilities for database environment. The Web sites include the CERT Coordination Center (www.cert.org), the Common Vulnerabilities and Exposures (CVE) (cve.mitre.org), Security Focus (www.securityfocus.com/bid), and Security Tracker (www.securitytracker.com/search/search.html). Major security vendors also post security alerts as a service to their customers. Additional resources are available at the end of this chapter for details on how to harden a database environment and security alerts from major vendors.

One thing worthwhile to mention is C2 security. C2 security is a government rating for security in which the system has been certified for discretionary resource protection and auditing capabilities. For example, SQL Server has a C2 certification; however, this certification is only valid for a certain evaluated configuration. You must install SQL Server in accordance with the evaluated configuration or to claim to be running a C2-level system.

Database Regulations and Compliance

Regulators have created a large and growing set of regulations aimed at enforcing protection of information, privacy, and transparency of information. Some of these regulations, such as HIPAA for health care and the Gramm-Leach-Bliley Act (GLBA) for financial services, are specific to certain market segments. Others are for a certain class of companies, such as the Sarbanes-Oxley Act (SOA) for public companies and California Senate Bill 1368 for companies that maintain personal information regarding residents of California. They all include stringent requirements dealing with information security and/or privacy, and all of them implement punitive consequences if compliance is not maintained. All regulations try to deal with a set of human behaviors such as untruthfulness, greed, sloppiness, laziness, and so forth. In doing this, the regulations use two main techniques: (1) guidelines so that people cannot too loosely interpret the regulations to their benefit and (2) segregation of duties.

A *reverse mapping* is helpful to ensure that a list of security and auditing provisions are implemented. We use HIPAA as an example to show how to map HIPAA regulations into technical implementation of database security. HIPAA 142.308 requires access controls as methods of controlling and restricting access to prevent unauthorized access to information. The database administration should employ authorization mechanisms including user-based, role-based privileges and optional context-related mechanisms to determine and assign privileges to users. HIPAA requires identification of the class of the user to restrict access to protected health information. This requires the adoption of authentication and identification mechanisms in administration of database security. HIPAA 164.308 requires implementing policies and procedures to prevent, detect, contain, and correct security violations. This requires techniques to enable database intrusion detection capabilities and SQL firewall capability. HIPAA requires mechanisms employed to examine and record system activity, and such monitoring and auditing should be in place.

Data mapping is very important in database security management because data is the target of protection. The data that maps into the protected information in regulations should be identified in the database. For example, if your enterprise is under the HIPAA regulation, the constituency of protected health information and the data subject to row-level security should be identified. If your enterprise needs to comply with SOX, you need to identify the tables that maintain financial data and the procedures needed to be monitored and controlled to ensure accuracy and integrity of financial reports. If your company needs to observe GLBA, you need to know where the sensitive data such as name, social security number, and income reside.

Access Control in Database Security

In order to ensure a successful implementation and avoid many frustrations, you should base the entire implementation on the concept of defining and implementing a security policy for your database environment. This will make sure that you do not lose a high-level overview and the end goals. Implementing database security policies is to map business needs into technical requirements. Security policies can be implemented through access control rules. Access control policies can be grouped into three main classes: *Discretionary access control* (DAC), *Mandatory access control* (MAC), and *Role-based access control* (RBAC). DAC policies associate identity of the subjects with privileges, which determines allowed operations on the requested objects. MAC policies label both subjects and objects and control access through a central authority. RBAC policies associate subjects with roles, and roles with privileges. In RBAC the access control rules state which privileges are allowed to users with given roles.

DAC policies of a database system can be implemented by the *access matrix model*, which regulates the privileges that a subject can have on an object. An access control system contains *subjects*, *objects*, and *actions*. The *subjects* will request and perform actions on the objects, which are the target of protection. An object can be a table, view, procedure, or any other database object. A subject can be a user, role, privilege, or a module. The access control matrix model uses a matrix to represent access control policies. Rows of the matrix correspond to subjects and columns correspond to objects. The intersection of row and columns is an action that a corresponding subject can execute on the corresponding objects. Access matrix can be practically implemented by an authorization table generally used in a DBMS systems access control list or capability list. In the access control list, each object is linked with a sequence of subjects and actions that the subject can execute on the object. The capability list links each subject with a set of objects and actions that the subject is allowed to execute on the object. The SQL Server, MySQL, Oracle Database, DB2, and Sybase support the implementation of access matrix. One thing that a database security administrator may need to pay attention to is the vulnerability of the discretionary policies. One vulnerability of DAC lies in the fact that there is no control on the flow of information. A Trojan Horse is one of the attacks that exploit such vulnerabilities. If we have a user called *Vicky* who is a top-level manager and has a file called *Market* about new products release, she can read and write the file *Market*. And we have another user called *John*, a subordinate of *Vicky*. He created a file called *Stolen* and allows *Vicky* to write on the file *Stolen*. He sent a Trojan Horse application to *Vicky* with two hidden operations: read operation on file *Market* and write operation on file *Stolen*. When *Vicky* runs the application, contents of *Market* will be read and written to the file *Stolen*. *John* has gained access to the file *Market* through a Trojan Horse application and DAC cannot control such exploits.

The MAC, also known as the multilevel security policy, labels subjects and objects using different security classification. Security classifications are ordered hierarchically including Top Secret (TP), Secret (S), Confidential (C), and Unclassified (U), where $TS > S > C > U$. MAC regulates the information flow, which prevents sensitive information from being leaked to unauthorized users. The security classification of an object represents sensitivity of the object, and the security classification of a subject represents clearance of the subject, which reflects trustworthiness and privileges of the subject. The Trusted Computer System Evaluation Criteria (TCSEC), a U.S. Department of Defense (DoD) standard, has details about MAC, which is also known as label security. The TCSEC, frequently referred to as the Orange Book, was replaced with the development of the Common Criteria for Information Technology Security Evaluation (C2) standard originally published in 2005.[2] Most of the database vendors can offer functions supporting label security through use of *row-level security* or *fine-grained access control*, which is one of the advanced security features in databases. Oracle calls it Fine-Grained Access Control (FGAC). DB2 currently only supports this feature on z/OS and calls it Multi-Level Security (MLS).[3] SQL Server only supports this feature in SQL 2005 and calls it Fine-Grained Privileges.

Role-based access control (RBAC) has its application in commercial databases such as Microsoft SQL Server and Oracle databases. RBAC attempts to specify and enforce enterprise-specific security policies in a way that maps naturally to an organization's structure. In RBAC, users are assigned roles based on their organizational responsibilities and then are given access to resources based on their assigned roles. Role-based policies break the user authorization into assignment of roles to users, and assignment of roles to permission, which is the authorization of access to objects. RBAC meets two basic design principles of a security model: least privilege and separation of duties. A user can log on to a DBMS and activate roles with the least privilege, which is necessary for the job he needs to perform. This reduces the risks caused by the lack of control on information flow. To realize separation of duties principle, no user will be assigned roles from different groups with a conflict of interests. Both SQL Server and Oracle databases support the concept of *roles*.

Virtual private database (VPD) is another implementation of access controls rules and data access at either the row or column level. VPD allows each user to access and update only the data that belongs to him or her when multiple users are sharing the same database. Microsoft SQL Server uses VIEW database object to implement VPD. VIEW objects are created to limit what users can access in a table; that is, a view is created to hide columns or rows from users. Oracle databases use application context to implement VPD. Application context is a function specific to Oracle that allows you to set database application variables that can be retrieved by database sessions. These variables can be used for security context-based or user-defined environmental attributes.

Securing Database Communications

The SQL Slammer worm uses a vulnerability of SQL Server to launch attacks from the network. One of the ways that network administers contain the worm is to filter outbound traffic from SQL Server, and not allow the UDP 1434 communications from one server to another. Therefore, it is necessary to monitor all database-to-database communications including both time and contents. The monitoring reports may consist of source programs that identify all database servers and its IP addresses. In addition to monitoring database-to-database communications, a baseline of interaction should be created to closely monitor any significant deviation.

A database link enables a user to perform Data Manipulation Language (DML) statements or any other valid SQL statement on one database while logged onto another database. In other words, a user can transparently issue a query that uses tables from database A and B. As a result, it is important to secure database links and watch for link-based elevated privileges. Monitoring access to link definitions is true for any database, even when there is less of a security vulnerability and even when passwords are not maintained in plain text. Accessing to link definitions includes any creation of database links, modification, and access to link information. In addition, usage of database links should be monitored, especially when the database A that is being linked is connected with another database B with weak security because the breach in database B can cause breach in database A.

Securing Replication Mechanism

Replication is the process of copying and maintaining database objects in multiple databases. Replication is one of the common advanced features in any database environment, and all major platforms support replication, even MySQL.

During database replication, we need to consider security of the replication mechanism and communication of files used by replication. The SQL Server replication architecture consists of publisher, distributor, and subscribers.[4] The publisher holds all the data to be replicated and the subscriber is the consumer of data on the publisher. The distributor buffers the data published by the publisher until it can be delivered to subscribers. The data always moves from the distributor to the subscribers, never from the publisher to the subscribers directly. The publisher delivers the data to the distributor, and then the distributor works with the subscribers to get the data into their databases. The published tables are called articles, and collections of articles are known as publications. On top of this architecture, there are three replication models, which are snapshot replication, transactional replication, and merge replication. In snapshot replication, the snapshot agent running on the distributor takes a "picture" of the data at a particular point in time and transfers that snapshot of the data to the distributor. The data is then transferred to the subscribers by the distribution agent. In transactional replication, the publisher keeps the subscribers updated with any changes by sending a stream of INSERT, UPDATA, and DELETE statements, reflecting the changes being made by users on the publisher. Merge replication allows changes to occur on both the publisher and the subscribers. It creates a consensus view of changes to the data, instead of a nice orderly flow to changes from the publisher to the subscriber.

When your replication scheme involves the creation of files, you must secure the *folder* where replication files are stored. For instance, when you set up the snapshot agent and the distribution agent in SQL Server, you specify which folder to use. By default, this network share is not a secure folder.[5] As a result, you should change the share path and configure NTFS permissions so that only the SQL Server Agent services on your SQL Server nodes can access and modify this folder. All replication schemes in Oracle use internal queues within the database, eliminating the need to worry about the security at file system level.[6] DB2 replication with the capture and apply component does not require securing files either.[7] The capture component looks for data modification from the log file and shores these modifications into control tables. The apply component runs on the replica database and pulls the data from the control tables to a local copy. One thing you need to know is that the capture program does write external diagnostics files in the CAPTURE_PATH directory, which should be protected appropriately.

We also need to secure and monitor replication *users* and *connections* because replication mechanism involves multiple connections and users. Moreover, we need to monitor *commands* that affect replication.

Database Auditing

There is no security without audit and therefore security and audit should be implemented in an integrated fashion. Auditing database activity and access can help identify security issues and resolve them quickly. Auditing as a function needs to play a central role in ensuring compliance because an audit examines the documentation of actions, practices, and conduct of a business or individual. It then measures their compliance to policies, procedure, process, and law. Two types of data are required to ensure compliance of the database environment. The first category includes audit trails and other logs, which are called auditing information. The second audit category involves security audits. They are sometimes called assessments, penetration tests, or vulnerability scans, and focus on the current state of a database environment rather than auditing data.

Many database auditing trails can be produced for a database environment, so we will discuss the categories of auditing. The first category of auditing that is required in most environments is a full audit trail of *logon and logoff*, and records all failed log-in attempts. Each log-in/log-off is recorded by its log-in name, timestamp, TCP/IP address, and the program that imitated the log-in/log-off. The second category is to audit *Data Control Language* (DCL) of the database. The DCL covers changes to privileges, user/log-in definition, and other security attributes. A complete audit trail of any changes made to the security and privilege model must be audited. The target of auditing in this category includes addition and deletion of users, log-ins, and roles, changes to the mappings between log-ins and users or role, password changes, and changes to security attributes at a server, database, statement, or object level. The third category is to audit *Data Definition Language* (DDL), which changes database schema. Some stealing information activities (e.g., Trojan Horse) may often involve a DDL command. For example, data can be copied to additionally created tables. Many regulations require auditing the modification of data schema such as tables and views. The fourth category is to audit changes to sensitive data via *Data Manipulation Language* (DML) activities. This auditing is particularly useful for a Sarbanes-Oxley project where accuracy of financial information is important. Through auditing DML activity we can record old and new values of sensitive records such as salaries. The auditing of a DML activity can be implemented by tools (e.g., log miner), external database audit systems, or customized triggers. The fifth category is to audit changes to sources of *stored procedures* and *triggers* where malicious codes can easily hide. The sixth category is to audit *database errors* because attackers will make many attempts before they get it right. The last but not the least category is to audit any changes made to the *definition of what to audit*.

An auditing solution has two indispensable parts: collecting the information and using the information. Auditing does not enhance security unless its trail is used. It is impossible to rely on a manual process to ensure that all the audit reports are checked and assessed. Automation and oversight become important parts of a sustainable solution. Automation can distribute the auditing data to the people who are reviewing them. A built-in oversight defines the review workflow and order, ensuring that the audit tasks are continuously activated and reviewers do not hold up the processes. Moreover, adopting an independent audit trail created by a third-party solution is a good practice to collect and use audit information because independent audit immune to bugs and vulnerabilities that the database may have. The third-party solution also helps to archive and secure audit information, and audit the audit system.

Concluding Remarks

Security in database management plays an important role in conforming to regulation that enforces protection of information and privacy. In this chapter we discussed how to manage secure database systems from both management and technical aspects. We explained database regulations and compliance and how to harden various database environments. Access control modules and database auditing are elaborated in this chapter because they are essential in the implementation of security policies of an organization. Securing database communications and replication mechanism are also covered.

In the future, we will work on security management of object-oriented databases and XML databases. Moreover, the techniques such as access control and database auditing will be investigated further.

Additional Resources

Hardening an Oracle Environment

- www.petefinnigan.com: Pete Finnigan is one of the world's foremost Oracle security experts, and he posts a lot of useful information on his Web site. See Pete Finnigan's Oracle security blog at www.petefinnigan.com/weblog/archives/

- www.dba-oracle.com/articles.htm#burleson_arts: Many good articles on Oracle and some on Oracle security published by Don Burleson.
- www.linuxexposed.com: A good resource for security includes an excellent paper, "Exploiting and Protecting Oracle."
- http://www.appsecinc.com/index.html: Application security Inc.'s white paper page, including a white paper titled "Protecting Oracle databases."
- www.dbasupport.com: Miscellaneous articles, resources and tips on Oracle.
- Oracle Security Handbook by Marlene Theriault and Aaron Newman.
- Effective Oracle Database 10g Security by Design by David Knox.
- Oracle Privacy Security Auditing by Arup Nanda and Donald Burleson.

Hardening an SQL Server Environment

- www.sqlsecurity.com: Web site dedicated to SQL Server security.
- http://www.sqlmag.com/: SQL Server magazine's security page.
- http://vyaskn.tripod.com/sql_server-security_best_practices.htm: Overview of SQL Server security model and best practices.
- http://www.appsecinc.com/index.html: Application Security Inc.'s white paper page, including a white paper titled "Hunting Flaws in Microsoft SQL Server White Paper."
- SQL Server Security by Chip Andrews, David Litchfield, Bill Grindlay, and Next Generation Security Software.

Hardening a DB2 Environment

- http://www.databasejournal.com/features/db2/: Database Journal for DB2.
- www.db2mag.com: DB2 Magazine.
- http://www.appsecinc.com/index.html: Presentations on various topics, including "Hacker-proofing DB2."

Hardening a Sybase Environment

- www.isug.com/ISUG3/Index.html: Sybase user group.

Hardening a MySQL Environment

- www.nextgenss.com/papers.htm: papers on various topics, including MySQL security (e.g., "Hacker-proofing MySQL").
- http://dev.mysql.com/doc/mysql/en/Security.html: Security section from MySQL manual.
- www.appsecinc.com/index.html: Presentations on various topics including "Hacker-proofing MySQL."

Oracle, SQL Server, DB2 and Sybase Security Alerts

Oracle security alerts: www.oracle.com/techonology/deploy/security/alerts.htm

SQL Server security: www.microsoft.com/technet/security/prodtech/dbsql/default.mspx

DB2 support page: www-306.ibm.com/software/data/db2/udb/support

Sybase support page: www.sybase.com/support.

References

Afyouni, Hassan, A. (2006). *Database Security and Auditing: Protecting Data Integrity and Accessibility*. Boston: Course Technology/Cengage Learning.

Common Criteria for Information Technology Security Evaluation, http://www.commoncriteriaportal.org/

Lewis, Morris. (2004). *SQL Server Security Distilled*. New York: Spinger-Verlag.

Natan, Ron Ben. (2005). *Implementing Database Security and Auditing*. Elsevier Digital Press.

Samarati, Pierangela, and Capitani de Vimercati, Sabrina. (2001). *Access Control: Policies, Models, and Mechanisms, Foundations of Security Analysis and Design*. ISBN 978-3-540-42896-1, pp. 137–196.

Endnotes

1. Natan, Ron Ben. *Implementing Database Security and Auditing*. Elsevier Digital Press, 2005.
2. Common Criteria for Information Technology Security Evaluation, http://www.commoncriteriaportal.org/
3. Natan, *Implementing Database Security*.
4. Morris Lewis, *SQL Server Security Distilled*. Apress, 2004. New York: Spinger-Verlag.
5. Natan, *Implementing Database Security*.
6. Ibid.
7. Ibid.

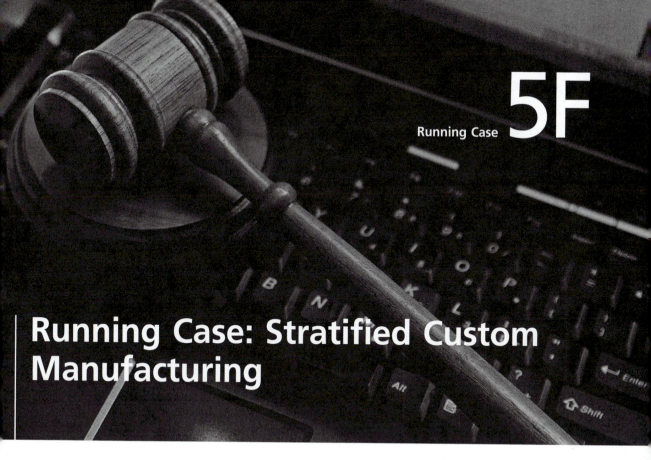

Running Case: Stratified Custom Manufacturing

Late one night not long ago, George Corday, SCM's Senior Manager of Information Systems noticed some heavier than usual traffic moving between three operational sites; Tokyo, Milan, and Tampa. The movement and the time of the traffic caught him as strange so he called the CSO, Tom Brown.

As usual Tom was at his desk when the call came in; some people claimed Tom slept and ate there. Tom answered "Hello, CSO Tom Brown speaking."

George answered: "Hi Tom, have you got a minute? I noticed something odd with our net traffic and wanted you to look at it."

Tom replied with a scripted answer, the first entry in the company incident response plan, "What do you think you saw, where and at what time or times?"

George gave Tom the information he had observed.

A few hours later Tom called George back to give him the initial report that someone had tapped into their system and was using it to transmit data around the world. The data was embedded in some typical transactions; however, the attacker had placed a worm in the system, which apparently had the potential for causing damage well beyond the company's system. He suggested to George that they could employ a track and trace procedure to attempt to isolate the attacker. Tom said he wanted to isolate those links in the system to prevent the attacker from launching attacks to other sites or hopefully to prevent the attacker from using their system to launch system attacks on the vendor and supply chain. Tom said he was more concerned over the ability of this worm to infiltrate their government contractors linked via VPN, which may have access to sensitive data and sites. The surprising part of the conversation turned out to be that an SCM laptop was being used to access the network.

In his phone call to Tom, George OK'd the use of the track and trace system Tom had created to find the attacker and disable their ability to use SCM's network. He wanted the identity of who had use of the laptop, and wanted to know if there was any potential for proprietary data being removed from their network or if the network was just being used as a carrier.

George also informed him that he would communicate the illegal use of their network to Takio Sumi, CIO, as soon as Tom had removed the attacker's ability to use their network.

Discussion Questions

1. Do you think any laws may have been violated by SCM in this investigation? Perhaps international laws?

2. Were any internal procedures violated by Tom and George?

3. The chain of events and type of attack should have required what type of response from the two employees?

4. At what point in time should SCM involve their contractors, vendors, and the government agencies? What is the appropriate way to do that?

Part 6

Information Security Program Management

Objective

The objective for this chapter of the text is an examination of the legal and ethical issues associated with the management of the security program itself. The information security program, like most organizational programs, must be effectively administered in order to provide value to the organization. Complicating issues in this area are the numerous legal and regulatory issues with impacts across the organization in privacy, financial, and other areas.

Contents

Jennifer L. Bayuk

As security professionals move to the executive ranks, they have been advised to speak in business terms. The direct translation of security measures to business terms has to date been risk reduction. So speaking in business terms has been to express information in terms of risk. It is very common to see panels of security experts nodding their heads in violent agreement that business risk is the most important factor to consider in designing security measures.

B Reading: Impact of Incomplete or Missing Information in a Security Policy

Wasim A Al-Hamdani

A security policy is a document that outlines the rules and practices for computers and it regulates how an organization protects, manages, and accesses its sensitive information. A security policy is often considered to be a "living document," meaning that the document is never finished, but is continuously updated as technology and employee requirements change. The fundamental elements of a security policy are audience, compliance, and consequences of non-adherence. This chapter looks at the results of missing one or more of the fundamental elements.

C Case: A Review of Information Security Management Requirements as Reflected in U.S. Federal Law

Jeffrey P. Landry

With federal regulation of information systems increasing, the need for greater understanding of the ethical and legal implications of information technology (IT) in society has never been greater. The need for legal and ethical acumen is even more pronounced for the management of information security in a government context. Federal agencies, for example, are large bureaucracies created and governed by laws, rules, and regulations, and the ethical principles embodied in these codes. The body of legislation relating to information security in federal agencies, along with evolving case law, is a rich context for understanding the ethical and legal impacts of IT for both the private and public sectors, and for both classified and nonclassified systems. A national training standard for senior systems managers identified more than a dozen laws relating to the management of information security. These laws will be used as a framework for investigating legal and ethical issues in information security management.

D Case: The Law in Information Security Management

Katherine H. Winters

This case study is designed to provide insight into the relationship between the law and information security management. A fictitious consulting company, K-LiWin Consulting, is used to provide cohesion. This fictitious company has four fictitious customers: a hospital, a financial securities firm, a record producer, and a nonprofit organization. Each of these organizations represents industries that have unique laws that impact their information security policy. Within the context of K-LiWin Consulting providing information security consulting services, some of these laws and regulations will be examined. This case will examine the impact of some of the major laws affecting information security such as HIPAA, the Sarbanes-Oxley Act of 2002 (SOX), the Gramm-Leach-Bliley Act of 1999, the Digital Millennium Copyright Act, and a Massachusetts statute dealing with privacy. A brief overview of each law is provided. The detail review of the law is left to the reader as an exercise. By no means is this an exhaustive list of important information security laws; it is intended to provide the reader with an appreciation of the importance of law in information security. A brief overview of the case and K-LiWin Consulting will be presented followed by details of each organization and one or more laws specific to that entity.

E Running Case

Information Security Metrics: Legal and Ethical Issues

Jennifer L. Bayuk
Stevens Institute of Technology

Jennifer Bayuk, CISM, CISSP, CISA, CGEIT, is an Information Technology due diligence consultant with direct experience in virtually every aspect of Information Security. Jennifer frequently publishes on IT Governance, Information Security Technology, and Audit topics, including two textbooks for the Information Systems Audit and Control Association. She lectures for organizations that include ISACA, NIST, and CSI. She is an industry professor at Stevens Institute of Technology and has master's degrees in Computer Science and Philosophy.

Overview

As security professionals move to the executive ranks, they have been advised to speak in business terms. The direct translation of security measures to business terms has to date been risk reduction.[1] So speaking in business terms has been to express information in terms of risk. It is very common to see panels of security experts nodding their heads in violent agreement that business risk is the most important factor to consider in designing security measures.

Introduction

An increasingly popular idea is that metrics with respect to information security should be reviewed at very high levels within an organization. There are publications that exhort members of boards of directors to ask questions about security and ensure that information security professionals are not censored as they present their information to influential decision-makers.[2]

The combination of these two notions, that the business language of information security is risk, and that information security metrics should be reviewed at high levels, has moved InfoSec into the realm of risk metrics. Risk management professionals are now called upon to use their skills to apply quantitative rigor to the InfoSec program.

This focus on risk has decoupled the honest presentation of progress in security measures from the metrics presented to executive management. Management reporting with respect to information security now focuses almost exclusively on risk to the organization rather than the goals and objectives of the information security program itself. Industry best practices exhort InfoSec professionals to report to management in the language of risk analysis.[3] This is evident given the plethora of products on the market that collect information security metrics that are collectively referred to as "ITGRC" solutions, which stands for "Information Technology Governance Risk and Compliance." They tout "Risk Management Dashboards" to be used for executive reporting, which abstract away details of program effectiveness and allow information security managers to arbitrarily color-code aggregate results so they can paint noncompliance of one target metric red while another appears green. Even the International Standards Organization places risk to the organization as the number 1 factor when considering security management: "This International Standard specifies the requirements for establishing, implementing, operating, monitoring, reviewing, maintaining and improving a documented Information Security Management System (ISMS) *within the context of the organization's overall business risks*."[4] Whether intentional or not, this risk focus often blurs facts concerning the true state of information security beyond recognition.

This paper describes metrics used to manage security in contrast with those often used to report on risk.

Security Metrics

Measurement is the process of mapping from the empirical world to the formal, relational world.[5] The measure that results characterizes an attribute of some object under scrutiny. Information security is not the object, nor a well-understood attribute. Attempts to create information security metrics fall into a wide variety of characterizations.[6] There are at least four types:

1. A—Activity-Related Metric: Metrics that Measure Work Activity
2. T—Target-Related Metric: Metrics that Have a Measurable Target (i.e., No Missing Logs)
3. R—Remediation Metric: Metrics that Show Progress toward a Goal
4. M—Monitor Related Metric: Metrics that Monitor Processes

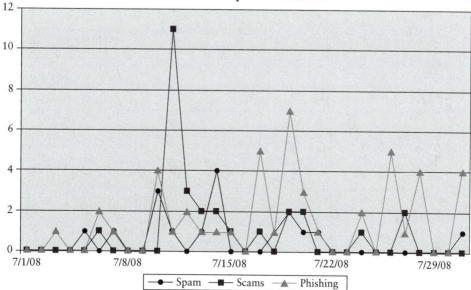

Note: *Blank lines indicate no incidents were reported, mostly weekends.*

Figure 6A-1 Activity Metrics

Courtesy Course Technology/Cengage Learning

Each type of characterization has its own utility in contributing information required to manage a security program.

Activity metrics are useful in resource allocation exercises. Figure 6A-1 shows activity metrics used to identify the number of incidents that security staff investigated over the course of the previous month. While there is no attempt at measuring the effectiveness of the incident investigation process, it is nevertheless useful in determining the number and type of activities that consume the time of security staff.

Target metrics are useful in verifying the correct implementation of technical security measures. The target is a total population that falls within the scope of a security measure. Figure 6A-2 provides an example of a target metrics where the target is a set of business unit applications and the attribute measured is whether they are all sending access logs to a central log collection server. Any deviation from 100% collected should immediately trigger an investigation. In this example, it appears that some technical difficulty was corrected midmonth, but resurfaced after a week or so of smooth operation.

Remediation metrics may be thought of as a subset of target where the scope of the target, thus the actual 100% measure, may not be known. Consider a case where an audit finding shows that user access is not properly terminated when employment is terminated because user ID strings are different in different systems and there is no correlation between those strings and any employee data record. A commonly agreed upon remediation for this situation is to deploy an identity management system to maintain such correlation. Figure 6A-3 is an example of remediation metrics that shows progress in the deployment of an identity management system. In this pre-production scenario, there are applications whose users are not yet

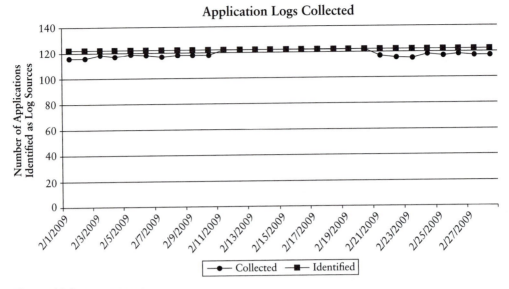

Figure 6A-2 Target Metrics

Courtesy Course Technology/Cengage Learning

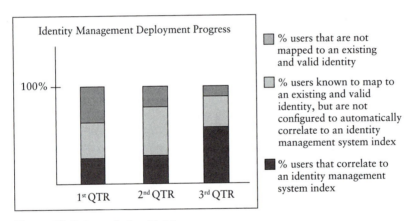

Figure 6A-3 Remediation Metrics

Courtesy Course Technology/Cengage Learning

identified by reference to an identity management system index, and they may or may not be mapped to an existing active and valid identity as the deployment continues. The number of users that are not correlated to the identity management system is considered a defect to be remediated and should become smaller as the deployment continues. A remediation metric is often used to determine the status of milestones in a security-related project plan.

Monitoring metrics are also useful in verifying the correct implementation of technical security measures, and in addition, they monitor security processes. Like target metrics, they have as a baseline the total population of a given universe. Figure 6A-4 illustrates how the correctness of firewall configuration may be measured. The top line represents the total number of firewalls in the organization. The line that sometimes dips below is the number of firewalls that were

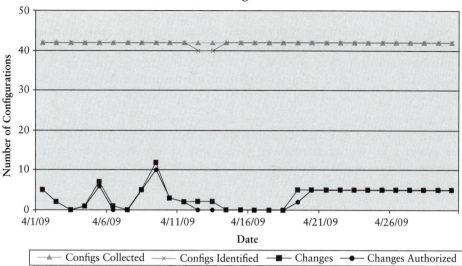

Figure 6A-4 Monitoring Metrics

Courtesy Course Technology/Cengage Learning

available during an automated daily configuration check. The lower lines on the chart represent the number of firewalls whose configuration check revealed changes from the previous day. The number of those changes is compared to the number of manual change control verifications that were performed by operations staff. A security manager can use this chart to verify both that automated controls are in place and that change procedures are properly executed. It can also be used to highlight systemic issues with a given process. In this case, it appears that there is a correlation between increases in the number of changes occurring on a daily basis and the occurrence of unauthorized changes.

These basic types of metrics are useful in managing a security program. Variations on them may be adapted to many situations and technologies encountered in day-to-day security tasks in the realms of policy, awareness and training, implementation, monitoring, and compliance.[7]

Case Studies

Following are three case studies that show the types of metrics most used in practice to demonstrate to auditors and regulators that information security goals are met. The activity that security personnel engage in to ensure security goals are met is observed during audit. The fact that management monitors that process is followed is also important. But it is the *result* of the staff activity and management monitoring that provides evidence control objectives are met. Auditors must gather evidence that they can use to verify that control objectives are actually met.[8] That type of evidence comes in the form of remediation and target metrics. The three cases show alternative approaches to the process of gathering target and remediation metrics.

Case 1: The Question-and-Answer Approach

Metrics of this type rely on a network of risk management professionals to monitor progress in meeting some sweeping organizational objective such as compliance with regulatory reporting requirements. The risk management professionals themselves are not usually responsible for meeting the objectives, just for identifying the right set of individuals who should address them, organizing a reporting framework, and periodically polling those accountable to see whether they have achieved compliance.

These types of metrics are often created using online surveys. The major challenge in this approach is devising methods of identifying organizational structure and individuals within them that can be held accountable for survey answers. The state of the art in survey metrics collection utilities are systems wherein the accountable person can be linked to the control they are reporting on in such a way that when they log in to the risk application, their log-in is treated as a digital signature. This, combined with strict management policy that questionnaires must be answered within strict timelines, allow the risk managers to report the results with firmwide authority. Figure 6A-5 provides an example of the type of online surveys an accountable manager may encounter.

From such a survey, metrics such as Figure 6A-6 may be derived. Risk management professionals reduce accountability to self-reported task completion. From Figure 6A-6, it may be inferred that all of the new applications introduced into operation in the first quarter are using the firm's single sign-on system for authentication, and are compliant with security policy, design, and change control standards. However, there were a few introduced in the second quarter that did not make use of single sign-on and were not policy or standards compliant. The pie charts in Figure 6A-7 show this line of business (LOB) in comparison with the

Application detail record for SALESAPP	
Application Acronym	**SALESAPP** CIO Owner: Doe, John L. (6043291)
Application Full Name	Salesperson Data Entry Application ▾
User Community	Line of Business - Services (Internal) ▾
Information Classification	Confidential (but not NPI) customer ▾ Information Class Definitions
Log-in method	Single Sign On ▾ Login Method Definitions
Is application design security policy compliant?	⦿ Yes ○ No
Is application implementation security policy compliant?	⦿ Yes ○ No
Is application change control process security policy compliant?	⦿ Yes ○ No
Does the application encrypt PCIS data?	⦿ Yes ○ No
Outsource Type	Customized Third Party Application run in house ▾
IT Manager	Jones, Janice (1638199)
Business Owner	Smith, Susan (6400809)
Status/DR Status	PROD ▾ Always Hot, Redundant Across Alternate Sites ▾

Figure 6A-5 Application Survey

Courtesy Course Technology/Cengage Learning

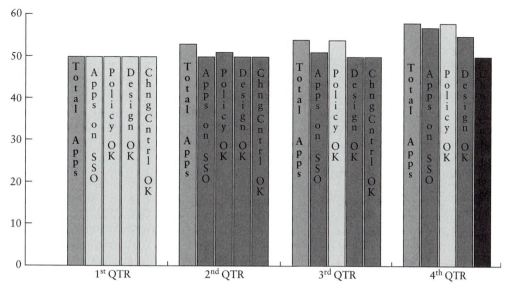

Figure 6A-6 Application Metrics

Courtesy Course Technology/Cengage Learning

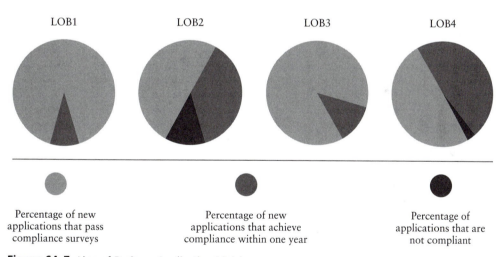

Figure 6A-7 Line of Business Application Metrics

Courtesy Course Technology/Cengage Learning

other LOBs in the firm. By comparison, LOB1 seems to have superior security deployment processes.

However, given that the data is based, not on automated measures, independent audit, or repeatable processes, but instead on data collection from accountable managers, all that can be inferred from Figure 6A-7 is that LOB1 *claims* to have fully compliant applications. The risk manager running the report is reduced to clerk status. These scenarios exist because the management objective on which the metric is modeled does not easily conform to available security measurement techniques. Suppose instead, there were automated verification procedures that could check to see if an application was in compliance, and there was a complete and accurate inventory of machines deployed in support of a given application. The inventory, in combination with automated verification procedures and/or technical configuration audits, could be used to establish that applications met firmwide security objectives. However, pressure for results in short timeframes sometimes require even the most technical of metrics professionals to resort to a question-and-answer method of data gathering.

These scenarios almost always suffer from real or perceived ambiguity in the way the "compliance" officer phrases overall goals and statements to be affirmed. For example, suppose an executive of a given organization is asked to affirm whether or not that organization has a policy to achieve compliance with a given regulation. The executive may sincerely respond in the affirmative, yet be thinking of a policy that states that the organization is fully committed to apply to all applicable regulation. At the same time, the executive may omit to mention that he or she does not believe that the regulation in question applies to that organization. Even when specific technology questions seem easy to verify, a respondent may find a question ambiguous enough for a misleading answer. For example, note the question in Figure 6A-5 that reads: "Does the application encrypt PCIS[9] data?" A manager who encrypts some but not all such data may honestly and misleadingly answer "yes." These examples and others like them leave a loophole of plausible deniability among those accountable for answering surveys while allowing the compliance officer to publish remediation metrics showing 100% compliance.

Case 2: The Risk Management Program

Risk assessment metrics with respect to security focus almost entirely on some adaptation of the risk management model prevalent in today's security literature:[10]

1. Assets
2. Threats to those assets
3. Vulnerabilities that may be exploited to enact threats
4. Probabilities that the exploits occur
5. Cost of controls that will reduce the likelihood the vulnerabilities can be exploited

Through a sound step-by-step approach, it is rare that an InfoSec professional will identify assets in any manner that would make sense from a business perspective. Performed correctly, the risk assessment would identify assets as products or services. However, there is overwhelming evidence in the security literature that assets are commonly construed to be computers themselves.[11] This makes threat identification easy, as a generic set of people who abuse computers can be easily identified: disgruntled employees, hackers, terrorists, and natural disasters. Vulnerabilities are also readily available as published sets of vulnerabilities from vendors as well as floods, fire, and hurricanes. Controls appear in this model as commercial off-the-shelf security products and services that will reduce the likelihood of threat.

So it is not too surprising that controls appearing as commercial off-the-shelf products and services are measured in similar ways by the InfoSec and risk management community. Automated tools can easily determine whether a given computer has a secure configuration. Figure 6A-8 demonstrates a metric commonly used in presentations of both InfoSec metrics and risk management metrics. It shows that there are a set of 27 computers in an organization all running the same operating system. There is an assumption that a secure

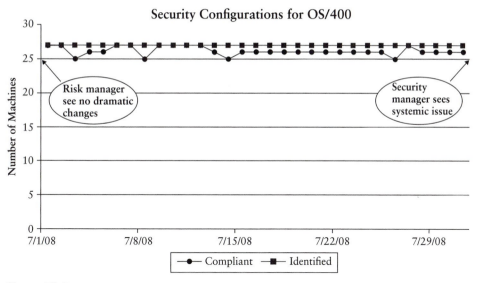

Figure 6A-8 Operating System Security Metric

Courtesy Course Technology/Cengage Learning

configuration of the operating system has been devised and is deployed on most of the computers in the set. However, it also shows that there are one or two machines that continually fall out of the secure configuration. To a risk manager, the lower line seems steady. The percentage of computers that are not secure seems low. The security configuration for the operating system as a whole seems stable. However, to the security manager, the same graph shows a target metric failed. The lower line indicates a weak link in the security operations support chain that could create a vulnerability to the entire platform. When this type of graph is presented to executives or auditors, it is almost always in the context of risk management.

Figure 6A-9 also demonstrates a metric commonly used in presentations of both InfoSec metrics and risk management metrics. It shows that some security control measure is in place for some type of platform that is deployed in different lines of business (LOB) in the organization. In both security management and risk metrics, it is intended to demonstrate that one business unit is more secure than another, to foster a sense of competition among business units. In the context of risk management, however, these metrics are instead used to explain different levels of risk and different approaches to the use of security controls as a risk reduction measure taken by different lines of business. Rather than walk away thinking that some LOB manager should be disciplined, executives are encouraged to compare the cost of security measures to the income produced by each line of business, and consider the probability that one of the known vulnerabilities indicated by the diagram may be exploited. A security manager seeing the same diagram sees a real and present danger.

It is an often glossed-over fact that the data presented in metrics like those in Figure 6A-8 reflect decisions based on judgments made by risk managers. An LOB may use Figure 6A-9 to determine that many of their noncompliance issues have to do with a single configuration parameter, that their machines are configured to "trust" others on their network. They may do a risk assessment on this configuration and decide that trust does not present a risk to

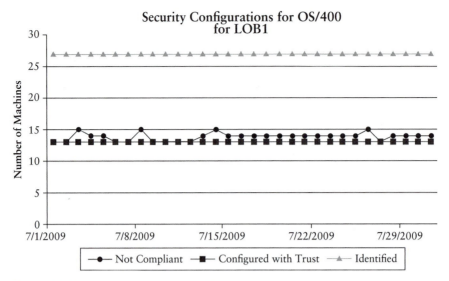

Figure 6A-9 Line of Business Platform Metric

Courtesy Course Technology/Cengage Learning

their environment. Where a security manager has been told that a LOB need not fix a vulnerability because their environment does not meet risk criteria necessary to fund a security fix, the group may mark that set of computers as the "equivalent" of having a compliant configuration. This may be recorded in a database that is consulted in the "automated" report that produces Figure 6A-8. To be clear on the potential impact of this risk management approach, the "Configured with Trust" line in Figure 6A-9 shows a number of computers that are not security policy compliant, but have been declared to be safe anyway due to a "risk acceptance" performed by line of business management. In Figure 6A-9, the 27 computers in Figure 6A-8 are represented as less than half policy compliant but half are not compliant due to a configuration that allows machines to trust each other. If a risk manager in the LOB finds the risk of trusting other computers acceptable in the course of their own risk assessment, the machines may be marked compliant. However, an auditor may only see Figure 6A-8 and not be told that different LOBs have different standards.

Moreover, even when configuration reports are produced with no exceptions, these risk management scenarios almost always concentrate on reported results of generic security software deployment packages. They rarely check to see if assets are protected through appropriate applications controls, or question whether management has allowed information to be disseminated too broadly rather than restricted by job function.

Case 3: The Sphere of Control

Organizations of this type have a centralized security function for most technology, while allowing some business units to independently manage business-unit-specific security measures. These distributed security functions usually have varying degrees of compliance with centrally published policies and procedures. However, when regulators and auditors come through, they are introduced to a person who is responsible only for security functions that

6A

overlap all business units, a *central* security officer, who proudly displays their metrics program while not mentioning that it does not cover 100% of the organization.

In contrast to the LOB-specific measures in Figure 6A-9, the central security function will gloss over technical differentiations in the data-gathering function. For example, measurements with respect to Windows operating systems are different than measurements concerning Linux. So normalizing these distinct measurements into industry-standard agreed-upon criteria for security measures seems like a commonsense exercise.

For example, Figure 6A-10 shows a set of security functions broken down by measureable features of operating systems that reflect them in a given environment. It does not necessarily matter that some operating systems implement security features better than others or that some instances of a given operating system are beyond the sphere of control of the central authority who generates the reports. It just demonstrates, whether, in the judgment of the central organization, these features are well implemented on the machines in scope. Such reports are meant to convey that the organization at least knows how to secure and measure things and that there should be no technology that requires security that would be beyond organizational expertise to deliver.

Central security organizations often feel justified in displaying this type of fuzzy target metric because they want to display true information but have been conditioned to allow the independent business units to evade their sphere of control. Where this is the case, they feel no responsibility to comment on the fact that their own management has allowed the independence. The lack of authority over LOBs could be perceived to indicate a lack of faith on the part of that management with respect to the security organization's ability to handle the special needs of the suborganization in the centralized program. The suborganization is acknowledged to be a stepchild under special care, like a child that is acknowledged to require special education whose efforts should not be averaged into the rest of the classroom because it would bring down the ratings for the school as a whole.

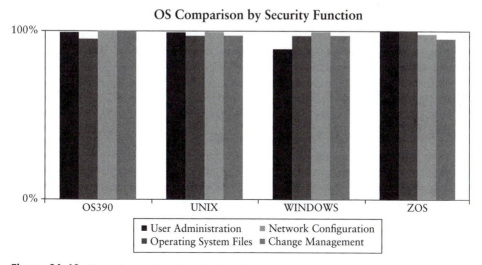

Figure 6A-10 Operating System Security Functions

Courtesy Course Technology/Cengage Learning

Conclusions

Let us suppose we are an InfoSec manager who needs to collect metrics to present to the board of directors (BOD). We are constrained on both time and level of detail. Suppose further we are new to the organization and not technical. We have no way to judge whether anything is secure or not for ourselves. In such a case, defining accountability and conducting surveys may be the only way to get the job done. The fact that the information is of dubious integrity is easily overlooked as the BOD meeting is short and is not expected to include technical details of how information was collected.

Even without the supposition that we are technical enough to evaluate information security risk ourselves, we are still constrained on both time and level of detail. Even when we know exactly where the problems are in the organization, it does not mean we have the solutions, especially when our sphere of control does not extend to LOB deployment programs. In this case, a security manager may feel that the program progress metrics are best served by presenting metrics as evidence of program evolution, that is, as charts that are clearly climbing uphill to meet targets. These normally leave the execs beaming about continuous improvements rather than upset about not meeting state-of-the-art, well-known, 10-year-old best practices.

A continuous improvement report where we do not meet targets is actually less preferable to present to the board than a presentation in which we are not at all expected to report on programs we do not control. Where we cannot even collect data from LOBs outside our control, we can simply omit mention of them and provide metrics on the deployment measures we fully control and endorse.

The metrics described in these cases will not tell the BOD whether the organization's information is secure. You know your information is secure when you have a security program and corresponding systems architecture. The way you know your program is working is via activity and monitoring metrics. The way you know your architecture is in place is via target metrics. When you find out you have a gap that leaves information exposed, you need remediation metrics. Metrics that correspond to a holistic security program demonstrate that management objectives for the program are (or are not) being met (or to what degree the gap). Without the explanatory guidance provided by the security program and information architecture, metrics represent collections of disconnected attributes, none of which are security. Every aspect of the security program need not be continuously measured to provide adequate assurance that the program is working. However, enough control points must be capable of being monitored often enough so that the combined measures of control points directly map onto the organization's requirements for information security. This mapping must be designed in such a way that there is capacity for demonstration that objectives are met.

Too often, target and remediation metrics absent program methodology and information architecture are mistaken for evidence of security program management. Executives on the receiving end of metrics often have a false sense of security. This type of blindspot, if it exists, does not extend to the rest of the organization nor even to its entire management team. Just as the product support team at Enron knew there was no broadband service offering,[12] the InfoSec managers and other technical managers know fully well that these types of metrics do not actually represent what they are implied to convey.

Endnotes

6A

1. See discussions of risk in Sherwood, John, Andrew Clark, and David Lynas, *Enterprise Security Architecture*, CMP Books, 2005.

2. *Board Briefing on IT Governance*, 2nd ed., IT Governance Institute (www.itgi.org), 2003.

3. See *Information Security Forum Standard of Good Practices*, SM3.3, www .securityforum.org. BS ISO/IEC 27001:2005 BS 7799-2:2005.

4. Ibid.

5. This is a fairly generic definition of measurement, but for more reading on the concept of metrics as applied to security, see Herrman, Debra, *Complete Guide to Security and Privacy Metrics*. Auerbach, 2007.

6. See Cohen, Fred, *IT Security Governance Guidebook with Security Program Metrics*. Auerbach, 2008.

7. For comprehensive treatment of each of these realms, see Bayuk, Jennifer, *Stepping Through the InfoSec Program*, Information Systems Audit and Control Association (ISACA), 2007.

8. See the Certified Information System's Auditor's *Code of Professional Ethics*, a Standard published by Information Systems Audit and Control Association (www.isaca.org).

9. PCIS in this context refers to data required to be encrypted according to the Payment Card Industry Security Standards published at https://www.pcisecuritystandards.org.

10. Such publications are based on practices described by Carnegie Mellon in Operationally Critical Threat, Asset, and Vulnerability Evaluation^{SM} (OCTAVE, http://www.cert.org/octave/), and National Institute of Standards and Technology in *Special Publication 800-30* (csrc.nist.gov/publications/nistpubs/800-30/sp800-30.pdf).

11. See Jaquith, Andrew, *Security Metrics*, Addison-Wesley, 2007, pp. 235–237.

12. McLean, Bethany, and Peter Elkind, *The Smartest Guys in the Room: The Amazing Rise and Scandalous Fall of Enron*. Penguin Group, 2003.

Impact of Incomplete or Missing Information in a Security Policy

Wasim A. Al-Hamdani and Wendy D. Dixie
Kentucky State University

Wasim A. Al-Hamdani is an Associate Professor of Cryptography and Information Security at Kentucky State University (KSU). He plays a leading role at KSU in developing the Information Assurance Master's Program and Information Security bachelor's degree. He was at the University of Technology in Baghdad from 1985 to 1999. He has published six textbooks and more than 53 papers dealing with computer science and cryptography and has contributed six chapters in research books.

Wendy D. Dixie received a bachelor's degree in computer science from Kentucky State University. She later received an MBA with a concentration in information technology from Eastern Kentucky University. She is currently pursuing a master's degree in computer science technology at Kentucky State University where she is working as a manager in the Information Technology Department.

Overview

A security policy is a document that outlines the rules and practices for computers and it regulates how an organization protects, manages, and accesses its sensitive information. A security policy is often considered to be a "living document," meaning that the document is never finished, but is continuously updated as technology and employee requirements change. The fundamental elements of a security policy are audience, compliance, and consequences of non-adherence. This chapter looks at the results of missing one or more of the fundamental elements.

Introduction

An information security policy is "typically a document that outlines specific requirements or rules that must be met within an organization. In the information/network security realm, policies are usually point-specific, covering a single area."[1] The purpose of the policy is to protect the company's information assets from all threats, whether internal or external, deliberate or accidental.[1] In particular, business continuity and contingency plans, backup procedures, avoidance of viruses and hackers, access control to systems, and information security incident reporting are fundamental to the overall organization's policy.

There are two types of policies: governing policies and technical policies.[2] Governing policies cover all aspects of information security at a higher level than technical policies. Technical policies have an audience of technical people who work with specific technologies. Technical policies include policies on authentication, backup, and configuration, to name a few. Any information security policy theoretically must have the following elements, even if they are not stated clearly:

- Subjects: active entity that causes information to flow among objects.
- Objects: passive entity is the part of a system that contains or receives information.

The remaining three elements of the security policy define the ways in which subjects and objects interact. These elements are the access attributes of a subject or an object, the access rules embody the policy that segregates information for the system and the privileges that determine a subject's ability to perform certain restricted system functions.

There are usually four key elements to a successful security policy document:[3]

- To whom and what the policy applies
- The need for adherence
- A general description
- Consequences of non-adherence

A more detailed security policy would cover:

1. Document information
2. Audience
3. Purpose
4. Scope
5. Policy
   - i) Objectives
     - (1) Confidentiality
     - (2) Integrity

6B

        (3)   Availability

        (4)   Non-repudiation

        (5)   Authentication

    ii) Compliance

        (1)   Reporting

        (2)   Consequence

    iii) Responsibility

    iv) Implementation

        (1)   Resources

        (2)   Access

        (3)   Security monitoring

    v) Controls

        (1)   Risk

        (2)   Awareness

        (3)   Incident response

        (4)   Disaster recovery

6.   Glossary

7.   Approval

An information security policy covers the following topics: organization security, network, access control, personal, data classification, physical, communication, electronic mail, firewall, and business continuity.

The main theme for this work is the study of "missing one or more elements of a policy or missing the whole policy." This chapter looks at different cases to study the impact on security.

Management Responsibility

Roles and Responsibility

It is essential to the implementation and credibility of a security policy that all system users across the organization have a role in implementing, supporting, and adhering to information technology security. The roles must be clearly defined at each level of responsibility. Additionally, support and commitment of management must be visible. The roles and responsibilities must be included in the job description and in employment contracts, which would include the consequences of not adhering to the policy. Additionally all users, including third-party vendors, who have access to sensitive information must sign a confidentially agreement.

Organizationally, in the absence of clearly defined and enforced roles and responsibilities, upper management will not be aware of the organization's role in the event that there is a security issue. If management is not aware of his or her role, then it will be evident that each level below management will not be aware of theirs. In the scenario of software piracy—students, faculty, or staff downloading copyrighted music or movies without paying or receiving permission—the university may take the posture that it is the individual's personal account that downloaded the copyrighted item; thus, the university has no responsibility in any legal issues that could arise. However, the user (for example, a student) may state that they were unaware that it was illegal to download the music because the university network allowed them to do so, thus putting the responsibility on the "system." Information technology could take the posture that the system allows the users to download because they do not have the tools to stop them because management has not approved the budget to purchase the tools or even that management does not support a policy of not allowing the system to be configured to stop the behavior. If each user knew their responsibility, then each user would know that each one of them has a responsibility in the prevention of software piracy.

Another scenario is related to information ownership. If responsibility of information does not exist, then access to systems/data can be given incorrectly. Who has the authority to give access will not be clear, and systems could be compromised, ultimately losing data. Organizationally, users (including management) may believe that information technology can give them access to or remove access to all systems without following any process or approvals from system owners. The users may not even be aware that owners even exist. For example, an employee may believe that they need access to a particular system. The user may come to information technology to get access. An employee in information technology may grant the user access because they are unaware of who owns the information or system procedures for granting access. Again, the users' roles have not been clearly defined and understood. If it is not defined who is responsible for information, the custodian may believe that it is only information technology's responsibility and not a conjunction of both areas.

Another scenario relates to maintenance of the security policies. Security policies and procedures must be reviewed, monitored, and kept up-to-date on a regular basis. If the policies are not reviewed, monitored, and updated, then the policies can become obsolete. Many times management and users may be unaware of the obsolete policy until a security violation occurs. If the user knows their responsibility in relation to updating the policies, then the policy will be updated and if not, then there would be consequences to the user.

Security Awareness and Training

In order to have an effective information security policy, all users of the systems must be informed of and trained on the organization's approach to managing information security on a regular basis. The policy must be clearly defined, communicated, and documented to the users in a manner that is "relevant, accessible, and understandable."[4] As part of management's support to security awareness, management must ensure that all users who have access to the computer systems of an organization participate in awareness and training programs as well as adhere to and confirm their understanding. Management must ensure that documentation is kept on record that training was conducted and who was in attendance.

In the absence of security and awareness training, users will not know what the security policies are, their role in the security policy, or how to identify or even report a security violation. More than likely, the user will not even know where the policies are located.

For example, in the event that a user receives an email asking them to send in his or her username and password, the user could send in their username and password to the "person" sending the email. However, if there was a security awareness program, users would know that information technology would never ask for his or her username and password. A security awareness program would also inform the user on how to respond to the incident and how to report the potential security threat.

All users who have access to the university's information systems must understand their role and how to protect the confidentiality, integrity, and availability of information systems. They must be given the supporting materials and any updates to the policy as the changes occur.

Physical Security

Physical security encompasses the environmental and physical access control of computer data centers, and information technology resources. It is vital to the overall security policy that physical security exists to prevent loss, damage, compromising of assets, and interruption of business activities. The very basics of environmental and physical access controls must be mandatory and enforced.

Environmental security controls can consist of uninterruptible power supplies, generators, temperature and humidity systems, as well as fire suppression units. In the absence of these environmental controls, the destructive impact that fire, water, and static electricity will have on a computing center is greater. For example, in the event that there is a power failure and there are no uninterruptible power supplies, there will be an immediate disruption of service, potentially causing data loss or hardware failure. The impact on users will be that they will not have access to the systems and the technology staff will not have had the opportunity to power down the systems in a proper way to prevent equipment failure.

Another environmental scenario could be in the event that there is a fire in the data center, if a fire suppression system does not exist; the entire computer center is subject to total destruction. A fire suppression system could rapidly detect and distinguish a fire prior to a large amount of damage to the computer system, without any disruption to business operations.

In addition to environmental controls, controlling access to computer facilities is just as important to a security policy. Ultimately, every office, computer room and work area containing sensitive information, or the means to access such information, must be a location that is secure and attended to only by authorized personnel.

Access control can be represented by special door locks and barriers, restricted access to authorized employees and escorted personnel, and processes for adding and removing personnel. A streamlined process should be executed for terminated employees. In the absence of access control, unauthorized personnel will have access to and expose computer systems to a number of computer security threats.

In the absence of an access control policy, if an authorized user of the computer room is called away on a support call or to a meeting and leaves an unauthorized person in the computer room, the unauthorized person will have access to unplug servers, review confidential information or printouts, steal equipment, or spill liquids on computer equipment. If an access control policy existed, the authorized user would know unauthorized users or visitors must have an authorized escort at all times in order to be in the computer room. The user would understand that the computer room and all data residing in the area are under a high level of security at all times and that any personnel in the area should only be in the area for authorized business. In another instance, the absence of access controls to support equipment, such as printers, photocopiers, or even fax machines, could lead to the release of sensitive information. For example, if a faculty member prints sensitive information regarding a student and the printer is in an unsecured location down two hallways or on another floor, in the time that it takes the faculty member to get to the printout, an unauthorized user could have reviewed or taken the information either intentionally or unintentionally.

Another consequence of the lack of an access control policy relates to change control. The technical staff may make changes to computer procedures, computer facilities, equipment, software, and systems without any formal approval, communication to others, or clear record of the change. In the event that there is a problem with the change, there will not be any documentation on how to recover from the change, those impacted by the change will be caught off guard, and information technology management may not have a clear understanding of what occurred and thus be unable to make accurate decisions on how to mitigate the incident.

Additionally, records must be kept and audited on a regular basis of who has access to the computer resources. In the absence of record keeping and auditing, a user who no longer should have access to the computer resources either because he or she has left the organization or because his or her position may have changed may still have access to the system. Auditing the system would readily identify users who have access and if the user should not, then his or her access could quickly be modified in accordance with the user's new role in the organization or completely removed.

Relating to physical security, there must be a policy for equipment that is taken to unprotected areas off the organization's property. The policy needs to be inclusive of the policy for securing the equipment while on the premises, in addition to how to protect the equipment while off the premises. The policy must explain that the equipment must not be unattended while in public places like an airport or hotel or even meeting rooms. In the event that this policy does not exist, the user may irresponsibly leave the laptop on the desk in the hotel, still logged in, exposing the data residing on the laptop or even exposing the laptop to theft. The policy would state that the user should store the laptop in the hotel's locked safety box or file cabinet.

In the absence of a policy for the secure disposal or surplus of equipment, information on the computer would be compromised. In one instance, a user will get a new computer and may delete items on the hard drive of the old computer, believing that he or she has completely removed any sensitive information, unaware that the data could be retrieved with special utilities. The old computer could be given away to charity or reused within the organization, increasing the likelihood that the information on the computer will be compromised. Additionally, if an old computer or hard drive is given to a member of information technology to dispose of properly, if the member of information technology does not have a procedure to follow for proper sanitizing of the storage media, then the member is also placing the information on the computer at the risk of being exposed.

Data Access Control and Security

In addition to physical security (environmental and physical), access to information must not be disclosed to unauthorized individuals or organizations that do not have legitimate reason for access to it; therefore, a policy must exist for the appropriate authentication into the computer system.

In the absence of an authentication policy, there is no way to identify who is accessing the computer system of an organization and it is difficult to keep unauthorized users off the computer system. For example, an unauthorized user can come to an organization, and without logging in, access the computer systems. The unauthorized user can install malicious code on the network, access sensitive or critical information, disable systems, or steal software. The user may even have access to use the organization's resources such as printing or copying. From a technical perspective, information technology would be unable to monitor not only who is on the system but also what information or services the user is accessing on the system as well as know when or how to add or remove users from the system. For example, if an official visitor is at an organization and needs to use the computer resources for legitimate reasons, the user may not get access to the system and will not be able to perform his or her work.

In direct connection to an authentication policy is an administrative guideline on username and password structure for computer systems. An advisory guideline should exist on how to handle usernames that are not being used, when employees are no longer employed at an organization, and removing default usernames. Additionally, guidelines should exist for how to create valid passwords and how to store passwords.

Usernames and passwords must be required for access to every system. The system must allow for the password to force "complex" passwords, meaning that the password must be reset after a number of days, the password cannot be reused within a certain number of times, the account must be locked out after a number of incorrect attempts, and the password must be a certain length and consist of a combination of letters, special characters, or numbers. In the event that a system cannot allow for that type of configuration, the greater the chance the system can be compromised.

In the event that a username or password guideline is not present, users will not have a clear understanding on how to create usernames or passwords. Users may use their social security number or other sensitive information for usernames or passwords. In the event that a password guideline does not exist, users may create weak passwords, share passwords, or even paste passwords on the computer unit they are logging into, ultimately causing the system to be compromised rather easily. There would not be any conformity of usernames within the system, thus making it difficult for system administrators to effectively and securely manage the system.

Additionally, the password guideline should address the storage of passwords. In the absence of a password storage guideline, users will write down their passwords and risk the password being lost, stolen, or exposed to another user.

Remote Access

Remote connectivity to an organization's network should be provided only to authorized users and on an as-needed basis. Users who access the system remotely are responsible for ensuring that unauthorized users are not allowed access to the network. The computer connecting must contain up-to-date antivirus software, and the computer equipment must be configured to comply with the organization's acceptable usage and security policy. Likewise, the user must understand that the computer connecting to the network is a de facto extension of the organization's network.

In the event that a remote access policy does not exist, any user who has access to an organization's network may have the ability to remotely access the network. The user may not realize the security violations that can occur if they are sitting in Starbucks and accessing sensitive information or if they are accessing the systems from a computer that is full of viruses or not on a secured network. Simply, if a policy for remote access is absent, computer systems and the data that resides on it can easily be compromised. Although the user may be an authorized user, the user still may not need access to the system remotely. In the absence of a remote access policy, the technical administrators may not set parameters to require authentication, or limitation of connection time. Another scenario may be that the user is working from home and leaves the laptop on the dinner table and has student information up on the screen, so anyone that comes by can eavesdrop or read the information that is on the screen.

Additionally, in the absence of a remote access policy, users may not realize the exposure of risk to the network systems by letting other individuals such as family members or friends use the equipment while still connected to the network or any sensitive information that is stored on the equipment. In the absence of a remote access policy, in the event that the organization uses VPN technology, there will not be a clear understanding of who is responsible for installing, configuring, and maintaining the connection.

Network and Communication Security

Network and communication security is more than securing Internet or email. It states how all assets, network connections, and interfaces stored on the network will be protected. Many of these policies, such as access control and remote access, have been addressed earlier in this chapter; however, there are other components that are essential to securing the entire network infrastructure.

General network policies should include network addressing and architecture. It should involve having a plan for segregating systems that have critical data or require special routing. In the absence of an addressing policy, a user may inadvertently get access to systems or data that they are not authorized to. One scenario would be that all authenticated users to the network could have access to network files saved by the president of an organization. If network parameters were set, users would have access only to the files that they have been granted access.

Essential to the network policy is the Internet security policy. This policy should consist of the minimum policies for managing data going out to and coming from the Internet, user responsibility, and Web site responsibilities.

In the absence of a policy to manage data imported from and exported to the Internet, unauthorized traffic or threats could come in and out of the network. In one scenario, a computer hacker would have the ability to place malicious code on a network and cause loss of data, services, hardware, and much more. In another scenario, a third-party vendor could have the ability to access servers on the network and get unauthorized access to information on the server. The organization could be exposed to Web hackers who could deface the Web site or even take sensitive information from the Web site.

Additionally, the firewall could be configured to not allow appropriate traffic to enter or leave the network. For example, authorized users may need access to a particular server to conduct actual business, but if a policy did not exist to allow for certain servers to have outbound traffic, then the users would not get access to the system.

In the absence of a user responsibility policy for the Internet, users would not know their responsibilities in appropriate use of the company Internet connection. Users of an organization may not realize that they are not to use the organization's Internet to download illegal files, files that contain viruses, or content that is explicit or illegal in nature. In one scenario, a user may access explicit content and be seen by another user. The user may report the information, but since the company does not have a policy against it, then there would not be much recourse for the company to use in the event that the user is fired from the organization and chooses to challenge his or her dismissal in a court of law.

In another scenario, the user may give too much information about the organization over the Internet. For example, the user may upload or send sensitive information about an organization without ensuring that the connection is secure or that the receiver of the information is legitimate.

In addition to protecting the data from external hackers, there needs to be a policy regarding the usage of data placed on the company Web site. In the absence of a Web site policy, any user could have access to update the Web site and place any type of information on or remove pertinent data from the Web site. For example, a user may believe that the Web site should contain photos of staff members partying or scantily dressed and then would have access to place the information on the Web site. A policy needs to exist that explicitly states who has privileges to update a company's Web site, and furthermore, what content can be added. The Web site system parameters should be set to support the policy.

Email Security

Email has become a critical communication tool for many organizations. An email security policy must involve proper access controls, as discussed earlier in this chapter, to ensure that only authorized users have access to an organization's email system. Additionally, an email policy needs to include administration of email, handling of email, and limiting the size of an individual email.

In the absence of an email policy, users will not be aware of their responsibility of knowing how to use email as correspondence. Many users may send sensitive data, harassing email, and spam emails to users from an organization's email system. For example, if there is not a clear policy on sending chain letters or other spam emails, a user may send chain letters to many, clogging up the email system, spreading viruses, or even misrepresenting the organization.

Another scenario in the absence of an email policy would be the storage of email. If there is not a policy on email box sizes, then users would use email as storage and have email boxes with an enormous amount of email in them. For example, a user can use email to store attachments, voice mail, and spam and have an email box that is over 20 GB. Having thousands of users with potentially 20 GB of data would put an enormous strain on servers and potentially cause service outage.

Viruses and Malicious Code

The need for protection against viruses and malicious code is another essential part of a security policy. As a baseline, a policy should at least include the mandatory installation of virus protection for every device connected to the network.

In the absence of a virus protection policy, an organization's network would be infected on a daily basis. Users could bring viruses from external devices, download from the Internet, or receive from email systems. Viruses could even be installed from third-party software vendors, as mentioned previously. Without a policy, a network could basically be rendered inoperable.

Additionally, the policy must also include a recommended timeframe for virus system scans and virus protection file updates. In the absence of this policy, the virus protection software could be present on a user's computer, but if the software is not updated or if the software scan is not run on a scheduled basis, new viruses could be present on a user's PC without the user even knowing it until they start having system problems.

Risk Management

Risk management is essential to ensuring that information technology resources are identified and protected. Additionally, understanding and documenting the risks from threats and vulnerabilities is critical to any security policy.

In the absence of a risk management policy, organizations will not know the threats they are facing. The organization would also not know the appropriate management actions to take in managing the risk nor how to implement controls to protect the organization from the risk. For example, management would not realize the organization is at risk for having a virus attack because the company's antivirus software has not been updated in years. Additionally, the organization would not know the impact of a virus attack as a result nor would they know how to implement controls to protect the organization from the risk. Additionally, a risk assessment must be conducted on a regular basis.

Security Incident Management

As stated throughout this chapter, the adherence to security policies is an essential responsibility that every user of a network holds. Just as it is important to adhere to the policy, the user's responsibility in reporting security violations cannot be underestimated.

In the absence of a security incident reporting policy, users will not know how to report an incident, when to report an incident, or even what is considered a security incident. Management would likely have the same type of unawareness; however, they have the added level of not knowing what to do if a security violation is reported.

For example, a user may not realize that burning a copy of a movie and then selling it to other coworkers is a security violation. But in the event a user realizes that this is a security violation, without a clear policy, the user will not know the procedure or how to report the violation; the organization is subject to copyright violations.

Another scenario could be that a user can report a security violation to the wrong person. The person who is receiving the security violation may not realize it is a violation or may not report it to anyone else. Thus, a violation has been reported but to the wrong person, and thus, no action could be taken.

Another scenario could be that a security violation is reported the right way to the right person but no disciplinary action taken against the violator. Other users will witness the non-action and not take the security policies or violation seriously.

Additionally, another scenario could be that a security violation is identified with a parameter setup of a system. The system administrator may identify the violation and fix the problem without reporting that a violation ever existed.

Business Continuity Management

To minimize the effect that security violations, disasters, and loss of service have on the operations of an organization, it is essential that a business continuity policy/plan exist. The policy must identify the risks, reduce the effects of the incidents, and provide a timely resumption of services.

In the absence of a business continuity plan, in the event that there is a service interruption, users and management would not know the steps needed to restore business operations. One scenario could be that a company's main generator malfunctions during a power outage, causing the organization to go on extended downtime during the company's prime time for services. If a plan is not in place, the company would not know how to continue the services that they provide. One plan could be to have another facility handle their operations, but in the absence of a plan, the company would be closed.

Another scenario, in the absence of a business continuity plan for each department within an organization, the user department may be experiencing problems and close down their operation because they do not have services. One plan could be for the company to go to a short-term manual process, but in the absence of a plan, the workers in the department may decide to take extended lunch breaks or just go home.

Another scenario could be that a business continuity plan exists but has never been tested. During the execution of the plan, the backup systems could fail, the equipment used as backup could be outdated, or the procedures may no longer be valid.

Another scenario could be that a business continuity plan exists but is not documented. During the execution of the plan, the system users, users who have a role in the execution of the plan, the system administrators, and affected third-party vendors may not know what to do. The organization would be operating in chaos.

Security Policy Section	Why it is needed	What happens if it does not exist
Roles and Responsibilities	So that users will know their roles and responsibilities regarding the security policy.	Users do not know their roles and responsibilities.
Security Awareness and Training	So that users will know what the security policies are, where they are located, and their responsibility in relation to it.	Users will be unaware of nature of policy, where they are located, or any new updates to policy.
Environmental Security	To ensure protection mechanisms are in place to protect the environment of the computer room.	Computing resources can be destroyed.
Physical Security	To ensure protection mechanisms are in place to protect the equipment and data resources.	Computing resources can be destroyed or compromised.
Access Control	To prevent unauthorized access to physical computing resources.	Unauthorized access to physical computing resources.
Password Policy	To make users aware of the risk of not protecting their password.	Unauthorized access to individual user data and possibly systems data.
VPN Policy	To establish remote access for individuals that need to access the network—the individual must be approved for this access.	Unauthorized users and hackers may gain access to the organization's computing resources and use them for personal gain or destructive reasons.
Network Policy	To protect the organization's network investment by defining all allowable devices and routes.	Users will connect unapproved and unacceptable devices to the network that will cause degradation in network services, possibly even halt network services.
Email Policy	To govern email usage, it needs to be spelled out that email is a tool of business and that personal messaging should be limited. Size and type of email will be defined as well.	Users will abuse email with respect to type of email, size of email, storage of email, etc.
Virus and Malicious	To protect and prevent viruses and malicious code from being introduced into the network. Also defines what steps to take in the event of a virus outbreak.	Virus and malicious code will be constantly running through the network preventing productive work.
Risk Management	Need to reduce or minimize known threats and be prepared for new and unknown threats to reduce or minimize major disruptions in service.	System downtime would be unpredictable with risk management in place.

Table 6B-1 Information Security Policy Components

6B

Security Policy Section	Why it is needed	What happens if it does not exist
Security Incident Policy	To have an organized and orderly process in place to systematically work through or debug an incident such as a virus attack or malicious code attack or power outage.	Incident resolution would be a guessing game at best, not sure how to go about resolving the incident. Just patching the problem and applying a permanent fix would be the most likely result.
Business Continuity Management	To ensure in the event of an extended period of downtime that a plan is in place that would allow the organization to efficiently operate without the use of its computing resources and networks so that service can still be rendered effectively.	The organization will more than likely shut down until systems are restored. Confusion, poor customer service, and chaos will be the end result of not having a business continuity plan.

Table 6B-1 Continued

Conclusion

The consequences of missing elements of a security policy can be devastating to an organization. Additionally, security awareness and education is essential. If management responsibility, support, and commitment are not present and the users are not educated, then the security policy basically does not exist.

Recommended Reading

Bacik, Sandy. 2008. *Building an Effective Information Security Policy Architecture,* 1st ed. CRC.

Barman, Scott. 2001. *Writing Information Security Policies.* Sams.

Diver, Sorcha. 2006. *Information Security Policy—A Development Guide for Large and Small Companies, V. 2.0.* Can be retrieved from http://www.sans.org/reading_room/ whitepapers/policyissues/

Easy2solve. 2005. *RU Secure.* Can be retrieved from http://www.rusecure.co.uk/

Greene, Sari. 2005. *Security Policies and Procedures: Principles and Practices.* Prentice Hall.

Information-Shield. 2005. *Information Security Policies Made Easy, Version 10.* Can be retrieved from http://www.informationshield.com/

ISACA.org. 2008. *Information Systems Audit and Control Association.* Can be retrieved from http://www.isaca.org/

ISO. 2005. *ISO/IEC 17799:2005 Information Technology—Security Techniques—Code of Practice for Information Security Management.*

Moskowitz, Jeremy. 2008. *Group Policy: Fundamentals, Security, and Troubleshooting.* Sybex.

Pearce_Pearce_Inc. 2008. *Information Security Policy.* Can be retrieved from https://www .pearceandpearce.com/

Peltier, Thomas R. 2001. *Information Security Policies, Procedures, and Standards: Guidelines for Effective Information Security Management,* 1st ed. Auerbach Publications.

Peltier, Thomas R. (ed). 2004. *Information Security Policies and Procedures: A Practitioner's Reference,* 2nd ed. Auerbach Publications.

SANS. 2008. *The SANS Security Policy Project.* Can be retrieved from http://www.sans.org/ resources/policies/

SearchSecurity.com. 2007. *Information Security Policy Definition.* Can be retrieved from http://searchsecurity.techtarget.com/dictionary/definition/what-is-security-policy.html

Technologies, CPCS. 2008. *Policy Samples: Sample Network & Computer Security Policies.* Can be retrieved from http://www.cpcstech.com/sample-network-computer-security-policies.htm

Ungerman, Mark. 2005. "Creating and Enforcing an Effective Information Security Policy." *Information Systems Control Journal,* Volume 6.

webopedia.com. *Security Policy Definition.* Can be retrieved from www.webopedia.com/

Endnotes

1. 2008 Pearce & Pearce, Inc., "Information Security Policy." Can be retrieved from https://www.pearceandpearce.com/

2. Sorcha Diver, *Information Security Policy—A Development Guide for Large and Small Companies,* V. 2.0, SANS Institute 2007. Can be retrieved from http://www.sans.org/ reading_room/whitepapers/policyissues/

3. Mark Ungerman, "Creating and Enforcing an Effective Information Security Policy," *Information Control Journal*, Volume 6, 2005.

4. ISO/IEC 17799: 2005, *Information Technology—Security Techniques—Code of Practice for Information Security Management.*

Case **6C**

A Review of Information Security Management Requirements as Reflected in U.S. Federal Law

Jeffrey P. Landry
University of South Alabama

Jeffrey P. Landry is a Professor in the School of Computer and Information Sciences at the University of South Alabama, where he teaches courses in information systems strategy and policy, project management, and human computer interaction.
Dr. Landry is developing risk assessments of voting systems for federal elections; has conducted risk management for a national, online certification exam; and has published on trust in the IS context, all following a ten-year software industry career.

Overview

With federal regulation of information systems increasing, the need for greater understanding of the ethical and legal implications of information technology (IT) in society has never been greater. The need for legal and ethical acumen is even more pronounced for the management of information security in a government context. Federal agencies, for example, are large bureaucracies created and governed by laws, rules, and regulations, and the ethical principles embodied in these codes. The body of legislation relating to information security in federal agencies, along with evolving case law, is a rich context for understanding the ethical and legal impacts of IT for both the private and public sectors, and for both classified and nonclassified systems. A national training standard for senior systems managers identified more than a dozen laws relating to the management of information security. These laws will be used as a framework for investigating legal and ethical issues in information security management.

Introduction

Historical events provide a context for understanding information security management in today's society. The Cold War, UFO sightings, Watergate, 9/11 attacks, Enron scandal, and Internet revolution are among the events that prompt periodic responses from the United States (U.S.) government. These responses often take the form of law. Legislative responses have officially authorized the upgrade of national security infrastructure and management for federal agencies, and affected the information rights and responsibilities for individuals and government. These laws embody an evolving historical response to information threats, and taken together, provide guidance for today's current and aspiring professionals.

The laws themselves authorize more information security education and training for government workers. Standards incorporating security training with legal and ethical coverage have been defined by the U.S. Department of Defense (DoD). One such directive is the Committee on National Security Systems (CNSSI) No. 4012—The National Information Assurance Training Standard (NIST) for Senior Systems Managers.[1] This document lists more than a dozen laws related to information security, and calls for coverage of legal and ethical issues.

NIST 4012 is one of several education and training standards defined by the DoD for various professional roles. The 4012 standard targets senior systems managers, otherwise known by titles such as Chief Information Officer (CIO), Designated Approving Authority (DAA), Chief Technology Officer (CTO), etc. The senior systems manager, who will also be called "CIO" or "IT manager" elsewhere in this chapter, refers to the overall leader of an organization's information systems function responsible for information systems success. This manager may sometimes share the responsibility of the Chief Information Security Officer (CISO) role, but recent federal legislation grants the CIO authority to create a separate CISO role.[2] When information security management is discussed, the issues may pertain to the CIO, CISO, or both.

The purpose of this chapter is to overview the 4012 laws related to the management of information security of federal computer systems, and to provide practical implications for information security managers in both public and private sectors. This chapter takes a broad managerial view of information security. With each law covered, the important implications for the management of information systems security and ethical considerations are discussed. Coverage consists of 11 laws, including the Privacy Act, Freedom of Information Act, FISMA, and the USA Patriot Act. Several cases are covered in-depth, demonstrating the legal and ethical dilemmas facing managers. The approach incorporates a viewpoint that legal and ethical considerations are inseparable.

Federal Laws Related to the Management of Information Security

Particularly useful for the understanding of legal and ethical issues in IT is 4012's identification of more than a dozen laws affecting information security. This set of laws, while not comprehensive, is nevertheless broad enough to gain insight into a variety of legislative issues and useful for a focus on professional development. See Function Three, Section A: "Laws Related to Information Assurance and Security" for the specific training standard.

The 4012 standards pertain particularly to national security systems managed by federal government and related entities. A national security system is defined narrowly as a government-operated information system for military or intelligence use, rather than routine administrative or business functions. See reference source[3] for a precise definition of national security system. Despite the specific focus on federal agencies and national security systems, the view taken in this chapter is that the 4012 standards have broader implications, pertaining both to classified and nonclassified systems. Many of the approaches used by government-issued standards, such as the risk management framework,[4] have broad applicability.

Table 6C-1 lists and describes federal laws that are specifically identified in the NIST 4012 standard. These laws are relevant to senior systems managers and federal systems, in particular, but also have a broader relevance. The table includes the major provisions of each law, its information security management implications, ethical considerations, and at least one private-sector information security issue that parallels the federal information security implication.

Each of the laws is discussed in the sections that follow.

National Archives and Records Act, and Electronic Records Management and Federal Records Act

These laws establish the National Archives and Records Administration, giving it the charge of collecting and preserving government and historical records. Best known for housing historical documents, such as the U.S. Constitution and Declaration of Independence, the National Archives primarily functions as an information classification and preservation body. Information accumulates, and all of it cannot be kept forever. When it is no longer useful or important, it can be thrown away. Other information is vitally important and must be preserved. The National Archives' charge is to work with government agencies to decide what is to be kept in the agency, what is to be destroyed, and what is to be historically preserved at the Archives.

Freedom of Information Act and Electronic Freedom of Information Act

The Freedom of Information Act[5] requires federal government agencies to make information available for public inspection. The public information includes rules, opinions, orders, records, and proceedings. Exceptions include national security concerns, interference with criminal investigations, certain financial data, and personal privacy invasions. The EFIA expanded the FOIA to require certain information to be made available electronically and accessible in reading rooms.

At the heart of this legislation is the principle that it is in the public good to know what its government is doing. Such legislation is often called transparency in government, or sunshine laws. Similar legislation in Florida allowed for public, televised hearings of voting boards considering the recount protests in the 2000 presidential election. In conflict with the public's right to know are those principles embodied in the exemptions—most notably, individual privacy and national security.

Legislation	Major Provisions	Information Security Implications	Ethical Considerations	Private-Sector Parallel
National Archives and Records Act	Charges the National Archives and Records Administration with collecting and preserving government and historical records	Preventing the destruction or loss of historical information needed for a very long time; as well as securing a limited amount of classified information	NARA has long-term obligations to keep historical information preserved and more easily accessible by the public, while dealing with reclassification controversies	Information classification and life-cycle policies within and across firms
Electronic Records Management and Federal Records Act	Establishes a program of records management for federal agencies with oversight provided by the NARA	Deciding whether a record is to be kept by the agency, transferred to archives, or destroyed	Requires responsible decision making to preserve and not destroy what is of value to society, and courage to face pressure to conceal or destroy information harmful to power groups	Inappropriate destruction of records in private firms, such as firms under investigation of wrongdoing
Freedom of Information Act and Electronic Freedom of Information Act	Gives individuals the right to access federal agency records, except for nine exceptions including national security, and that certain records be stored and accessible in electronic form	Nine exemptions include issues of national security, internal personnel policies, exemptions by other statutes, trade secrets, privileged memos or letters, unwarranted invasion of personal privacy, law enforcement exemptions, sensitive financial data, and exempt information about gas or oil wells	Balance of the privacy vs. Access trade-offs and possible misuses of exemptions to conceal information	Requiring public disclosure of certain information in private firms by agencies such as the SEC
Privacy Act	Individuals have the right to access and request corrections to their personally identifiable information held by federal agencies	Administrative and physical security systems are mandated to be in place to prevent unauthorized disclosure	How far should information privacy rights be extended?	Privacy policies for customers doing e-business; access policies for personnel records; management and technical countermeasures for information security; HIPAA, FERPA

Table 6C-1   Summary of NIST 4012 Laws Affecting Information Security Management

6C

Legislation	Major Provisions	Information Security Implications	Ethical Considerations	Private-Sector Parallel
Federal Managers Financial Integrity Act of 1982	Require ongoing evaluations and reports of the adequacy of the systems of internal accounting and administrative control of each executive agency	Requires accurate reporting and controls to safeguard funds, property, and other assets are safeguarded against waste, loss, unauthorized use, or misappropriation	Responsibility to safeguard public assets; duty to the citizen as taxpayer	SOX compliance; duty to corporate shareholders
Federal Property and Administration Service Act	Created the General Services Administration, an independent agency to support the functioning of other agencies	The GSA issues a federal standard glossary of telecommunications terms	Responsibility for updating standards to adapt to changing technologies and needs	Updating standards that pertain to private firms, such as telecommunications standards
Government Paperwork Elimination Act	Requires that federal organizations use electronic forms, electronic filing, and electronic signatures to conduct official business with the public	Ensure that the creation, collection, maintenance, use, dissemination, and disposition of information by or for the federal government is consistent with laws relating to privacy and confidentiality, security of information, and access to information; and to ensure the integrity, quality, and utility of the federal statistical system	The goals of cost savings and convenient access to information should be balanced with privacy and security issues	Business B2E and B2C uses of it to automate existing work processes
E-Government Act of 2002	Improve the management and promotion of government services, such as citizen access to government information and services, using Internet and related technologies	Provide enhanced access to government information and services in a manner consistent with laws regarding protection of personal privacy, national security, records retention, and access for persons with disabilities	Calls for balancing enhanced access with protection of personal privacy and national security; records retention policies; and access to government information and services by citizens, including persons with disabilities	E-business strategies, such as B2E, B2C, and B2B; using IT to improve products and services, and supply chain management

Table 6C-1   Continued

Legislation	Major Provisions	Information Security Implications	Ethical Considerations	Private-Sector Parallel
Title III, Federal Information Security Management Act (FISMA), 17 Dec 02	Improve computer and network security within the federal government and affiliated parties, such as government contractors, by mandating processes to be followed	Establishes an information security chain of authority; requires security awareness and training; requires that computer systems be secured; and requires security-related documentation, assessment, and continuous improvement	Beginning in 2008, requires more detailed reporting of annual privacy reviews, including redress of complaints; requires accurate, timely, and complete incident reporting; and management, operational, and technical control mechanisms	Role of CIO; rise of the CISO and corporate information security management; CMMI; disaster planning and business continuity
Computer Fraud and Abuse Act, P.L. 99- 474, 18 U.S. Code 1030	Prohibits intentional, unauthorized access to computers for a variety of purposes	Specifically prohibits unauthorized computer access for: obtaining national security data, financial data, any government department or agency data; fraudulently obtaining anything of value; interstate or foreign communication	IT managers must weigh the societal benefits of reporting cybercrimes against the negative impacts of bad publicity	Corporate cybercrime and management countermeasures
USA Patriot Act	To deter and punish terrorist acts in the United States and around the world and to enhance law enforcement investigatory tools	Enables enhanced surveillance, warrantless searches and seizures of information by the government in cases of suspected terror, expanded voluntary disclosure rights for information service providers, and improvements in cyber security forensic investigation capabilities	Creates ethical dilemmas that balance safety and security against privacy and freedom	Corporate security policies; workplace monitoring; relationship with government and law enforcement

Table 6C-1   Continued

Case-in-Point: Reclassification of Government Archives

The case of the 2006 reclassification controversy illustrates the interplay of various issues and statutes, in this case the National Archives and FOIA, that affects the management of information and its security. At the center of this controversy is the information security manager's issue of dealing with various reasons for classifying, concealing, or destroying data, and making the right choice.

In 2006, a researcher attempted to access a previously viewed Air Force document at the Archives, but discovered it was missing. Moreover, there was no indication of what had happened to it, or that it had even existed in the first place. Puzzled archivists used the Freedom of Information Act to query the Air Force about the missing document. The Air Force did not reveal the document, citing national security concerns, but they were forced to disclose parts of a secret memo that revealed an agreement with Archives to reclassify public documents. Usually, documents go from classified to declassified and enter the public domain. Reclassification is like reversing the decision with declassified documents going back to classified, for national security reasons, usually. Congressional hearings discovered that more than 55,000 documents had been reclassified in the program, carried out by the Air Force and other unnamed agencies in the unrevealed parts of the memo. Archivists speculated that Air Force concerns over secret Cold War spy balloon projects, such as the Project GENETRIX—that fueled the UFO craze of the 1950s and government conspiracy theorists—might have triggered the reclassification program. A copy of the secret memo is available from the Department of Justice.[6]

Privacy Act

The Privacy Act of 1974[7,8] establishes policies regarding information that the government collects about individuals. Enacted during the Watergate scandal, the law was intended to curb the maintaining of secret surveillance files by federal agencies, and as such, applies only to federal agencies. The act aims to restrict disclosure of personal records, grant individual access rights, allow individual amendment rights, and create a code of fair information practices for agencies to follow.

The Privacy Act gives individuals, including citizens and legal aliens, the right to access and request corrections to their personally identifiable information. If the government collects information on a person, then that person can request and access it. One notable exception is that the information has to be "personally identifiable." That means that it has to be indexed or looked up by a name or unique personal identifier to be legally accessible by subjects. Some information is exempt from access, including the IRS taxpayer investigations database.[9] Amendment rights means that individuals can request that their personally identifiable records be amended, or changed. The modifications allowed are usually only factual corrections. With regard to the use of social security numbers, the Privacy Act makes it "unlawful for any Federal, State or local government agency to deny to any individual any right, benefit, or privilege provided by law because of such individual's refusal to disclose his social security account number."[10]

The Privacy Act contains privacy and security provisions similar to other statutes, and commonly practices in organizations. The Privacy Act contains a specific provision for information security, mandating that administrative and physical security systems be in place to prevent unauthorized disclosure of information. Organizations that conduct e-commerce or Web sites that collect personal information will often publish a privacy policy that embodies a specific version of fair information practices similar to those upon which the Privacy Act is based. The Health Insurance Portability and Accountability Act of 1996 (HIPAA) is a privacy statute that applies to the collection and use of an individual's medical information.

Federal Managers Financial Integrity Act of 1982

This law requires ongoing evaluations and reports of the adequacy of the systems of internal accounting and administrative control of each executive agency.[11] It requires accurate reporting and controls to safeguard funds, property, and other assets against waste, loss, unauthorized use, or misappropriation. From an information security standpoint, it makes federal agencies responsible for safeguarding public assets.

FMFIA is somewhat analogous to the Sarbanes-Oxley (SOX) regulations. Both laws make organizations financially accountable to important stakeholders. Whereas FMFIA protects government stakeholders—citizens as taxpayers—the SOX shields corporate investors—the shareholders.

Federal Property and Administration Service Act

This law created the General Services Administration, an independent agency to support the functioning of other agencies. The information security-related aspect of the GSA is that it issues a federal standard glossary of telecommunications terms as one means of supporting IT security in the federal government. These standards need to be updated periodically as technologies and needs evolve.

Government Paperwork Elimination Act

The Government Paperwork Elimination Act was enacted in 1998, requiring that by 2003, federal organizations use electronic forms, electronic filing, and electronic signatures to conduct official business with the public.[12] This requires government-to-employee (G2E) and government-to-citizen (G2C) use of IT by the federal entities by automating existing work processes and reaching the consumer with Internet-based products and services. This theme continues with the E-Government Act of 2002, discussed next.

The government's use of the Internet makes it vulnerable to security threats and requires improved information security practices that eventually are mandated by FISMA. See below.

E-Government Act of 2002

The E-Government Act of 2002's stated purpose is to improve the management and promotion of electronic government services and processes. The law establishes a CIO-type role within the OMB office, and calls for the use of the Internet and related technologies to improve citizen access to government services, for example. The law has led to the creation of Web sites for government job applications (USAJobs.gov), benefits management (GovBenefits.gov), government services (USA.gov), grants administration (Grants.gov), and tax filing services (IRS Free File). This act greatly expands the GEMA's G2C strategy.[13] The law also promotes interagency collaboration in providing electronic government services, a G2G use of IT.

The E-Government Act provides specifically for information security management: "To provide enhanced access to Government information and services in a manner consistent with laws regarding protection of personal privacy, national security, records retention, access for persons with disabilities, and other relevant laws."[14] The E-Government's security mandate is more specific than the language of the Privacy Act, but not as detailed as FISMA, described next.

Title III, Federal Information Security Management Act (FISMA)

6C

At about the same time, FISMA[15] was enacted to improve computer and network security within the federal government. FISMA applies to federal agencies and affiliated parties, which includes government contractors. A clear chain of command is established with a CISO reporting to the CIO who reports to the agency head. The CISO's role is to carry out the security requirements of FISMA. These requirements include:

- security awareness and training
- computer system security
- security-related documentation
- periodic risk assessment
- continuous improvement
- accurate, timely, and complete incident reporting
- management, operational, and technical control mechanisms
- annual reporting to Congress

Beginning in 2008, FISMA requires more detailed reporting of annual privacy reviews.[16] Agencies will be required to document how it addressed all of the privacy complaints it receives.

The practices required by FISMA include a strong CIO role reporting directly to the CEO, a separate CISO, and corporate security policies that include risk management, continuous improvement, annual reporting and disaster planning, and business continuity planning.

One of the most important FISMA requirements is that federal agencies submit an annual security report to Congress. For each of the past eight years, the reports have been graded on FISMA-related criteria by the House Oversight and Government Reform Committee.[17,18] In 2007, the 24 executive branch agencies scored an overall C, up from C– in 2006 and D+ in 2005. However, performance varied widely, with seven agencies scoring A's and five scoring F's. See Table 6C-2.

Computer Fraud and Abuse Act

Passed by Congress in 1986, this Act was passed to stem the increase in threats such as hacking and viruses. The Act prohibits intentional, unauthorized access to computers to commit a variety of offenses, specifically:

- accessing national security data
- accessing financial data
- accessing any government department or agency data
- obtaining anything of value
- conducting interstate or foreign communication

It was amended in 1996 and again in 2001 by the USA Patriot Act. The Patriot Act upped the penalties for hacking from 5 years to 10 for a first offense, and from 10 years to 20 for a second-time offender, and added to the list of offenses to include damages to the computers themselves.[19]

Agency	Grade
Department of Justice	A+
Environmental Protection Agency	A+
Agency for International Development	A+*
National Science Foundation	A+*
Social Security Administration	A+*
Housing and Urban Development	A
Office of Personnel Management	A–
Department of Energy	B+
Department of Homeland Security	B+
General Services Administration	B+
Department of Health and Human Services	B
Small Business Administration	B
National Aeronautics and Space Administration	C
Department of State	C*
Department of Education	C–
Department of Commerce	D+
Department of Labor	D
Department of Transportation	D
Department of Defense	D–
Department of Agriculture	F
Department of the Interior	F
Department of Treasury	F
Department of Veterans Affairs	F
Nuclear Regulatory Commission	F

Table 6C-2 **Computer Security Report Cards**

Source: House Oversight and Government Reform Committee

The law will most likely continue to be amended in the future as technology and the nature of cyber threats change. In 2008, the U.S. Justice Department has used the CFAA and related cyber laws to prosecute cases in the following areas:[20]

- spam prosecutions
- online frauds affecting financial institutions
- online identity thefts

6C

- worms, Trojans, and botnets
- online fraud schemes
- computer intrusions to steal data or damage computers

Corporate intellectual property is an area affected by the CFAA. A case in point is Oracle's suit of SAP under the Act.[21] In March 2007, Oracle Corporation sued SAP, the German software firm, for intellectual property theft. A subsidiary firm of SAP, TomorrowNow, had used passwords of Oracle customers to illegally download Oracle's copyrighted support software. SAP later admitted to the inappropriate downloads. Oracle claimed that SAP could offer cut-rate, third-party support to Oracle customers, using illegally obtained, copyrighted software products and other support materials, and eventually lure customers away from Oracle. SAP denied these claims, made personnel changes at TomorrowNow, and is "winding down"[22] operations at its third-party support firm, while the case is still ongoing.

A key ethical consideration is that IT managers must weigh the societal benefits of reporting cybercrimes against the negative impacts of bad publicity. Despite the teeth put into cyber law enforcement by the Computer Fraud and Abuse Act, and with its strengthening by the Patriot Act, organizations do not report security intrusions to law enforcement most of the time. According to the 2007 CSI/FBI Computer Crime and Security Survey,[23] only 29% of respondents said that they reported to law enforcement following a security incident. By contrast, the three most common actions following an incident were: attempted to identify perpetrator (61%), did your best to patch security holes (54%), and installed security patches (48%). The reasons cited for failing to report the incidents included: negative publicity (26%), believed law enforcement couldn't help (22%), and competitors would use to their advantage (14%).

USA Patriot Act

The Patriot Act, as it is commonly called, was established in response to the 9/11 attacks "to deter and punish terrorist acts in the United States and around the world, to enhance law enforcement investigatory tools," among its purposes.[24] As it pertains to the management of information security, the act:

- enables enhanced surveillance
- permits warrantless searches and seizures of information by the government in cases of suspected terror
- expands voluntary disclosure rights for information service providers
- funds improvements in cyber security forensic investigation capabilities

One of the sections of the Patriot Act amended the criminal code, giving information providers more freedom to report protected information to law enforcement parties. The law in question is crimes and criminal procedures section 2702.[25] Providers of remote computing services or electronic communications services, such as Internet service providers and cell phone companies, now have the right to divulge customer records to law enforcement agencies when people are in danger. Normally, these information providers are prohibited from divulging the content of customer records to third parties, except in the following situations. Providers may voluntarily divulge records:

- to the National Center for Missing and Exploited Children if the information pertains to missing or abused child cases,

- to law enforcement authorities if they believe that the information pertains to the commission of a crime, and

- to law enforcement authorities if the information involves the danger of death or serious injury to any person.

Section 816 of the Patriot Act calls for the development and support of cyber security forensic capabilities, providing $50 million per year for the Attorney General to use for forensic analysis of seized cyber terror evidence, training and education of federal, state, and local law enforcement in forensic analysis, and to assist all three levels of law enforcement.

One of the most controversial provisions of the Act, Section 505, gives federal law enforcement expanded powers to issue national security letters (NSLs). An NSL is a form of administrative subpoena that can be used by the FBI and certain other federal agencies to obtain information without a judicial warrant, without probable cause, and with a gag order on the recipient. Prior to the Patriot Act, the NSLs could be used only in cases pertaining to a foreign power. The Patriot Act eliminated that restriction, and also lowered the standard for the information so as to be related to a terrorism investigation rather than a terrorist suspect. Thus, the FBI could seek information on individuals who were nonsuspects, as long as the information sought was related to an investigation.[26,27] The congressional reauthorization of the Patriot Act and court cases (see below) subsequently weakened the use of NSLs somewhat. A sample NSL can be found at the Electronic Freedom Foundation Web site: http://www.eff.org/files/filenode/ia_v_mukasey/Nov2007_NSL.pdf

The following two cases illustrate how managers can get caught in legal and ethical dilemmas brought on by FBI investigative searches.

Case: *Doe v. Ashcroft*[28,29]

Facts of the Case

An unnamed Internet service provider (ISL) was served with multiple national security letters (NSLs) by the FBI. Under the Patriot Act, the ISL was prohibited from disclosing that it had been served—the gag order provision. The ISL protested, claiming its Fourth and First Amendment rights had been violated. A search was authorized without judicial oversight, and the ISL had no ability to publicly protest such action, except through the courts.

Decision

In 2007, Judge Marrero of the Southern District of New York ruled that the FBI's use of the letters, and the gag order provision in particular, violated the First Amendment and separation of powers guarantees of the Constitution. The recipients of the letters, the judge wrote, remain "effectively barred from engaging in any discussion regarding their experiences and opinions related to the government's use" of the letters.

Ramifications

A preliminary ruling by the judge was followed by Congress's amendment of the Patriot Act in its 2006 reauthorization, providing additional judicial oversight of NSLs. In light of the gag order provision being dropped, in the future the burden of going to court would be on the FBI if they wanted to suppress free speech rights of NSL recipients to disclose the existence of the NSL.

Ethical Considerations

IT managers are stewards of the information in their corporate databases. When faced with government orders to search and seize information, under what circumstances would you decide to challenge in court rather than comply?

This next case illustrates an FBI cyber crime search and seizure on a different issue.

Case: *United States vs. Ziegler*[30,31]

Facts of the Case

In May of 2003, Ziegler, an employee of Frontline Processing, Inc., was indicted on child pornography charges. He had been accessing child pornography Web sites from a Frontline computer. The FBI investigated after it received a tip from Frontline's Internet Service Provider. Frontline's IT administrator confirmed from a firewall and another monitoring device that it was the plaintiff's computer. Using a key obtained from the CFO, the IT administrator unlocked Ziegler's office to make copies of the hard drive at the request of the FBI. Ziegler filed a pretrial motion to suppress the evidence. Ziegler claimed that the FBI violated his Fourth Amendment rights by conducting a warrantless search of his computer.

Decision

The U.S. Court of Appeals for the Ninth Circuit held that the defendant's employer maintained the authority to consent to the search of his workplace environment. The resulting evidence collected from the computer, images of child pornography, were therefore admissible.

Ramifications

Managers, not their individual employees, are responsible for deciding whether to comply with law enforcement searches and seizures in the workplace. It is up to managers to decide whether to waive Fourth Amendment protections to permit warrantless searches of workplace computers.

Ethical Considerations

In a managerial, i.e., decision-making role, in an organization, what responsibilities do you have regarding employee and customer records that you possess?

Managers should carefully weigh their responsibility to protect the privacy of their employees with their duty to cooperate with law enforcement. They should not defer this decision to the employees themselves. They should consider what is best not only for the employee and the company but all of society, in deciding the right thing to do. They should ask ethical questions like "Whose rights are more important?" "What action will produce the best overall outcome?"

The NSLs remain the subject of much debate and court battles. Privacy advocates have fought and won battles against the use of NSLs. The Department of Justice, on the other hand, insists that the NSLs have been extremely helpful in successfully fighting cyber crimes and the War on Terror.

We have seen in the legislation reviewed herein and in several recent cases that managerial rights and responsibilities vary from situation to situation. You might have the responsibility to secure and protect that information from disclosure to third parties. But, if you are issued a warrant or national security letter by law enforcement agencies, you will be compelled by law to disclose some portion of the information you possess unless you challenge the government's action in court. You might also have the right to voluntarily disclose information to law enforcement in certain situations, such as suspecting a crime has occurred, someone might be harmed, or children are being exploited or abused. And, as the manager, you retain the right to permit searches and seizures of employees' property in the workplace, including a company-owned computer.

Implications for IT Managers in Government

Law enforcement should seek information useful for investigative goals while acting in strict compliance with legal requirements in evidence gathering, using strategies that are more likely to garner public trust and cooperation rather than suspicion and opposition.

Government agencies in implementing G2C e-government initiatives should follow FISMA's guidance in bringing about improved information security along with education, training, and awareness of IS security in its workforce, while respecting the privacy of citizens, and disclosing what the Freedom of Information Act requires.

Implications for IT Managers in Organizations

6C

Organizations in general need to be prepared for encounters with law enforcement, balancing the legal and ethical requirements to protect sensitive information with the legal and ethical obligations to cooperate with criminal and terrorist investigations; take advantage of its access to government data and services; and understand the privacy rights of its employees and its responsibility to customers.

Conclusions

Clearly, there are fundamental differences in managing corporate vs. federal government organizations. On the contrary, the examination of legislation affecting information security management in federal agencies suggests that major information security issues are similar. Information security managers should:

- Carefully manage data across the life cycle, from generation to destruction
- Prevent inappropriate destruction of data and safeguard information to be preserved
- Be transparent and accountable to stakeholders with a vested interest
- Establish information access and use policies
- Manage security in an e-enabled world that harnesses the Internet for working inward, outward, and across
- Continuously adapt and improve operations to cope with evolving technologies and emerging cyber threats
- Develop comprehensive information security management capabilities, including a chain of command, risk management, countermeasures, security audits, continuous improvement, education, training, and awareness
- Protect and defend intellectual property
- Investigate and prosecute cybercriminals
- Manage ethical dilemmas where conflicts arise among principles, such as privacy, safety, and the right-to-know

These laws, taken together, reveal the interweaving of a myriad of information technology issues at the heart of information security management. These issues include information life cycle issues, individual privacy, national security, public access to information, financial integrity, and the societal benefits of information use. In many cases, issues and laws are in conflict with one another. When conflicts arise, IT managers are faced with tough decisions. IT managers need to exercise intelligence, wisdom, integrity, and good judgment to make sound decisions. Sometimes it is the courts who decide.

The overview of federal information security-related legislation also has implications for educators. With a sense of history, a background in legal concepts, and a basic foundation in ethics, the law itself is a teacher.

Endnotes

1. Committee on National Security Systems—CNSS, *National Information Assurance Training Standard for Senior System Managers: CNSSI No. 4012.* National Security Agency, June 2004. Available from http://www.cnss.gov/Assets/pdf/cnssi_4012.pdf

2. NIST, *Federal Information Security Management Act of 2002: Title III—Information Security,* 2002, p. 52. Available from http://csrc.nist.gov/drivers/documents/FISMA-final .pdf

3. ATIS, *ATIS Telecom Glossary 2007.* Retrieved August 2, 2008 from http://www.its .bldrdoc.gov/projects/devglossary/_national_security_system.html Alliance for Telecommunications Industry Solutions, PRQC Committee. Available from: http://www.its .bldrdoc.gov/projects/devglossary/

4. C. Herrod, "The Role of Information Security and Its Relationship to Information Technology Risk Management," in M. E. Whitman and H. J. Mattord (Eds.), *Readings and Cases in the Management of Information Security,* Volume I, Boston: Thompson Course Technology, 2006, pp. 45–61.

5. United States Department of Justice, *The Freedom of Information Act,* 2002. Retrieved August 5, 2008 from http://www.usdoj.gov/oip/foiastat.htm

6. National Security Archive, *Secret Agreement Reveals Covert Program to Hide Reclassification from Public.* George Washington University, 2006. Retrieved August 5, 2008 from http://www.gwu.edu/~nsarchiv/news/20060411/index.htm

7. Department of Justice, *Overview of The Privacy Act of 1974,* 2004 Edition. Retrieved August 5, 2008 from http://www.usdoj.gov/oip/1974polobj.htm

8. Wikipedia contributors, Privacy Act of 1974. *Wikipedia, The Free Encyclopedia.* Retrieved August 5, 2008 from http://en.wikipedia.org/wiki/Privacy_Act_of_1974.

9. M. J. Quinn, "Privacy Act of 1974," in *Ethics for the Information Age.* Boston: Pearson Addison Wesley, 2005, pp. 208–209.

10. Department of Justice, "Overview of The Privacy Act of 1974, 2004 Edition: Social Security Number Usage," 2004. http://www.usdoj.gov/oip/1974ssnu.htm

11. Office of Management and Budget, *P.L. 97-255—(H.R. 1526): Federal Managers Financial Integrity Act of 1982.* Retrieved August 4, 2008 from http://www.whitehouse.gov/ omb/financial/fmfia1982.html

12. Webcontent.gov, *Government Paperwork Elimination Act (GPEA),* 2005. Retrieved August 2, 2008 from http://www.usa.gov/webcontent/reqs_bestpractices/laws_regs/gpea .shtml

13. E-Gov, *Report to Congress of the Benefits of the E-Government Initiatives,* U.S. Office of Management and Budget, 2008. Retrieved August 3, 2008 from http://www .whitehouse.gov/omb/egov/g-10-Benefits_Report.html

14. Wikipedia contributors, E-Government Act of 2002. *Wikipedia, The Free Encyclopedia.* Retrieved August 2, 2008 from http://en.wikipedia.org/wiki/E-Government_Act_of_2002

15. NIST, *Federal Information Security Management Act of 2002: Title III—Information Security*. Available from http://csrc.nist.gov/drivers/documents/FISMA-final.pdf

16. M. Mosquera, "OMB Wants Privacy Review Details in FISMA Reports," *Federal Computer Week (FCW.COM)*, January 2008. Retrieved August 2, 2008 from http://www.fcw.com/online/news/151386-1.html

17. B. Krebs, "Govt' Earns 'C' on Computer Security Report Card," *Washington Post*, May 2008. Retrieved August 4, 2008 from http://blog.washingtonpost.com/securityfix/2008/05/govt_earns_grade_of_c_for_comp.html

18. T. Davis, "Eighth Report Card on Computer Security at Federal Departments and Agencies," *House Oversight and Government Reform Committee*, 2008. Retrieved August 5, 2008 from http://republicans.oversight.house.gov/media/PDFs/Reports/FY2007FISMAReportCard.pdf

19. U.S. Department of Justice, *18 U.S.C. 1030. Fraud and Related Activity in Connection with Computers*, January 24, 2002. Retrieved August 6, 2008 from http://www.usdoj.gov/criminal/cybercrime/1030_new.html

20. U.S. Department of Justice, *Fact Sheet: Department of Justice Efforts to Combat Cyber Crimes*, August 5, 2008. Retrieved August 6, 2008 from http://www.usdoj.gov/criminal/cybercrime/CCFactSheet.pdf

21. R. Mark, "SAP Admits Wrongdoing in Oracle Suit," *InternetNews*.Com. Jupiter Media Corporation, July 3, 2007. Retrieved August 5, 2008 from http://www.internetnews.com/bus-news/article.php/3686891

22. TN Lawsuit Information, *SAP to Wind Down Operations of Tomorrow Now*. SAP, July 2008. Retrieved August 6, 2008 from http://www.tnlawsuit.com/uploads/SAPPressReleaseonTNWindDown.pdf

23. R. Richardson, *2007 CSI Computer Crime and Security Survey*. San Francisco: Computer Security Institute. Retrieved August 5, 2008 from http://i.cmpnet.com/v2.gocsi.com/pdf/CSISurvey2007.pdf

24. The Library of Congress, H.R. 3162, 2001. *Thomas*. Retrieved August 3, 2008 from http://thomas.loc.gov/cgi-bin/bdquery/z?d107:h.r.03162

25. Onecle, *Crimes and Criminal Procedure—18 USC Section 2702*, April 2006. Retrieved August 8, 2008 from http://law.onecle.com/uscode/18/2702.html

26. Wikipedia contributors, *National Security Letter*, 2008. Retrieved August 8, 2008 from http://en.wikipedia.org/wiki/National_Security_Letter

27. U.S. Department of Justice, "A Review of the Federal Bureau of Investigations Use of National Security Letters," *Office of the Inspector General*, 2007. Retrieved August 8, 2008 from http://cryptome.org/fbi-nsl/fbi-nsl.htm

28. A. Liptak, "Judge Voids F.B.I. Tool Granted by Patriot Act," *The New York Times*, September 7, 2007. Retrieved August 8, 2008 from http://www.nytimes.com/2007/09/07/washington/07patriot.html?_r=2&oref=slogin&oref=slogin

29. Wikipedia contributors, "National Security Letter": *Doe vs. Ashcroft*, 2008. Retrieved August 8, 2008 from http://en.wikipedia.org/wiki/National_Security_Letter#Doe_v._Ashcroft

30. FindLaw, *U.S. Constitution: Fourth Amendment*. Retrieved August 8, 2008 from http://caselaw.lp.findlaw.com/data/constitution/amendment04/

31. Additional Developments—Cyberlaw, *United States v. Ziegler. Berkeley Technology Law Journal*, Vol. 22, Issue 1, 2007, p. 600.

Case **6D**

The Law in Information Security Management

Katherine H. Winters
University of Tennessee at Chattanooga

Ms. Winters has M.S. degrees in engineering management and computer science from the University of Tennessee at Chattanooga. Her research interests are in security in software engineering and integration of security throughout the computer science curriculum. She has authored papers on these areas in refereed journals, conferences, and symposiums. She is a member of the ACM and Upsilon Pi Epsilon.

Overview

Information security is built on three basic tenets: integrity, confidentiality, and access. The job of the information security professional is to balance the integrity and confidentiality of the maintained data while providing needed access to the data by authorized individuals. To further complicate the situation, the organization's information security implementation must assure that the organization is able to accomplish its mission and goals while complying with relevant laws and regulations.

In order to accomplish these goals, the information security professional (InfoSecProf) must understand the laws, regulations, and policies that impact their organization and design the necessary controls and protections with consideration given to applicable laws and regulations. The InfoSecProf must have the necessary skills for keeping abreast of the continual change in this area. Laws affecting an organization may be state, local, or federal statutes. This case study will not examine any local ordinances. Some states have enacted privacy and information security laws affecting business and citizens of that particular state. One such law that will be examined is a Massachusetts privacy law. Most federal laws are enacted to protect an individual's right to privacy from government intrusion, information and information systems belonging to the government, or are designed to protect a specific industry and have information security implications such the Health Insurance Portability and Accountability Act of 1996 (HIPAA). Federal laws affecting information security are limited and state statutes can vary state by state as well as industry by industry. A study of applicable laws can be very tricky. For example, in the area of the disclosure of sensitive personal information, no single law or regulation provides comprehensive oversight. In the area of the disclosure of this type of information, requirements are dependent on factors such as: the information owner, the type of organizations, the type of information, and the medium or format in which the information is kept. As of January 2008, 39 states have enacted data security laws requiring organizations to notify a person if their personal information, such as individual's names, addresses, phone numbers, account numbers, and social security numbers, has been disclosed.[1] The federal government is considering a similar law. There are few, if any, organizations exempt from this type of regulation. An organization could be subject to multiple laws and regulations affecting its operations. While the Information Security professional must stay abreast of the changing laws, they are no substitute for legal help and guidance. The Information Security professional must know when to solicit help. It is their job to implement the necessary training, education, and technology to assure compliance with laws. It is the job of the legal professional to interpret and determine the applicability of the laws.

The following case study is designed to provide insight into the relationship between the law and information security management. A fictitious consulting company, K-LiWin Consulting, is used to provide cohesion. This fictitious company has four fictitious customers: a hospital, a financial securities firm, a record producer, and a nonprofit organization. Each of these organizations represents industries that have unique laws that impact their information security policy. Within the context of K-LiWin Consulting providing information security consulting services, some of these laws and regulations will be examined. This case will examine the impact of some of the major laws affecting information security such as HIPAA, the Sarbanes-Oxley Act of 2002 (SOX), the Gramm-Leach-Bliley Act of 1999, the Digital Millennium Copyright Act, and a Massachusetts statute dealing with privacy. A brief overview of each law is provided. The detailed review of the law is left to the reader as an exercise. By no means is this an exhaustive list of important information security laws; it is intended to provide the reader with an appreciation of the importance of law in information security. A brief overview of the case and K-LiWin Consulting will be presented and then followed by details of each organization and one or more laws specific to that entity.

The Case Study

For many organizations, the regulations and laws with which they must comply are largely driven by the product or service provided. Each organization is unique; to fully implement an effective information security policy, the information security specialist must have an understanding of the organizations in which they are employed and make the direct connection between the laws, as interpreted by the legal department, and their impact on the information security of the organization. This is especially evident in some industries. Four examples of such an organization include a health care company, a financial securities company, a music production company, and a nonprofit organization. An examination of specific laws pertinent to each of these diverse organizations provides the security professional with the opportunity to explore and investigate how laws affect the data management of the organization. This case will first briefly discuss laws applicable specifically to each of these organizations and then discuss laws that are general in nature and may have an impact. A full exploration of the applicable laws, their provisions, and regulations is left to the student as an exercise. This is a fictitious consulting company.

K-LiWin Consulting

K-LiWin Consulting is a consulting firm that provides professional security advice and services to a wide variety of customers who use information systems and networks in their organizations. Their services bridge the gap between real-world business needs and specific security functions required to protect the organization. K-LiWin Consulting provides both comprehensive security advice at the management level and detailed support at the technique level.

For each customer, K-LiWin Consulting provides a complete portfolio of security solutions to meet the specific organization need. The consulting team can provide any or all of the following services:

1. Identify legal and regulatory requirements of each company.
2. Perform risk assessment, which identifies virtual and physical assets, potential threats, and vulnerabilities.
3. Propose security policies to protect assets and manage risks.
4. Map security policies into detailed techniques that consist of cryptography selection, firewall configuration, IDS setup, deployment of physical security, personnel training, and security maintenance.

At the current time, K-LiWin Consulting has acquired four new clients, a small hospital (Metro Hospital), a private securities firm (Secure Securities), a music producer (ChattTown Records), and a nonprofit organization (Homeless Helpers of Massachusetts). Each of these customers has unique regulatory and information management issues. In order to develop a comprehensive plan to meet their individual information security needs, it is necessary to understand the laws and regulations affecting their organizations. The first client is Metro Hospital.

Client: Metro Hospital

Metro Hospital is a small community hospital with 50 beds. It is non-teaching hospital; however, one of the doctors runs a small research facility focusing on the role genetics plays in a patient's ability to heal after surgery. The hospital has a staff of about 200. All information technology (IT) work is done in-house but the hospital is considering outsourcing this work. A Chief Information Security Officer (CISO) has just been hired but his background is in finance and not information management. He has little understanding of information security but a strong background in management. The CISO recognized his lack of expertise in this area and hired K-LiWin Consulting to make sure the hospital is in compliance with all applicable laws and regulations. There is a legal staff that will provide detailed legal advice. K-LiWin's role is to provide management advice and technical expertise on implementing security policies and practices that assure compliance with the applicable laws. To date, the legal staff has identified two laws, HIPAA, and The Common Rule with direct applicability. Both are discussed briefly below.

Applicable Health Care Laws   The legal department has identified the Health Insurance Portability and Accountability Act of 1996 as the law with the largest information security impact at Metro Hospital. It has a profound effect on how information is managed. This particular law has provisions for the establishment of electronic transmissions of health care records. **Subtitle F—Administrative Simplification SEC. 261. Regulation** states:

> *It is the purpose of this subtitle to improve the Medicare program under title XVIII of the Social Security Act, the Medicaid program under title XIX of such Act, and the efficiency and effectiveness of the health care system, by encouraging the development of a health information system through the establishment of standards and requirements for the electronic transmission of certain health information.*[2]

Within that law, Congress included provisions to address the need for safeguarding electronic health information.[3] This law and its provisions have a number of requirements for the transmittal, storage, and privacy of health care information. Specifically in the area of information security, there are eighteen information security standards. These standards fall into three distinct areas: administrative, physical, and technical safeguards. The administrative safeguards document policies and procedures for daily operations, while the physical safeguards protect the computer systems themselves. The technical safeguards deal with how to use technology as safeguards.[4]

Because Metro Hospital is engaged in research, another directly applicable law is The Federal Policy for the Protection of Human Subjects, referred to as The Common Rule and adopted by a number of federal agencies in 1991. Each institution engaged in research covered by The Common Rule is required to provide written assurance that it will comply with The Common Rule. This assurance is written and legally binding.[5] Among other provisions the regulation requires "a statement describing the extent, if any, to which confidentiality of records identifying the subject will be maintained."[6] Additional laws may be applicable and are discussed in the section entitled Laws with General Application.

Client: Secure Securities

Secure Securities is a publicly held securities firm. Their function is to provide clients with financial and wealth management services. Secure Securities offers a full range of financial planning and wealth management services with twenty associates handling approximately $20 million dollars in assets at any given time. Personnel as well as client data is stored on a centralized server owned by the company and located within its suite of offices. The company contracts all server services to a local company. There are no information technology employees on staff or any expertise in information security. Any legal issues are handled by a local firm on an as-needed basis. There is only one office and payroll is handled in-house. Secure Securities approached K-LiWin Consulting after an internal audit revealed they were not in compliance with all of the information security management aspects of the Sarbanes-Oxley

Act of 2002 (SOX). In addition, one of the employees read an article, which stated you must have a disaster recovery plan under SOX and Secure Securities has no such plan. K-LiWin Consulting was contracted to help in both these areas and provide general assistance for the implementation of any controls or security policies necessary for Secure Security to be in compliance. Their legal counsel will identify the compliance issues and K-LiWin will address the information security needs.

Applicable Financial Securities Laws After the collapse of Enron, the WorldCom accounting irregularities, and other high-profile accounting problems, the government established the Sarbanes-Oxley Act of 2002 (SOX).[7] The law begins with these words: "To protect investors by improving the accuracy and reliability of corporate disclosures made pursuant to the security laws and for other purposes."[8] The impact of this act has been compared to the business reforms of Franklin Roosevelt. Reporting, record keeping, and accountability changes resulting from SOX were designed to enhance corporate responsibility and financial disclosures and combat corporate and accounting fraud.[9] Information security is not specifically addressed by this act; however, modern financial systems are highly technology dependent. Internal controls for information security systems are necessary to assure the reliability of the internal controls of the financial system. Section 302 dealing with corporate responsibility for financial reports, and Section 404 addressing management assessment of internals, are of particular importance to the information security professional.[10] In addition, Section 409 requires real-time reporting of the event, which affects a company's status and earning. This section of the law has been interpreted to include real-time monitoring of computer systems including firewalls, intrusion detection, and other technology security controls.[11]

The Public Company Accounting Oversight Board (PCAOB) was also created to oversee the activities of the auditing profession.[12] The PCAOB was also created to provide guidance to auditors. This guidance provides details on types of necessary controls specifically addressed as information technology general controls. Again, the reasoning of this guidance is that financial system controls are dependent on the technology controls.[13]

SOX is far reaching in its impact. Its provisions impact everything from security access, segregation of duties, repeatable and audible processes covering all aspects of IT: hardware, software, physical access, and change management. SOX's requirements must be met even in the case of a disaster. "SOX clearly states a harsh set of fines and other punishments for failure to comply with the law; however, it doesn't offer any leeway when it comes to being unable to meet your requirements due to a disaster or other data-loss event. You must be able to file your reports and have the data to back them up, no matter what else may be going on in the organization or its data center. The bottom line is that even in the case of large-scale disasters, your company could be held liable if you cannot meet the requirements of the regulations."[14]

The Gramm-Leach-Bliley Act of 1999 also has some implications for Secure Securities. It has several provisions that address issues of privacy:

- *Requires clear disclosure by all financial institutions of their privacy policy regarding the sharing of non-public personal information with both affiliates and third parties.*

- *Requires a notice to consumers and an opportunity to "opt-out" of sharing of non-public personal information with nonaffiliated third parties subject to certain limited exceptions.*

- *Addresses a potential imbalance between the treatment of large financial services conglomerates and small banks by including an exception, subject to strict controls, for joint marketing arrangements between financial institutions.*

- *Clarifies that the disclosure of a financial institution's privacy policy is required to take place at the time of establishing a customer relationship with a consumer and not less than annually during the continuation of such relationship.[15]*

Additional laws may be applicable and are discussed in the section entitled Laws with General Application.

Client: ChattTown Records

ChattTown Records is an independent recording label founded in 2004 by Charlie, a recording artist. Charlie posted one of his songs on YouTube and had over 2 million hits. Realizing people liked his music, he decided he would record a CD. Charlie went online and found that if he signed with a major music label, he would receive only a very small percentage of the sales. He and Barry, a friend with a recording studio, decided to produce the CD themselves. It was very successful and they were able to establish distribution and marketing channels. Based on this success, together they founded ChattTown Records. At the current time, ChattTown Records has five individuals on full-time employment and produces records for Charlie, as well as four additional artists. ChattTown does its own payroll and financial record keeping and stores the data on a server located at the company. In addition to being used for record keeping, the server is used for the storage of musical recordings. There is no IT department; all server and routine IT maintenance are handled by a contractor who has limited information security knowledge.

Of particular concern to the owners of ChattTown Records is music pirating. Recently the business manager read an article on music pirating from the Institute for Policy Innovation, which stated: "Piracy of recorded music costs the U.S. sound recording industries billions of dollars in lost revenue and profits. These losses, however, represent only a fraction of the impact of recorded music piracy on the U.S. economy as a whole. Combining the latest data on worldwide piracy of recorded music with multipliers from a well-established U.S. government model, this study concludes that recorded music piracy costs American workers significant losses in jobs and earnings, and governments substantial lost tax revenue."[16] The article states that the U.S. economy loses $12.5 billion annually.[13,17] ChattTown Records did not want to become a part of that statistic and wanted to take all reasonable precautions to prevent the pirating of their recordings. Because of the limited knowledge of their current IT consulting firm, K-LiWin Consulting has been contracted by ChattTown Records to address information security, specifically what information management practices can be implemented to assure compliance with applicable laws and safeguard its information resources and assure employee privacy.

Applicable Copyright Laws On October 12, 1998, the U.S. Congress passed the Digital Millennium Copyright Act and two weeks later, on October 28th, President Clinton signed the Act into law. The general provisions of the law include:

- Makes it a crime to circumvent anti-piracy measures built into most commercial software.

- Outlaws the manufacture, sale, or distribution of code-cracking devices used to illegally copy software.

- Does permit the cracking of copyright protection devices, however, to conduct encryption research, assess product interoperability, and test computer security systems.

- Provides exemptions from anti-circumvention provisions for nonprofit libraries, archives, and educational institutions under certain circumstances.

- In general, limits Internet service providers from copyright infringement liability for simply transmitting information over the Internet.

- Service providers, however, are expected to remove material from users' Web sites that appears to constitute copyright infringement.

- Limits liability of nonprofit institutions of higher education—when they serve as online service providers and under certain circumstances—for copyright infringement by faculty members or graduate students.

- Requires that "Web casters" pay licensing fees to record companies.

- Requires that the Register of Copyrights, after consultation with relevant parties, submit to Congress recommendations regarding how to promote distance education through digital technologies while "maintaining an appropriate balance between the rights of copyright owners and the needs of users."[18]

Additional laws may be applicable and are discussed in the section entitled Laws with General Application.

Client: Homeless Helpers of Massachusetts (HHM)

HHM is a nonprofit organization whose mission is to provide comprehensive services to the homeless in the community. It offers temporary shelter and meals to homeless families throughout Massachusetts. HHM also provides homeless families with resources to acquire long-term housing, job training, employment, student tutoring and counseling. HHM coordinates with other service organizations and provides each family with a comprehensive plan to accomplish the goal of becoming self-sustaining members of the community. In order to accomplish this goal, HHM must collect and maintain personal information about each of its clients.

The HHM offices are collocated in a facility that houses a day center, training room, case worker offices, and health care services. HHM has only three employees and relies heavily on volunteers. Physical access to the HHM offices is limited to staff and volunteers only and within the HHM offices, there are five computers that are networked together with a server located on the premises. The server stores all donor, client, and employee information. All IT services are handled by a local IT firm, which volunteers its time and resources. There is no on-staff IT support. Legal services are provided by an attorney who works pro bono. The attorney was notified of a new privacy law enacted in Massachusetts directly affecting organizations that store personal information about Massachusetts's citizens. The attorney immediately recognized its potential impact to HHM and notified the director. Together they realized they did not have the expertise or knowledge to determine its impact on their organization or what needed to be done to be in compliance with the law. HHM contacted K-LiWin Consulting to help them with this and any other relevant laws impacting their information security practices, policies, or procedures.

Applicable Privacy Laws On September 22, 2008, Massachusetts adopted a law that requires organizations to implement comprehensive information security program if the organization, no matter its location, maintained or used personal data about Massachusetts residents. California and Nevada have similar laws, although they are far less reaching in scope.[19] The Massachusetts law requires an organization to have a written security program.[20] The law requires that:

1. one individual be responsible for the data system
2. each of the organization's employees having design, development, operations, maintenance, or use of the personal data be informed of the regulations
3. the data holder not allow unauthorized access to the data
4. the data must be protected from fire, theft, flood, natural disasters, or other physical threat
5. the holders of the data maintain a record of access
6. the holders of the data provide access to a citizen concerning his own personal data
7. the holders of the data assure accuracy of the data
8. upon their request inform the citizen that their personal data is being held
9. establish procedures that all the data subject to contest any information held and make any necessary correction
10. maintain procedures that will notify an individual of any legal demand for data in time to stop the action
11. only reasonably necessary data be maintained on any individual[21]

The majority of the federal laws relating to privacy is applicable to federal agencies and intended to protect citizens against an invasion of their privacy by the federal government. These laws are not intended to regulate nonprofit organizations. However, there are standards and good practices that should be adhered to by nonprofit entities. In *The NonProfit Times*, Jon Biedermann provides some important practices that should be used. They include:

- Back up your data
- Use strong passwords
- Store passwords with a high level of encryption
- Never display passwords on a screen
- Passwords and user ID should have a predetermined expiration date
- Limit unsuccessful log-in attempts to three
- Limit access to the data
- Provide audit trails for data usage
- Limit physical access to your computers and servers
- Conduct user security awareness training
- Beware of phishing schemes
- Secure your database systems[22]

6D

While these are excellent best practices, they are not laws. There is currently no federal law that requires organizations to implement information security or to encrypt personal data. Laws of this nature are left to the individual states. However, forty-six U.S. states and the District of Columbia do have laws requiring organizations to notify their clients of any breach of their personal information.[23]

HHM may also be subject to additional privacy laws as discussed in the following section.

Laws with General Application

There are federal laws that impact the information management security practice, which are not specific to any single organization. These laws are generic in nature but have an impact on a good information security policy. These statutes are designed to criminalize or decriminalize some computer activities, and an information security professional should be familiar with these laws and their impact on the organization. Perhaps one of the laws having the broadest impact is the Computer Fraud and Abuse Act (CFAA), which was enacted in 1986 to reduce hacking of computer systems. It was amended in 1994, in 1996 by the National Information Infrastructure Protection Act, in 2001 by the USA Patriot Act, and again in 2006 by the USA Patriot Improvement and Reauthorization Act. This law is designed to criminalize "hacking" and other malicious acts to a computer system.[24]

There are several privacy acts that govern the use of information maintained on individuals and the disclosure of that data. Falling under this category would be the Electronic Communications Privacy Act of 1986 and the USA Patriot Act of 2001. In addition, the Privacy of Customer Information Section of the Common Carrier Act protects data from being used for marketing purposes. On a separate note is the Economic Espionage Act of 1996, designed to prevent theft of corporate trade secrets. One last law of note is the Security and Freedom through Encryption Act of 1999, which defines the use of encryption for people in the United States.[25]

Problem

K-LiWin Consulting has been contacted by four distinct companies to advise them on their information management needs as related to security. Each company has differing needs based on the regulation and laws pertaining to their specific industry. Each student should provide a thorough review of one of the laws listed above. They should prepare a report and make a presentation as to the provisions, if any, that apply to the associated company. In the case of laws that may have an impact on multiple companies, the student should determine which provisions apply to which company. Each report should at a minimum give an overview of the law, define the provisions impacting the respective company or companies, define how those provisions impact the information security management of the data, and provide some guidance on what controls and information security practices should be placed in the organization's security policy to assure compliance with all applicable laws. In addition, if during the investigation other laws are encountered, they should be noted.

Endnotes

1. Gina Marie Stevens, CRS Report for Congress, April 3, 2008.

2. Health Insurance Portability and Accountability Act of 1996. Public Law 104-191. Viewed 6/24/2008. http://www.cms.hhs.gov/HIPAAGenInfo/Downloads/HIPAALaw.pdf. page 2

3. Federal Register, February 20, 2003, Part II, 45 CFR Parts 160, 162, and 164, Health Insurance Reform: Security Standards; Final Rule. Viewed 6/24/2008. http://www.cms .hhs.gov/SecurityStandard/Downloads/securityfinalrule.pdf

4. Viewed 1/2/09. http://www.sans.org/resources/policies/

5. Marisue Cody, PhD, RN. *Ethical Considerations: The Common Rule*. Office of Research and Development. Program for Research Integrity Development & Education (PRIDE). Department of Veterans Affairs. Viewed 7/14/08. http://www.research.va.gov/ programs/pride/resources/Common_Rule_Flyer.pdf

6. Office for Human Research Protections (OHRP). OHRP Informed Consent Frequently Asked Questions. Viewed 1/12/2009. http://www.hhs.gov/ohrp/informconsfaq.html#q1

7. Viewed 1/2/08. http://searchcio.techtarget.com/sDefinition/0,,sid182_gci920030,00.html

8. Viewed 7/15/2008. http://fl1.findlaw.com/news.findlaw.com/hdocs/docs/gwbush/ sarbanesoxley072302.pdf

9. The Laws That Govern the Securities Industry. Viewed 6/25/2008. http://www.sec.gov/ about/laws.shtml#sox2002

10. Gregg Stults, *An Overview of Sarbanes-Oxley for the Information Security Professional*. May 9, 2004. GP Assignment, SANS Institute 2004. Viewed 1/2/2009. http://www.cs .jhu.edu/~rubin/courses/sp06/Reading/soxForInfoSec.pdf

11. E. Eugene Schultz, *Sarbanes-Oxley Compliance and Information Security Data Correlation*. High Tower White Paper. Viewed 1/2/2009. http://www.high-tower.com/docs/ SoX_ITsecurity_white_paper.pdf

12. Viewed 7/15/2008. http://fl1.findlaw.com/news.findlaw.com/hdocs/docs/gwbush/ sarbanesoxley072302.pdf

13. Stults, *An Overview of Sarbanes-Oxley for the Information Security Professional*.

14. Mike Talon. "Understand the Impact of Sarbanes-Oxley Compliance on Your Disaster Recovery Plan," *Tech Republic*. 2/27/2006. Viewed 7/15/2008. http://articles .techrepublic.com.com/5100-10878_11-6043448.html

15. *Financial Services Modernization Act*. U.S. Senate on Banking, Housing, and Urban Affairs. Viewed 7/16/2008. http://banking.senate.gov/conf/grmleach.htm

16. Stephen E. Siwek, *The True Cost of Sound Recording Piracy to the U.S. Economy*. Institute for Policy Innovation: Policy Report # 188. 8/21/2007. Viewed 1/2/2009. http://www.ipi.org

17. Ibid.

18. The Digital Millennium Copyright Act. The UCLA Online Institute for Cyberspace Law and Policy. Viewed 7/15/08. http://www.gseis.ucla.edu/iclp/dmca1.htm

19. Randy Gainer, *New State Laws Require Extensive Data Security Plans and Encryption.* Viewed 1/5/2009. http://www.dwt.com/practc/privacy/bulletins/09-08_DataSecurityPlans (print).htm

20. Bart Lazar, "Data Privacy, Security Laws Have Far-Reaching Impact." *NETWORK-WORLD,* November 7, 2008. Viewed 1/5/2009. http://www.networkworld.com/news/ 2008/110708-data-privacy-security-laws-have.html?hpg1=bn

21. *Part I. Administration of the Government Title X. Public Records Chapter 66A. Fair Information Practices.* The General Laws of Massachusetts. Viewed 1/5/2009. http:// www.mass.gov/laws/mgl/66a-2.html

22. Jon Biedermann, "Information Security Is Threatened Every Day," *The NonProfit Times.* Viewed 12/17/2008. http://www.nptimes.com/technobuzz/TB20080325_3.html

23. Gainer, *New State Laws Require Extensive Data Security Plans and Encryption.*

24. Michael E. Whitman and Herbert J. Mattord, *Principles of Information Security,* 3rd ed. Course Technology, Cengage Learning, 2009, pp. 90–91.

25. Ibid.

6D

Running Case: Stratified Custom Manufacturing

Running Case: Stratified Custom Manufacturing

James Mburi has been making an effort to get more data for use by the marketing team to prove its viability and to push toward a new bespoke customer base he has been trying to court. He calls in his marketing and business intelligence guru Nubrio Nutahsi to discuss the best way to push this project even though current preliminary data does not support moving to the new customer base.

James calls Nubrio and asks him to check out a new vendor for conducting their business intelligence surveys that would help him prove the worth and value of the new customer base. James said he had heard great things about the Nigerian Data Consortium (NDC) and he would like Nubrio to use them for the data gathering and analysis phase of the project.

Nubrio mentions that this is outside the normal policies regarding contractor use; however, if James directed him to do so, he would call them first thing after lunch. James calls him on the telephone and directs him to proceed in the project using NDC.

James then calls his wife to have her call her brother, CEO of NDC, and tell him to get data to support the project no matter what it takes. She makes the call.

Six weeks later Drew Cubbins and David MacIntosh are reviewing the cost and further outlays to NDC right after James makes a powerful and compelling presentation for his plan to expand his marketing and sales efforts using data supplied by NDC.

After the meeting, in a private conversation, David says to Drew, "The costs of this project seem to be a bit high, don't you think?"

Drew says, "Yes, they do seem to be out of line with what I was expecting, and why did James use this new vendor instead of our usual data provisioning service? Also, I was wondering how they obtained the necessary internal data without access codes and passwords to work with that sensitive data? I checked with the provisioning group and found that they had not been given access to our VPN nor had they signed the required nondisclosure agreements."

"Let me check into it," David says and walks off with the spreadsheets stacked under his arm.

Later he asks his research assistant, Sally Etheridge, to find out all she can about NDC.

Her initial report handed to David later that afternoon was shocking. It appeared that James had violated a number of corporate policies, and that NDC was nothing more than a shell company. Sally said the trail of data appeared to have been partially constructed from internal data and data located outside their protected net. The how and when the data had been constructed was a serious question. And the determination of who had done the work, whether inside the corporation or external, was now a second serious set of questions. The validity of the data was suspect as well because it had to have come from outside their protected network.

Discussion Questions

1. What specific policy, ethical rules, and legal rules did James break, if any?

2. What should Nubrio have done when asked to perform a questionable task with a vendor that had not gone through the company's strict accreditation process for vendors? Do you think he will come to regret having let this contract without a paper trail?

3. What happens when a major stockholder and founding member violates company rules, procedures, and processes?

Part 7

Information Security Governance and Regulatory Compliance

Objective

The objective for this chapter of the text is an examination of the legal and ethical issues associated with strategic planning and governance in the face of regulatory issues. As with the rest of the organization, information security governance provides strategic direction for the domain, integrating it into the strategic planning for the rest of the organization, ensuring it supports rather than competes with other areas. Without an understanding of key regulatory issues, the organization will continually find itself "putting out legal fires" instead of doing good business.

Contents

The pervasiveness and convenience of computers and the Internet tend to make most of society deeply dependent on information technology. This technology has provided tremendous benefits to society in regard to areas such as commerce, the distribution of knowledge, and the ability of persons to communicate with one another. Unfortunately, it has also opened up vulnerabilities that did not exist outside of networked computer systems.

B Reading: Global Information Security Regulations, Case Studies, and Cultural Issues

Guillermo A. Francia, III, and Andrew P. Ciganek

The pervasiveness of the Internet has created a new challenge to legislators around the globe: the enactment of regulations that will preserve and protect the country's information technology (IT) infrastructure and its integrity in delivering secure products and services. This paper examines the global, and yet unilateral, attempts of various countries in ratifying their own information security legislations.

C Case: Collaboration and Compliance in Health Care: A Threat Modeling Case Study

Divakaran Liginlal, Lara Z. Khansa, and Jeffrey P. Landry

The objective of this case study is to examine the strategic advantages of collaboration and information sharing in today's health care marketplace, and the resulting threats that hinder regulatory compliance. Building an illustrative case around a major health care provider in the U.S. Midwest, the study first explores how collaboration technologies play a crucial role in delivering enhanced health care services. The important elements of information sharing in inter-organizational systems—a key ingredient of collaboration—and related regulatory compliance needs are then presented. This is followed by a discussion of threat modeling methodologies and tools, along with a framework for modeling threats associated with collaboration. Two threat modeling use cases are developed for scenarios involving collaboration, namely, unauthorized access by insiders and abusive use of instant messaging applications. Each use case is accompanied by the related formal threat models, enterprise best practices, and lessons learned for collaborative health care, given the need for regulatory compliance. The use cases are described so as to facilitate their modeling using the Microsoft Threat Modeling Tool (TMT), which has the ability to uncover threats that might otherwise go unnoticed.

D Running Case

Security Compliance Auditing: Review and Research Directions

Guillermo A. Francia, III, and Jeffrey S. Zanzig
Jacksonville State University

Dr. Guillermo A. Francia, III, received his Ph.D. in computer science from New Mexico Tech. In 1996, Dr. Francia received one of the five national awards for Innovators in Higher Education from Microsoft Corporation. Dr. Francia served as a Fulbright scholar to Malta in 2007. His research interests include computer security, digital forensics, visualization, data mining, and performance dashboards. Currently, Dr. Francia is serving as Director of the Center for Information Security and Assurance at Jacksonville State University.

Dr. Jeffrey S. Zanzig received his Ph.D. in accounting from the University of Mississippi. His research interests include accounting history, computer security, internal auditing, financial reporting, and auditing.

Overview

The pervasiveness and convenience of computers and the Internet tend to make most of society deeply dependent on information technology. This technology has provided tremendous benefits to society in regard to areas such as commerce, the distribution of knowledge, and the ability of persons to communicate with one another. Unfortunately, it has also opened up vulnerabilities that did not exist outside of networked computer systems.

Introduction

The vast number of federal and state regulations over technological security presents a daunting task for organizations to ensure compliance:

- Section 404 of the Sarbanes-Oxley Act of 2002 deals with weaknesses in financial reporting,
- Gramm-Leach Bliley Act is concerned with financial data privacy,
- California's Senate Bill 1836 promotes public disclosure of breaches of data, and
- Health Insurance Portability and Accountability Act requires privacy and security for medical records.

It is believed that there is a common thread of security issues interwoven within technological security legislation. Some of these common elements include:

- Risk assessment process to continually assess security risks,
- Access controls so that only authorized individuals can enter various areas of a system, and
- Security logs to monitor the system's handling of security issues and maintain accountability for system users.

There has been a tremendous amount of literature on compliance auditing practices and tools to accomplish information and technological security. These practices typically attempt to achieve continuous data protection by determining levels of company data that should be subject to differing security requirements, hardware and software to achieve the security, ensuring compliance with legislation, and regular testing of the effectiveness of the security system.

This chapter begins by considering some of the security legislation regarding the collection and processing of information through the use of technology. This legislation provides a driving force behind the need for a manageable approach that will ensure compliance over information security. It is therefore followed by a discussion regarding common characteristics of compliance to illustrate that, although there are numerous pieces of legislation, there is a common set of requirements that allows them to be addressed as a group. However, in addition to finding commonality regarding security issues in legislation, there is the need to combine what are traditionally separate evaluations of accounting internal control and technological security issues. This situation is therefore described along with why it is important to integrate the evaluations. Next the discussion moves into the development of formal models and expert systems as a means of implementing a compliance model. The importance of implementing appropriate measurement and benchmark components into the model is also addressed. The discussion concludes with suggested research directions and concluding comments.

Security Legislation

In the middle of the twentieth century, when computers began to catch on as a means of storing and processing information, the security of the actual computer was generally treated the same as the security over its data and processing. In these early days, computer processing was centralized on mainframes that received inputs from decks of punched cards that were batch processed to produce printouts. Access to these items and the computers could be physically controlled. In the later part of the twentieth century, the advent of computer networking significantly improved the ability of computers to provide benefits in regard to commerce, the distribution of knowledge, and the ability of persons to communicate with one another. Unfortunately, it also opened up significant vulnerabilities that did not previously exist.[1]

Johnson provides some examples of cases that led to the conclusion that there is a trend in the courts that the possessors of a database of confidential information have a legal duty to protect someone's personal information.[2] In a case in the New York Court of Appeals known as the *Palsgraf v. Long Island Railroad Co.*, the justice concluded that the railroad did not have a duty to protect a patron, Helen Palsgraf, from an explosive placed on the train in a newspaper-wrapped package by a man who was running from the train. The basis for the finding was that the risk was not "within the range of reasonable apprehension." In another case known as *Kline v. 1500 Massachusetts Avenue Apartment Corp.*, the court held that a landlord was responsible for an assault on one of his tenants because he was aware of a growing assault problem in the area and took no reasonable steps to prevent the harm. This thought process along with current legislation over technological security led to the conclusion that due to the fact that the possessor of a database of confidential information can reasonably perceive the danger of harm when this information is hacked, there is a duty of care established within both common and legislative law for protection of this data.

Society's concern over the protection of information has resulted in numerous pieces of legislation to deal with security issues. Table 7A-1 provides some examples that are further discussed in the following paragraphs.

Title of Legislation	Basic Provisions
California Security Breach Information Act	Businesses in California have an obligation to safeguard personal customer information.
Computer Fraud and Abuse Act	It is illegal to inappropriately obtain access to information on computers of governmental and financial institutions, or those involved in interstate and foreign commerce.
Federal Information Security Management Act of 2002	Requires government agencies to provide security for both their information systems and the information that they use to support their operations.
Gramm-Leach-Bliley Act	Primarily applies to financial institutions and deals with the collection, disclosure, use, and protection of what is considered to be personal information of a nonpublic nature.
Health Insurance Portability and Accountability Act	The Privacy Rule established in connection with this legislation helps to ensure that personal health information is protected as it moves through appropriate channels to promote quality health care.
Sarbanes-Oxley Act of 2002	Designed to strengthen the financial reporting process for public companies.

Table 7A-1 Summary of Legislation

California Security Breach Information Act

Although this legislation does not attempt to determine what a reasonable level of security is, it does make it clear that California businesses have an obligation to safeguard personal customer information. Therefore, customers are eligible for recovery of damages when a business breaches this duty of care.[3]

Computer Fraud and Abuse Act

The primary cyber security law in the United States is known as the Computer Fraud and Abuse Act (CFAA), passed by Congress in 1984. Chan and Rubiner provide a description of the CFAA and how it has recently affected employee hiring practices.[4] This piece of legislation arose primarily out of a desire to stop the unauthorized access of computer information. Although originally structured to protect information on the computers of governmental and financial institutions, the reach of the CFAA was significantly extended in 1996 when the law was modified to include any computer used in interstate and foreign commerce. Liability under the CFAA can be established by the plaintiff showing that the defendant "(1) either fraudulently or 'intentionally' accessed a protected computer 'without authorization or [in excess of] authorized access' and (2) that, as a result of such conduct, caused damages of at least $5,000."

It is interesting that although early CFAA cases dealt with situations involving unauthorized access to a protected computer database, employers are now using it as a tool to continue to exert influence over prior employees. For example, an employee could be subject to the CFAA when they interview with a competitor and continue to work with their current employer for a period of time. To avoid this situation, the former employee must be able to prove that any access to the prior employer's system, after the interview for new employment, was to perform their job duties rather than for the benefit of the new employer. It is also suggested that employers put a structure in place that, as part of the interview process, ensures that the interviewee is aware that they are not to gather any information that could be used to the competitive disadvantage of the former employer. Then after hiring, the employee should be asked to certify that they have returned all information to the prior employer.

Federal Information Security Management Act of 2002

The Federal Information Security Management Act (FISMA) applies to government agencies and requires them to provide security for both their information systems and the information that they use to support their operations.[5]

Gramm-Leach-Bliley Act

The Gramm-Leach-Bliley Act (GLBA) is a piece of legislation from 1999 that primarily applies to financial institutions and deals with the collection, disclosure, use, and protection of what is considered to be personal information of a nonpublic nature. However, this legislation also covers information security requirements for accountants involved in the preparation of individual tax returns and the offering of nonbusiness advice regarding taxes and financial planning.[6]

Health Insurance Portability and Accountability Act

The Health Insurance Portability and Accountability Act of 1996 (HIPAA) was enacted on August 21, 1996. The Privacy Rule established in connection with this legislation helps to ensure that personal health information is protected as it moves through appropriate channels to promote quality health care. The provisions of the Privacy Rule apply to covered entities that include: individual and group health plans providing or paying for medical care, health care providers making use of electronic transmissions of health information regarding certain transactions, and health care clearinghouses (i.e., an entity that processes information between a standard and nonstandard format). The rule protects all types of information classified as "individually identifiable health information," which includes demographic and other information relating to:

- A person's past, present, or future mental or physical health or condition.
- The provision of health care to the person.
- A person's past, present, or future payment for the provision of health care.
- Individually identifiable information such as a name, address, social security number, and birth date.

The basic principle behind the Privacy Rule is that, unless permitted by the rule, a covered entity cannot use or disclose the protected health information without written authorization from the individual or their personal representative.[7]

Sarbanes-Oxley Act of 2002

The Sarbanes-Oxley Act of 2002 (SOX) includes a number of provisions designed to strengthen the financial reporting process for public companies. One of the provisions provides that the management of public companies provide an annual assessment of their internal controls over financial reporting. In addition, the company's external auditor must now report on both the fair presentation of the financial statements and also provide a written assessment of their client's system of internal controls. Another provision of SOX created the Public Company Accounting Oversight Board (PCAOB) and charged it with the responsibility to establish or adopt standards in regard to auditing, ethics, independence, and quality control in the preparation of public company audit reports.[8]

Common Characteristics of Compliance

There have been numerous attempts to develop an approach to address issues of security legislation by considering some of the common characteristics of security compliance issues. A set of common characteristics begins to emerge from a review of even a small number of technology security frameworks. This section provides some background on a few of the frameworks and guidance that exists in regard to the security of information and the technology that processes it. It concludes with a brief summary of some common characteristics that are interwoven within the frameworks.

Committee of Sponsoring Organizations

In regard to the compliance issues set out in the Sarbanes-Oxley Act of 2002, the PCAOB issued Auditing Standard No. 5, entitled *An Audit of Internal Control Over Financial Reporting That Is Integrated with An Audit of Financial Statements*. This standard was issued on June 12, 2007, and supersedes prior guidance provided in the PCAOB's Auditing Standard No. 2. Auditing Standard No. 5 provides that "the audit of internal control over financial reporting should be integrated with the audit of the financial statements."[9] The importance of this requirement is tied to the idea that an understanding of internal accounting controls could allow the auditor to assess control risk at a low level when performing a financial statement audit. Control risk is the risk that a company's internal controls will fail to detect a situation that could result in the financial statements being materially misstated. When internal accounting controls function appropriately to prevent misstated financial statements, an auditor could perform less audit work in forming an opinion regarding the fair presentation of the financial statements.

Auditing Standard No. 5 also provides that "the auditor should use the same suitable, recognized control framework to perform his or her audit of internal control over financial reporting as management uses for its annual evaluation of the effectiveness of internal control over financial reporting." In 1992, the Committee of Sponsoring Organizations of the Treadway Commission (COSO) developed a framework that is often adopted by many organizations and their auditors for the evaluation of internal accounting controls. Minter provides a well-developed background regarding the history of the COSO framework.[10] The framework came into being as a result of concern in the mid-1980s regarding fraudulent financial reporting by public companies in the United States. To address this situation, the National Commission on Fraudulent Financial Reporting was formed and chaired by a prior commissioner of the Securities and Exchange Commission named James C. Treadway. Although the Treadway Commission functioned independently of its sponsoring organizations, it included an Advisory Board made up of members from various organizations including its sponsoring organizations. The composition of the sponsoring organizations included the following:

- American Institute of Certified Public Accountants (AICPA)
- Institute of Internal Auditors (IIA)
- Financial Executives International (FEI), then known as Financial Executives Institute
- Institute of Management Accountants (IMA), then known as the National Association of Accountants (NAA)

Although the COSO framework was developed with the idea of strengthening internal accounting controls, the five basic components of this framework could be considered to be equally applicable to the development and maintenance of the internal controls of any system. COSO's five interrelated components of internal control are described in *The Internal Control—Integrated Framework*. The following summarizes the components:

- Control Environment—reflection of the control consciousness of organizational personnel as set by senior management. It serves as the foundation for all of the internal control components since it provides for the structure and discipline for the overall process of establishing and maintaining internal controls.
- Risk Assessment—organizations establish objectives and face risks that could interfere with their ability to achieve those objectives. A common quantitative method of

analysis involves taking each potential loss times its probability of occurrence to determine an exposure value. These values can be ranked in order of significance to provide a means of prioritizing risks that the organization wishes to protect itself against. Since some risks are difficult to quantify, it is also advisable to view risks while considering qualitative factors in addition to exposure values.

- Control Activities—involve policies and procedures established by management to basically lessen the probability of occurrence of the potential financial loss associated with the various risks an organization faces.

- Information and Communication—are needed to ensure that organizational personnel are aware of their internal control responsibilities and that information is exchanged to facilitate the management of company operations. This includes an organization's accounting information system.

- Monitoring—recognizes the fact that organizations operate in a dynamic environment and that internal controls may need to be modified to make them more effective. It is therefore imperative that management keep its hands on the pulse of the organization and make adjustments to internal control policies when necessary.[11]

The IT Governance Institute addresses the application of the COSO framework to information technology.

IT Governance Institute

A framework, known as Control Objectives for Information and Related Technology (COBIT), provides a comprehensive approach for dealing with risk and control issues in an information technology (IT) environment, including: four domains, 34 information technology processes, and 215 control objectives.[12] Lahti and Peterson provide a brief description of the four domains:

1. Plan and Organize—planning is concerned with the development of strategic IT plans that provide support for business objectives. This generally involves a two- to five-year projection period.

2. Acquire and Implement—acquisition involves acquiring new applications along with the acquisition or development of staffing skill needed to carry out the plans. Implementation deals with areas of identification, certifying, maintenance, and testing of changes necessary to ensure the continued availability of both new and existing systems.

3. Delivery and Support—provide assurance that implemented systems continue to function in accordance with expectations over time.

4. Monitor and Evaluate—allows a proactive approach to be taken to ensure that the system meets baselines established in subsequent phases.[13]

An approach to applying the COSO framework to information technology processes has been proposed by the IT Governance Institute to consider how the components of COSO interact with COBIT control objectives. The IT Governance Institute was created in 1998 to promote international thinking and standards development to assist in controlling and directing the information technology of organizations. In the second edition of their report entitled *IT Control Objectives for Sarbanes-Oxley—The Role of IT in the Design and Implementation of Internal Control Over Financial Reporting*, they provide a mapping of COBIT to COSO. The linking of COSO and COBIT by the IT Governance Institute seems to be a good step in improving the adaptation of internal control evaluation from the manual to the information technology environment.[14]

The Security Matrix Elements

Dennis C. Brewer provides a discussion of considerations regarding information technology controls in his book entitled *Security Controls for Sarbanes-Oxley Section 404 IT Compliance: Authorization, Authentication, and Access.*[15] The section on seven essential elements of the security matrix illustrates one classification scheme of common characteristics:

1. Identification—different items such as a social security number and driver's license can be used along with references and background checks to help verify a user. System access should not be granted until such techniques are used to help verify the identity of a potential system user. After such background checks, digital identification normally consists of usernames.

2. Authentication—used to increase the level of confidence that can be placed on identity, messages, and sources by providing additional security regarding whether a particular username is genuine. It commonly consists of requiring a password, in addition to a username. It should be kept in mind that some systems allow a method of simple user-selected passwords where the identity of the user is not verified. Such a system may be fine for zero-risk resources and data. However, authentication methods for protected resources should verify the identity of the end user before assigning a username and password.

3. Authorization—used to determine a relationship between usernames and the resources and/or data stores that the user is permitted to access. These authorization decisions should primarily be based on operational decisions rather than technological personnel. The entire authorization process should be sufficiently documented so that an audit trail exists showing exactly what rights each end-user has. Rights to generic type resources (i.e., resources not subject to external regulatory influences) can normally be granted on the basis of user groups. Other areas deal with protected information, and authorization must normally be restricted using more unique characteristics of the end-user.

4. Access Control—used to enforce the authorization requirements. On the basis of authorization rules, access is granted to only certain resources and information. Access controls can also be layered, such as requiring additional authorization information to move to various areas within a system. It is imperative that access controls provide an audit trail in the form of a log that indicates when access is granted along with any changes made to information or processes while there.

5. Administration—the functioning of the security system must be documented to include everything from how information is to be protected to recovery from malicious code. If this information needs updating, the process should prioritize what should be worked on first by considering the worst things that could happen as a result of procedures being improperly documented. The most dangerous exposures should be addressed first.

6. Auditing—the audit process should include tests of compliance for established security controls. Internal audits can be used to correct deficiencies in an organization's handling of security before testing is performed by external compliance auditors.

7. Assessment—the following steps could be used to assess the vulnerabilities of an organization's system:

   - A list is prepared that defines any threats that contribute to vulnerabilities.

   - These threats can be classified as either those that cannot be eliminated due to operational reasons or those that can be eliminated.

   - Continuously perform a reevaluation of any remaining threats to see if new strategies or tools become available to eliminate them.

   - Any remaining threats are added to a to-do list for possible elimination in the future. This list should be prioritized with some cost-benefit considerations.

   The overall goal is to eliminate a threat if possible and constantly monitor those that cannot be reduced to a nuisance level.

Other

Schattner, Pletsshner, Bhend, and Brouns attempted to determine guidelines for computer security in the health industry in Australia by reviewing literature, analysis of current practices, and interviews with key stakeholders.[16] Their work produced a security checklist covering nine categories, including: (1) use of a computer security coordinator, (2) having procedures for setting IT security policies and procedures, (3) access control, (4) disaster recovery plans, (5) backups, (6) viruses, (7) firewalls, (8) network maintenance, and (9) secure electronic communication. Each of these categories has accompanying tasks that a reviewer can mark as to whether they have been completed.

The Reymann Group provides a whitepaper that discusses what they refer to as "The 15 Security Compliance Threads."[17] Their conclusions are based on various conversations and projects that they were engaged in over a period of several years. Table 7A-2 presents a brief summary of the security compliance threads.

Some Common Characteristics

In general terms, some of the common characteristics contained within the frameworks of this section include:

- Risk assessment
- User identification
- System access according to data classifications
- Establishment of operating procedures
- Administration of operating procedures
- Proper documentation that is regularly updated
- Regular assessment and monitoring

Compliance Thread	Summary Points
1. Risk Assessment	Organizations should maintain a risk assessment program.
2. Access Controls	Access should be limited to authorized individuals.
3. Protect Sensitive Data	Measures should be in place to provide administrative, technical, and physical safeguards over nonpublic data.
4. Vulnerability and Threat Assessment	Networks should be periodically scanned to look for vulnerabilities.
5. Firewalls	Management should establish a firewall policy in accordance with their process of ongoing security risk assessment.
6. Intrusion Detection and Prevention	Organizations should establish activities to both detect and prevent intrusion.
7. Patch Management	Procedures should be in place to identify, evaluate, approve, test, install, and document software patches.
8. Change Management	Any system changes should be authorized and documented.
9. Configuration Management	Procedures for establishing baseline versions of hardware, software, security, and documentation should be put in place. Any changes should be carefully evaluated and approved before being distributed.
10. Logging	Security logs should be maintained to monitor and enforce security policies.
11. Monitoring	Organizations should have the ability to determine new threats, actual attacks, and determine security effectiveness.
12. Reporting	Procedures should be in place to report material events to management.
13. Rapid Response	Procedures should be in place that set out response actions for material events.
14. Intrusion/Incident Response	Containment procedures should be in place to respond to intrusions and assure system restoration.
15. Business Continuity	Management should periodically test their backup systems to minimize risk associated with system failures and intrusions by unauthorized personnel.

Table 7A-2 Summary of Security Compliance Threads

The Separation of Accounting and Technological Security Issues

The evaluation of internal accounting controls to ensure the reliability of the financial reporting process has traditionally been largely separated from the evaluation of technological security. This may be largely due to the fact that professionals in these two areas need more of a common understanding of each other's fields and how they relate to one another. The following discussion begins by presenting a brief review of some literature regarding metrics in these two fields and concludes with a discussion of the urgent need for their processes being integrated.

Internal Control Metrics

The evaluation of internal accounting controls provides a means of measuring the effectiveness and efficiency of the organization's execution of its activities in order to achieve its goals or objectives while preserving the integrity and accuracy of its accounting data. The following discussion summarizes some of the published works on the evaluation and monitoring of internal control systems.

Meservy, Bailey, and Johnson present an examination of the tasks involved in reviewing and evaluating internal controls.[18] The tasks were formalized and used to create a computational model, which was subsequently implemented as an expert system to automate the entire process and simulate the processes of expert auditors in auditing internal controls. In their document entitled *Guidance on Monitoring Internal Control Systems*, the Committee on Sponsoring Organizations provides guidance to assist organizations in effectively monitoring the quality of their systems of internal control. The guidance includes directions on establishing a baseline for monitoring, the implementation of monitoring procedures, and the assessment of results.[19]

Brewer and List propose time metric measurement of the operational effectiveness of internal controls, including: (1) the time of detection, (2) the time that the damage caused by the event is fixed or resolved, and (3) the time limit before an impact penalty is incurred if the problem is not corrected.[20] These time metrics are basically independent of external factors and therefore best reflect the level of effectiveness of an organization's internal control system. The metrics are structured around a classification scheme involving preventive, detective, and reactive controls. The preventive controls tend to prevent the adverse conditions from occurring or having an impact if they do occur. The detective controls tend to detect the adverse conditions and react to the problem within the shortest time possible. The reactive controls are those control classes in which a Business Continuity Plan (BCP) should be in place in the event that adverse or unanticipated conditions occur and are not detected in a timely manner.

Information Security Metrics

The motivation to measure information security is primarily driven on the basis of various regulatory requirements. The National Institute of Standards and Technology, an agency under the Department of Commerce, has published *Special Publication (SP) 800-55, Revision 1, titled Performance Measurement Guide for Information Security.*[21] This document covers the development and collection of three types of metrics: (1) implementation measures for security policy implementation measurement, (2) effectiveness measures for security services delivery measurement, and (3) impact measures for measurement of the effect of security events on business operations. The document also provides a number of sample measures that organizations can use as starting security metrics templates to measure the performance of their information security programs. These template measures include the security budget, vulnerability management, access control, awareness and training, audit and accountability, configuration management, contingency planning, incident response, etc.

Herrmann presents metrics on measuring compliance with security and privacy regulations and standards.[22] Herrmann wades through a number of regulations including GLBA, SOX, HIPAA, FISMA, etc. Suggested metrics on compliance are enumerated for each of the regulations. A common thread among the provided metrics is that almost all of them involve quantified measures. Qualitative measures have been, for not so obvious reasons, omitted. In addition, it should be pointed out that the following details need to be specified and delineated when metrics are developed: (1) the process of collection, (2) the responsible party, (3) its purpose, (4) the frequency of collection, and (5) the reporting format. In fairness, Herrmann made a valiant attempt to address such a daunting task on security metrics that her work will surely be highly appreciated by practitioners and academicians alike.

Integrating Internal Accounting Controls and Information Security

The Sarbanes-Oxley Act of 2002 requires that both company management and their financial statement auditor provide an assessment of internal controls over financial reporting. The financial statement auditor is subject to strict rules of independence to keep them from being biased in their evaluation of their client's financial statements and internal controls. However, there is also the area of internal audit where the auditors are not subject to the same level of independence requirements as the external auditor who issues a report on financial statements. In contrast, internal auditors are often employees of the same company that they audit. However, internal auditors are also subject to professional guidelines that require them to make objective evaluations in carrying out their duties. It is often the internal audit function who primarily assists company management in the design, maintenance, and evaluation of a system of internal controls. Such assistance provides a valuable resource to company management in ensuring that appropriate internal controls are designed, placed in operation, and periodically assessed. Internal audit can also assist in ensuring compliance with the provisions of various types of security legislation. However, do internal auditors normally have the expertise to deal with technological security issues?

Zanzig compared the perceptions of internal auditors with various organizational personnel in regard to the functioning of internal auditing in a field study involving six organizations.[23] One of the comparisons related the perceptions of internal auditors with the customer group of management information systems (MIS) and data processing personnel. Although both internal auditors and this customer group agreed that internal auditors strive to maintain business skills beyond the areas of accounting and finance, MIS and data processing personnel felt significantly more strongly than internal auditors that additional skills were needed by internal auditors. At the time of this study, the Institute of Internal Auditors was using the following for its *Statement of Responsibilities of Internal Auditing*:

> *Internal auditing is an independent appraisal function established within an organization to examine and evaluate its activities as a service to the organization.*[24]

Chapman points out that this statement was revised in June 1999, as the internal auditing profession attempted to better capture its areas of responsibility:

> *Internal auditing is an independent, objective assurance and consulting activity designed to add value and improve an organization's operations. It helps an organization accomplish its objectives by bringing a systematic disciplined approach to evaluate and improve the effectiveness of risk management, control, and governance practices.*[25]

Chaney and Kim point out that "all internal auditors need to understand core IT control concepts and risks to provide assurance in today's technology-based business world."[26] They also make the observation that they perceive a knowledge gap between internal auditors and IT auditors in that many internal auditors see technology issues as the domain of IT auditors. In support of this perception, they point out that many organizations schedule simultaneous but separate audits of the business and IT. It is only at the reporting phase that the separate audits are pulled together. Such an approach can lead to "inadequate scoping and execution of integrated audits, unclear accountability between the roles of business and IT auditors, and inadequate identification and testing of automated controls." This approach should be replaced with a truly integrated audit process. The area of expert systems is one of the tools that can be of assistance in bridging this gap and assisting both company management and their auditors in addressing technological security issues in a truly integrated audit with other business processes. A formal model integrating these areas is imperative in today's society where financial and other private data are communicated and processed through the use of technology.

Formal Models

A formal model for security evaluation over the processing and storage of information involves aspects of both an underlying theory of security issues and a means of implementing the model in a technological framework where it can be used by organizational personnel. The theoretical portion of the model provides the expertise to ensure that appropriate issues are evaluated. The computational portion provides the technological structure or tools to apply the theoretical model in an effective and efficient manner. This section presents some literature regarding formal security models representing underlying security theory and computational models for their implementation.

Formal Security Models

Seminal works on formal security models include the Bell-LaPadula Model, the Biba Model, and the Information Flow Model. The Bell-LaPadula Model focuses on the confidentiality of information.[27] A subsequent work, the Biba Model, introduced the concepts of integrity levels and policies.[28] The Information Flow Model is based on the lattice structure of security levels.[29] In this structure, security is enforced by requiring that all information transfers obey the flow relation among security classes. Landwehr provides an extensive literature review of research works on formal modeling of information security.[30]

A formal framework for information system security is the Trusted Computer System Evaluation Criteria (TCSEC), which was superseded by *DoD 5200.28-STD, 1985* in 1985.[31] It is also known as the "orange book." The four classes of protection that are defined by the document are (1) minimal, (2) discretionary, (3) mandatory, and (4) verified. These formal models and framework on information security have a significant impact on regulatory compliance implementation and auditing. A primary reason for this is that the three tenets of security (i.e., confidentiality, integrity, and availability) need to be upheld in both security implementation and auditing processes.

Computational Models

A computational model is a computer simulation of a process or a set of processes. The model can be built using computational modeling tools such as programming languages and shells.[32] LISP and Prolog are the traditional programming languages that are used for this modeling. However, the rapid expansion of the Web and the popularity of object orientation brought about a new generation of meta-languages such as the Business Process Modeling Language (BPML), Extensible Markup Language (XML), Unified Modeling Language (UML), and Systems Modeling Language (SysML). Shells are software packages that provide the infrastructure for rapidly building a model. Examples of shells are EMYCIN, ExShell, Clips, JESS, and EXPERT. Meservy, Bailey, and Johnson,[33] Lovata,[34] Changchit and Holsapple,[35] and Chang, Wu, and Chang,[36] all present research on the application of computational modeling in the evaluation of internal controls.

Meservy, Bailey, and Johnson present a formalization of auditor processes as a computational model where the evaluation of internal accounting controls by experienced auditors was simulated and validated.[37] The research made use of one expert auditor to build the model, while the validation phase was conducted by a team including this same auditor and six other auditors. The implemented computational model included approximately 300 conditional statements, where 10% to 25% of the statements were used in any given evaluation. The model's performance was evaluated using two major features: (1) tests of the quality of model processes and of cue usage, and (2) tests of sufficiency or adequacy of model outcomes. With very few exceptions, the model performed the tasks in a manner similar to the auditors.

Changchit and Holsapple argue for the notion that managers should have easy access to internal control evaluation knowledge.[38] The argument is based on the facts that (1) managers are responsible for establishing and supervising internal controls rather than external auditors, (2) decisions that are made by managers may or may not have a serious impact on internal controls, and (3) managers have a better perspective on the company's operations, including internal controls, than external auditors. The paper described the design, implementation, and testing of an expert system on internal control evaluation for practicing managers. The results provide evidence that such a system can be a valuable and effective means of supporting management's decision-making process regarding internal controls.

The computer-based auditing system described in Chang, Wu, and Chang is specifically geared toward the internal controls that govern the purchasing and expenditure cycle of an Enterprise Resource Planning (ERP) system.[39] The system was primarily created to comply with Section 404 of the Sarbanes-Oxley Act. The results of using this system indicate that it is capable of providing both management and external auditors with a means of identifying incorrect financial statements and fraudulent activities. The use of expert systems provides a form of computational model that can function extremely well in representing the theoretical framework of formal security models.

Expert System Models

The use of expert systems came into being as a form of artificial intelligence around the late 1970s. Expert systems offer the advantage of being able to perform qualitative reasoning in addition to traditional quantitative analysis. However, their use is somewhat restricted in that

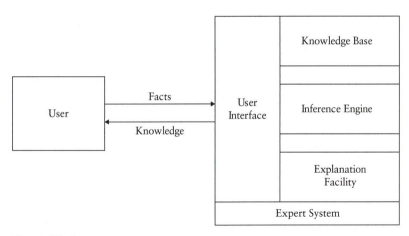

Figure 7A-1 Expert System Components

Courtesy Course Technology/Cengage Learning

the problems they address must involve situations where there are clearly defined facts and decision rules in an application area with known boundaries. Accounting's use of expert systems has traditionally involved "in-house" development by larger CPA firms and other organizations that possess enough expertise and funding to take on the task. Once developed, these organizations are normally reluctant to make the expert systems available to others. This is often attributed to the fact that incorrect decisions resulting from these systems could subject the developer to legal liability.[40]

Components of an Expert System

Baldwin-Morgan describes an expert system as being composed of four basic components.[41] First, there is a knowledge base that represents the collective knowledge of the human expert. The second component is an inference engine that is actually a computer program that identifies the appropriate knowledge bases for the problem and manipulates them to identify a solution. The third component is an explanation facility that helps the user to understand how the suggested solution has been determined. The fourth component is a user interface that facilitates communication between the system and user by collecting facts from the user and providing the solution and accompanying explanation. Figure 7A-1 illustrates the interrelationship among the components of an expert system.

Expert System Reasoning

Foltin and Smith describe that expert system reasoning use either forward chaining or backward chaining.[42] Both methods of reasoning make use of a set of rules in the form of "if-then" statements. Forward chaining is the more intuitive of the approaches since it is like a traditional reasoning process that proceeds as follows:

1. A rule is evaluated to see if the "if" portion of the rule is met.

2. When the "if" portion of the rule is met, a conclusion is reached that the "then" portion of the rule is true. This serves to provide new data.

3. The new data is compared to the "if" portion of other rules to see if they can be met.

4. The system progresses in this manner until the system reaches a conclusion.

Forward chaining is often thought of as moving down a decision tree. For example, an auditor could conclude that when certain control procedures are not followed ("if" portion of a rule), there are certain weaknesses in a system ("then" portion of a rule). The extent of the weakness would depend on how the system progresses through the rules. In contrast, backward chaining involves working up a decision tree as follows:

1. A conclusion is drawn and a "then" portion of a rule is searched to see if there is a match.

2. If the conclusion matches a "then" portion of a rule, the "if" portion of the rule is evaluated to see if it is true based on the particular situation.

3. When the "if" portion is true, the system treats it as a new conclusion to find another "then" portion of a rule that matches it.

4. The system progresses in this manner until the system reaches a conclusion or determines that the problem has an unknown solution.

Using the same illustration of an auditor evaluating a system of internal controls, the auditor would use backward chaining by starting with a conclusion regarding the strength of internal controls ("then" portion of a rule), and see if the "if" portion for the rule is supported on the basis of the circumstances. If the auditor can find a clear path backwards through the rules in support of the conclusion, it may be determined that the initial conclusion is supported.

Use of Expert Systems in Auditing

Three areas that expert systems have been used in auditing include the development of audit programs, internal control evaluation, and specific technical assistance. Brown and Murphy conducted a survey of some of the expert systems used by auditors describing some examples in these areas.[43] It is believed that these examples are also typical of what can be done with expert systems in auditing today. In considering audit programs, it is imperative that the structure of the audit process be planned in a way that collects appropriate evidence regarding the fair presentation of the financial statements in a manner that collects a sufficient, but not excessive, quantity of the necessary information to form a proper opinion. The extent to which audit procedures are applied on an audit is often dependent on the quality of the client's system of internal controls. If internal controls are strong, less evidence is required regarding the numbers in the financial statements. In addition, although there are standard audit procedures that are required on practically any audit, other procedures will depend on characteristics of the client and their industry. In regard to the use of expert systems in auditing, Brown and Murphy point out that one accounting firm used a system known as "Expertest" that made use of information about the firm's audit strategy and the business of the client to develop an audit program from 19 general audit programs contained in its knowledge base.[44]

In the area of internal control evaluation, another firm made use of a system known as "Internal Controls Expert" to assess the probability that the management of the audit client would prepare fraudulent financial statements. The risk assessment process made use of a system of weighted factors rather than a rule base. The auditor would be presented with a set of questions to answer regarding whether certain factors were present in the system. The system would then weight the factors to provide a fraud score. On the basis of this scoring, the system would classify the client as (1) a low probability of fraud, (2) an uncertain risk, or (3) a relatively high level of risk. The application of this system today is extremely relevant given the additional responsibility put on both company management of the client and their auditors for assessing internal accounting controls under the Sarbanes-Oxley Act of 2002.[45]

Finally, in the area of technical assistance expert systems, another firm made use of a system known as "Loan Probe" to perform an analysis of bank loans to determine if the banks had an appropriate level of loss reserves on their books for bad debts. The Loan Probe System made use of over 8,500 rules representing the knowledge of top professionals in the banking industry. Depending on the situation, the system would (1) state that a loan loss reserve was not needed, (2) specify a recommended reserve within a certain range, or (3) state that there was insufficient information to draw a conclusion. This system hits very close to today's world where subprime loans are resulting in massive home foreclosures and a plummeting of the value of the securities of financial institutions on the stock exchanges.[46]

Criticisms of Expert Systems in Auditing

The use of an expert system in the audit process is not without resistance from some in the profession. Some feel that using machine processing to replace the ability of a professional auditor to draw proper audit conclusions is inappropriate. In June 2006, an article entitled "Assessing Materiality: A New Fuzzy Logic Approach" appeared in *The CPA Journal*. In the article, the authors Rosner, Communale, and Sexton proposed the use of an expert system and fuzzy logic as a tool to aid an auditor in judging the materiality of audit issues. One of the journal's readers took an opposing position to the article. The authors of the article later responded to the criticism in the section of the journal for Letters to the Editor. Two of the reader's issues raised in opposition to expert systems in auditing are summarized as follows:

1. There is substantial litigation risk that arises from drawing an incorrect audit conclusion. It is therefore inappropriate to allow a computer system to overly influence the decision process of a seasoned auditor.

2. Since expert systems work best in situations that involve a certain domain of results, they are inappropriate in a financial statement audit because the domain of such an evaluation is far from being limited.

The authors of the article conceded that both arguments have some validity, but stated that there are supporting points that can be made to counter them. In regard to overreliance on the expert system, the authors point out that an auditor should not use an expert system to reach a conclusion that some audit issue is immaterial when classical audit approaches already indicate a material issue. To the contrary, the use of expert systems should be used to allow the auditor to be even more conservative in judgments and thus form a conclusion with the expert system that an issue is material when classical audit approaches fail to indicate materiality. In regard to the domain issue, the authors counter that although each engagement must be evaluated on its unique characteristics, it does not mean that no similar situations exist in certain areas where expert systems could be extremely helpful as a decision aid while allowing the auditor to weigh all evidence to reach an appropriate conclusion as an experienced professional.[47]

Model Development

Any endeavor requires a solid foundation upon which it is based. A formal model for security compliance auditing is necessary to assist organizations in developing and selecting security products. A continuously updated version of this model is also necessary to ensure continued compliance with security issues. Similarly, there is a need for a compliance auditing tool that will allow ease of updating for changes in the model and adaptability to the uniqueness of individual organizations. The components of the formal security model upon which this system is based should provide for two important aspects of evaluation. First, there must be some means of measuring the elements of the formal security model to capture an image of an organization's security posture. Second, there needs to be some means of benchmarking it against a yardstick to provide an indication of how the security situation measures up to appropriate security practices. The next two sections address these issues.

Measurement Approaches

There has been a plethora of measurement mechanisms appearing in the literature: the Goal/Question/Metric (GQM) approach (i.e., Basili and Weiss,[48] Basili, Caldiera, and Rombach[49]), the Quality Function Deployment (QFD) approach (i.e., Kogure and Akao[50]), the Six Sigma Quality approach (i.e., Harry[51] and Harry and Lawson[52]), and the Time Metrics approach (i.e., Brewer and List[53]).

The Goal/Question/Metric Approach

The GQM paradigm came into being roughly 20 years ago and lays the foundation for software processes requiring that (1) goals are identified, (2) questions are formulated in quantifiable terms, and (3) metrics are defined. The successful implementation of the paradigm has been demonstrated in a number of industrial settings including Motorola and Digital Equipment (i.e., Daskalantonakis,[54] Basili and Rombach,[55] Fuggetta, Lavazza, Morasca, Cinti, Oldano, and Orazi,[56] and Basili[57]). Although the literature shows that the GQM approach has been widely adopted and studied, it has also been widely criticized due to its perceived weaknesses. Some of the shortcomings include the following: it provides very little flexibility, it has the narrow focus of being a goal-driven approach, it has limited applicability, and it becomes unmanageable when confronted with expanding goals.

Basili, Heidrich, Lindvall, Munch, Regardie, and Trendowicz point out one limitation and propose a new measurement approach to improve the original technique by extending it to what is known as GQM+Strategies.[58] Their paper describes the difficulty of GQM in linking software measurement goals with higher-level goals of the organization where the software is being developed. They further argue that, without this linkage, software measurement data may possibly not be afforded the chance to influence important company decisions. Their proposal of GQM+Strategies as a measurement approach adds several extensions on top of the GQM model. These extensions include making business goals and strategies explicit, linking software goals with business strategies, and attaching information about relationships between goals, relevant context factors, and assumptions.

The Quality Function Deployment Approach

The QFD approach focuses on improving process quality by assuring that organizational processes and actions at various stages conform with established standards or benchmarks.[59] QFD is primarily geared toward satisfying the customer needs and has been successfully applied in various business and industrial settings as well as in software development.[60]

The Six Sigma Approach

The Six Sigma approach uses a structured methodology for accelerated process improvement that aims for virtually error-free business processes.[61] The five cyclic phases of the Six Sigma process (DMAIC) are: (1) define, (2) measure, (3) analyze, (4) improve, and (5) control. The define phase involves stating or restating the goals. The measure phase involves the establishment of reliable metrics to help monitor the progress toward the project goals. The analyze phase includes the evaluation of the strengths and weaknesses of the current state and its distance from the stated goal. The improve phase takes the results of the analyze phase and provides improvements to the process. The control phase is concerned with monitoring and continuous improvement.

The Time Metrics Approach

For each adverse event, the Time Metrics approach determines the time duration relative to a baseline with which the event occurred.[62] The approach measures the effectiveness of operational controls in their capabilities to deter and detect the occurrence of an adverse event and to minimize its impact through immediate rectification. The metrics define costs that are directly proportional to the time duration associated with the adverse event.

Benchmarks and Performance Dashboards

A benchmark is a point of reference for measurement. It is used as the standard with which the measures of performances of product or service can be uniformly compared. Security and compliance benchmarks are available at the Center for Internet Security (CIS).[63] The CIS benchmarks are developed by information security professionals and organizations using a global consensus process. The CIS benchmarks and scoring tools cover multiple computer systems and are widely accepted for regulatory standard compliance, including the International Organization for Standardization (ISO). There are two levels of CIS benchmarks. The level-1 benchmarks define the minimum level of security to which all users should conform. The level-2 benchmarks go beyond the minimum level and are based on specific network architecture and server functions. These benchmarks reflect the best security practices in use by CIS member organizations.[64]

A framework and benchmark of best control practices developed by the Information Systems Audit and Control Association (ISACA) is the Control Objectives for Information Related Technology (COBIT). Tuttle and Vandervelde provide an empirical study on COBIT's conceptual consistency as it applies to the operational, compliance, and financial audit settings.[65] The paper reports the following findings: (1) COBIT's conceptual model is internally consistent and useful when applied to auditing IT controls; (2) COBIT is an appropriate supplement to COSO; and (3) COBIT needs additional work in reference to risk assessments for IT processes

	Conforms to Specifications	Meets Consumer Expectations
Product Quality	Accuracy and Completeness of Information	Usefulness of Information Product
Service Quality	Service Dependability	Quality of Information Delivery

Figure 7A-2 Product and Service Model for Information Quality

Courtesy Course Technology/Cengage Learning

and additional studies on how some of the IT processes described therein relate to audit settings.

Information quality has a great impact on security compliance and has been widely studied (i.e., Pitt, Watson, and Kavan,[66] Reeves and Bednar,[67] and Strong, Lee, and Wang[68]). The need for benchmarks and models to measure the level of information quality across organizations is evident. The development of an information quality (IQ) benchmark using the product and service performance model for information quality (PSP/IQ) is presented in Khan, Strong, and Wang.[69] The model uses a two-dimensional table where columns represent quality in conformance with specifications and in a state that meets or exceeds consumer expectations. The rows capture the quality from an organization's products and services. Thus, four quadrants represent the model as illustrated in Figure 7A-2.

The first quadrant, which is the Product Quality/Conforms to Specifications cell, represents a data repository that meets the standards of accuracy and completeness. A high-quality measure on this quadrant represents information that approaches perfection in accuracy and completeness. In measuring regulatory compliance, this can serve as a benchmark for the quality of coverage and accuracy of record keeping. The second quadrant, the Product Quality/Meets Consumer Expectations cell, represents the usefulness of the information that was supplied as a product. This can be used as a benchmark for measuring the quality of tools and processes necessary for meeting regulatory compliance. The third quadrant, the Service Quality/ Conforms to Specifications cell, represents a measure of service dependability. In measuring regulatory compliance, this can be used to measure the quality of compliance audit process. The fourth quadrant, which is the Service Quality/Meets Consumer Expectations cell, represents quality of the delivery of information for immediate utilization. Simply stated, the quality of information delivery is directly proportional to the degree with which it can add value to a task at hand. In measuring regulatory compliance, this quadrant can serve as a benchmark for quality of services that facilitates regulatory compliance such as accurate report generation, data protection through encryption, and complete record keeping.

A performance dashboard, also known as a performance management system, is an information system with built-in business intelligence and data integration infrastructure that provides three main sets of functionality: (1) monitor, (2) analyze, and (3) manage.[70] The monitoring function keeps track of business processes using business performance metrics and triggers alerts when potential problems arise. The analyze function provides the tools for problem evaluation using visual analytics and drill-down techniques. The manage function facilitates the administration of people and processes by steering them toward effective decisions, optimized performance, and streamlined operations.

There are three types of performance dashboards: (1) operational, (2) tactical, and (3) strategic.[71] Operational dashboards, which are used to monitor operations, are mostly used by lower management and specialists. Tactical dashboards, used mainly by middle managers and analysts, are intended to monitor and measure progress. Strategic dashboards, which are mainly for executives and higher management staff, are used to monitor the execution of company strategies. Strategic dashboards are mostly implemented using Balanced Scorecards. Kaplan and Norton describe the benefit of Balanced Scorecard as follows:

> *By combining the financial, customer, internal process and innovation, and organizational learning perspectives, the balanced scorecard helps managers understand, at least implicitly, many interrelationships. This understanding can help managers transcend traditional notions about functional barriers and ultimately lead to improved decision making and problem solving. The balanced scorecard keeps companies looking—and moving—forward instead of backward.[72]*

Where does a performance dashboard fit in security compliance auditing? A performance dashboard can be an extremely relevant tool for monitoring the state of regulatory compliance, for analyzing compliance metrics and problems associated with compliance efforts, and for managing people and processes that are relevant to the implementation of the regulatory requirements.

Research Directions

The discussion presented in this chapter raises issues that present several avenues for future research directions. The empirical study on COBIT as an internal control framework by Tuttle and Vandervelde suggests the following research topics: (1) a study on control deficiencies that produce variations in audit practices and opinions, and (2) the development of a formal theory on internal control as it relates to information technology.[73] A study on the validation process for the formal theory is a logically extension to the research.

On the issue of the development of a computational model for compliance auditing, it is suggested that future research address the design and development of an automated and intelligent compliance audit tool that will simulate the process of manual auditing. This work must be supported by empirical studies. In addition, it would perhaps also be wise to develop some formal arguments to counter opposition to the use of expert systems in the audit process.

The design and development of a compliance management and performance dashboard will surely be appreciated by the public. An empirical study on the usefulness and efficacy of such a tool should follow.

Several studies on benchmarks and metrics are found in the literature. They generally deal with areas such as software development, information security, internal control evaluations, and business processes. Apparently, there is also a need for benchmarks and metrics that apply specifically to security compliance auditing. A future research work in this area will most likely find a unified approach that will meld the previous works on those four areas.

Concluding Comments

The difficulty of complying with various types of legislation over the security of information processing is certainly a daunting task, but not one involving completely separate issues. There is a great deal of literature available about appropriate considerations that the compliance model should address. The theoretical portion of the model must address measurement issues and benchmarking. The computational portion of the model must provide an easily updatable model to consider changes in theoretical requirements while providing the computational ability to allow effective and efficient compliance evaluations by organizational personnel. The use of expert systems provides one such avenue that could serve this need. Future research is certainly needed to consolidate and extend current literature over the security of information and the technology on which it is stored and processed.

Endnotes

1. Whitfield Diffie, "Information Security: 50 Years Behind, 50 Years Ahead," *Communications of the ACM*, January (2008): 55–57.

2. V. R. Johnson, "Data Security and Tort Liability," *Journal of Internet Law*, January (2008): 22–31.

3. Ibid.

4. Paul S. Chan and John K. Rubiner, "Access Denied: Using the Computer Fraud and Abuse Act to Restrict Employee Mobility," *The Computer and Internet Lawyer*, June (2006): 12–18.

5. Robert W. Hall and Anne Layne-Farrar, "Law and Economics of Software Security," *Harvard Journal of Law and Public Policy*, Fall (2006): 283–353.

6. Mary J. Hildebrand and Matthew Savare, "Privacy Principles for Accountants' Legal Issues and Business Opportunities," *The CPA Journal*, May (2008).

7. United States Department of Health and Human Services, *Summary of the HIPAA Privacy Rule*. Last revised 05/03. Viewed on June 27, 2008. <http://www.hhs.gov/ocr/privacysummary.pdf>

8. United States Congress, *Sarbanes Oxley Act of 2002*. H.R. 3763. 23 Jan. (2002).

9. Public Company Accounting Oversight Board (PCAOB), *Auditing Standard No. 5, An Audit of Internal Control Over Financial Reporting That Is Integrated with An Audit of Financial Statements*, June 12 (2007).

10. Frank C. Minter, "Do You Remember COSO?" *Strategic Finance*, February (2002).

11. American Institute of Certified Public Accountants (AICPA), *Financial Reporting Alert, Internal Control Reporting—Implementing Sarbanes-Oxley Act Section 404*. (2005–06).

12. IT Governance Institute, *IT Control Objectives for Sarbanes-Oxley—The Role of IT in the Design and Implementation of Internal Control Over Financial Reporting*, 2nd ed., September (2006).

13. Christian Lahti and Roderick Peterson, *Sarbanes-Oxley IT Compliance Using COBIT and Open Source Tools*. Rockland, MA: Syngress Publishing, Inc., 2005.

14. IT Governance Institute, *IT Control Objectives for Sarbanes-Oxley*.

15. Dennis C. Brewer, *Security Controls for Sarbanes-Oxley Section 404 IT Compliance: Authorization, Authentication, and Access*. Indianapolis, IN: Wiley Publishing, Inc., 2006.

16. Peter Schattner, Catherine Pleteshner, Heinz Bhend, and Johan Brouns, "Guidelines for Computer Security in General Practice," *Informatics in Primary Care* (2007): 73–82.

17. Reymann Group, Inc., "Third Brigade: A New Approach to Addressing Regulatory Compliance." Access page to request paper was viewed on July 3, 2008. <http://resources.thirdbrigade.com/newapproach>

18. R. D. Meservy, A. D. Bailey, and P. E. Johnson, "Internal Control Evaluation: A Computational Model of the Review Process," *Auditing: A Journal of Practice and Theory*, Vol. 6, no. 1 Fall (1986).

19. Committee of Sponsoring Organizations of the Treadway Commissions (COSO), "Guidance on Monitoring Internal Control Systems." Accessed date: July 10, 2008. <http://www.coso.org/guidance.htm>

20. D. Brewer and W. List, "Measuring the Effectiveness of an Internal Control System." Accessed date: July 1, 2008. <http://www.gammassl.co.uk/topics/time/time040317.pdf>

21. National Institute of Standards and Technology (NIST), Special Publication (SP) 800-55, Revision 1. *Performance Measurement Guide for Information Security (Draft)*. September (2007).

22. Debra S. Herrmann, *Complete Guide to Security and Privacy Metrics: Measuring Regulatory Compliance, Operational Resilience, and ROI*. Boco Raton, FL: Auerbach Pub. Taylor and Francis Group, 2007.

23. Jeffrey Zanzig, *Perceptual Gaps Between Internal Auditors and Audit Customers*, UMI Dissertation Services, 1998.

24. The Institute of Internal Auditors, *Standards for the Professional Practice of Internal Auditing*, 1997.

25. Christy Chapman, "On the Road of Change," *Internal Auditor*, June (2004): 41–47.

26. Christine Chaney and Gene Kim, "The Integrated Auditor," *Internal Auditor*, August (2007): 46–51.

27. D. E. Bell and L. J. LaPadula, "Secure Computer Systems: A Mathematical Model," ESD-TR-73-278, vol. 2, ESD/AFSC, Hanscom AFB, Bedford, MA, 1973 (MTR-2547, vol. 2, MITRE Corp., Bedford, MA).

28. K. J. Biba, "Integrity Considerations for Secure Computer Systems," ESD-TR-76-372, ESD/AFSC, Hanscom AFB, Bedford, MA, 1977 (MTR-3153).

29. D. E. Denning, "A Lattice Model of Secure Information Flow," *Communications of the ACM*, 19, no. 5 (May 1976): 236–243.

30. C. E. Landwehr, "Formal Models for Information Security," *Computing Surveys*, 13, no. 3 (1981).

31. DoD 5200.28-STD, "Department of Defense Trusted Computer System Evaluation Criteria," 1985. Accessed date: July 16, 2008. <http://nsi.org/Library/Compsec/orangebo.txt>

32. E. Hayes-Roth, D. A. Waterman, and D. B. Lenat (eds.), *Building Expert Systems*, Addison-Wesley, 1983.

33. R. D. Meservy, A. D. Bailey, and P. E. Johnson, "Internal Control Evaluation: A Computational Model of the Review Process," *Auditing: A Journal of Practice and Theory*, 6, no. 1 (Fall 1986).

34. L. M. Lovata, "Audit Technology and the Use of Computer Assisted Audit Techniques," *Journal of Information Systems* 4, no. 2 (1990): 60–68.

35. C. Changchit and C. W. Holsapple, "The Development of an Expert System for the Managerial Evaluation of Internal Controls," *Intelligent Systems in Accounting, Finance, and Management*, 12 (2004): 103–120.

36. S. Chang, C. Wu, and I. Chang, "The Development of a Computer Auditing System Sufficient for Sarbanes-Oxley Section 404-A Study on the Purchasing and Expenditure Cycle of the ERP System," *Information Systems Management*, 25 (2007): 211–229.

37. Meservy, Bailey, and Johnson, "Internal Control Evaluation."

38. C. Changchit and C. W. Holsapple, "The Development of an Expert System for the Managerial Evaluation of Internal Controls," *Intelligent Systems in Accounting, Finance, and Management* 12 (2004): 103–120.

39. S. Chang, C. Wu, and I. Chang, "The Development of a Computer Auditing System Sufficient for Sarbanes-Oxley Section 404—A Study on the Purchasing and Expenditure Cycle of the ERP System," *Information Systems Management* 25 (2007): 211–229.

40. L. Craig Foltin and L. Murphy Smith, "Accounting Expert Systems," *The CPA Journal*, November (1994).

41. A. A. Baldwin-Morgan, "Integrating Artificial Intelligence into the Accounting Curriculum," *Accounting Education*, 4, no. 3 (1995): 217–229.

42. Foltin and Smith, "Accounting Expert Systems."

43. Carol E. Brown and David S. Murphy, "The Use of Auditing Expert Systems in Public Accounting," *Journal of Information Systems* (1990).

44. Ibid.

45. Ibid.

46. Ibid.

7A

47. Rebecca L. Rossner, Christie L. Communale, and Thomas R. Sexton, "Letters to the Editor—Regarding 'Assessing Materiality: A New Fuzzy Logic Approach'," *The CPA Journal* (October 2006): 12–14.

48. V. R. Basili and D. M. Weiss, "A Methodology for Collecting Valid Software Engineering Data," *IEEE Transactions on Software Engineering*, SE-10, no. 6 (November 1984): 728–738.

49. V. R. Basili, G. Caldiera, and D. Rombach, "Goal/Question/Metric Paradigm," *Encyclopedia of Software Engineering*, Vol. 1 (J. C. Marciniak, ed.). New York: John Wiley and Sons, 1994, pp. 528–532.

50. M. Kogure, and Y. Akao, "Quality Function Deployment and CWQC in Japan," *Quality Progress* (October 1983): 25–29.

51. M. J. Harry, "The Nature of Six Sigma Quality," Government Electronics Group, Motorola, Inc., Schaumburg, IL (1989).

52. M. J. Harry and J. R. Lawson, *Six Sigma Producibility, Analysis and Process Characterization*. Reading, MA: Addison-Wesley, 1992.

53. D. Brewer and W. List, "Measuring the Effectiveness of an Internal Control System." Accessed date: July 1, 2008. <http://www.gammassl.co.uk/topics/time/time040317.pdf>

54. M. K. Daskalantonakis, "A Practical View of Software Measurement and Implementation Experiences Within Motorola," *IEEE Transactions on Software Engineering*, 18, no. 11 (1992): 998–1010.

55. V. R. Basili and D. Rombach, "The TAME Project: Towards Improvement-oriented Software Environments," *IEEE Transactions on Software Engineering*, 14 (1988): 758–773.

56. A. Fuggetta, L. Lavazza, S. Morasca, S. Cinti, G. Oldano, and E. Orazi, "Applying GQM in an Industrial Software Factory," *ACM Transactions on Software Engineering and Methodology*, 7, no. 4 (1998): 411–448.

57. V. R. Basili, "Applying the Goal/Question/Metric Paradigm in the Experience Factory," *Software Quality Assurance and Measurement: Worldwide Perspective* (N. Fenter, R. Whitty, and Y. Lizuka, eds.). International Thomson Computer Press, 1995, pp. 21–44.

58. V. R. Basili, J. Heidrich, M. Lindvall, J. Munch, M. Regardie, and A. Trendowicz, "GQM+Strategies—Aligning Business Strategies with Software Measurement," Proc of the First International Symposium on Empirical Software Engineering and Measurement (ESEM), 2007, pp. 488–490.

59. K. Liu, Y. Sun, G. Kane, Kyoya, and K. Noguchi, "QFD Application in Software Process Management and Improvement Based on CMM," *ACM SIGSOFT Software Engineering Notes*, 30, no. 4 (July 2005): 1–6.

60. R. E. Zultner, "Quality Function Deployment (QFD) for Software," *American Programmer* (1992).

61. T. Pyzdek, *The Six Sigma Handbook*. New York: McGraw Hill, Inc., 2003.

62. D. Brewer and W. List, "Measuring the Effectiveness of an Internal Control System." Accessed date: July 1, 2008. <http://www.gammassl.co.uk/topics/time/time040317.pdf>

63. Center for Internet Security (CIS), "CIS Benchmarks." Accessed date: July 11, 2008. <http://www.cisecurity.org/bench.html>

64. C. Kreitner and B. Miuccio, "The Center for Internet Security: Global Security Benchmarks for Computers Connected to the Internet," *Information Systems Control Journal*, 6 (2001). Accessed date: June 30, 2008. <http://www.isaca.org>.

65. B. Tuttle and S. D. Vandervelde, "An Empirical Examination of CobiT as an Internal Control Framework for Information Technology," *International Journal of Accounting Information Systems*, 8 (2007): 240–263.

66. L. F. Pitt, R. T. Watson, and C. B. Kavan, "Service Quality: A Measure of Information System Effectiveness," *MISQ*, 19, no. 2 (1995): 173–188.

67. C. A. Reeves and D. E. Bednar, "Defining Quality: Alternatives and Implications," *AMR*, 19, no. 3 (1994): 419–445.

68. D. M. Strong, Y. W. Lee, and R. Y. Wang, "Data Quality in Context," *Communications of the ACM*, 40, no. 5 (1997): 103–110.

69. B. K. Khan, D. M. Strong, and R. Y. Wang, "Information Quality Benchmarks: Product and Service Performance," *Communications of the ACM*, 45, no. 4 (2002): 184–192.

70. Wayne W. Eckerson, *Performance Dashboards Measuring, Monitoring, and Managing Your Business*. John Wiley & Sons, Inc., 2006.

71. Ibid.

72. R. S. Kaplan and D. P. Norton, "The Balanced Scorecard—Measures that Drive Performance," *Harvard Business Review*, 70, no. 1 (Jan-Feb 1992): 71–79.

73. B. Tuttle and S. D. Vandervelde, "An Empirical Examination of CobiT as an Internal Control Framework for Information Technology," *International Journal of Accounting Information Systems*, 8 (2007): 240–263.

Global Information Security Regulations, Case Studies, and Cultural Issues

Guillermo A. Francia, III
Jacksonville State University

Andrew P. Ciganek
University of Wisconsin at Whitewater

Dr. Guillermo A. Francia, III, received his Ph.D. in computer science from New Mexico Tech. In 1996, Dr. Francia received one of the five national awards for Innovators in Higher Education from Microsoft Corporation. Dr. Francia served as a Fulbright scholar to Malta in 2007. His research interests include computer security, digital forensics, visualization, data mining, and performance dashboards. Currently, Dr. Francia is serving as Director of the Center for Information Security and Assurance at JSU.

Dr. Andrew P. Ciganek is an Assistant Professor of information technology and business education at the University of Wisconsin at Whitewater. He earned his Ph.D. from the University of Wisconsin—Milwaukee in 2006. His research interests include examining the managerial and strategic issues associated with the decision-making process of innovative technologies. He has had several refereed publications and has also published book chapters examining topics related to Mobile Computing Devices and Enterprise Application Integration.

Overview

The pervasiveness of the Internet has created a new challenge to legislators around the globe: the enactment of regulations that will preserve and protect the country's information technology (IT) infrastructure and its integrity in delivering secure products and services. This paper examines the global, and yet unilateral, attempts of various countries in ratifying their own information security legislations.

Introduction

In 2005, Thomas Friedman wrote on the subject of a perceivable economic change that was brought about by globalization.[1] He suggested that the world has gone "flatter" in the sense that the competitive field between established and emerging market economies have leveled. Among the so-called "flatteners" that Friedman defined are "outsourcing" and "offshoring." These two concepts induce the tapping of "economically viable" job markets in countries such as China and India. As a consequence, information security regulations have to reach out as well. Countries that need to stay viable need to legislate their own information security regulations that are in line with those in the country where their counterparts are located. However, one of the most difficult aspects of creating and passing a national legislation that is in conformity with international regulations is the need to accommodate differing cultures, varying structural and governmental models, and the intricacies of making it consistent with existing public policies and regulations.

The issue of preserving "economic viability" in the global job market is not the only compelling reason for a country to strengthen its information security legislations and regulations. Other possible reasons may include the following:

- the protection of its citizens' fundamental right to privacy;
- the security of the country's critical infrastructures;
- the preservation of the intellectual property rights of its public and private constituents;
- the upholding of the country's integrity and its international reputation;
- the protection of consumers, investors, financial market, and banking system; and
- the adherence to internationally recognized standards and protocols that apply to cyberspace and information handling.

Mitrakas and Portesi raise the issue of whether there is a real need to regulate network and information security and the conditions with which it can be taken up by legislators.[2] They suggest using the soft law approach[3] in creating regulations due to sporadic instances of ineffective legislations. Soft law, self-regulation, and co-regulation are alternative regulatory instruments that can be used to shape the processes of self-regulation, to determine an alternative to legislation, and to complement existing legislations. But no matter what approach a certain country, region, group, or union decides to follow, the resulting information security regulation should be founded on the following guiding principles: respect for basic human rights, fairness and timeliness, protection of privacy rights, and sensitivity to moral and ethical issues.

The remainder of the reading includes an extensive literature review of and case studies on global information security regulations, guidelines, and directives. In addition, a discussion on the cultural issues influencing the legislations and their enforcements are presented. Specific to the subject at hand will be a case study on the state of information security regulation in Thailand. Thailand is uniquely situated on the opposite ends of every national culture dimension with the United States, and in some instances, the most extreme ends.[4] For example, the United States is characterized as one of the most individualistic cultures (loose bonds with others), while Thailand represents one of the most collectivist cultures (everyone takes responsibility for others). Similar dichotomies exist among both cultures in each of the other national culture dimensions and have been shown to significantly influence differences in perceptions.[5] Such differences in culture offer opportunities to reveal insights into the various activities that prevail within each country to protect data. The reading concludes with an analysis of the similarities of different information security regulations worldwide, a discussion on the need for harmonization, and descriptions of future research opportunities related to the subject matter.

The Regulations, Acts, and Directives

The following literature review on information security regulations are organized according to affected sectors: privacy protection, financial and banking services, electronic commerce, government, publicly traded entities, and general population.

Privacy Protection

Iceland Iceland has been actively amending its *Data Protection Act*, which is also known as *Act on the Protection of Privacy as Regards to the Processing of Personal Data*. The law has been amended four times: *Act No. 90/2001, Act No. 30/2002, Act No. 81/2002*, and *Act No. 46/2003*. Its basic provision is "to promote the practice of personal data processing in accordance with fundamental principles and rules regarding data protection and privacy, and to ensure the reliability and integrity of such data and their free flow within the internal market of the European Economic Area."[6] The law is very comprehensive in that it includes, among others, the following sensitive and personal data:

- data on origin, skin color, race, political opinions, religious beliefs, and other life philosophies;
- data on criminal suspicion, indictment, prosecution, or conviction;
- health data;
- data on sex life and sexual behavior; and
- data on trade-union membership.

Its provisions are clearly delineated by Articles dealing with (a) risk analysis, security, and integrity of data; (b) internal audit; (c) rights of access; (d) notification of data usage; and (e) transfer of data to other countries that may or may not provide adequate data protection.

Malta Malta's *Electronic Communications (Personal Data and Protection of Privacy) Regulations (SL 399.25)* requires that if there is a significant risk of a breach of network security or when the contents of communications have been unintentionally made known to other parties, the entity that provides the electronic communications services should inform the affected consumers of (a) that risk; (b) any remedies appropriate to afford safeguards against that risk the subscribers themselves might take; and (c) the costs involved in relation to such remedies. This regulation is a bit dated and, essentially, has not fully addressed computer data and its protection.

Romania Romania's *Law no. 506/2004. Processing of Personal Data and the Protection of Privacy in the Electronic Communications Sector* states that the provider of an electronic communications service must take appropriate security measures to safeguard its service. Further, the measures taken should ensure a level of security appropriate to the current risk and the state of the technology. In case of a particular risk of a breach on network security, the provider of the service must: (a) inform the subscribers of such risk and of the possible ensuing consequences; (b) inform the subscribers of any possible remedies; and (c) inform the subscribers of the likely costs involved by eliminating the risk. This law is very similar to Malta's privacy protection law and should be amended and expanded.

Singapore Singapore has no dedicated or overarching legislation for privacy protection. However, personal information is protected under sector-specific laws such as the *Banking Act*, the *Statistics Act*, the *Official Secrets Act*, and the *Statutory Bodies and Government Companies (Protection of Secrecy) Act*.

USA Among the provisions of the Health Insurance Portability and Accountability Act[7] (HIPAA) of 1996 is the protection of the privacy of personal health information. This ensures that all types of collected information are secured as they are transmitted in electronic form along a network of health care providers, insurers, clearinghouses, and payment processing centers. Compliance with this law entails, among others, the installation of access control mechanisms, intrusion detection and prevention systems, encryption systems, reporting systems, and a robust and secure network infrastructure.

The United States has passed its own consumer privacy protection laws to supplement existing federal laws. A representative sample taken from a comprehensive list[8] is shown as follows:

- *Arizona SB 1338* requires notifying the customer of any breach in the security of unencrypted computerized personal information. A thorough investigation that deems that there is no likelihood of damage exempts the company from performing the notification.

- *California Civil Code Sec. 1798.82-84* requires that any business entity in the state must disclose any breach in system security that may compromise the unencrypted personal information of its customers.

- *Massachusetts Public Law 82-2007* states that an entity that maintains, stores, or owns data that includes personal information about a resident of the commonwealth should provide notice when such entity has reason to believe that the personal information of such resident was compromised.

- The states of Ohio (*HB 104*), Oklahoma (*Okla. Stat. 74-3113.1.*),Oregon (*SB 583*), Michigan (*SB209*), and Tennessee (*HB2220*) have essentially the same requirements.

Wisconsin's *Wis. Stat. 895.507* law extends the characterization of private information to include DNA and biometric data.

Financial and Banking Services

International The Revised Framework on *"International Convergence of Capital Measurement and Capital Standards"* (also known as the new *Basel Capital Accord* or *Basel II*) represents a significant and complex best practice agreement that requires internationally active banking institutions to adopt risk management practices for tracking and publicly reporting exposure to operational, credit, and market risks.[9] Essentially, *Basel II* is built on three main requirements: minimum capital to cover credit risk, supervisory review, and market disclosure of capital adequacy and intrinsic banking risks.

The Council of European Union adopted in June 2006 two directives that, in essence, adopted the Basel II agreement into EU law. The two directives are the recast *Directive 2000/12/EC* on the business of credit institutions and *Directive 93/6/EEC* on the capital adequacy of investment firms and credit institutions.

In July 2008, the Office of the Comptroller of the Currency of the U.S. Department of Treasury, the U.S. Federal Reserve System, and the Federal Deposit Insurance Corporation released a document entitled "Supervisory Guidance: Supervisory Review Process of Capital Adequacy (Pillar 2) Related to the Implementation of the Basel II Advanced Capital Framework."[10]

In Asia, the influence of Basel II is quite noticeable. All Malaysian banks started applying the Standardized Approach for credit risk and Basic Indicator Approach for operational risk in January 2008; most of the locally incorporated authorized institutions in Hong Kong have adopted the Standardized Approach for credit risk starting in January 2007; and the Monetary Authority of Singapore (MAS) started to implement Basel II for all Singapore-incorporated banks on January 1, 2008.

USA The *Financial Services Modernization Act* of 1999, also known as the *Gramm-Leach-Bliley Act*[11] (*GLBA*), includes provisions to safeguard customer records and information held by financial institutions. The three principal parts to the privacy requirements of GLBA are the Financial Privacy Rule, the Safeguards Rule, and the Pretexting provisions. The Financial Privacy Rule requires financial institutions to give consumers privacy notices and to offer them the right to limit the sharing of their information. The Safeguards Rule requires all financial institutions to implement reasonable safeguards to protect customer information. This includes administrative, technical, and physical safeguards. The Pretexting provisions of GLBA essentially make it illegal to use fraudulent statements or instruments to obtain customer information from a financial institution or directly from its customer.

Electronic Commerce

Malta The *Electronic Commerce Act of Malta*[12] (*Cap 428*) was enacted in 2002 and last amended in 2007. The Act requires the establishment of the validity of an electronic transaction; the acceptance of the equivalency of documents in electronic and written forms; the recognition of the legality of an electronic signature; the retention of electronic documents and communications; the formation of electronic contracts; the protection of the integrity of electronic documents and communications; and the specifications of the responsibilities of service providers. This Act is closely aligned with the United Nations Commission on International Trade Law's (UNCITRAL) work on the use of electronic communications in international contracts.

Philippines The authority of the implementation and promotion of the *Electronic Commerce Act of the Philippines (Republic Act No.8792)* is assigned to the Department of Trade and Industry.[13] Among the provisions of the Act are the following: the development of a technology-aware workforce that will sustain electronic commerce; the promotion of electronic commerce through enhanced public awareness; the assurance of network security, connectivity, and technological neutrality; the legal recognition of electronic documents and signature; the responsibilities of service providers; and the protection of users' rights to privacy, confidentiality, and anonymity.

The *Electronic Commerce Act of the Philippines* is also closely aligned with *UNCITRAL's Model Law on Electronic Commerce*,[14] which was expanded by the United Nations Commission on International Trade Law's work on the use of electronic communications in international contracts in 2005.

Singapore Singapore's *Electronic Transactions Act*[15] (ETA) (*Cap. 88*) contains provisions that pertain to the following:

- Electronic contracts;
- Electronic records and signatures;
- Secure electronic records and signatures;
- Effect of digital signatures and duties relating to such signatures;
- Duties of Certification Authorities and their subscribers;
- Regulation of Certification Authorities;
- Government use of electronic records and signatures; and
- Liability of network service providers.

Singapore's ETA follows closely *UNCITRAL's Model Law on Electronic Commerce*.

United Nations In 2005, the United Nations Commission on International Trade Law (UNCITRAL) finalized its work on a convention that was formally entitled "*The Convention on the Use of Electronic Communications in International Contracts.*" The convention contains provisions that facilitate international electronic commerce. These provisions enable the two principles at the core of any electronic transaction's legislation:[16]

- Functional equivalence—paper documents and electronic transactions are treated equally by the law; and
- Technology neutrality—the law does not discriminate between different forms of technology.

The convention was formally adopted by the UN General Assembly on November 23, 2005, and has been open for signature since January 16, 2006. Prominent provisions that are included in the convention are the legal recognition of an electronic contract; the acceptance of electronic communication as legally equivalent to a written form; the requirements for the integrity of an electronic signature and preservation of electronic documents; and the determination of time and place of dispatch of an electronic communication.[17]

USA There is no federal regulation that is specific to electronic commerce. Rules and regulations that apply to online retailers and service providers are found in other federal laws and regulations. For instance, the protection of customers' privacy and security is required by GLBA. Children's online privacy is protected by the *Children's Online Privacy Protection Act (COPPA)*, whose basic requirement is a prominently visible privacy policy that explains what types of personal information are collected, how those data are being used, and whether those data are shared and with whom.[18] Additional guidelines[19] on how to comply with laws and regulations related to ecommerce in the United States are published by the U.S. Small Business Administration. The set of guidelines covers the protection of customer privacy, collecting sales taxes, selling internationally and exporting, online advertising and marketing, and digital rights and copyrights.

A very important component of ecommerce is online payment through credit cards. Payment account data security is self-regulated and is covered by a standard developed by the Payment Card Industry Security Standards Council. The standard, *Payment Card Industry Data Security Standard*[20] (*PCI DSS*), facilitates the broad adoption of globally consistent data security measures.

Government

USA The *Federal Information Security Management Act (FISMA)* applies to U.S. federal government agencies and requires them to provide security for both their information systems and the information that they use to support their operations.[21] FISMA's provisions fall into three major categories: assessment, enforcement, and compliance. Assessment pertains to determining the adequacy of the security of federal assets and operations. Enforcement requires that key information security management processes must be integrated with agency strategic and operational planning and execution processes. The third category compliance provisions for the management of each agency's information security program and the accountability of each agency for compliance and reporting. In addition, FISMA requires the reporting of significant deficiencies; i.e., agencies must continuously identify and track material weaknesses and report any progress.

Canada The Canadian counterpart of the U.S. *Federal Information Security Management Act (FISMA)* is called the *Operation Security Standard: Management of Information Technology Security (MITS)*. It defines baseline security requirements that federal departments must comply with to ensure the security of information and information technology assets under their control.[22] The standard defines and describes the roles and responsibilities of IT security personnel, the required departmental IT security policy, the management controls, the need for periodic IT security assessment and audit, and the importance of regular IT security training. Further, it provides guidance on technical and operation safeguards such as an active defense strategy, preventive tools and measures, detection of incidents, and response and recovery.

Publicly Traded Entities

USA The *Sarbanes-Oxley (SOX)* Act of 2002 was enacted by the U.S. Congress mainly to address the crisis brought about by the WorldCom and Enron debacle to the financial markets. The law is ratified to enforce accountability for financial record keeping and reporting of publicly traded corporations. The Chief Executive Officer (CEO) and the Chief Financial Officer (CFO) are directly responsible for the completeness and accuracy of their institution's financial reporting and record-keeping systems.[23,24] The Public Company Accounting Oversight Board (PCAOB) is a private-sector, nonprofit corporation created by the Sarbanes-Oxley Act.

Australia The *Corporate Law Economic Reform Program (CLERP)*, also known as *Audit Reform and Corporate Disclosure Act 2004* or *CLERP 9*, governs corporate law in Australia. *CLERP 9* requires companies to have adequate measures, processes, and procedures for auditing and company financial reporting. These requirements are embodied in four regulatory policies: auditor registration, disclosure for on-sale of securities and other financial products, reporting obligation of an auditor to the Australian Securities and Investments Commission, and transaction-specific disclosure.[25]

Canada In 2004, the *Canadian Securities Administrators (CSA)* introduced a series of rules called *Multilateral Instruments (MI)*, and *National Instruments (NI)* to closely align with the *U.S. SOX Act* and, with the same effort, to address the unique nature of the Canadian financial market. *MIs* are securities rules that cover all Canadian provinces and territories, while *NIs* are rules in force in each Canadian province and territory that elects to adopt those instruments.[26]

European Union (EU) *Directive 2004/109/EC of the European Parliament* established the transparency requirements in relation to information about issuers whose securities are admitted to trading on a regulated market or operated within a Member State.[27] Important provisions of the Directive include the effective protection of investors and the proper operation of regulated markets; the designation of a single competent authority in each Member State to oversee compliance; the removal of barriers and the effective enforcement of controls; the transparency of the securities market through the disclosure of accurate, comprehensive and timely information about security issuers; and the mandatory reports required on issuers of securities on regulated markets.

Japan In June 2006, the Japanese legislative body passed the *Financial Instruments and Exchange Law*, which contains provisions that are unofficially referred to as the "J-SOX" requirements. Compliance is effective for fiscal years beginning on or after April 1, 2008. While this legislation in Japan is different from the contents of the *U.S. Sarbanes-Oxley Act*, the specific requirements are very similar to the *Sarbanes-Oxley Act Sections 302 (Management Certification)* and *404 (Management Evaluation and Report on Internal Controls)*.[28] Among the provisions of J-SOX are that (a) management is required to evaluate the efficacy of its internal control for financial reports and draw up a report on it and (b) the external auditor who already carries out the audit for the financial reporting must also conduct an audit to determine the appropriateness of the management's evaluation of the effectiveness of the internal control for financial reports.

General Population (Cyber Crime)

7B

Norway The Odelsting, a chamber in the Norwegian Parliament, recommended in March 2005 an Act amending the Penal Code and the ratification of the *Budapest Council of Europe Convention on Cybercrime*. The Act was enacted in April 2005 and entered into force and the ratification of the *Budapest Council of Europe Convention on Cybercrime* was made in November 2005. The amendment to *Penal Code 145* includes a penalty for unlawful access to data or programs that are stored electronically. *Penal Code 151* has been amended to include a penalty for destroying, damaging, or putting out of action any data collection instrument. The *Budapest Council of Europe Convention on Cybercrime* contains the remaining provisions for fighting cyber crime in Norway.

Pakistan Pakistan has enacted its *Electronic Crimes Act* in 2006. The law includes deterrence against cyber attacks such spoofing, spamming, fraud, forgery, malicious code distribution and authoring, cyber stalking, and cyber terrorism. In addition, the federal government is given the broad power to collect electronically transmitted data in real time. Some very interesting provisions of this Act include life imprisonment for anyone who willfully defiles, desecrates, or damages the Quran or the prophet Mohammed.

USA Laws against cyber crime in the United States are part of four major regulations:

- The *Prosecutorial Remedies and Tools Against the Exploitation of Children Today Act* (PROTECT Act)
- The *Homeland Security* Act of 2002
- The *USA Patriot Act* of 2001
- The *US Code Title 18 Part I Chapter 47 Section 1030* "Fraud and Related Activity in Connection with Computers"

The *Patriot Act* contains the *Computer Crime and Intellectual Property Section* (CCIPS), which includes the authority to intercept voice communications; the facility to obtain voice mail and other stored voice data; allowing the use of a subpoena for collecting electronic evidence; utilization of pen/trap orders to intercept evidence; and deterrence and prevention of cyberterrorism.

Case Studies

Privacy Protection/Health Care Regulations

In October 2003, workers in Bangalore, who are employed by an outsourcing company in Ohio, threatened to reveal confidential medical records unless they received financial payoff. A similar threat was received by the University of California in San Francisco (UCSF) Medical Center just three weeks earlier from a Pakistani woman who was transcribing the hospital's files.[29]

The above incident puts a serious doubt on the safe handling of customers' confidential information by outsourcing companies located abroad. A nonprofit public interest organization, Public Citizen, publicly exposed the inadequacy of the U.S. law regarding privacy protection overseas compared to the protection afforded by the corresponding European Union (EU) law.[30]

The EU law that restricts the offshore transfer of personal data is *Directive 1995/46/EC of the European Parliament and of the Council of 24 October 1995* on the protection of individuals with regard to the processing of personal data and on the movement of such data.[31]

Financial and Banking Regulations

The following case study on a legal decision concerning the GLBA could have broad implications for financial institutions.

Sinrod[32] writes that a court ruled a student loan company was not negligent and did not have a duty under the Gramm-Leach-Bliley statute to encrypt a customer database. The student filed a federal lawsuit in Minnesota, claiming that Brazos Higher Education Service Corporation, Inc. negligently permitted an employee to maintain unencrypted, private customer data on a laptop computer, which ultimately was stolen from the employee's home.

Judge Richard Kyle dismissed Guin's lawsuit and stated, in his ruling, that

> "the statute does not prohibit someone from working with sensitive data on a laptop computer in a home office," and does not require that "any nonpublic personal information stored on a laptop computer should be encrypted."[33]

E-Commerce Regulations

In June 2007, the Ninth Circuit disagreed on an earlier ruling by the district court that favored the notion that merely posting a Web link to a new contract on the phone company's Web site constitutes sufficient notice to change contracts with existing customers. The opinion of the Ninth Circuit in *Douglas v. U.S. District Court for the Central District of California* is based on the principles of contract law, which essentially makes any new term in a contract nonbinding if the other party has not been notified of the changes. Further, the court noted that the customer had no duty to visit the phone company Web site and thus, may never have received such notice.[34]

One of the most important provisions of a legislation affecting e-commerce is the establishment of the equivalency of paper documents with electronic forms. How can one reconcile this provision with the ruling that a company link is not a sufficient notice of a change in the contractual agreement?

Government Regulations

A press release on June 5, 2008, by the U.S. Department of Justice in Louisiana reported that three individuals were indicted by a federal grand jury with conspiracy to exceed authorized access of a government computer. According to the indictment, the indicted supervisor, in the District Attorney's office in Covington, used her work computer to generate NCIC criminal histories and sold the criminal history reports to the other two defendants. If convicted, the defendants face at most 5 years' imprisonment, a $250,000 fine, or both.

This case has a number of interesting what-if scenarios. If the criminal history reports have not been used to gain profit, would the indictment occur? If a government computer at work were used to send personal emails or download information for personal use, would it constitute an abuse of authorized use?

Corporate Governance Regulations

In *Bechtel v. Competitive Technologies, Inc.*, a Connecticut District Court ruled for the two plaintiffs, Bechtel and Jacques, and ordered Competitive Technologies, Inc. (CTI) to reinstate the employment of the two former employees who made whistle-blower claims under the Sarbanes-Oxley Act.[35] The SOX Act authorizes an employee to bring a retaliation claim against his/her employer if the employee is terminated, demoted, or threatened as a result of the employee's reporting of securities law violations. A few months after CTI was required to reinstate Bechtel, an Administrative Law Judge ruled that CTI had not, in fact, terminated Bechtel for his alleged whistle-blowing but for financial reasons and, thus, had not violated the Sarbanes-Oxley Act.[36]

The Bechtel case has underlined the significance of the SOX Act in regard to protecting whistle-blowers even though the initial ruling was overruled by another legal technicality. This opens up an issue that requires serious consideration: the justification of the Sarbanes-Oxley requirement of job reinstatement even before the conclusion of litigation.

Cyber Crime Regulations

In September 2007, Spanish authorities arrested Sergiu Daniel Popa, a 22-year-old Romanian national, on behalf of the United States. Popa was indicted in June, 2007, on three counts of possession of 15 or more stolen credit card numbers and three counts of aggravated identity theft by the U.S. Attorney's Office for the District of Minnesota. The indictment alleges that Popa, within a span of almost 3 years, conducted a "phishing" scheme to steal bank and personal information. He was extradited to the United States in May and made his first appearance in federal court in June 2008.

The FBI started investigating Popa in January 2005 and executed search warrants directed to Internet Service Providers (ISPs) to track down and document Popa's online activities. The indictment alleges that, in a span of almost 3 years, he instigated several illegal activities that include the selling of stolen personal data through email, the selling of a phishing toolkit and hardware devices capable of copying magnetic information at the back of credit cards, and the possession of a machine capable of creating fake credit cards and driver's licenses. If convicted, Popa faces 10 years in jail for every credit card number possession and mandatory statutory 2-year penalty for identity theft.

This case has several important implications on international cyber crime legislations. What if Spain does not have any law that addresses cyber crime? Would the FBI be able to track Popa's activities had the ISPs not made a backup of all electronic transactions? If Popa went back home to Romania, can he be extradited? Assuming that all the allegations are properly and legally obtained, what allegation may stand out to be the hardest to prove?

In regard to the Pakistani cyber crime law, what consequences of international proportion will it create if a person has desecrated the Quran or the prophet Mohammed over the Internet and Pakistan decides to pursue the matter through extradition?

Cultural Issues

Background

Culture is theorized to shape the behavior of a collection of individuals[37] and has been shown to have a significant impact on decision-making processes.[38] Culture is defined as the "interactive aggregate of common characteristics that influence a human group's response to its environment."[39] Culture establishes social norms and values, which in turn affect individual behaviors and beliefs. Hofstede identifies five different dimensions of national culture that explain the similarities as well as differences of behavior and belief among individuals in different societies; high/low power distance, individualism/collectivism, masculinity/femininity, high/low uncertainty avoidance, and long-term/short-term orientation.[40] Each of these dimensions, with respect to the United States and Thailand, are summarized in Table 7B-1.

Since the United States and Thailand are on the opposite ends of every national culture dimension, and in some instances, the most extreme ends,[41] we anticipate that there are many insights specific to ISA policies in the United States that can be gained by examining how a disparate culture from the United States resolves these same challenges. For example, Thailand is characterized as having a low tolerance for uncertainty, which should have an impact on the specific organizational policies and procedures in place. The successes and/or challenges that Thai organizations encounter as a result of their ISA polices, while facing the same security threats as U.S. firms participating in the global economy, should lead to some key insights for future research directions.

Case Study: Thailand's Computer Crime Act (CCA)

The Computer Crime Act (CCA) took effect on July 18, 2007, with the aim of ensuring Internet security and enhancing electronic commerce in Thailand by creating a safer environment that was more conductive to Internet users. A primary goal of the CCA was to eliminate loopholes in existing Thai laws to empower law enforcement agencies to more effectively deal with cyber crimes like hacking and spamming. As a result, the CCA requires all Internet Service Providers (ISPs) to keep log files of bandwidth consumption, Internet traffic, and records of individual users for 90 days. Without this law, it is argued that law enforcement officials would be unable to apply the Criminal Code and criminal procedures in order to go after cyber criminals.[42] The CCA was based on the ISO/IEC 27001 information security management system standard and also follows the U.S. Department of Defense Directive 8570.1 to ensure that computer forensic examiners are trained and certified to effectively defend information, information systems, and information infrastructures.

Uncertainty Avoidance Uncertainty avoidance describes the tolerance for uncertainty and ambiguity that is considered acceptable in one country over another. Though the CCA was based on internationally accepted standards, there are a few aspects of its implementation in which Thai culture (high uncertainty avoidance) is reflected. First and foremost, true

Power Distance: Extent less powerful members of organizations accept and expect power distributed unequally	
United States:	**Thailand:**
<ul><li>Greater equality between societal level</li><li>Cooperative interaction across power levels</li><li>More stable cultural environment</li></ul>	<ul><li>High level of inequality of power and wealth, not necessarily forced upon the population, but accepted by the society as a part of their cultural heritage</li></ul>
Individualism/Collectivism: Degree to which individuals are integrated into groups	
United States:	**Thailand:**
<ul><li>More individualistic attitude</li><li>Relatively loose bonds with others</li><li>Self-reliant</li></ul>	<ul><li>Close, long-term commitment to the member "group"</li><li>Loyalty is paramount</li><li>Strong relationships; everyone takes responsibility for others</li></ul>
Masculinity/Femininity: The distribution of roles between the genders	
United States:	**Thailand:**
<ul><li>High degree of gender differentiation of roles</li><li>The male dominates a significant portion of the society and power structure</li></ul>	<ul><li>Less assertiveness and competitiveness</li></ul>
Uncertainty Avoidance: Tolerance for uncertainty and ambiguity	
United States:	**Thailand:**
<ul><li>Fewer rules</li><li>Does not attempt to control all outcomes and results</li><li>Tolerance for a variety of ideas, thoughts, and beliefs</li></ul>	<ul><li>Strict rules, laws, policies, and regulations are adopted</li><li>Goal is to control everything to avoid the unexpected</li><li>Does not readily accept change, very risk adverse</li></ul>
Long-/Short-Term Orientation: Concern with virtue regardless of truth	
United States:	**Thailand:**
<ul><li>Fulfills its obligations</li><li>Appreciation for cultural traditions</li></ul>	<ul><li>Emphasis on thriftiness and perseverance</li></ul>

Table 7B-1 Summary of National Culture Dimensions (Adapted from Hofstede, 2007[4])

to its characterization as a culture that is very risk-adverse or does not readily accept change, Thailand is several years behind the lead of many other countries in implementing cyber crime legislation. Interestingly, the origins of the CCA could be traced back to the Internet Promotion Act forwarded back in 1997 in Thailand and many other policies proposed thereafter. However, all legislation has faced intense opposition by the elected Thai government, which has made laws slow to react to the demands and vulnerabilities of today's security environment and has ultimately made such policies out-of-date even before they are ever enacted.

Another feature of the CCA that can be tied to Thai culture is how strict this law is in comparison to cyber crime legislation implemented elsewhere in the world. Several national and international human rights groups, including Reporters Without Borders and the Asian Human Rights Commission, have criticized Thai legislation like the CCA as both restrictive and repressive. Earlier drafts of the CCA included the death penalty and life imprisonment for computer crimes that cause damage to computers and/or people, but have since been revised to maximum sentences of 20 years and significant fines.

Individualism-Collectivism The cultural dimension individualism-collectivism refers to the degree that individuals are integrated into groups, which in Thailand is relatively high and collectivist. With respect to a collectivist culture where there are strong relationships that exist and everyone takes responsibility for others, this can be seen directly in some of the language of the CCA. In Thailand, for example, it is possible that individuals or parties be held responsible for cyber crimes even though they did not initiate the crime themselves. Under section 14 of an earlier draft of the CCA, "Any service provider knowing of the perpetrating of an offence under Section 13 [which includes libel, falsifying data, national security breaches, viewing porn or sending porn to friends] within a computer system under their control but failing to delete immediately the computer data contained therein shall be subject to the same penalty as that imposed upon a person committing an offence under Section 13."[43] Consequently, any "service provider," which is language vague enough to include all organizations from Internet Service Providers to local Internet cafés, can face the same fines or penalties (up to 5 years' imprisonment) as if they had committed the cyber crimes themselves.[44]

Another feature of a collectivist culture is one in which loyalty is the dominant guiding rule in society. This is best illustrated in lèse majesté crimes, or insults against the king of Thailand, who is wonderfully revered and respected by all Thais and is considered a father-like figure, which carry some of the severest penalties for such crimes in the world.[45] In other instances where loyalty is paramount, section 20 of the CCA prohibits data from being disseminated, which "might be contradictory to the peace and concord or good morals of the people," however, no description is provided of what might cause damage to national security or contradict peace and morality.[46] As a result of the lack of any clear direction, this provision could be interpreted to include not only the owners of the content that is perceived as offensive to the country, but those that view that content as well. As stated above, however, what is clear is that a "service provider" can be held liable for any illegal content that is located on their servers. Although the CCA never refers to censorship because censorship is illegal and unconstitutional in Thailand, there is incentive for service providers to self-censure to ensure that they are compliant. Consequently, it is not uncommon in Thailand for content to be available from one service provider while blocked by another.[47]

Power Distance Power distance refers to the extent that less powerful members of a society accept and expect power distributed unequally. This type of behavior is exhibited through the enforcement of the CCA in Thailand in which Thai officials are sometimes viewed as being above the law. Whether such behavior is deliberate or unintentional, it is best described as a "corruption of policy," since it is acceptable practice for Thai officials to describe their potentially illegal action as being in the interest of "national security." For example, as stated above, censorship is illegal in Thailand, but if a Web site is deemed to be offensive to the country or having lèse majesté content, it may be blocked. At times, the "offensive" content that is blocked through the enforcement of the CCA is actually content from opposing political parties or simply opposing political viewpoints.[48,49]

7B

Analysis and Research Directions

Common Threads on Regulatory Provisions

A careful examination of the various international regulations, guidelines, and directives on information security reveals a recurring theme: a common thread of provisions. This section aims not to present an exhaustive list of common threads, but to illustrate a representative sample of those common threads. These common threads and their respective descriptions are depicted in Table 7B-2.

The recognition of the existence of these common threads in two or more information security regulations can translate to cost-effective and efficient compliance measures for an

Common Threads	Descriptions
Privacy Protection	Privacy protection is found in almost all regulations. At the very least, electronic data and transactions must be encrypted to be in compliance.
Monitoring	The monitoring of computing activities such as data transfer, queries, access, etc. is required by SOX, FISMA, HIPAA, MITS, and UNCITRAL's Model Law on Electronic Commerce.
Reporting	Reports on audit of internal controls and other system activities are required by SOX, FISMA, HIPAA, MITS, and the MI 52-109 of Canada.
Security Audit	Periodic security audit is required by most regulations to ensure compliance through the protection of systems that process and store sensitive data.
Vulnerability and Risk Assessment	This requires that a vulnerability and risk assessment process should be conducted on a regular basis. Proactive and immediate corrective measures must be identified, documented, and implemented by the security team.
Access and Authentication	This requires authentication mechanisms such as two-factor controls to protect system access.
Logging	The logging of system, device, and physical access and activities are required to be strictly enforced by most regulations.
Data Protection and Preservation	Data protection and preservation are important control objectives that are required to restore or retrace certain events, messages, documents, or transactions.
Physical and Component Access	Physical and component access and transport are required to be strictly monitored.
Trusted Path or Channel	Some regulations require the utilization of secure channels such as Virtual Private Networks (VPN) or Secure Socket Layers (SSL) for data communications.
Change and Patch Management	This control requires that a management process must be in place to ensure that the system patches are constantly monitored and installed. It also requires that any system change is properly documented.

Table 7B-2 Common Threads in Information Security Regulations

organization. A prototype of an implementation of a regulatory compliance toolkit that took these common threads into consideration is described in a recently published work.[50]

Harmonization of Information Security Regulations

The rapid expansion and adoption of the Internet as a tool for business, social, political, and scientific communication has been made possible by devices and systems software that are working in complete harmony. Not only did the Internet spawn beneficial and trustworthy activities, but also malevolent activities and organizations as well. As such, the proliferation of legislations and regulations, whose primary goal is to control both types of activities and entities, came about. This worldwide phenomenon presents a new challenge that has never been seen before. Although long-standing and established cooperation and recognition in criminal matters have existed between countries, cyberspace and information security laws and regulations, which are globally accepted, are just starting to emerge. Prominent examples of global harmonization of cyberspace and information security laws and regulations are the following:

- The *Council of Europe Convention on Cybercrime*[51] in Budapest on November 23, 2001, is the first multilateral agreement drafted specifically to address the problems posed by the international nature of computer crime. It requires signatory countries to institute and enforce stiff penalties for computer crime, to adopt domestic procedural laws to investigate computer crimes, and to provide a framework with which collaborative enforcement of international laws can operate in eradicating computer crimes.

- The *Basel II Capital Accord* is being adopted and implemented as best practices standards in international banking.

- The *Sarbanes-Oxley Act* has been partially emulated in Japan, Australia, Canada, and the European Union for controls on financial instruments and securities.

- The *Trusted Computer Systems Evaluation Criteria* (TCSEC), also known as the Orange Book, was developed in the early 1980s by the U.S. Department of Defense (DOD). In 1990, the European Commission harmonized the security evaluation efforts of several European countries by establishing the TCSEC equivalent, the *Information Technology Security Evaluation Criteria* (ITSEC). These groups of criteria evolved into the *Common Criteria* (CC), which was subsequently adopted by ISO to form an international standard, *ISO 15408*.[52]

Since almost all of the developed and developing countries are now heavily dependent on networked computers and the Internet, the danger of being attacked from domestic and foreign locations has escalated to an unprecedented level. The national security of a country is especially threatened when its critical infrastructures, such as those in the military, banking, business, transportation, commerce, and utilities sectors are computer-system dependent. Indeed, there is a great need to harmonize and standardize these laws and regulations across territorial boundaries just like what has been done to the hardware and software components that sustain the cyberspace infrastructure. A well-crafted multilateral agreement that minimizes jurisdictional hindrances in prosecuting computer-related crimes is mutually beneficial to all those involved. In 2006, the European Network and Information Security Agency (ENISA) formed a working group to study the regulatory aspects of network and information security. The report[53] of the group proposes guiding principles on the harmonization of laws, regulations, and processes that influence network and information security. Additional descriptions and analysis of various events and efforts toward the harmonization of legal approaches to cyber crime are published by Schjolberg and Hubbard.[54]

Research Directions

The discussions presented in this chapter bring up issues that usher several avenues for future research directions. In the area of legislation, an approach that requires further investigation and validation is the utilization of soft law, co-regulation, and self-regulation. In 2003, the European Parliament adopted the Inter-institutional Agreement on better law-making and a general framework for the use of co-regulation and self-regulation mechanisms within the EU context.[55] The focal point of possible research in this area will be on two main themes: the effectiveness of those alternative instruments in establishing regulations and the portability of the approach across cultures and shifting ethical standards.

Although there has been some progress in the area of global harmonization of regulatory standards and criteria, there remain a number of pressing issues that are yet to be resolved. Research topics in this area may include the following:

- the development and validation of a formal regulatory model that is devoid of cultural and current technological influences;
- the creation of regulatory templates that can be used as bases for information security legislations; and
- an in-depth study on the harmonization of global security regulations and ways to address the issues that influence its successful implementation.

An area of research that is partially covered by this chapter is that on the influence of culture on the legislation or non-legislation of information security regulations. As the initial case from Thailand has shown, there are some stark differences that exist in information security regulations between the United States and Thailand. Consequently, further examination of additional cases in Thailand as well as in other countries would likely lead to additional insights into the impact that culture has on information security policies. We believe that the successes and/or challenges that organizations from disparate cultures encounter, while facing the same security threats as American firms participating in the global economy, will lead to key insights that can be communicated as best practices to follow. Additional topics that are worthy of academic pursuit include: the provisions that may seem extraordinary in other cultures, the length of time it takes to legislate a law, the factors that influence the depth and breadth of legislative provisions, and the degree of affinity of similar information security legislations in countries that belong to the same region.

Endnotes

1. Thomas L. Friedman, *The World Is Flat: A Brief History of the Twenty-First Century.* Farrar, Straus, and Giroux Pub., 2005.

2. A. Mitrakas and S. Portesi, "Regulating Information Security: A Matter of Principle?" *ISSE/SECURE 2007 Securing Electronic Business Processes. Highlights of the Information Security Solutions Europe/SECURE 2007 Conference* (N. Pohlmann, H. Reimer, and W. Schneider, eds.) Vieweg Pub., 2007, pp. 3–17.

3. Linda Senden, "Soft Law, Self-Regulation and Co-regulation in European Law: Where Do They Meet?" *Electronic Journal of Comparative Law*, 9, no. 1 (Januray 2005). www.ejcl.org

4. G. Hofstede, *Geert Hofstede Cultural Dimensions*, 2007. Viewed on October 10, 2007, <http://www.geert-hofstede.com>

5. A. P. Ciganek, S. Jarupathirun, and H. Zo, *The Role of National Culture and Gender on Information Elements in e-Commerce: A Pilot Study on Trust.* Paper presented at the Tenth Americas Conference on Information Systems (AMCIS), 2004, New York, New York.

6. Personuvernd, "The Data Protection Act," Iceland, 2008. Viewed on July 18, 2008. http://www.personuvernd.is/information-in-english/greinar//nr/438

7. United States Department of Health and Human Services, *Summary of the HIPAA Privacy Rule*, last revised 05/03. Viewed on July 18, 2008. http://www.hhs.gov/ocr/privacysummary.pdf

8. Consumers Union, "Notice of Security Breach State Laws." Viewed on July 20, 2008. <http://www.consumersunion.org/campaigns/Breach_laws_May05.pdf>

9. Andreas Mitrakas, "Information Security and Law in Europe: Risks Checked?" *Information & Communications Technology Law*, 15, no.1 (March 2006): 33–53.

10. Office of the Comptroller of the Currency, "Supervisory Guidance: Supervisory Review Process of Capital Adequacy (Pillar 2) Related to the Implementation of the Basel II Advanced Capital Framework," 12 CFR Part 3 [Docket ID OCC-2008-0009], July 2008.

11. Federal Trade Commission (FTC), "The Gramm-Leach-Bliley Act." Viewed on July 21, 2008. <http://www.ftc.gov/privacy/privacyinitiatives/glbact.html>

12. Malta Ministry for Justice and Home Affairs, "Chapter 426 Electronic Commerce Act." Viewed on July 16, 2008. http://docs.justice.gov.mt/lom/legislation/english/leg/vol_13/chapt426.pdf

13. LawPhil Project, "Republic Act 8792. An Act Providing and Use of Electronic Commercial and Non-Commercial Transactions, Penalties for Unlawful Use Thereof, and Other Purposes." Viewed on July 21, 2008. http://www.lawphil.net/statutes/repacts/ra2000/ra_8792_2000.html

14. United Nations Commission on International Trade Law (UNCITRAL), "2005—United Nations Convention on the Use of Electronic Communications in International Contracts." Viewed on July 17, 2008. http://www.uncitral.org/uncitral/en/uncitral_texts/electronic_commerce/2005Convention.html

15. Infocomm Development Authority of Singapore (IDA), "Electronic Transactions Act (ETA) (Cap. 88)." Viewed on July 20, 2008. http://www.ida.gov.sg/Policies%20and%20Regulation/20060420164343.aspx

16. C. Connolly and P. Ravindra, "First UN Convention on eCommerce Finalized," *Computer Law & Security Report*, 22, no. 1 (2006): 31–38.

7B

17. UNCITRAL, "2005—United Nations Convention on the Use of Electronic Communications in International Contracts."

18. Federal Trade Commission-Children's Online Privacy Protection Act (FTC-COPPA), "Introduction to COPPA." Viewed on July 21, 2008. <http://www.ftc.gov/bcp/conline/edcams/coppa/intro.htm>

19. United States Small Business Administration (US-SBA), "Online Business." Viewed on July 20, 2008. http://www.business.gov/guides/online-business

20. Payment Card Industry Security Standards Council (PCI-SSC), "About the PCI Data Security Standard (PCI DSS)." Viewed on July 20, 2008. https://www.pcisecuritystandards.org/security_standards/pci_dss.shtml

21. Robert W. Hall and Anne Layne-Farrar, "Law and Economics of Software Security," *Harvard Journal of Law and Public Policy* (Fall 2006): 283–353.

22. Treasury Board of Canada Secretariat, "Operational Security Standard: Management of Information Technology Security (MITS)." Viewed on July 20, 2008. http://www.tbs-sct.gc.ca/pubs_pol/gospubs/TBM_12A/23RECON_e.asp

23. Public Company Accounting Oversight Board (PCAOB), "Sarbanes-Oxley Act of 2002." Viewed on June 13, 2008. http://www.pcaobus.org/rules/Sarbanes_Oxley_Act_of_2002.pdf

24. M. Whitman and H. Mattord, *Management of Information Security,* 2nd ed. Course Technology/Cengage Learning, 2007.

25. Commonwealth of Australia, Parliamentary Joint Committee on Corporations and Financial Services, "Corporate Law Economic Reform Program (CLERP). Corporate Reporting and Disclosure Law." Senate Printing Unit, Parliament House, Canberra, 2004.

26. Tara Gray, "Canadian Response to the U.S. Sarbanes-Oxley Act of 2002: New Directions for Corporate Governance." Library of Parliament, PRB 05-37E, Canada, 2005.

27. European Union, "Directive 2004/109/EC of the European Parliament and of the Council of 15 December 2004," *Official Journal of the European Union.* L390: pp. 38–57. Viewed on August 1, 2008. <http://eur-lex.europa.eu/LexUriServ/LexUriServ.do?uri=OJ:L:2004:390:0038:0057:EN:PDF>

28. Protiviti-Japan, "J-SOX Insights-Frequently Asked Questions about J-SOX" (2007). Viewed on July 20, 2008. https://www.sdn.sap.com/irj/sdn/go/portal/prtroot/docs/library/uuid/40d44037-09aa-2910-e5b0-edd182ed9cec

29. David Lazarus, "Extortion Threat to Patients' Records," *San Francisco Chronicle.* April 2, 2004 issue, p. A-1.

30. Public Citizen, "Offshoring and Privacy Protection," *Global Trade Watch.* Viewed on July 24, 2008. <http://www.citizen.org/trade/offshoring/privacy/>

31. European Commission, "Legislative Documents-Data Protection." Viewed on July 24, 2008. <http://ec.europa.eu/justice_home/fsj/privacy/law/index_en.htm>

32. E. J. Sinrod, "A Federal Court Rules That a Financial Institution Has No Duty to Encrypt a Customer Database," 2006. *FindLaw Thomson Reuters Business*. Viewed on July 24, 2008. http://writ.news.findlaw.com/commentary/20060220_sinrod.html

33. Ibid.

34. Lothar Determan, "Electronic Contracting," *Electronic Commerce & Law Report*, 12, no. 32 (2007).

35. Lori R. Clark, "The Sarbanes-Oxley Act Provides Significant Protection to Employee Whistleblowers," *Labor and Employment Newsletter* (Fall 2005). Tyler Cooper & Alcorn, LLP. Viewed on July 28, 2008. http://www.tylercooper.com/publications/Detail .aspx?ID=23e2263a-daf2-4416-8739-092908419aab

36. Ibid.

37. G. Hofstede and G.-J. Hofstede, *Cultures and Organizations: Software of the Mind*. New York: McGraw-Hill, 2004.

38. A. P. Ciganek, E. Mao, and M. Srite, "Organizational Culture for Knowledge Management Systems: A Study of Corporate Users." *International Journal of Knowledge Management*, 4, no. 1 (2008): 1–16.

39. Hofstede and Hofstede, *Cultures and Organizations*.

40. Ibid.

41. Hofstede, *Geert Hofstede Cultural Dimensions*.

42. "New Law Takes Aim at Cyber-Criminals," *The Nation* (2007, July 18). Retrieved July 22, 2008 from www.nationmultimedia.com

43. "Draft Cybercrime Bill, Freedom Against Censorship Thailand" (2007, March 8). Retrieved July 16, 2008 from facthai.wordpress.com

44. D. Sambandaraksa, "When Webmasters End Up in Jail," *Bangkok Post* (2008, June 11). Retrieved July 26, 2008 from www.bangkokpost.com

45. "Government Steps Up Online Censorship," (2008, May 20), Reporters Without Borders. Retrieved July 26, 2008 from www.rsf.org

46. "Unintelligible Computer Law Passed Under Junta's Watch" (2007, July 25), Asian Human Rights Commission. Retrieved July 26, 2008 from www.ahrchk.net

47. D. Sambandaraksa, "How ISPs View the Cyber Law," *Bangkok Post* (2008, June 11). Retrieved July 26, 2008 from www.bangkokpost.com

48. "Media Rights Group Condemns Thai Censorship in Name of King," Agence France-Presse (2008, June 5). Retrieved July 22, 2008 from afp.google.com

49. Prachatai, "Exploring 29 Websites Alleged by Democrat Party to Lave Lese Majeste Content (2008, May 30). Retrieved July 22 from www.prachatai.com

50. G. Francia, B. Estes, R. Francia, V. Nguyen, and A. Scroggins, "The Design and Implementation of an Automated Security Compliance Toolkit: A Pedagogical Exercise," *Journal of Digital Forensics, Security and Law*, 2, no. 4 (January 2008).

7B

51. Council of Europe, "Convention on Cybercrime," ETS No. 185. Budapest, November 23, 2001.

52. Gurpreet Dhillon, *Principles of Information Systems Security: Text and Cases.* Hoboken, NJ: John Wiley and Sons, 2007.

53. European Network and Information Security Agency (ENISA) Working Group on "Regulatory Aspects of Network and Information Security" (WG RANIS), 2006. "Inventory and Assessment of EU Regulatory Activity on Network and Information Security (NIS)."

54. S. Schjolberg and A. M. Hubbard, "Harmonizing National Legal Approaches on Cybercrime," International Telecommunication Union WSIS Thematic Meeting on Cybersecurity. Document CYB/04. June 2005.

55. Senden, "Soft Law, Self-Regulation and Co-regulation in European Law."

Collaboration and Compliance in Health Care: A Threat Modeling Case Study

Divakaran Liginlal
Carnegie Mellon University at Qatar

Lara Z. Khansa
Virginia Polytechnic Institute and State University

Jeffrey P. Landry
University of South Alabama

Divakaran Liginlal (Lal) is an Associate Teaching Professor of Information Systems at Carnegie Mellon University in Qatar and is affiliated to the College of Humanities and Social Sciences at CMU. Lal received a BS in communication engineering, MS in computer science and engineering from the Indian Institute of Science, and a Ph.D. in management information systems from the University of Arizona. His research has been published in such journals as CACM, IEEE TKDE, IEEE SMC-A, EJOR, DSS, Fuzzy Sets and Systems, and Computers & Security. Contact him at liginlal@cmu.edu.

Lara Khansa is Assistant Professor of business information technology. She received a Ph.D. in information systems, MS in computer engineering, and MBA in finance and investment banking from the University of Wisconsin, Madison, and BE in computer and communications engineering from the American University of Beirut. Her primary research interests include the economics of information security and related regulations, and the implications for IT innovation and the IT industry landscape. Contact her at larak@vt.edu.

Jeffrey P. Landry is a Professor in the School of Computer and Information Sciences at the University of South Alabama, where he teaches courses in information systems strategy and policy, project management, and human computer interaction.
Dr. Landry is developing risk assessments of voting systems for federal elections; has conducted risk management for a national, online certification exam; and has published on trust in the IS context, all following a 10-year software industry career.

Overview

The objective of this case study is to examine the strategic advantages of collaboration and information sharing in today's health care marketplace, and the resulting threats that hinder regulatory compliance. Building an illustrative case around a major health care provider in the U.S. Midwest, the study first explores how collaboration technologies play a crucial role in delivering enhanced health care services. The important elements of information sharing in inter-organizational systems—a key ingredient of collaboration—and related regulatory compliance needs are then presented. This is followed by a discussion of threat modeling methodologies and tools, along with a framework for modeling threats associated with collaboration. Two threat modeling use cases are developed for scenarios involving collaboration, namely, unauthorized access by insiders and abusive use of instant messaging applications. Each use case is accompanied by the related formal threat models, enterprise best practices, and lessons learned for collaborative health care, given the need for regulatory compliance. The use cases are described so as to facilitate their modeling using the Microsoft Threat Modeling Tool (TMT),[1] which has the ability to uncover threats that might otherwise go unnoticed.

Industry, Organization, and Business Problem Definition

Industry Overview

The health care industry is among the world's largest and fastest-growing industries, typically consuming, on average, over 10% of the gross domestic product (GDP) of most developed nations. It is projected to grow at approximately 18% per year over the next several years. About 580,000 establishments make up the health care industry. Varying greatly in terms of size, staffing patterns, and organizational structures, the health care industry spans a wide range of medical services covering hospitals, physicians' offices, dental facilities, and nursing homes. There are over 500,000 health care institutions in the United States that are employing over 12 million people. Hospitals constitute only 1% of these health care organizations; but they employ as much as 35% of all workers. Although the health care industry is a profit-generating industry, it provides an even more important service, that is, patient care.

Enterprise Description

7C

The UWM Health System consists of 60 clinics and over 1,100 primary care physicians. In recent years, it has been consistently ranked among the top 50 of the nation's major medical centers by *U.S. News and World Report*. UWM has one of the top ten most innovative facilities in health care and is among the nation's "100 Most Wired." With operating revenues of nearly $1 billion, this independent and nonprofit organization has over 5,000 full-time employees. It integrates multispecialty medical centers and provides clinical and hospital care with research and education. While UWM has seen tremendous advances in medical technology to improve patient diagnoses, such as three-dimensional MRIs and CT scans, its back office and operational information systems have failed to keep pace. In order to serve its patients most effectively, UWM has to manage patient care information in a reliable and efficient manner, while ensuring patient privacy and compliance with regulations such as HIPAA. Adoption of regulatory standards necessitates increased documentation and reporting requirements, and requires the implementation of scalable, secure, and cost-effective information systems throughout the organization.

Business Problem Definition

The most common approach to patient care is face-to-face delivery, a practice adopted in general medicine in most countries. However, health care is not always face-to-face; telemedicine and in-absentia health care is becoming commonplace. Advances in information technology continue to improve patient care and worker efficiency. For instance, the use of mobile devices enables a doctor or nurse to electronically record notes about a patient by the bedside or on the move. Information on vital signs and orders for tests can be electronically transferred to a main database. This process eliminates the need for paper and reduces record-keeping errors. Further, practitioners and patients may communicate over the phone, or through video conferencing, the Internet, email, text messages, or other forms of non-face-to-face communication. Access to patients' medical records from multiple places when doctors and caregivers collaborate is an important need. Another need is to eliminate the use of film imaging for X-rays and other imaging diagnostics. Further, UWM needs seamless communication among its various networked units, partners, and insurance and pharmaceutical companies to facilitate collaboration and meet both administrative and treatment needs. Vast amounts of health information need to be shared and protected. The infrastructure has a very high critical uptime, and the need to collaborate in real time across several locations is high. There is also a need to contact staff who are off-site or visiting patients whose locations are not immediately known.

To ensure regulatory compliance and enhance collaboration across all of its organizational units and strategic partners, UWM embarked on a mission to convert all its paper-based patient records to electronic formats, known as Electronic Health Records (EHR) (see Concept Definition box on page 339 for details). Although the implementation of EHR systems offers considerable benefits ranging from operational efficiencies to improved patient health care, UWM needs to address the additional challenges of various security and privacy risks that are faced by the entire health care industry. Between February 2005 and June 2006, medical organizations accounted for 11% of worldwide data breaches, making the confidentiality, integrity, and availability of patient data a primary concern.

In this case study, we devote our attention to two important risks that UWM faces, which relate to insider threats in collaboration: (1) unauthorized use and (2) abusive Internet access by employees. The first risk is associated with dishonest insiders who have privileged access to sensitive patient information, and who are likely to steal or sabotage information for personal gains, vendetta, or pure thrill. In the second case, employees often use instant messaging applications to share sensitive information with no regard to breach risks. In short, the business problem facing UWM is the need to provide enhanced patient care by strategically deploying collaborative technologies, while minimizing the associated risks.

Building the Business Case for Collaborative Health Care

Business Drivers of Collaborative Health Care

Baggs et al.[2] defined *collaboration* as individuals "working together to achieve a common goal via information-sharing, joint decision-making, and coordination of activities." The IT value hierarchy[3] is a simple model, based on Maslow's hierarchy of needs,[4] which articulates the progressive desire to use sophisticated IT applications within competitive organizations. It provides a good framework for discussing strategy, prioritization, and resource allocation. It also helps depict the need for collaborative technologies in UWM, with emphasis on the more sophisticated or innovative applications that may provide competitive advantage. Accordingly, Table 7C-1 presents this IT-enabled collaboration in health care at the five levels of maturity. At the most basic level, UWM's infrastructural needs have to be met to ensure performance and usability. The next level encompasses security, reliability, and availability considerations for the network and applications. The integration level ensures the existence of collaborative applications that bring together doctors, nurses, administrators, and caregivers, while the competitive level envisages use of state-of-the-art technologies, particularly those derived from Web 2.0. Finally, the adoption of 3-D virtual collaboration technologies, such as Nortel's proposed Web.Alive project, ensures that UWM is at the cutting edge of technologies.

The benefits of internal and external collaboration reach all parties involved in a health care system, as shown in Figure 7C-1.

Internal Collaboration   Cohn et al.[5] studied the effects of conflicts among doctors and administrators. They argued that cultural strife leads to errors, which hurts patients,

Paradigm Shifting	3-D virtual collaboration (e.g., Nortel's Web.Alive project)
Competitive	Use of state-of-the-art technology (Blackberry for key employees), social networks for enhanced patient care, ubiquitous access
Integration	Interorganizational information sharing and enterprise applications
Safety	CIA (Confidentiality, Integrity & Availability) privacy safeguards
Infrastructural	Speed, usability considerations

Table 7C-1 IT-enabled Collaboration in Healthcare

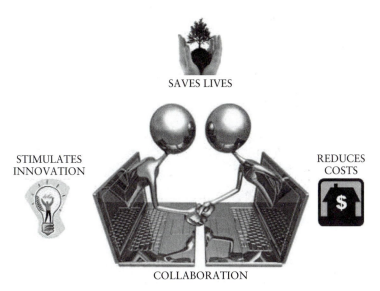

SAVES LIVES

STIMULATES
INNOVATION

REDUCES
COSTS

COLLABORATION

Figure 7C-1 Business Case for Collaboration

Courtesy Course Technology/Cengage Learning

communities, and all other stakeholders. Effective collaboration, on the other hand, produces the following key benefits:

1. *Saves lives:* Internal collaboration via information sharing and joint decision making improves the quality of care and performance of health care organizations. A longitudinal study[6] of 23 neonatal intensive care units showed that collaboration among front-line staff, that is, employees directly delivering services to users and managers, results in improved patient outcomes and is associated with a reduced chance of infant mortality.

2. *Reduces costs:* A study at Rocky Mountain tertiary care facility showed how collaboration among practicing physicians and hospital administrators led to over $500,000 in sustainable long-term cost savings.[7]

External Collaboration

1. *Reduces the costs of unnecessary duplicate care:* With more collaboration comes centralization and coordination, which, at the least, eliminate the need for multiple medical tests when patients move from one facility to another (e.g., from a hospital to a rehabilitation facility). There is a need for policy leadership to coordinate the various fragmented health care entities from insurance companies to front-line staff. EHRs offer a common repository accessible to doctors when needed. Disabled or gravely ill patients are more often than not unable to remember their medical history, which necessitates such a centralized system to carry patients' EHRs. Because of the ability of EHR systems to save lives and reduce costs, their benefits, by far, outweigh the risks and costs of data sharing.

2. *Can reduce medical errors:* In 1999, the National Academy of Sciences released a report[8] entitled "To Err Is Human: Building a Safer Health System," in which they revealed that at least 44,000 and as many as 98,000 Americans die yearly as a result of medical errors. These errors have been partly attributed to the lack of collaboration and

communication among the health care body. The Patient Safety and Quality Improvement Act of 2005 was enacted and signed into law on July 29, 2005, with the goal of improving voluntary and confidential reporting of medical information that adversely affects patients. The Act calls for the creation of Patient Safety Organizations (PSOs) to collect, aggregate, and analyze confidential information, in an effort to eliminate patient safety risks and hazards. The Act also calls for enhancing collaboration through the establishment of a Network of Patient Safety Database (NPSD) to provide an interactive resource for providers, PSOs, and other entities. The NPSD, supported by the Department of Health and Human Services, promotes interoperability among various reporting systems and promotes expedited services to patients through building a network of health care providers.

3. *Stimulates innovation:* Collaboration among physicians and various other health care institutions, such as pharmaceutical companies, is instrumental in offering the best state-of-the-art services and products to patients. Not only is collaboration in health care capable of boosting health care innovation, but more importantly, it encourages innovation in information technology. This innovation consists of designing integrated mobility solutions within medical systems and equipment, enabling professionals to quickly and collaboratively treat patients at the point of care. For example, Cisco's Unified Wireless Network (UWN) and health care–specific applications offer the possibility of deploying a medical network that offers instant access to information, while maintaining secure information and safeguarding patient privacy. This networking solution allows collaboration among physicians, nurses, and administrators at each of Orlando Regional's eight facilities. The hospital's chief technology officer, Alex Veletsos, noted,[9] "All of our clinical information, electronic medical records, and even our employee payroll, human resources and purchasing information can be accessed via the wireless network. The network allows our staff to become more efficient and productive, which results in improvements across the board, and most importantly with the care of our patients."

Balancing the Scorecard

The current health care system suffers from many gaps that hamper its ability to protect patients. First, without PSOs, the system would suffer from a severe disconnect because there is no central entity to keep up-to-date patient information where it would be instantly accessible as needed. Second, there is no linkage or framework that ties health entities together. Third, there are no established standards, best practices, or performance gaps. All these three limitations hamper effective collaboration among various health care entities. When it comes to health care, it is important to achieve consensus on nomenclature, concepts, and priorities, and what and how to measure the effectiveness of collaboration. A balanced scorecard is a strategic measurement-based system, instrumental in monitoring performance of strategic goals over time. Kaplan and Norton[10] defined a balanced scorecard as a "multi-dimensional framework for describing, implementing and managing strategy at all levels of an enterprise by linking objectives, initiatives, and measures to an organization's strategy."

When constructing a balanced scorecard for UWM, the first step consists of defining the vision and mission of the institution. The goal of any health care institution ought to be adequate care for all patients. Essentially, the patients' well-being and satisfaction are what matter; thus, everything within the organization has to revolve around the patient. If the patient

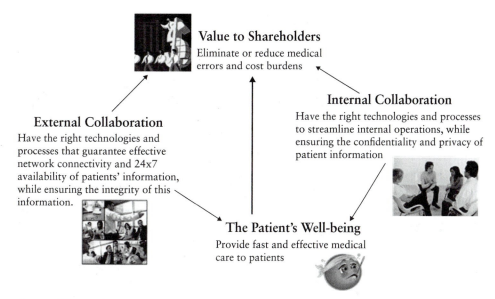

Value to Shareholders
Eliminate or reduce medical errors and cost burdens

Internal Collaboration
Have the right technologies and processes to streamline internal operations, while ensuring the confidentiality and privacy of patient information

External Collaboration
Have the right technologies and processes that guarantee effective network connectivity and 24x7 availability of patients' information, while ensuring the integrity of this information.

The Patient's Well-being
Provide fast and effective medical care to patients

Figure 7C-2 Holistic Benefits of Collaboration

Courtesy Course Technology/Cengage Learning

is cared for, employees are rewarded and shareholders benefit. Collaboration plays a crucial role not only within UWM, among employees and personnel, but equally important outside of UWM, among partners to ensure expediency and accuracy of care. Based on our analysis of UWM, we define UWM's vision and mission in the framework shown in Figure 7C-2. We then materialize UWM's vision and mission into a set of objectives and measures that can be used to assess UWM's progress toward their goals. Table 7C-2 presents these goals and measures, in addition to attainable targets and implementable initiatives.

1. Effectiveness of internal collaboration: Internal collaboration among employees within UWM is essential for adequate care. Three important measures of internal effectiveness are as follows:

   a. Employee turnover: Employees are the backbone of any successful institution and it is important that they be satisfied to be productive. A good measure of employee satisfaction has traditionally been employee turnover.

   b. Effectiveness of training: It is important for employees at all levels to undergo training and development programs. This training should not only be targeted toward medical care but should also ensure the confidentiality and privacy of patients. It is important to tie training and development programs to employee performance and to the overall performance of the organization. Ultimately, the goal is to show the capacity of the organization to learn on a sustained basis. Therefore, it is important to undergo frequent assessments of employees at all levels.

   c. Ensuring patient privacy: Several incidents in the recent past involved deliberate release of medical records by insiders to health organizations, for financial gain. UCLA fired workers for snooping into Britney Spears's and Farrah Fawcett's medical records in 2008. As many as 40 doctors and other employees at the

Objectives	Measures	Targets	Initiatives
Effectiveness of internal collaboration and operations	Staff satisfaction Physician satisfaction	>75% satisfaction	Employee satisfaction initiative Employee involvement and coordination initiative Greater staff/budget for HIPAA enforcement Tracking access to medical records Enforcing better control over medical records databases
	Low employee turnover	<7% turnover	
	Rate of medical errors	<.5%	
	Number of complaints, such as illegally releasing patients' medical records, either intentionally or otherwise (violation of HIPAA)	<2 per year	
Effectiveness of external collaboration	Rate of medical errors due to problems with external communication or lack of coordination of care externally	<.5%	Patient Safety Organizations (PSOs) Network of Patient Safety Databases (NPSD) Establishing a central framework to ensure private and secure sharing of health information
Shareholder value	Net increase in revenues from prior period	>20%	Reducing "defects," i.e., anything that does not meet customers' expectations, through Six Sigma or other similar initiatives
	Return on investment	>15%	
	Patient base, bed occupancy	>90%	
	Patient-reported satisfaction		
	• Adequate communication/ information	95%	
	• Controlled wait times		
	• Consistent message from multiple providers		

Table 7C-2 **Scorecard for Collaboration in Health Care**

Palisades Medical Center were suspended for knowingly leaking confidential information about George Clooney and his girlfriend in 2007. These incidents have forced health care organizations to enforce better audits and controls for their databases of medical records.

2. Effectiveness of external collaboration in reducing medical errors: One of the main problems identified in the National Academy of Sciences report is the unavailability of the right information when needed, which could result in medical errors that jeopardize the well-being of patients. The best measure to assess effective external collaboration is, thus, the reduction in the number of medical errors compared to prior periods.

3. Shareholder value: If UWM is functioning well, that would transcend into more profitability. Return on investment (ROI) has been widely used as a financial performance measure. ROI should also be complemented with qualitative measures extracted from employee satisfaction surveys and patient follow-up surveys. Customer satisfaction could be reached through organization-wide initiatives, such as enforcing Six Sigma throughout the organization's operations.

Discussion Questions

1. Discuss ways that collaboration and information sharing would benefit UWM.

2. What set of attainable objectives would generate business value for UWM?

3. What are measures that UWM can use to assess their progress toward these goals?

4. List initiatives that can be implemented by UWM to reach their target measures. What do you think is the most important objective in the case of UWM? Discuss ways that UWM can attain this objective.

Information Sharing in Collaboration: Security and Privacy Threats

Information Sharing in Collaborative Health Care

Information sharing is crucial to health care collaboration. The key drivers of information sharing for UWM are their ability to: (i) communicate health care information on a timely basis, (ii) classify information based on a need to know basis, and (iii) permit ease of electronic exchange and visualization of information. Two conflicting objectives consist of ensuring: (i) the trustworthiness of the source of information and (ii) the confidentiality, integrity, and availability of such information. Tools for collaboration need to balance the requirements of ease of use and accessibility with trust and security. Not only does a health care organization, such as UWM, have to function properly from within, but it also has to be an effective, albeit secure, link within its network. It is, therefore, crucial to ensure that patient privacy is maintained. This is an important focus of our study.

Understanding the information sharing practices of people in the context of the enabling technologies is crucial to ensuring the security of the information shared. Obviously, electronic means of sharing information is of interest to us. The tools that facilitate such information sharing need to be tightly integrated into the collaborative environment. While traditional modes of communication, such as file attachments in email or instant messenger, are feasible, a topic worth investigating relates to how safe these communications means are and how confident the users are in using them. Consider, for instance, IBM's Lotus Instant Messaging and the Web Conferencing (Sametime) product and platform for real-time collaboration. It is based on three on-demand concepts:

1. Presence awareness. See, in advance, whether a person(s) or application(s) is available to collaborate, share information, and/or take an action.

2. Instant messaging. Be able to converse virtually through the exchange of text-, audio-, and/or video-based information in real time.

3. Web conferencing. Share information, an application or an entire desktop, or engage in team white boarding.

Table 7C-3 depicts tools and environments that facilitate information sharing.

Method	Features
Telephone	Most common form of communication; cheap; available
Voice Mail	Asynchronous; allows storage; high cost; quite popular
Facsimile	Common form of communication; fast; cost effective; allows storage and automation
Email	Most popular; security and spam issues; costly but allows storage and automation; decentralized information; can be processed through filtering, sorting, and prioritization
Video Conferencing	Costly; desktop video conferencing more available and popular now
Integrated Messaging	Combines some of the other methods; becoming commonplace; enhances productivity; standards are emerging
Groupware	Combines messaging and database technologies; primarily designed for collaboration; integrates all of the other primary techniques, information organization, centralized source of information; can also integrate project management features such as calendaring, scheduling, and data tracking
Document Management Systems (DMS)	Administrative, collaborative, and computer document management systems; integrates groupware features and evolving XML standards of data representation; functions include document scanning, search and retrieval, data vaulting, document/file linking, workflow automation, document archiving, and review and markup
Electronic Patient Record Management System	Has all the capabilities of DMS, plus configuration management, change management and may be integrated with ERP systems
Virtual Reality (VR)	Allows user interaction with the underlying model, inclusive VR permits better visualization of 3-D objects through a set of manipulations; interactive VR is focused on interacting with objects within the scale and constraints of the environment in which the products are situated

Table 7C-3 List of Environments and Tools Facilitating Collaboration

To investigate trust and security in information sharing, it is absolutely necessary to understand the types of information shared. Table 7C-4 provides a listing of different data types and formats used in information sharing in a collaborative environment.

Three models of information sharing from an inter-organizational perspective may be noted:

1. Decentralized: Information is maintained and controlled by each individual partner in the collaboration and is released only on a need-to-know basis and subject to tight controls.

2. Coordinated: Limited sharing among trusted partners where information is commonly maintained for each subset of trusted partners.

3. Centralized: All information is maintained in a common repository and is accessible by all partners subject to user-level restrictions.

Three models of information sharing from a systems perspective may also be identified.[11] In the information transfer model, one is looking at a scenario where one party transfers information to the other who maintains it in a private database. In the third-party model, a trusted third party collects information and maintains it in a database for use by other parties in a collaborative venture. In the information hub model, the third party is replaced by a common

Data Type	Traditional Data Format	Web Format
Images	TIFF, GIF, JPG	GIF, JPG
Unformatted documents	TXT	XML, HTML, TXT
Formatted documents	MSWord, Postscript	PDF, MS Word
Forms	Lotus 123, MS Excel	HTML
Database sectors	Database file	XML, HTML
Audio	WAV, etc.	MP3
Video	MPEG, etc.	MOV
Animations	Flash, etc.	VRML, SVG

Table 7C-4 **Types of Information Shared in a Collaborative Design Environment**

information hub. Thus, there need not be a physical system in existence. Rather, a distributed component object model such as Web services–enabled infrastructure would suffice.

HIPAA Compliance Issues in Information Sharing

The Health Insurance Portability and Accountability Act (HIPAA) was formed with the intention of moving the health care system to the information era and to fulfill the need for a nationwide security standard. The key objective of the U.S. Congress was to enact standards that provide fundamental privacy rights for patients and define responsibilities for those who serve them. HIPAA recognizes that privacy is a fundamental right protected by the Constitution. The Act provides a standard terminology to communicate and considers the privacy of the patient as an important asset. It facilitates securing all devices with patient information, allows for privacy educational sessions for all employees, stipulates the monitoring and tracking of access to patient records, and mandates that patients have the right to inspect their medical records. Title II of HIPAA, "Preventing Health Care Fraud and Abuse, Administrative Simplification, Medical Liability Reform," sets standards for Electronic Data Interchange (EDI), privacy, and security; standardizes manual and electronic transactions; and is designed to prevent occurrences of fraud in the system.

HIPAA mandates that private medical information and other patient identifying data be accessible only on a need-to-know basis by physicians who are in direct connection with patients. The 45 CFR 160.102 mandate in HIPAA's privacy rule considers health care providers "covered entities" and requires them to be HIPAA compliant. A "covered entity" can share "protected health information," or PHI, with other entities under some circumstances. Information pertaining to a patient's "physical or mental condition or functional status" is considered PHI. Per HIPAA's 45 CFR 164.508, a client's information can be shared when an authorization is signed by the patient, or whoever is specified as authorized parties. PHI can be shared to provide effective treatment or other health care operations, as well as to process payments. Per HIPAA's 45 CFR 164.501, "treatment means the provision, coordination, or management of health care and related services by one or more health care providers, including the coordination or management of health care by a health care provider with a third party; consultation between health care providers relating to a patient; or the referral of a patient for health care from one health care provider to another."

HIPAA requires that all health care employees, including contractors, be trained to comply with the HIPAA privacy and security policies by maintaining and upholding patients' privacy and security. HIPAA also implies the necessity to install technologies that secure the transmission of private data within and across health care organizations over the Internet. According to these rules, collaboration is permitted among doctors and other health care givers to provide the patient with the best services. In an effort to ensure compliance with HIPAA, the Patient Safety and Quality Improvement Act provides federal, legal, privilege, and confidentiality protections to information that is assembled and reported by providers to a PSO or developed by a PSO. The Act significantly limits the use of this information in criminal, civil, and administrative hearings and includes provisions for monetary penalties for violating confidentiality or privilege protections.

Discussion Questions

1. Discuss the benefits and risks of Electronic Health Records compared to paper-based records for UWM.

2. How important are Electronic Health Records to UWM from a HIPAA compliance perspective?

3. What are the barriers to the adoption of Electronic Health Records for small and medium health care enterprises? What, in your opinion, are the attendant risks of not adopting EHR?

Threat Modeling for Collaborative Technologies

Swidersky and Snyder[12] provide definitions of terms that are essential to comprehend before initiating the threat modeling process.

- **Asset.** A system resource, such as data in a database or in a file system.

- **Threat.** A potential occurrence, malicious or otherwise, that might damage or compromise the system's assets.

- **Vulnerability.** A system's weakness that makes a threat possible. Vulnerabilities might exist at the network, host, or application levels.

- **Attack (or exploit).** An action taken by someone or something that harms an asset. This could be someone following through on a threat or exploiting a vulnerability.

- **Countermeasure.** A safeguard that addresses a threat and mitigates risk.

Threat modeling is a structured approach that helps system designers to systematically identify and rate the threats that are most likely to affect their systems. The purpose of threat modeling is to identify all possible threats, vulnerabilities, and attacks in a complex system, regardless of their probabilities of occurrence, and help define the necessary countermeasures in the context of the system scenario. By identifying threats, vulnerabilities, and possible attacks, threat modeling provides the foundation upon which the rest of the security system is built and, thus, supports developing realistic and meaningful security requirements, and enables the creation of a robust security strategy.

7C

Concept Presentation
Electronic Health Record (EHR)

I. Concept Definition (Source: Legislative Analyst's Office, CA)

Also known as Electronic Medical Records (EMRs), EMRs consist of electronically stored information about an individual's health history, medical treatments, and other related information maintained by a health care provider. An EMR may be designed with varying complexity and may include information in a variety of forms, such as X-rays or computerized scan results. Functionality offered by EMRs includes viewing patients' medical histories, ordering prescriptions and lab work, and treatment advisory functions.

Related Information Classes

Electronic Prescribing (eRx)
The eRx tools will help create, process, and communicate prescriptions for medication. In its most basic form, an eRx could consist of the physicians' using computers instead of a paper pad to write and manage prescriptions. More advanced versions can include treatment advice and communication across organizations. eRx could take the form of a software that comes as a stand-alone product, or may be incorporated into a package of EHR systems or software.

Computerized Physician Order Entry (CPOE)

These products are clinical information technology tools, frequently used in hospitals, that physicians and other providers can use to enter orders into a computer system for further patient action, such as prescription drugs or lab tests.

II. Illustrative Example

Type of Health Record Used, by Practice Size, 2005

No. of full-time physicians in practice	Paper medical record filed in cabinet	Scanned image filed electronically using a document image management system (DIMS)	Dictation and transcription system combined with DIMS	EMR in a relational database	Other
5 or fewer	78.0	2.3	6.3	12.5	0.9
6-10	73.9	3.0	7.2	15.2	0.7
11-20	67.0	1.6	11.7	18.9	0.9
21 or more	65.8	3.1	10.7	19.5	1.0
All practices	75.3	2.5	7.2	14.1	0.9

Type of record (%)

In 2005, electronic health records were least common among small physician groups, as shown in the above table adapted from Gans et al.[13] A report in the *New England Journal of Medicine* (Oct. 4, 2008) states that, although doctors who use electronic health records say overwhelmingly that such records have helped improve the quality and timeliness of care, only less than 20% of the nation's doctors have started using such records.

III. Connect—Clinical Decision Support

These are software tools that assist care providers by offering advice or diagnosis for a patient's situation, based on information about the individual patient and a database of recommended procedures. These capabilities are now frequently incorporated into EMR, CPOE, and eRx products.

The threat modeling process helps in the following ways:

- Identify potential threats and the conditions that must exist for an attack to be successful.
- Provide information on how existing safeguards affect required attack conditions.
- Provide information about which attack conditions and vulnerability remediation activities add the most value.
- Understand which conditions or vulnerabilities, when eliminated, mitigate multiple threats, thus optimizing investment in security.

The critical decision for the designer is to evaluate all vulnerabilities and decide which merit immediate attention. One of the basic tenets of risk management is that not all vulnerabilities present a threat to assets. Only a vulnerability that can be exploited constitutes a threat to the asset. A threat modeling methodology that is focused on collaborative technologies would enable UWM's management to objectively identify and evaluate threats to their infrastructure. Thus, such a methodology translates the associated risks into business impact; empowers business groups to accept, avoid, transfer, or reduce the identified risks; and creates awareness among security and information technology teams concerning their interdependencies and assumptions.

Methodologies and Tools

Creating a satisfactory threat model requires a systematic and repeatable process to ensure that all known and unknown threats and vulnerabilities are addressed. A number of threat modeling approaches have been used in recent years.[14] A common thread of threat modeling activities begins with gathering, organizing, and consolidating already known system information, such as components, data, roles, external dependencies, and compiling it into a threat model document. Using this information, the security profile of the system is created by breaking it down into its functionality and network topology. Identifying the assets is a crucial step because it forms the foundation for the threat modeling exercise. An asset inventory needs to be drawn up and assets ought to be classified based on their relative importance to the business. Having defined the assets of the system, the threat identification step follows. A good approach toward threat identification is Microsoft's STRIDE, which is a goal-based approach, where an attempt is made to get inside the mind of the attacker by rating the threats against Spoofing identity, Tampering with data, Repudiation, Information disclosure, Denial of service, and Elevation of privilege. A different approach consists of using an exhaustive threat list, walking through every one of the listed assets, and evaluating them in the light of their rankings and security contexts.

A detailed analysis of threats from the perspectives of network, hosts, and applications is crucial. Once all the threats have been enumerated, they need to be rated to determine the degree of countermeasures that need to be undertaken. A rating system used for threat analysis is Microsoft's DREAD methodology, in which threats are rated against the following:

> Damage potential—What would be the extent of the damage if the threat were to happen in reality?
>
> Reproducibility—How easy is it to repeat the attack?
>
> Exploitability—How easy is it to launch an attack?
>
> Affected users—How many users would be affected by the attack?
>
> Discoverability—How easy is it to find the vulnerability?

Once the threat modeling process is completed, threats may be measured and analyzed using risk management techniques, based on the impact to the business and the probability of occurrence. A decision must be made on whether to accept, avoid, reduce, or transfer related risks. The last step of the threat modeling process is the definition of the security requirements and the countermeasures for mitigating the prioritized threats identified during the risk management stage. Four alternative threat modeling systems are good candidates for investigation where the Microsoft approach fails: Trike, AS/NZS 4360:2004 Risk Management, CVSS, and OCTAVE. We refer the reader to the OWASP site (http://www.owasp.org/index.php/Threat_Risk_Modeling) for more information.

Modeling Threats in Collaborative Applications: A Conceptual Framework

A conceptual framework for threat modeling encompasses the three orthogonal dimensions of source, target, and extent of threat as shown in Figure 7C-3. Threats may arise from several sources: internally or externally; from people or organizations; and could be targeted at data or applications. Taking control of key applications would, in turn, result in compromising critical data. The impact of compromising either application or data or both may stay within the organization or may affect the entire strategic alliance and results in loss of intellectual assets and/or financial losses, and consumption of resources to contain, thwart, or recover from the resulting detrimental effects. The points of attack, history of vulnerabilities, and the implications of new technologies are all crucial to ensuring that adequate countermeasures are put in place.

Without understanding the processes and their involved applications, it is impossible to uncover all the possible ways that an attacker is likely to use to compromise a system. Methods used in modeling threats include use cases, sequence diagrams, and component models. These models evolve with better understanding of the application. A use case in software engineering and systems engineering is a description of a system's behavior as it responds to

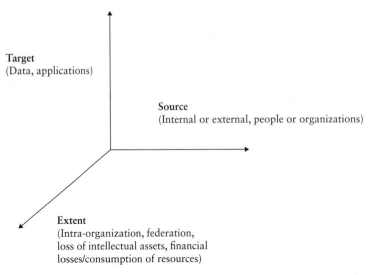

Figure 7C-3 A Conceptual Framework to Model Threats and Assess Risks

Courtesy Course Technology/Cengage Learning

a request that originates from outside of that system.[15] The use case approach is used widely within Microsoft during the software development process.[16] Sequence diagrams that trace the data flow between system components are very useful, especially for examining component to component communications and understanding the message transformations that occur at each component.

Assets are the resources that an attacker aims at either stealing or modifying, and that, therefore, need to be protected. The next step consists of defining these assets. Assets are classified as physical, such as Web servers, computers, buildings, Web pages, source code, etc., or intangible, such as intellectual property, goodwill, and electronic organizational records (e.g., customer records and sales data). The establishment of an information security program will always require organizations to establish an asset classification regime. Asset classification is used to break data down into types of data and data sets with various protection requirements.

Vulnerabilities can be classified into technical, managerial, and operational. While other areas of this testing framework create tests specifically aimed at extracting these vulnerabilities (particularly technical vulnerabilities), it is useful to explore them during the development of a threat model. Many issues become obvious before traditional testing takes place. A list of potential vulnerabilities should be created by looking at the data flow and state transitions of each asset, and its operational environment. Technical vulnerabilities may include issues such as a lack of encryption between the data flow end points, or no input validation. Management issues might include a lack of policy or standards for components developed in specific languages, or a lack of configuration guidelines for a database server. Operational vulnerabilities include issues such as having no defined process to review audit logging information, or changing control procedures for component updates. All of the potential vulnerabilities that affect each asset should be grouped and listed.

By systematically exploring attackers' motives, it is possible to construct a threat matrix outlining what threats affect which assets. The important thing to note when devising a threat matrix is the concept of prevalence. It is important to document realistic threats by asking questions to determine what attackers would do, how they would do it, how hard it would be to do, or the likelihood of that happening. Mitigation strategies should be created after gaining a solid understanding of the development project, and creating lists of system assets, potential vulnerabilities, and possible threats. The chosen risk handling tactic for each threat should be added to the development procedures to mitigate, accept, or transfer the risk.

Threat Modeling Use Cases

One of the greatest dangers associated with UWM's collaboration infrastructure is insider threat. Every employee launching a Web-based collaborative application can open a gate into UWM's enterprise network. The resulting backdoors create a frightening array of new challenges arising from active content, Botnets, and susceptibility to phishing attacks.

Concept Presentation
Insider Threat

I. Concept Definition

An "insider" is anyone who has been authorized to access an information system. Insider threat, also referred to as "unauthorized user threat," represents the behavior of trusted adversaries, such as internal employees or partners, that can potentially cause direct financial losses to a company, lead to the theft or impairment of intellectual property, or compromise customer data.

Classification of Insider Threats (Source: Oakley Networks)

Deliberate Malfeasance: Patient credit and medical information theft, hacking, fraud.

Lost Productivity: Chat, personal email usage, gambling, porn.

Employee Morale: Internal protests, organize labor, whistle-blower, press leaks.

Privilege Abuse: Snooping, rights escalation, technical arrogance, insider trading.

Hostile Environment: Hazing, discrimination, racial slurs, hate sites.

II. Examples

According to the 2007 CSI-FBI survey, insider abuse of network access or email edged out virus incidents as the most prevalent security problem in the organizations surveyed, with an average cost of nearly $2.9 million. A former systems administrator at

Medco Health Solutions planted a logic bomb that cost $70,000–$120,000 to repair. He faces up to 10 years in prison.

Verizon's 2008 Data Breach Investigations Report, which looked at 500 breach incidents over the last 4 years, determined that, although outsider attacks were more frequent, insider threats tend to be more costly. The report states that this supports the principle that privileged parties are able to do more damage to the organization than outsiders.

III. Connect—Collaboration

HIPAA stipulates a set of rules for the handling, security, and retention of health care information. Hospitals are required to submit detailed reports on patient care quality, patient safety, and organizational performance indicators to government agencies. Thus, there is a strong need to capture, retain, and access large historical patient data to remain in compliance with HIPAA. Also, there are new initiatives, such as the Medicare pay-for-performance (P4P), which will make reimbursements to hospitals dependent on the ability to accurately document patient care plans and data. The foundation of effective pay-for-performance initiatives is collaboration with providers and other stakeholders, to ensure that valid quality measures are used, that providers aren't being pulled in conflicting directions, and that providers have support for achieving actual improvement. Consequently, to develop and implement these initiatives, UWM is collaborating with a wide range of other public agencies and private organizations. UWM is also providing technical assistance to a wide range of health care providers through its Quality Improvement Organizations (QIOs). Through these collaborative efforts, UWM is developing and implementing a set of pay-for-performance initiatives to support quality improvement in the care of Medicare beneficiaries. In addition to the initiatives for hospitals, physicians, and physician groups described below, UWM is also exploring opportunities in nursing home care—building on the progress of the Nursing Home Quality Initiative—and is also considering approaches for home health and dialysis providers. Finally, recognizing that many of the best opportunities for quality improvement are patient-focused and cut across settings of care, UWM is pursuing pay-for-performance initiatives to support better care coordination for patients with chronic illnesses.

We next discuss two use cases associated with insider threats from UWM employees. The first relates to unauthorized access, while the second relates to abusive use of instant messaging. Both use cases bring out the risks associated with collaborative technologies for UWM. The absence of proper security processes and technologies would allow computer users to wander through the UWM network virtually unimpeded. Most inside users may have no malicious intent; but a few are likely to have interests that range from criminal to prurient. Often, the inability to control access to sensitive medical data creates holes for insiders and outsiders to slip through. The use cases are described in a way that makes it easy to model using the Microsoft Threat Modeling Tool (MTM). The tool facilitates the modeling of a use case as conventionally defined, but when configured properly, facilitates the generation of associated threats and countermeasures. The authors are willing to share the threat models that were created to capture the threats corresponding to these scenarios for use as teaching aids in the classroom.

Use Case 1: Insider Threat—Unauthorized Access

Description of Scenario Billing agents and pharmacists use UWM's collaborative system based on EMR to access the patients' billing records and prescription information. However, at any time, the billing agent or the pharmacist—in this case malicious insider— may compromise the system by launching an insider attack. A typical scenario involves a billing agent using the EMR system accessing an EMR application, which accesses or updates an associated database, such as billing information, prescription information, or links to an insurance company Web service. When this scenario is modeled, it could potentially yield threats corresponding to the STRIDE categorization. Following are three examples of threats generated by the threat modeling process. The first threat is to confidentiality of protected health or financial information of a patient when the billing agent steals credit card and insurance information. The perpetrator could potentially sell it to malicious outsiders who might use this information to commit fraud or identity theft. The second threat jeopardizes the integrity of the data when, for instance, a pharmacist alters a patient's prescription to steal prohibited drugs and make profits. The third class of threat relates to the availability of critical information when a disgruntled insider sabotages the collaboration infrastructure by launching a Denial of Service attack.

Identified Threats and Associated Risks

- *Spoofing identity*: A billing agent spoofs a physician's credentials to access patients' protected health information (PHI).
- *Tampering with data*: A pharmacist tampers with prescription either by increasing the quantity or by adding prohibited drugs to personally make profit.
- *Repudiation:* System administrators collude with malicious insiders to obfuscate audit logs to help perpetrate fraud.
- *Information disclosure*: A billing agent sells PHI to malicious outsiders to commit insurance fraud.
- *Denial of service*: A disgruntled insider sabotages EMR.
- *Elevation of privilege*: A nurse uses a physician's credentials to tamper with patients' treatment records.

An example of a DREAD model derived from our use case is shown in Table 7C-5.

Criteria	Evaluation	Rating	Justification
Damage potential	*How great is the damage if the vulnerability is exploited?*	*HIGH*	HIPAA violation would result in penalties for the organization.
Reproducibility	*How easy is it to reproduce the attack?*	*HIGH*	The reproducibility is high for an insider exploiting a weakness in the system.
Exploitability	*How easy is it to launch an attack?*	*MED*	The protection measures in place by UWM do not make it easy for an insider to launch a serious attack.
Affected users	*As a rough percentage, how many users are affected?*	*LOW*	Depending on what kind of information or data an insider can compromise, the number of impacted users is usually low.
Discoverability	*How easy is it to find the vulnerability?*	*LOW*	It is well documented that insider threats are very difficult to detect. When they are found, it is often too late to correct them.

Table 7C-5 Sample DREAD Model for UWM's Insider Threat Use Case

Recommended Mitigations Several solutions exist for health care organizations to effectively counter and mitigate the risks of insiders. Some prominent Insider Threat Management (ITM) solutions include Oakley Networks SureView 3., Vontu 5.0, Reconnex iGuard 2.1, and Tablus Content Alarm 3.0 Beta. These products implement behavioral profiling solutions that monitor user activity. They provide monitoring of system administrators, application-based monitoring and analysis, correlation analysis across multiple monitoring mechanisms, and differential and adaptive monitoring.

The important driver for UWM for adopting insider threat management solutions is compliance with standards like HIPAA and PCI (when payment is made to insurance companies), PHI protection, and protection from liabilities and lawsuits that arise from deliberate or unintentional leakage of data. CERT/CC has published a report called *"Commonsense Guide to Prevention and Detection of Insider Threats."* The information is based on an analysis of more than 150 known cases of malicious insiders. The report notes, "insider threats are influenced by a combination of technical, behavioral, and organizational issues, and must be addressed by policies, procedures, and technologies. Therefore, it is important that management, human resources, information technology, and security staff understand the overall scope of the problem and communicate it to all employees in the organization."

UWM's experience with insider threats provides several important best practices for health care organizations that are currently considering the adoption of collaborative technologies. First, periodic enterprise-wide risk assessment is an important deterrent to internal threats. Organizations should monitor activities such as copying files to removable media, printer output, DVD/CD-burning, off-line user activity, and capturing incidents of users with company laptops. They should also analyze, inventory, and track the flow of sensitive and confidential information on all network assets. In addition, organizations should be able to generate audit trails for compliance requirements and provide incident replay for forensics and investigation. Organizations should institute periodic security awareness training for all employees, and ensure separation of duties and least privilege. The CERT/CC report provides several useful tips and best practices for organizations to combat insider threats.

7C

**Concept Presentation
Problematic Internet Usage**

I. Concept Definition

Problematic Internet Usage (PIU) can be defined as the "use of the Internet that creates psychological, social, school, and/or work difficulties in a person's life."[17] PIU is also characterized as a distinct pattern of Internet-related cognitions and behaviors that result in negative life outcomes.

Perspectives

a. Internet addiction perspective: This entails a "psychological dependence on the Internet, and is characterized by (1) an increasing investment of resources on Internet-related activities, (2) unpleasant feelings (e.g., anxiety, depression, emptiness) when off-line, (3) an increasing tolerance of the effects of being online, and (4) denial of problematic behavior.[18]

b. Specific PIU involves overuse or abuse of content-specific functions of the Internet (e.g., gambling, stock trading, and viewing sexual materials).

c. Generalized PIU is conceptualized as a multidimensional overuse of the Internet itself that results in negative personal and professional consequences. Symptoms of generalized PIU include maladaptive cognitions and behaviors related to Internet use that are not linked to any specific content. Rather, generalized PIUs occur when an individual develops problems due to the unique communicative context of the Internet. In other words, they are drawn to the experience of being online, in and of itself, and demonstrate a preference for virtual, rather than face-to-face, interpersonal communication contexts.[19]

II. Examples

Instant messaging (IM) applications in the workplace lead to considerable loss of productivity. A recent survey shows that 58% of IM use is for non-work-related activities. Another example of inappropriate use is sending offensive material to another party. The greatest danger arising from Instant Messaging is the possibility of backdoor Trojan horses.

III. Connect—Backdoors

A backdoor Trojan horse is a specific malware installed to allow an intruder to fully control a given system in secrecy. Backdoors are harmful in several respects: (i) all files on a computer can be shared using an instant messaging system; (ii) even if users use a dynamic IP address, the screen name never changes; (iii) intruders receive notification each time the user is on the system; (iv) applications do not open a new port; instead they use already open instant messaging ports making firewalls useless. Backdoor attacks can compromise an entire patient database resulting in the (i) release of patient information; (ii) change of payment addresses; (iii) denial of authorized claims; (iv) compromise of firm integrity; and (v) selling or release of critical data related to customer service representatives.

Use Case 2: Instant Messaging

Instant messaging (IM) is a communication tool that provides the characteristics of email and phone. There is immediate awareness of the availability of the person being contacted. In a typical usage scenario, client A, who wishes to initiate communication, logs on to see if any of his/her contacts are online. Once the link is established, clients can start communicating directly. IM became popular in the consumer market in 1997 with the introduction of the AOL instant messenger. There were 170 malicious code attacks in 2007 on consumer-grade IM platforms. It is estimated that, of the enterprises that use IM, only 26% use enterprise-grade products.

Description of Scenario   Instant messaging allows instant chatting among providers and multiple UWM customer service representatives that are available online. Some third-party vendors facilitate customizing an IM application by requiring the provider to input beneficiary information, which allows the desired information to be relayed more quickly to the provider. Thus, instant messaging permits quick access of UWM employees to critical information, and allows other parties to directly converse with a UWM representative and transfer information through a third-party IM host. A typical use scenario is described as follows: UWM needs immediate access to critical information about a patient. A hospital employee or customer service representative establishes a direct conversation with an insurance provider through a Web-based interface facilitated by the IM host. Patient information is transferred through the IM host, which could be a third-party host. The insurance provider's representative, in turn, accesses a data Web service through a remote service client to obtain health history and coverage information for the queried patient. The resulting data is then transferred to UWM via the IM host.

Identified Threats and Associated Risks   The risks associated with IM include the possibility of virus injection, intellectual property leakage, eavesdropping, Spam Over Instant Messaging (SPIM), and security risks associated with mobile devices. Below is an example of a STRIDE model of risks, most of which will be automatically generated by the MTM tool when the use case scenario is modeled.

- Spoofing: Unauthorized access to client information by a third party.
- Tampering: Changing client history or coverage.
- Repudiation: Provider's denial that certain messaging transactions ever took place.
- Information disclosure: Exposing protected health information (PHI) in transit.

7C

Criteria	Evaluation	Rating	Justification
Damage potential	How great is the damage if the vulnerability is exploited?	HIGH	Could prohibit users from accessing crucial emergency data by flooding IM third-party host
Reproducibility	How easy is it to reproduce the attack?	HIGH	Easy to reproduce; involves overloading the server with requests; almost anyone can do it
Exploitability	How easy is it to launch an attack?	HIGH	Infection by Trojans would result in take-over of host system and in turn compromise the network
Affected users	As a rough percentage, how many users are affected?	LOW	Any remote system users
Discoverability	How easy is it to find the vulnerability?	HIGH	Even script kiddies are aware that most sites are vulnerable to denial of service attacks

Table 7C-6 Sample DREAD Model for UWM's Abusive Internet Use

- Denial of Service: Inability of providers to quickly access the data in case of emergency, due to system congestion.
- Elevation of Privilege: Launching a phishing attack through a cleverly crafted message. This will involve the affected party clicking on a URL link, resulting in outsiders' gaining access to the system.

The associated DREAD model is shown in Table 7C-6.

Several HIPAA provisions exist that have direct impact on IM. For instance, once you're a covered entity under HIPAA and use any form of communication that uses personal or health communications, it is necessary to keep this information logged and archived for several years. It is necessary to have measures in place to protect confidential patient information. There must be measures that prevent violation of data integrity. Patient data must not be made available to third parties intentionally or unintentionally. Necessary safeguards need to be in place to authenticate users and manage user access.

Recommended Mitigations As an organization, UWM needs to commit to keeping its customer data secure prior to exposing its internal data stores to direct external access. It is important to have strict policy enforcement, internally within UWM, and externally among UWM's partners and providers upon accessing shared assets. Enterprise solutions today have end-to-end conversation encryption. They block file transfers and have integrated virus and content filtering. This can, to some extent, prevent or mitigate the adverse effects of inappropriate use over the network. Often, logging conversations are not only important to maintain compliance but they can also be used as a preventative measure to mitigate inappropriate use internally. Strong authentication schemes must be implemented to ensure proper access to shared resources.

The three largest application vendors in the marketplace, IBM, Jabber, and Microsoft, all have end-to-end encryption and the ability to record traffic. They can also all be set up to only allow internal users and, to some extent, provide support for mobility. IBM's Lotus Sametime supports more than one platform and is priced much lower than Jabber and Microsoft Enterprise Messenger 3. The IBM platform has been the choice of many *Fortune 500* companies and allows a broader range of appliances and mobile services. Some of the notable vendor solutions for secure collaboration are Akonix, Baracuda, Facetime, and Symantec. Akonix is a market leader in IM security management appliances, while Baracuda's IM Firewall provides a secure channel and blocks public IM. It can also store up to 5 years of logs. The data loss prevention tool from Vericept Corporation monitors IM traffic and alerts the security team about any serious breaches. All these appliances have network inventory tools that can detect IM traffic and notify the organization of unauthorized IM traffic including VoIP, and P2P, a centralized server to log conversations, an enterprise integration feature to manage user accounts, file transfer blocking, virus protection, and built-in restrictions on incoming URLs.

Studying UWM's deployment of their IM infrastructure provides glimpses of important best practices for enterprises. It is important to ensure that IM products be kept up to date with the latest patches and security updates. A few other best practices may be identified: (i) enabling the latest antivirus software on all IM management servers; (ii) blocking public instant messaging programs; (iii) avoiding the use of third-party IM hosts; (iv) blocking file sharing with external agencies; (v) designing an acceptable use policy that dictates what information can be shared in IM communications; and (vi) installing screen locking software to prevent unauthorized user access to the IM system.

UWM had a tough time making a compelling case for decision makers to consider adopting these technologies. Upon examining UWM's successful IM deployment, we identified the following drivers, which serve as justification to the adoption of these technologies: (i) online visibility of customer service representative to third parties; (ii) ability to share and collaborate in real time without the inherent delay of emails or pagers; (iii) facilitating interactive and instantaneous conversation; (iv) setting expectation for immediate response; (v) providing the ingredients of a face-to-face interaction. Another important lesson learned is with respect to the adoption of enterprise-grade features that provide the level of security or compliance/readiness that they need. This helped them minimize exposure of patient data to the various security threats identified earlier.

Discussion Questions

1. Discuss ways UWM can prevent inappropriate use of IM.

2. What technical safeguards should be in place in user workstations within UWM to prevent such inappropriate use from their system?

3. Do you think it is wise for the health care industry to implement IM across their system?

4. Assume you are the CIO of UWM. You are asked to justify the deployment of enterprise IM. Argue why the benefits outweigh the associated costs and risks.

Conclusion

We examined the threats associated with collaborative technologies in a regulatory context through a case study of the UWM Health System. We identified several important contributions: (i) a one-dimensional scorecard composed of a set of objectives, measures, and attainable targets that lays out the business value of collaborating and information sharing in health care; (ii) a framework for analyzing the threats to information sharing in the context of HIPAA compliance; and (iii) two interesting use cases that clearly detail threats to HIPAA.

From a pedagogical perspective, this study provides several useful teaching aids. First, the outline of the case study itself has been tested by the authors for several years in the classroom as a template for student projects, which consisted of a case presentation and a case write-up. A second notable feature is the presentation of three key concepts. This method of presenting a case study is derived from a well-known pedagogical technique called the concept tutor. Third, the use cases serve both as practical exercises for students to gain better insights into the problem and exemplars for similar threat modeling exercises.

The value of this case study extends beyond a pedagogical role to the business world, through teaching the reader how to embed strategic concepts (business drivers, scorecard) with real-world technology (threat modeling). The use cases presented can be easily modeled with the Microsoft Threat modeling (MTM) tool. Each use case has been developed by first presenting the most important related concept, followed by a use scenario and the corresponding STRIDE and DREAD models, and finally by suggested enterprise best practices and lessons learned.

Endnotes

1. Swidersky, F., and Snyder, W. (2004). *Threat Modeling* (1st ed.). Redmond: Microsoft Press.

2. Baggs, J. G., Schmitt, M. H., Mushlin, A. I., Mitchell, P. H., Eldredge, D. H., Oakes, D., and Hutson, A. D. (1999). "Association between Nurse-Physician Collaboration and Patient Outcomes in Three Intensive Care Units." *Critical Care Medicine*, 27(9), 1991–1998.

3. Urwiler, R., and Frolick, M. (2008). "The IT Value Hierarchy: Using Maslow's Hierarchy of Needs as a Metaphor for Gauging the Maturity Level of Information Technology Use within Competitive Organizations." *Information Systems Management*, 25 (1), 83–88.

4. Maslow, A. (1943). "A Theory of Human Motivation." *Psychological Review*, 50, 370–396.

5. Cohn K. H., and Allyn, T. R. (2005). "Making Hospital-Physician Collaboration Work." *Healthcare Financial Management*, 59(10), 102–108.

6. Nembhard, I. M., Tucker, A. L., Bohmer, R. M. J., Horbar, J. D., and Carpenter, J. H. (2007). "Improving Infant Mortality Rates: The Impact of Front-Line Staff Collaboration on Neonatal Care." Harvard Business School Working Paper, No. 08-002.

7. Cohn K. H., Wise A. S., and Bellhouse, D. E. (2005). "What Physicians and Hospital Leaders Can Teach Each Other about Marketing," in Cohn, K. H., *Better Communication for Better Care: Mastering Physician-Administrator Collaboration*. Chicago: Health Administration Press.

8. Kohn, L. T., Corrigan, J. M., and Donaldson, M. S. (Eds.). (2000). *To Err Is Human: Building a Safer Health System*. Washington, DC: National Academy Press.

9. "Cisco Drives Innovation in Healthcare With Enhanced Mobility Solutions, Industry Collaboration; Cisc." (2008). *Internet Wire*, Feb. 25 Issue.

10. Kaplan, R. S., and Norton, D. P. (1996). *Balanced Scorecard: Translating Strategy into Action*. Harvard Business School Press.

11. Lee, H. L., and Whang, W. (2000). "Information Sharing in a Supply Chain." *International Journal of Technology Management*, 20(3/4), 373–387.

12. Swidersky, F., and Snyder, W. (2004). *Threat Modeling* (1st ed.). Washington: Microsoft Press.

13. Gans, D., Kralewski, J., Hammons, T., and Dowd, B. (2005). "Medical Groups' Adoption of Electronic Health Records and Information Systems." *Health Affairs*, 24(5), 1323–1333.

14. Torr, P. (2005). "Demystifying the Threat Modeling Process." *IEEE Security & Privacy Magazine*, 3(5), 66–70.

15. http://en.wikipedia.org/wiki/Use_case

16. Swidersky, F., and Snyder, W. (2004). *Threat Modeling* (1st ed.). Washington: Microsoft Press.

17. Beard, K. W., and Wolf, E. M. (2001). "Modification in the Proposed Diagnostic Criteria for Internet Addiction." *Cyberpsychology and Behavior*, 4, 377–383.

18. Kandell, J. J. (1998). "Internet Addiction on Campus: The Vulnerability of College Students." *Cyberpsychology and Behavior*, 1, 11–17.

19. Davis, R. A. (2001). "A Cognitive-Behavioral Model of Pathological Internet Use." *Computers in Human Behavior*, 17, 187–195.

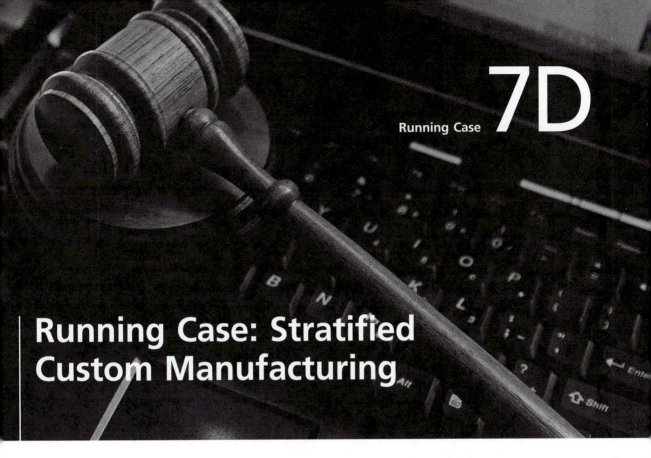

Running Case: Stratified Custom Manufacturing

The operations group was a well-knit bunch of guys even though they were scattered all over the world. Periodically they would get together either face-to-face in meetings or via a conference call process. As with many groups that came from diverse backgrounds with common work objectives, they shared work-related information as well as personal data both verbally and via emails. Some of the personal data was outside the company's guidelines for email usage and could be considered inappropriate and adult-oriented under U.S. guidelines. But, within the context of the virtual locker room they shared every day, none of them felt it was out of the ordinary for the countries where SCM had operations. The managers of some of the operations' group members allowed this to continue and even added to the dialogs, conversations, and viewings of some interesting materials. The materials and emails were confined to the operations network and were not widely distributed except to the intended recipients.

Shortly after the revision of standards and policies that was implemented in 2009 by corporate, some of these materials seeped into several of the administrative systems and were viewed by people outside the operations group. A group of vendors that had access to the administrative systems network inadvertently gained access to the materials. One CEO, Shelia Strong, of Make Right Products LLC., felt greatly offended and discussed possible legal action with her legal team.

They filed a civil suit and began their discovery phase. Ellen Winter was the Administrative Security manager and got involved immediately by requiring all data from the systems to be held pending the outcome of the suit. Takio Sumi met with his four senior managers to discuss their roles in the suit and how to properly prepare data for the lawyers. He specifically had Robert Germain, his senior manager of Information Security meet with his three managers, which included Ellen Winter, to make sure that SCM had complied with federal rules as well as corporate policy.

During their investigation Curtis Northman and Ellen found that their standing policies and practices regarding retention of both emails and voice mails had been deleting files that were now needed for the lawsuit by the prosecutors. The technicians in charge of maintaining the databases had been overwriting disks to save money and disk space. Now it was determined that data needed to comply with the court's discovery directive had been destroyed or had its embedded native file viewers removed so the data was unable to be decrypted. Their actions were part of a set of policies that had not been enforced since the early 2009 reorganization, but instead seemed to have come online as soon as rumors of the lawsuit began to circulate. They followed guidelines that they knew were no longer valid corporate policy, and their managers did not realize it until the legal action called upon them to restore emails and saved voice mails.

Discussion Questions

1. What U.S. federal laws apply to this situation?

2. Pick a U.S. state or another national government as a point of reference to research and determine which laws apply to this situation.

3. What is one of the primary problems found during the implementation planning for the e-discovery project?

4. How does a corporation handle situations like the above where policy nonenforcement or selective enforcement becomes a larger problem?

5. The information systems involved were administrative and operational and had little to no sensitive information on them. How does one go about protecting data at a level that is commensurate with its sensitivity, value, and criticality when those parameters can change due to circumstances such as a lawsuit?